THE
SOCIALIST REGISTER 1984

THE
SOCIALIST REGISTER
1984

EDITED BY

RALPH MILIBAND

JOHN SAVILLE

and

MARCEL LIEBMAN

THE MERLIN PRESS
LONDON

First published in 1984
by the Merlin Press Ltd
3 Manchester Road
London E14

British Library Cataloguing in Publication Data
Socialist register.—1984
1. Socialism—Periodicals
335'.005   HX3

ISBN 0-85036-324 1
ISBN 0-85036-325 x Pbk

Printed in Great Britain
by Whitstable Litho, Whitstable, Kent

Typesetting by Heather Hems
The Malt House, Chilmark, Wilts.

TABLE OF CONTENTS

PREFACE

This twenty-first volume of *The Socialist Register* differs from its predecessors on two counts: first, because it has had three editors instead of the usual two. Marcel Liebman is the author of *Leninism under Lenin* and other works, and is Professor of Political Science at Brussels University. The second new feature of this issue of the *Register* is that it is entirely devoted to one theme, anti-communism. We began work on this volume with the conviction that anti-communism was a crucial aspect of the politics of the twentieth century, and that it needed much more detailed attention from the left than it has usually received. The articles which appear in this volume confirm our view that neither the internal politics of capitalist countries nor international politics can be understood without the closest reference to the role which anti-communism has played in both. The volume does not of course discuss every manifestation of anti-communism; but we believe that what is presented here provides sufficient information and analysis to show what is involved in an anti-communist enterprise which decisively shapes the present epoch.

The introductory article discusses the main arguments upon which anti-communism has been based, and offers some reflections on the uses to which anti-communism has been put by conservative forces everywhere. The following five articles document and discuss some major historical manifestations of anti-communism in the early years of the Cold War. Thus, Reg Whitaker presents a comparative survey of anti-communist measures and policies in the immediate post-war years in the United States, Britain, Canada and Australia. John Saville reviews the third volume of Alan Bullock's biography of Ernest Bevin, and shows the critical role which Bevin played, as Foreign Secretary in the Labour Government that was elected in 1945, in the early history of the Cold War. Martin Eve recalls one important episode in that history, namely British and American intervention in Greece to ensure the victory of the forces of conservatism. For his part, Rudi van Doorslaar provides an unusually detailed account of anti-communist endeavours in Belgium before and during World War II; and Jon Halliday offers an important reassessment of the origins and character of the Korean War, an episode which he rightly describes as a turning point in the history of our times.

William Graf's article is a detailed survey of the ways in which anti-communism was articulated and practised in the Federal Republic of

Germany from 1945 onwards; and Alan Wolfe presents an interpretation of the reasons which made anti-communism the central element in the shaping of American foreign policy. The following two articles are concerned with anti-communism in Central America: Philip Brenner surveys American policies in the region, while James Petras and Morris Morley examine the consequences which American intervention in Guatemala in the name of anti-communism have had in that country since the coup which overthrew the Arbenz government in 1954. Xavier Zeebroek provides a close analysis of Soviet and American nuclear strength, and exposes the myth of Soviet superiority. Roland Lew and Jean Pierre Garnier analyse the ways in which the disappointment of the hopes which many left intellectuals in France placed on the 'Third World' in the sixties and early seventies have helped to feed the extreme anti-communism of parts of the left which has been such a notable feature of French intellectual and political life in recent years; and Pascal Delwit and Jean-Michel Dewaele document this phenomenon by reference to the political trajectory of two prominent and prolific French ex-Communists, Annie Kriegel and Pierre Daix. Last but not least, François Houtart reflects on a subject of great and growing importance, the attitudes of the churches to anti-communism.

Among our authors, Reg Whitaker is Professor of Politics at York University, Toronto. Rudi van Doorslaar is a Research Fellow at the Centre d'Etudes sur la Second Guerre Mondiale in Brussels. Jon Halliday is well known for his writings on the Far East. William Graf teaches politics at Guelph University, Ontario, and Alan Wolfe is in the Department of Sociology at Queen's University, New York. Philip Brenner teaches foreign policy at the American University in Washington and is a Fellow of the Institute of Policy Studies. Morris Morley is also at the American University and James Petras is Professor of Sociology at the State University of New York, Binghamton. Xavier Zeebroek is engaged in research and writing on the arms race. Roland Lew is a Research Fellow at the Institute of Sociology, Brussels, Jean Pierre Garnier is a Research Fellow at CNRS and François Houtart teaches at the Catholic University of Louvain. Pascal Delwit and Jean-Michel Dewaele are graduate students at Brussels University.

We are very grateful to our contributors for their help; to David Macey for his translations; and also to Martin Eve, of Merlin Press, who also appears in this volume as a contributor. As usual, we wish to stress that neither the editors nor the authors should be taken to agree with everything that appears in the following pages.

August 1984   R.M.
                                                                 J.S.
                                                                 M.L.

REFLECTIONS ON ANTI-COMMUNISM*

Ralph Miliband and Marcel Liebman

Ever since the Bolshevik Revolution of October 1917, anti-communism has been a dominant theme in the political warfare waged by conservative forces against the entire left, Communist and non-Communist; and since 1945 and the onset of the Cold War in particular, anti-communism has been ceaselessly disseminated by a multitude of different sources and means—newspapers, radio, television, films, articles, pamphlets, books, speeches, sermons, official documents—in a massive enterprise of propaganda and indoctrination. No subject other than 'communism' has received anything like the same volume of criticism and denunciation. The intensity and forms of this propaganda have varied from country to country and from period to period, with the United States well in the lead among capitalist democracies in the intensity and pervasiveness of its anti-communism; but at no time since 1917 has anti-communism failed to occupy a major, even a central, place in the politics and policies of the capitalist world. Different Communist countries have at various times been the main target of attack—China at the time of the Korean war, Vietnam at the time of the Vietnam war. But it is the Soviet Union which has always been taken to be the principal and most dangerous enemy; and it is with anti-communism as it refers to the Soviet Union that we shall be mainly concerned here.

For all the diverse forms which it has assumed, anti-communism is based on two fundamental contentions: the first is that 'communism' is a supreme and unqualified evil; and the second is that it is an evil which the Soviet leaders are seeking to impose upon the rest of the world. It is these two contentions which we propose to discuss here; and we do so from an independent socialist position which, although very critical of many aspects of Soviet 'communism', is also very sharply at odds with anti-communism.

I

From the first days of the Bolshevik Revolution, anti-communism has painted Soviet 'communism' in the darkest possible colours. For their

---

* Many thanks are due to John Saville for his very helpful comments, criticisms and suggestions in regard to an earlier version of this article.

part, Communists and many other people on the Left sought, from 1917 until the 20th Soviet Communist Party Congress of 1956 and Khrushchev's 'secret speech', to paint the regime in the brightest possible colours, and resolutely dismissed all criticism of the Soviet Union as mere bourgeois propaganda, inventions and lies. A great deal of it undoubtedly was: anti-communism has always relied on, and has itself produced, much false and tendentious information about the Soviet Union. But a lot of the adverse information and comment, even of an extreme kind, was not lies and inventions at all; and it was grievously misguided for the defenders of the Soviet Union to give total and unqualified endorsement to everything that the Soviet regime did, if only because no regime, whatever its intentions and even its achievements, should ever be given this sort of endorsement. The point is valid at all times, but has exceptional force in relation to the years of Stalin's rule, from the late twenties to his death in 1953, when immense crimes were committed by the regime.

There are many reasons to account for the wholehearted support which Communists and others on the left gave to Stalinist policies and actions; and it is worth dwelling on them, since they are usually ignored by anti-communists. One such reason is that alongside massive repression and murder, there was also great construction and advance; and the latter served to occlude the former. So did the derelictions and crimes of western capitalism and imperialism strengthen the will to believe that the Soviet Union, poor, beleaguered and vilified, was a land where socialism was being built: on no account must its endeavours be weakened and its enemies strengthened by adverse comment. The rise of Nazism enormously encouraged this view; so did the appeasement of the fascist dictators by Britain, France and other capitalist regimes. The Soviet Union and Communist parties at its command played their own considerable part by insisting that anyone on the left who did criticise the Soviet Union was 'objectively' allied to reactionaries and fascists, and must be mercilessly denounced. After World War II, there was also the appreciation of the immense contribution which the Soviet Union had made to the defeat of Nazism; and there was also the resumption of the old ideological and political warfare in the Cold War, and the determination of the West to stem the radical pressures generated by the war.

All such reasons—and the list could easily be extended—only serve to explain rather than justify the tragic submission to Stalinism of a vast army of activists in labour movements everywhere who were among the most dedicated and courageous participants in the class struggles of their times; and it needs to be said, given the denigration to which they have been subjected, not least by people who were themselves Stalinists, and by others who never lifted a finger on behalf of any decent cause, that these were the people everywhere who fought hardest against conservative, reactionary and fascist forces, with no thought of personal gain or advancement, but on the contrary at great cost to themselves, often at the sacrifice of liberty and life.[1]

These defensive reflexes about the Soviet Union have by no means disappeared. But the reality of Stalinist rule has long been acknowledged on the left; and there has also been a wide measure of recognition that the post-Stalinist regime, while immeasurably less tyrannical than its predecessor, has remained exceedingly intolerant of dissent, and that its actions in this area as well as any other should be subject to intransigent socialist criticism. The extent of criticism varies greatly from one part of the left to another, but there is at least no disposition now to take the Soviet regime as a 'model' of socialism: indeed, there is now a widespread disposition on the left to think of the Soviet regime as an 'anti-model'. How could it be otherwise, given some of the most pronounced features of that regime? The socialist project means, and certainly meant for Marx, the subordination of the state to society. Precisely the reverse characterises the Soviet system. Moreover, the domination of the state in that system is assured by an extremely hierarchical, tightly controlled and fiercely monopolistic party aided by a formidable police apparatus. Outside the Party, there is no political life; and inside the Party, such political life as there exists is narrowly circumscribed by what the Party leadership permits or ordains—which means that there is not much political life in the Party either. Essential personal, civic and political freedoms are limited and insecure. Intellectual freedom in any meaningful sense is virtually non-existent; and the treatment of 'dissidents' of every kind is a scandal and a disgrace for a country which proclaims its dedication to socialism and Marxism. Much the same, with greater or lesser emphasis, is also true of all other Communist regimes. To call this 'socialism' is to degrade the concept to the level assigned to it by its enemies.

There have been people on the left, belonging to different and conflicting tendencies, groups and parties, who have ever since the first years of the Soviet regime been extremely critical of it. It is in fact from within the Marxist left that has been produced some of the most cogent critiques of the Soviet regime, notably from different strands in the Trotskyist tradition, beginning with Trotsky himself. But these critics have also very firmly rejected, as we do, any assimilation of their position to that of anti-communism; and we must now turn to the grounds on which our rejection of it is based.

One of these grounds is that anti-communism is an essentially conservative stance, which uses the experience of Soviet-type regimes as a further means—there are many others—of combating as utopian, absurd, dangerous and sinister any transformative project which goes beyond the most modest attempts at 'piecemeal social engineering'. Socialists are well aware by now of the difficulties of every kind which are bound to attend the creation of a cooperative, democratic and egalitarian commonwealth.

But this does not make them renounce their commitment to it; and the experience of the Soviet regime, or of China or Cambodia or anywhere else cannot be taken as of decisive relevance elsewhere, least of all in countries whose economic, social, political and cultural circumstances are vastly different from those in which Communist regimes have been implanted. Nor would most socialists want to divorce the communist project envisioned by Marx from the meaning of socialism. On the contrary, they see it rather as representing the fulfillment, however distant, of the promise of socialism.

Anti-communism is also grossly selective in its view of Communist regimes, and systematically presents a highly distorted picture of their reality. In particular, it casts into deep shadow or ignores altogether their positive side and their economic, social and cultural achievements. The two-sided nature of Soviet-type regimes is an intrinsic part of their being. As in the case of the Stalinist era in the Soviet Union, there is, in most if not all Soviet-type regimes, advance and progress as well as dictatorship and repression.

Anti-communism not only understates or ignores altogether the advances that are made, but also pays very little if any attention to the conditions and circumstances in which they have been made. Communist regimes have generally come to power in countries the vast majority of whose population has traditionally suffered from varying degrees of economic under-development, in some cases of an extreme kind, from fierce local and foreign exploitation; and from one form or other of authoritarian rule, including colonial rule. Moreover, many of these countries were ravaged by civil war and foreign intervention before or after coming under Communist rule, as in the case of the Soviet Union, China, Korea, Vietnam, Laos and Cambodia; and their regimes were also subjected to economic warfare, waged under the leadership of the United States, as in the case of Cuba. In other words, all Communist regimes have started out with fearsome handicaps and burdens. This combination of under-development and exploitation on the one hand and of capitalist hostility and destruction on the other, does not annul or explain away the negative aspects of these regimes. But it is highly relevant to any serious assessment of their nature and dynamic; and it makes their advances and achievements all the more noteworthy.

Anti-communism is also tendentiously selective in another respect. It condemns the political and human abuses of Communist dictatorships, but very often condones or simply ignores the abuses and crimes of right-wing regimes. Such regimes, however tyrannical and criminal they may be, can count on the steadfast support of the United States and other capitalist states, all of course in the name of the defence of democracy and freedom. At most, perfunctory and general regrets may be expressed at the evil deeds which right-wing regimes may commit (though this is not how it is put), with pious hopes also being voiced that the time may soon arrive when such abuses as occur may cease. But the contrast between this indulgence and the fierce denunciation of abuses in Communist regimes is very striking, and says much about the genuineness of anti-communist concern for human rights, democracy and the rest. We will return to the point later.

Mrs Jeanne Kirkpatrick, formerly a professor of Political Science and at present chief US delegate to the United Nations, has sought to justify this difference of attitude to right-wing dictatorships and Communist regimes with the argument, *inter alia,* that the former were only 'authoritarian', whereas the latter were 'totalitarian'. Authoritarian dictatorships of the right are capable of reform and change in the direction of 'democracy', whereas Communist and left 'totalitarian' regimes are not.[2] These notions warrant some comment.

First, 'authoritarian' regimes supported by the West only become less repressive and more 'democratic' under the impact of extreme crisis and challenge. The crisis itself is the result of pressure and struggle, including armed struggle, against the regime in question; and it is a challenge which the regime, with the full support of the United States, seeks to defeat, usually by savage repression. It is only when it is unable to achieve the obliteration of challenge that reform may follow. The grim irony of this scenario is that it is not the successes of the policies of the United States, but American inability to shore up a tyrannical regime, which produces concessions.

Secondly, these concessions usually leave intact the repressive structures of the regimes, their police and military apparatus, and all the forces which sustained the authoritarian regime in the first place. Death squads, systematic and extensive torture, the imprisonment and killing of opponents may no longer be in fashion; and that is indeed a great gain. But most of the people responsible for the crimes of the regime remain in positions of power and influence and continue to be an important force in public affairs. There is no very good reason why their turn should not come again.

Thirdly, and relatedly, the changes that are made in the political realm, such as they are, leave quite intact the economic and social structures which form the permanent source of 'social oppression' for the vast majority of the population; and they also leave intact the predominant position of foreign interests and international capital in these countries. For the vast majority, exploitation, subjection, hunger and malnutrition, chronic disease and early death, all remain largely or wholly unaffected by the 'democratic' changes which may have occurred in a remote and alien capital; and attempts to resist and reduce 'social oppression' on the part of those subjected to it are not much less liable to harsh suppression than they were under the dictatorship. The only real hope of significant progress lies in the revolutionary transformation of the economic, social and political system, and in the overthrow of the conservative forces in society and the state which have been dominant hitherto; and this of course must include powerful foreign capitalist interests. This is not a sufficient condition of progress; but it is nevertheless an essential one.

It is precisely the purpose of local oligarchies and their foreign protectors to prevent, contain, neutralise or crush attempts at revolutionary change: 'democratic' reforms, reluctantly conceded when outright repression has failed, is viewed as a means of maintaining the status quo, not in the least of transforming it.

It is the revolutionary transformation which occurred in Cuba that makes possible the kind of Reuter report from Havana which the London *Times* carried at the end of 1983 under the headline 'How Castro has created a welfare state to be envied', and which is worth quoting at length:

> Even Fidel Castro's harshest critics would have difficulty in belittling the progress made by Cuba's revolution, twenty five years old on January 1, in creating a welfare state worthy of a much richer country.
>
> A guarantee to free education and public health services has been one of the main goals of Cuba's Communist Government which inherited a far different society when Dr Castro's guerilla army took power in 1959.
>
> Official statistics, backed by United Nations specialists working here, illustrate the transformation that has taken place in this tropical, largely agricultural island.
>
> The average life expectancy of a Cuban born in the 1950s was around 50 compared with 73 today, while infant mortality has been slashed from about 60 per 1,000 births to 16. Inoculation campaigns and improved diet, sanitation and living conditions have all but eliminated diseases which still wreak havoc in most Third World countries. No cases of polio, malaria, diphtheria or infantile tetanus, ailments which once killed thousands of Cuban youngsters, have been registered in the past decade.
>
> Cradle-to-grave social benefits ensure that even the poorest families do not go hungry and have equal access to medical treatment and schooling. Government spending on education and health takes up more than 20 per cent of the national budget. The number of hospitals and doctors has tripled and the new Hermanos Ameijeiras hospital in central Havana is symbolic of the new authorities' near obsession with providing the best in medical treatment.[3]

Of no comparable capitalist country in the 'Third World' could such a report be written; but it concerns an aspect of Communist reality which anti-communism chooses to occlude.

Also, the 'totalitarian' label which is attached to Communist regimes is more useful as denunciation than as description. For whatever the intentions of their leaders may be, the notion of total domination which the term conveys is belied in actual experience. Not only do these regimes have to cope with diverse oppositions, but, repressive though they are, they do have elaborate mechanisms of participation and consultation which make possible the expression of a multitude of demands, promptings, grievances and discontents at the grassroots. Some of these are heard and heeded, others are not. But the picture which anti-communism seeks to convey of an Orwellian world of *1984* is inaccurate. For those people who transgress the shifting bounds of orthodoxy imposed by the Party and the state, life is likely to be bitter and cruel, and this is a standing indictment of the regimes in question. All the same, they are not, generally speaking, regimes in which crushed populations live as Orwellian 'proles' under effective 'totalitarian' control. The notion that they are is part of ideological warfare, in which truth, as in all wars, is an early casualty. One of the purposes of this propaganda is the celebration, in C. Wright Mills's formulation, of capitalist democracy, better known as democracy, and the blurring of the pressures in these capitalist democratic regimes towards enforced conformity.

It is also inaccurate to say that Soviet-type regimes, being 'totalitarian', are incapable of change. They are all 'modernising' regimes; indeed, some of their major problems have been produced by a 'productivist' megalomania, aggravated by the lack of effective political checks. At any rate, the dynamic that carries them forward requires them to experiment, change and adapt. Here too, nothing could be further from the stagnant world of *1984*. It is true, on the other hand, that the many reforms that are undertaken do not extend to the erosion, let alone the abrogation, of the monopolistic role of the Communist Party, translated as its 'leading role'. But even this needs some qualification. For erosion of this 'leading role' of the Party has on occasion occurred, notwithstanding the resistance of its leadership. Czechoslovakia in the Spring of 1968 showed how much change could be forced from within upon a system that has been a byword for rigidity; and Poland in 1980 and after also has shown that change was both possible *and* extremely difficult to sustain in the face of Soviet opposition. The Czech Spring was stopped by Soviet tanks, and the Polish stirrings by a novel form of Communist Bonapartism, induced by Soviet pressure, and made possible, it is important to add, by Soviet contiguity. This does not, however, diminish the significance of these experiences in terms of what they betoken for the future.

Nor even should the extent of the changes which have occurred in the Soviet Union itself since Stalin's death be underestimated. There is a crucial sense in which the system has not changed; but within an outwardly rigid framework, much in its functioning has indeed been transformed from the days of unbridled tyranny, so much so that it is not at all unrealistic or 'utopian' to think that 'Czech' and 'Polish' experiences will, in due course and in their own way, make themselves felt in the Soviet Union itself.

The 'totalitarian' label is part of ideological warfare in another way as well—in so far as it covers both Communist and Fascist regimes, and is thereby intended to suggest that they are very similar systems. More specifically, the suggestion is that Communism and Nazism are more or less identical. This may be good propaganda but it is very poor political analysis. There were similarities between Stalinism and Nazism in the use of mass terror and mass murder. But there were also enormous differences between them. Stalinism was a 'revolution from above', which was intended to modernise Russia from top to bottom, on the basis of the state ownership of the means of production (most of those 'means of production' being themselves produced as part of the 'revolution from above'); and Russia was indeed transformed, at immense cost. Nazism, on the other hand, was, for all its transformative rhetoric, a counter-revolutionary movement and regime, which *consolidated* capitalist ownership and the economic and social structures which Hitler had inherited from Weimar. As has often been observed, twelve years of absolute Nazi rule did not fundamentally change, and never sought to change fundamentally, the social system which had existed when Hitler came to power. To assimilate Nazism and Stalinism, and equate them as similarly 'totalitarian' movements and regimes of the extreme right and the extreme left is to render impossible a proper understanding of their nature, content and purpose.

Two further points need to be made about the movements which have been the prime targets of anti-communist attack and denunciation. The first is that the revolutionary movements which have come to prominence in the years since World War II have not been Communist-led or dominated. A profound difference has in this respect come upon the revolutionary scene from the first half of the twentieth century to the second. In the first half, at least after 1917, revolutionary movements of the left across the world were mostly Communist-led; and those who led them accepted allegiance to the Communist International, meaning in effect its Russian leadership, and believed this to be synonymous with, or at least in no way opposed to, their allegiance to their own national struggles. Those who did not take this view did not long remain leaders.

In the second half of the century, on the other hand, revolutionary movements have not been of this type at all, even though Communists have often been one of their constituent elements. The Cuban revolutionaries, for instance, were not Communists when they set out on the road which ultimately led them to Havana in 1959. Nor are the Sandinistas in Nicaragua, or the liberation forces in El Salvador.

Furthermore, no revolutionary movement anywhere in the world, whether it calls itself 'Marxist–Leninist' or not, believes that it owes any particular allegiance to Moscow, or that the interests which it defends are necessarily synonymous with those of the Soviet Union. All such movements are imbued with very strong nationalist sentiments; and one of the strongest impulses which animates them is precisely the desire to free their country from foreign domination, notably that of the United States. The idea that they are willing to exchange one form of foreign domination and dependence for another is absurd, and is not least derived from a rather racist view that hitherto dominated people in the 'Third World' cannot really be as keen to be free from foreign domination as the people of the United States or Britain, and that their governments, for their own good, require tutelage, whether they want it or not. Revolutionary movements and regimes may be forced by Western hostility and intervention to seek Soviet support, and to enter into close relations with the Soviet Union. Cuba is an excellent example of this process: there is every reason to suppose that its ties with the Soviet Union would not have become nearly so close if the Cuban revolutionary regime had not been faced with the implacable determination of the United States to inflict whatever damage it could upon the country and ultimately to bring down its government. The same applies to other revolutionary movements and regimes driven to seek support from the Soviet Union by American hostility.

The second point concerns Communist parties in advanced capitalist countries. There is a weak sense in which these remain 'revolutionary' parties—in the sense that they remain committed to the fundamental transformation of their countries in socialist directions. In this sense, however, a good many social democratic parties can also claim to be 'revolutionary'. Communist parties further stress their commitment to class struggle, use its language much more emphatically than do their social democratic counterparts, and proclaim their attachment to 'Marxism–Leninism', or at least to Marxism. But they are also thoroughly committed to working within a strictly constitutionalist framework, and in terms of a strategy which accords priority to electoral and parliamentary gains. As noted earlier, most of them have moreover ceased to accept dictation from the Soviet Union; and they are greatly concerned to emphasise that they will follow their own road to socialism, in accordance with their own national traditions, circumstances and needs. Notwithstanding such proclamations, most of these parties retain close and even intimate links with the Soviet Union and its allies. But it is nevertheless only in the haunted world of anti-communism that these parties appear as mere outposts of Soviet power, burning with the desire to bring their countries into the Soviet fold.

This view, however, applied on a world scale, is essential for the purpose of legitimating anti-revolutionary action against revolutionary movements and regimes; and these do not have to be 'officially' Communist to be denounced as Trojan horses or fifth columns. Any kind of revolutionary movement or regime of the left will do. This is the basis on which the United States seeks to justify the claim that, say, Nicaragua under the Sandinistas poses a direct threat to the security of the United States. The claim can only be taken out of the realm of pure fantasy on the assumption that the Sandinistas *want* to bring the Soviet Union into their country. This assumption, however, itself belongs to the realm of what might be described as functional nonsense.

But there is another assumption which accompanies this one, namely that the Soviet Union is itself desperately concerned to go into country after country, in pursuit of that 'expansionism' which, as we noted at the beginning, is the second core proposition of anti-communism. It is to this alleged 'expansionism' that we now turn.

II

Since World War II, a deafening anti-communist chorus in the West has turned into conventional wisdom the notion that the Soviet Union was an imperialist and expansionist power, whose leaders seek world domination, and whose hegemonic designs are a threat not only to its neighbours but to the whole world. The exact terms of the indictment, and explanations of this alleged Soviet 'expansionism' vary, and so do conceptions of what ought to be done about it, but the basic point remains: the Soviet Union poses a permanent threat to all free countries—a threat even more menacing, in the eyes of many anti-communists, than did Nazism, because it is more insidious and pervasive. The least this requires is containment and deterrence by way of the military might of the United States and its partners in NATO and beyond, in vigilant awareness of the proven dangers of 'appeasement'.

Before discussing this, it is relevant to recall that violent hostility to the Soviet Union was a guiding principle of the diplomacy of the great powers long before there was any question of Soviet 'expansionism'. It was after all in the first days of the Bolshevik regime that the armies of a dozen countries and more went into Russia with the task, as Winston Churchill put it at the time, of 'strangling Bolshevism in its cradle'. Marx and Engels had proclaimed in the *Communist Manifesto* in 1848 that 'a spectre is haunting Europe—the spectre of Communism'. But here was no longer the spectre of 'communism', but its dreaded reality. For the first time in history, a state had been turned into the embodiment of 'communism'; and a state, moreover, which claimed sovereignty over the largest country in the world. No wonder that the representatives of the old order tried to destroy it; and that, having failed to do so, they should have been concerned to contain and reduce its impact in the world, without much need to invoke Soviet 'expansionism'. Anti-communism in its pure form, so to speak, was good enough.

In a book entitled *Politics and Diplomacy of Peacemaking* and subtitled *Containment and Counterrevolution at Versailles,* Professor Arno Mayer has noted that 'the Paris Peace Conference made a host of decisions, all of which in varying degrees, were designed to check Bolshevism'.[4] This could well serve as a *leit-motiv* for British and French diplomacy in the inter-war years: at least, the diplomatic and political history of those years cannot properly be written without making this a central element in the account. For British diplomacy in particular, the containment of 'communism' and of its spread through the British Empire remained throughout a major preoccupation, much more so than Nazism.

Similarly, it is anti-communism which dictated much of the grand strategy of the Western Allies in World War II. Scarcely a single major episode in the war from 1942 onwards can be explained without close reference to the fears which they had of social upheaval at the end of the war, and of the contribution which Soviet military successes and advances might make to revolutionary transformation in liberated countries.[5] Nor of course was this only a matter of saving Europe alone from 'communism': the concern was global and encompassed British, French and other colonial territories aflame with the expectation of national and social liberation.

In fact, it was not 'communism' which was then at issue at all, but radical change in which Communists were certain to play an important role, but not a monopolistic one. In Western Europe, Communist parties played a crucial stabilising role at a time of great social and political upheaval, and rejected out of hand any 'adventurist' policies, meaning any policies that might have endangered their continued participation in the bourgeois governments they had entered. This strategy was of immense help in maintaining social discipline in the working class; and it was a strategy which these Communist parties pursued in full accord with the Soviet leaders, and in the sure knowledge that any other strategy would have been fiercely opposed by these leaders.

Nor even did the Soviet Union then insist on the 'stalinisation' of Eastern Europe at the end of the war: it was not until 1947 and the aggravation of the Cold War that fully-fledged Communist regimes were installed in the countries which Stalin wanted in the Soviet sphere of influence, with the inclusion of Czechoslovakia by way of a Communist take-over in 1948. It is also noteworthy that Stalin was perfectly prepared to abandon the Greek Communist resistance to the bitter fate reserved for it by British-backed Greek reactionaries, and to see Greece come into the British, and then the American, sphere of influence.

What the Western Allies were seeking to achieve at the end of World War II was precisely what they had sought to achieve at the end of World War I, namely to restore and stabilise an old order convulsed by war and threatened by the radicalism fostered by war. This endeavour took many different forms; and it involved confrontation with the Soviet Union at many different points. It was this, and not Soviet 'expansionism', which set in motion a dialectic of escalation and counter-escalation which has defined the whole history of the post-war years.

In this perspective, the term 'Cold War' is somewhat misleading: it implies a state to state antagonism, which is indeed real enough, but which obscures the fact that what is at the core of this antagonism is the determination of the Western powers to contain revolutionary movements everywhere and even for that matter reformist movements, a purpose to which the Soviet Union, for its own reasons and in its own ways, is something of an obstacle. The notion of 'international civil war', which Professor Mayer among others also uses, is closer than 'Cold War' to the real nature of the confrontation.

Since 1939, the Soviet Union has absorbed Eastern Poland, the Baltic states, the western part of the Ukraine and Byelorussia. These territories were of course part of the Czarist empire before 1917. This is no justification for the absorption of countries which, as in the case of Lithuania, Latvia and Esthonia, had achieved independence as a result of the downfall of Czarism. But it is a fact which is nevertheless relevant to a judgment of the kind of considerations which determine the actions of the Soviet leaders—in this instance, a mixture of nationalism, a particular view of what Soviet security requires, a complete indifference to what the people concerned may or may not want, possibly combined with a belief that they must eventually come to see the benefits of their return to a Russian state that is now a Soviet commonwealth.

Since 1945, the Soviet Union has also brought Poland, Hungary, Bulgaria, East Germany and Czechoslovakia within its sphere of domination. Its relationship with Rumania is more ambiguous, and amounts to a great deal less than control. In 1979, it met by force of arms the threat to its control of Afghanistan, as it had done in Hungary in 1956 and in Czechoslovakia in 1968. It has close ties with Vietnam and Cuba. On the other hand, its relations with other Communist states are uncertain, and range from the more or less friendly, as in the case of North Korea and Yugoslavia, to the frankly hostile, as in the case of China and Albania. Its relations with other self-proclaimed 'Marxist–Leninist' states, such as South Yemen, Ethiopia, Mozambique and Angola, are good but do not give it anything like control over these countries.

What does this tell us about the dynamic of Soviet foreign policy? For anti-communism, the answer is blindingly simple and obvious: it tells us of a Soviet imperialism combined with traditional Russian imperialism; of relentless totalitarian expansionism, of Communist aggression and of an implacable will to achieve world domination. But there is a different view, which is altogether more realistic and grounded in actual history rather than ideological fantasies, namely that Soviet foreign and defence policies are dominated by the will on the part of Soviet leaders to ensure the security of the Soviet Union in what they conceive to be a profoundly hostile and threatening context.

This Soviet belief in the existence of a hostile and threatening capitalist world is often deplored and derided in the West as 'neurotic', 'pathological' and totally unwarranted, but the record says otherwise, and does tell of the unremitting hostility which all capitalist powers have displayed towards the Soviet Union ever since the Bolshevik Revolution. That hostility is at times more pronounced, and at other times less: but it is never absent from the West's dealings with Russia. Different capitalist powers have relayed each other, so to speak, in assuming the leadership of the anti-communist camp—first Britain and France, then Nazi Germany, then the United States. But it is not very remarkable that the Russians should remember much more clearly than people in the West the fact that this hostility has found extremely costly expression for them on at least two occasions: one of them was the wars of intervention which capitalist powers waged against the Bolshevik regime in the first years of the revolution; the other, much more traumatic, was the war which Germany and its allies waged against the Soviet Union. Britain and the United States were then Russia's allies, more or less. But it was neverthleess the Soviet Union which was left to bear the brunt of Germany's military might from 1941 until 1944, and it was upon the Soviet Union that devolved the main task of destroying the German war machine, a task which was only accomplished at horrendous human and material cost.[6] On this record alone, the notion of capitalist hostility—and Nazi Germany *was* a capitalist power, which enjoyed quite friendly relations with other capitalist powers until its expansionist appetites grew too large—is not some kind of paranoid phantasm, but a simple reality. And that hostility has not only been expressed in episodic military terms, but in terms of consistently hostile economic, diplomatic and strategic policies as well. It is only in anti-communist propaganda that the adverse attitudes towards the Soviet Union which have been the guiding thread of Western policies since World War II, and particularly of American policies, have all been 'the fault of the Russians'. The hostility was there from the start: what can be laid at the door of the Russians, apart from their repressive actions within their own domain, is that what they conceived to be required for their security led them to act in ways which made it easier for American and other Western leaders to convince their populations that the hostility was justified; and the grossly rebarbative aspects of Soviet-type regimes have made this easier still. A great and dangerous *non sequitur* is in this latter respect at work here. Because the Soviet regime is repressive, it is widely believed and even taken for granted that it must also be imperialist and 'expansionist'. This, however, does not at all follow. It is perfectly possible for a regime to be tyrannical *and* free from any imperialist ambitions. On the other hand, the fact that the United States is a capitalist democracy, and in the eyes of its own leaders and people a democracy *tout court,* easily generates the view that it cannot have imperialist and hegemonic designs. This does not follow either. The most that can be said about capitalist democracy in the late 20th century on this score is that it makes the pursuit of imperialist designs rather more difficult than it used to be, because of the internal opposition they generate. Unfortunately, it does not make their pursuit impossible.

The Soviet actions which have most usefully served to buttress the thesis of Soviet 'expansionism'—the stalinisation of the East European regimes, and the invasion of Hungary, Czechoslovakia and Afghanistan— are in fact much more reasonably explained by the Soviet leaders' concern for security. The same goes for the rash actions in which Soviet leaders have occasionally engaged since World War II, for instance the Berlin blockade of 1948 and the installation of Soviet missiles in Cuba in 1962.

It is also significant in the present context that Stalin acted with a good deal of caution when confronted with the 'defection' of Yugoslavia from the Communist bloc in 1948, and that the Soviet response was confined to the denunciation of the Yugoslavs by Communist parties throughout the world as renegades, fascists and agents of Western imperialism, and to some attempts at the 'destabilisation' of the Tito regime. Similarly, the Soviet leaders accepted the 'loss' of China when the Sino-Soviet dispute erupted, and also confined their response to the abrupt cutting off of aid, to attempts at 'destabilisation', and to denunciations which were richly reciprocated by the Chinese themselves.

These do not seem to be the responses of rulers driven by an irresistible impulse to territorial expansion and military adventure. They suggest rather a generally cautious approach to international relations, a good deal less 'ideological' and interventionist, in fact, than the approach which the United States has brought to world affairs since 1945. Since the end of World War II, the United States has intervened in every part of the globe to defeat revolutionary movements and to maintain a status quo favourable to its own purposes. Indeed, it has intervened not only against revolutionary movements and regimes, but against moderately reformist ones as well, as in the case of Guatemala in 1954 and of Chile between 1970 and 1973, when it did everything it could to 'destabilise' and bring down a constitutional and 'pluralist' government in favour of a military junta which it has supported unswervingly ever since—all in the name of national security, freedom, democracy, etc. Nicaragua's reforming regime is the latest to bear the brunt of United States hostility; but it will not be the last. In the light of this consistent record of anti-revolutionary intervention in the name of American security, it cannot be said that there is anything very abnormal in the Soviet leaders' own preoccupation with 'security', however much one may disapprove of their conception of it or of the paths in which it leads. All in all, the record shows that Soviet leaders have been a great deal less reckless than American ones in invoking 'national security' in the defence of what they took to be their interests. They have, in fact, often displayed a remarkable degree of restraint in times of crisis: their actions, or non-actions, in the crisis provoked by the Israeli invasion of the Lebanon in the summer of 1982, illustrate the point, and contrast markedly with American military intervention in the area. Nor is it to be overlooked that the Russians have on occasion accepted quite meekly what amounted to a 'reversal of alliances' on the part of countries from which they found themselves humiliatingly expelled, notwithstanding all the aid they had given them: Egypt is the best case in point. Somalia is another.

Of course, Soviet leaders do seek to win friends and gain influence wherever they can, and view the establishment of revolutionary regimes anywhere as of advantage to themselves, whether these regimes proclaim themselves to be 'Marxist–Leninist' or not. The main reason for this is clear, and has already been suggested earlier, namely that all such revolutionary regimes, whatever their ideological dispositions, have it as one of their main aims to remove their country from the American sphere of influence, more properly described, for many countries, as the American sphere of domination. Inevitably, any such weakening of American global power is viewed by Soviet leaders as a net gain.

In this perspective, the really remarkable thing is not that the Soviet Union should extend aid to revolutionary movements and to newly-established revolutionary regimes, but that it is quite cautious in what it does in this respect. However, it does voice support and extend aid to such regimes, and provides an important counterweight to American power and purpose by virtue of its presence on the international scene. On occasion, this has quite decisive consequences. It is for instance very likely that the Cuban regime would have gone under without Soviet support and material help. Similarly, Cuban military intervention in Angola was decisive at a critical point for the revolutionary forces. Whether Cuba was acting on its own initiative or at the behest of the Soviet Union is not here very important: for it could not have acted at all if it had not itself received support from the Soviet Union.

In this light, it is perfectly true that the existence of the Soviet Union and its active presence on the international scene is or can be 'subversive', and that it often does run counter to the anti-revolutionary purposes of the United States and its allies. It is a naive illusion of the more primitive devotees of anti-communism that all revolutionary movements would cease, or would cease to be revolutionary, if the Soviet Union did not exercise its baleful and sinister influence in the world. But it is true that such movements would, generally speaking, be easier to deal with if the Soviet Union did not exist or could somehow be prevented from extending any help to revolutionary movements. In this sense at least, and from a conservative perspective, anti-communism does have a point.

Any attempt to redress the 'balance of blame' is naturally anathema to anti-communism, and is automatically denounced as an apologia for the repression of dissidents, the Gulag Archipelago, Stalinism and everything else that is wrong with the Soviet regime. This is a form of moral terrorism and political blackmail that must be resisted. Quite apart from pointing to the actual as opposed to the mythical record, a simple question may be asked from those who have made subscription to the belief in Soviet 'expansionism' an article of political intelligence, decency, morality, etc: what reasons can anti-communism advance to justify the view that everything which the Soviet leaders do is motivated by 'expansionist' ambitions and purposes? What, in other words, are the *reasons* which can be invoked to explain these 'expansionist' ambitions?

On examination, the reasons advanced turn out to be exceedingly flimsy. One of them is that the Soviet leaders have an insatiable desire for power. But the question is not whether the Soviet leaders want power. This may be taken for granted, though it can hardly be said to be a trait unique to them. All leaders everywhere want power: otherwise, they would not be leaders. But Soviet leaders already have all the power they can handle, and more; and there is nothing in the record to suggest that this kind of pseudo-psychological construction has anything to offer by way of a plausible explanation of Soviet foreign policy.

Indeed, as has already been noted, there have been many occasions when Soviet leaders, far from supporting revolutionary developments which might have been favourable to an increase in their power abroad, have in fact been opposed to what they viewed as revolutionary 'adventurism', and as running counter to their view of what Soviet security demanded. It should be recalled, in this connection, that both the Yugoslav and the Chinese revolutions would have been stalled at the end of World War II if their leaders had accepted Soviet advice, which was for Tito and Mao to enter into coalition with their enemies. Had the advice been taken, the result would have been a curbing not an extension of Communist power; and Stalin was as willing to accept this as he was willing to see another such Communist retreat which we noted earlier, namely that of the Greek Communists.

Nor was this suspicion of revolutionary movements and the fear of 'adventurism' peculiar to Stalin. It has also been exhibited by his succesors, as was shown, for instance, by the extreme reserve observed by the Soviet leaders in regard to the 'May events' in France in 1968, and their approval of the French Communist Party's own rejection of 'adventurist' policies.

These instances also serve to undermine another reason advanced to justify the notion of Soviet 'expansionism', namely that the Soviet leaders are driven by a compelling ideological proselytism, and that they will not rest until the whole world has been converted, by force if necessary, to their particular brand of 'Marxism–Leninism'. Here too, the record gives no support to any such view. Soviet leaders may welcome the proclamation by this or that revolutionary regime of its 'Marxist–Leninist' convictions. But we have already noted that their approval is based, not on any great ideological zeal, but on the more mundane consideration that such proclamations, whether they betoken good relations with the Soviet Union or not (and they may not) almost certainly betoken bad relations with the United States. 'Marxism–Leninism' may sustain Soviet leaders, just as 'democracy' or 'freedom' or whatever may sustain Western leaders. But ideological considerations have nevertheless always played a very secondary role in Soviet foreign policy; and such considerations have never prevented Soviet leaders from actions inspired by the starkest notions of *real-politik*: the Hitler–Stalin alliance, which lasted from 1939 until Hitler attacked the Soviet Union in 1941 is the most spectacular illustration of the point; but there have been many others.

In any case, it must also be said that there is nothing in 'Marxism–Leninism', not to speak of Marxism, which requires their disciples to proselytise at the point of bayonets. On the contrary, it is one of the firmest tenets of Marxism revolutionary theory that revolutions are not for export and must be made at home. Proletarian internationalism demands that revolutionary movements should be supported; but that is hardly the same thing as the export of revolution. Anti-communists often speak as if the Soviet leaders were passionate converts to the Trotskyist doctrine of 'permanent revolution'. They are not. The support they do give to revolutionary movements is based upon very different considerations, paramount among which is what they take to be the Soviet 'national interest' and Soviet security. None of these perceptions entails the kind of global 'expansionism' which anti-communism proclaims to be at the core of Soviet purposes.

III

We have so far referred to anti-communism as if there was only one version of it. There are in fact a good many; and it may be useful to point to distinct positions, emphases and nuances within a common framework of anti-communism.

There is, to begin with, an absolutist position, which finds many different expressions, but whose common denominator is a total, unqualified and vehement rejection of 'communism' as the embodiment of evil, the work of Satan, the product of the darkest and most sinister impulses of the human spirit, the negation of civilisation and enlightenment, and much else of the same kind. This anti-communism, couched in extreme moralistic terms, often with strongly religious connotations, sees the Soviet Union as the material incarnation of evil and as the main source of the dissemination of evil. Consequently, its disappearance from the face of the earth is a prime condition of human regeneration and salvation, and something to be prayed and worked for, fought and died for.

The beauty of this position is that it admits and indeed invites every kind of hyperbole and does not require validation by way of evidence, analysis or anything else. It is enough that it should be expressed, preferably in a suitably exalted rhetoric. Nor is it encumbered by any notion of prudence, compromise, negotiation and accommodation. Any such notion is itself a token of corruption, weakness and perversity. How can one seek accommodation with ultimate evil?

This absolutist position is held by very diverse people, from the primitive anti-communists of the John Birch Society and other such ultra-right organisations in the United States and other capitalist countries, to sophisticated American and European intellectuals, many of them ex-Stalinists, ex-Maoists, former ultra-left revolutionaries or would-be revolutionaries of one sort or another, who now bring to their present commitments the same unrestrained and apocalyptic ardour which they brought to the old ones. Their ranks are constantly added to by Soviet and East European emigrés whose understandable bitterness and hatred brings valuable support to this section of the anti-communist camp.

The absolutist position has of course very strong political resonances. But it is not a position which Western conservatism can readily adopt, save for the purposes of ideological warfare, on the lines of President Reagan's reference to the Soviet Union as the 'empire of evil'; and even such rhetoric has normally to be used sparingly by politicians, lest it should frighten an electorate which does not want dangerous and expensive crusades. Western conservatism is not less anti-communist than the ultras of the Right, but its leaders must perforce seek to deal with the Soviet Union in less inflamed terms, from which negotiation and even compromise cannot be excluded.

A range of positions is to be found here, whose occupants all want to achieve the containment of revolutionary movements everywhere, and the curtailment or stoppage of Soviet help to such movements. At one end of this conservative spectrum, there lurks the hope—even the belief—that rather more than containment may eventually become possible, and that 'communism' may be rolled back in a number of countries where it has come to prevail, and even that this may yet come to be possible in the Soviet Union itself. At the other end of the spectrum, the 'liberal' end, there is the belief, entirely justified, that such aspirations must generate policies and actions which make war, up to and including nuclear war, more rather than less likely; and there is also at this end the hope that the Soviet Union might be induced to play a 'moderate' (and moderating) role in the world, on terms which would be economically and politically advantageous to it. The Soviet Union must be 'deterred': but it is from extending help to revolutionary movements that it must be 'deterred', rather than from launching a military attack on the West, an eventuality in which no serious politician truly believes.

Alongside conservative anti-communism, there has existed from the first days of the Bolshevik Revolution a fierce social democratic anti-communism, which has been of great political consequence. The divisions between right and left in the labour movements of capitalist societies were bitter and profound long before Lenin was ever heard of. But the victory of the Bolsheviks deepened them much further and gave them new institutional forms; and the repressive nature of the Soviet regime, combined with Communist attacks on social democratic leaders, served to reinforce in these leaders tendencies that were already well developed towards a 'socialism' which held no threat to the established order. Anti-communism was a major factor in the insertion of social democratic movements into that established order, and provided a powerful ideological basis of agreement between social democratic leaders and their conservative opponents. From 1945 onwards, it also provided the basis for a broad consensus between them on foreign and defence policies; and social democratic leaders played a major role in the legitimation of the Cold War and in the mobilisation of labour movements behind the banner of anti-communism.

In many countries, anti-communism has also been a valuable weapon in the hands of social democratic trade union and political leaders in their struggles inside unions and parties against Communists, and also against left activists who sought to challenge their positions. It has often been very convenient to meet the challenge with anti-communist denunciations, supplemented in many cases by measures of exclusion of the critics from positions of power and influence, and by expulsion from party membership.

It is, however, to conservative forces in capitalist countries that anti-communism has been of the greatest value in their struggle against the whole left, social democracy included. It has in fact been their favourite weapon: in no legislative or presidential election in a capitalist-democratic regime since 1918 (not to speak of 'elections' in capitalist-authoritarian ones) have conservatives failed to exploit the Communist and Soviet 'menace', even though 'communism' has usually been totally irrelevant to the issues in contention, with Communists very often, as in the United States, virtually or totally absent from the scene. Once 'communism' could be turned into the issue, however implausibly, argument could be laid aside and invective and denunciation could take over, and be directed against anyone who did not wholly subscribe to the basic tenets of anti-communism, or to whatever notions and policies anti-communists chose to propound. However much social democrats and liberals might vie with their conservative opponents in their anti-communist proclamations, the latter were virtually unbeatable on this terrain.

Moreover, the fact that 'communism' could be identified with the Soviet Union, and that the Soviet Union was after 1945 proclaimed to be a dire and urgent threat to 'national security' made it possible for anti-communists to denounce anyone who opposed them not only as godless, immoral, unpatriotic and subversive (that had been said since 1917, and for that matter long before then as well), but also as supporters, allies or agents of their country's greatest enemy. Some anti-communists generously conceded that all those they denounced might not actually be 'traitors', but only weak and naive dupes; but that did not diminish the need to denounce them and their views.

The identification of 'Communists' with the Soviet enemy has also been of the greatest value in legitimating witchhunting at the level of the state. The existence of witches requires efficient witchhunters, and this requirement has greatly helped to justify the vast enlargement of the control and surveillance functions of the state, and the vast increase in the scope and powers of the security services. Anti-communism and the 'strong state' are closely linked: the more pervasive and extreme the former, the stronger the movement towards the latter. Once 'communism' is proclaimed to constitute a clear and present danger of subversion at home and of military aggression from abroad, it is much easier to argue that the times do not admit the luxury of libertarian squeamishness.

The same reasoning goes for society at large. Faced with the Communist threat, it is not only the state which must be strong and vigilant, but all institutions in society where subversion is most insidious and dangerous—the media, schools, universities, firms engaged in work related to defence, or even unrelated to it. Exclusion of people deemed politically 'unreliable', 'unsound', potentially subversive, in other words too far to the left, need not always be explicit; the important thing, from the anti-communist perspective, is that exclusion should be practised, and that it should serve as a warning to others. The extent to which this occurs also varies, depending on the country and the period; but even if the more spectacular forms of McCarthyism are now discredited, a creeping version of it has come to form part of the life of many if not most capitalist countries.

Anti-communism has in recent years made great use of a rhetoric which assigns a very large place to human rights, political and civic freedoms, and so forth. These are indeed precious values, which is why they are at the very heart of the socialist project. Anti-communists, on the other hand, cannot, as such, be taken to be true defenders of these values. We have already noted the selectivity which they bring to their defence of human rights and political freedoms, and the indulgence which they are willing to extend to the most repressive regimes, provided they are not 'communist'. It may be noted in addition that it is among these same defenders of freedom and human rights in Communist regimes that are to be found the most dedicated advocates of the curtailment of civic and political freedoms in their own countries, and the most ardent supporters of interventionist policies designed to shore up tyrannical regimes.

There is, however, something else to be noted about the ways in which anti-communists view human rights, quite apart from the selectivity with which their concern for these rights is usually manifested. This is the extremely *circumscribed* meaning which they attach to human rights. These rights are taken—quite rightly—to be violated when people are deprived of the chance to exercise elementary civic and political rights, and are persecuted for their opposition to their government or regime. But human rights are also violated, and dreadfully violated, when men, women and children are denied the elementary requirements of life, as they are in the 'Third World', and not only in the 'Third World'. Hunger, disease induced by destitution, the lack of clean water, early death, are great violations of human rights.[7] But these are not the violations which anti-communist defenders of human rights are much given to attack, or even to acknowledge. On the contrary, their anti-communism leads them to acquiesce in, and even to support, the social order which is responsible for these violations, and to oppose the movements which seek to undo the status quo. These crusaders purport to fight for human rights; but their crusade in fact entails support for everything that makes for the denial of such rights.

In the anti-communist crusade, we also suggested earlier, the bogey of a Soviet military threat of world-wide dimensions plays an absolutely essential part. For it serves to legitimate American and other interventionist enterprises in every part of the world against revolutionary and even reformist movements, on the principle that these movements, if allowed to grow and to succeed, are bound to 'let the Russians in', that they must produce a 'domino effect', and that they must inevitably threaten vital economic and strategic Western interests. Everything is permissible to prevent this from happening, including the massacre in military operations of large numbers of men, women and children.[8]

The Soviet bogey also has a uniquely important role in legitimating the arms race. Nothing else could possibly persuade the populations of capitalist countries to support the expense, the waste and the risks of that race. Arms themselves do not produce wars. But the need to justify the arms race generates campaigns of anti-communist propaganda which contribute to a tense and fraught international climate; in that climate, confrontation between the United States and the Soviet Union becomes more likely and more dangerous.

The danger of such a confrontation is in any case already high. For in a world astir with challenge to the status quo, anti-communist insistence that any such challenge must be opposed by the United States and met by American intervention means in effect that the avoidance of confrontation between the 'super-powers' depends on the Soviet Union's acquiescence in American intervention, wherever it may occur. This is not a safe basis on which to rest the maintenance of peace.

Anti-communism has to be fought. The struggle against it is made much harder by the nature of the Soviet regime and by many of its policies and actions, from the treatment of Sakharov and other 'dissidents' at one level, to the invasion of Afghanistan at another. But it is nevertheless a struggle that must not be shunned, for the sake of peace, of democratic rights, and of socialist advance.

NOTES

1. For a self-critical analysis by an ex-Stalinist, notable for its dignity and sobriety, see M. Rodinson, *Cult, Ghetto and State* (London, 1983), Ch. 2.

2. See J.J. Kirkpatrick, *Dictatorships and Double Standards*, (New York, 1982), Ch. 1.

3. *The Times*, 30 December, 1983.

4. A.J. Mayer, *Politics and Diplomacy of Peacemaking. Containment and Counter-revolution at Versailles. 1918-1919*, (New York, 1967), p. 9.

5. These fears, in relation to the Far East and the projected entry of the Soviet Union in the war against Japan, may not have been the only reason for the decision to drop atom bombs on Hiroshima and Nagasaki. But they were part of the calculations which went into the making of that decision.

6. It is well known that the Russians lost up to twenty million people killed in the war. But the material damage which they sustained was also immense, with, according to official Soviet statements, the total or partial destruction of fifteen large cities, 1,710 towns and 70,000 villages, six million buildings, more than 30,000 enterprises, etc., etc. (D. Horowitz, *The Free World Colossus*, (London, 1964), p. 51, fn. 3.

7. Thus, Norman Geras notes that '40,000 children die every day; that of the 122 million born in 1979, 17 million (nearly 14 per cent) will die before they are five; that between 350 and 500 million people are disabled, the major cause of this being poverty: about 100 million have been disabled by malnutrition; that 180 million children are not getting enough food to sustain health and minimal physical activity: protein deficiency, which can lead to mental retardation, affects 100 million under five in developing countries. . . over half the people in the third world have no access to safe water and that water-borne diseases kill some 30,000 people every day and account for about 80 per cent of all illnesses: every year 400 to 500 million are affected by trachoma and six million children die of diarrhoea. . . that in the tin mines of Bolivia a miner's life expectancy is reduced to 35 because of silicosis and tuberculosis; that 375,000 or more people in the third world will this year be poisoned by pesticides. . .' (N. Geras, *Marx and Human Nature: Refutation of a Legend*, (London, 1983), p. 105).

8. Thus, the French in Indochina and Algeria, the British in Malaya and Kenya, and the Americans in Korea and Vietnam. The devastation which the United States inflicted on Vietnam and Cambodia is not yet quite forgotten. On the other hand, the devastation inflicted on Korea by bombing is seldom remembered. The head of Bomber Command in the Far East described it in the following terms: 'I would say that the entire, almost the entire Korean peninsula is just a terrible mess. Everything is destroyed. There is nothing standing worthy of the name. . . Just before the Chinese came in we were grounded. There were no more targets in Korea', (Horowitz, *op. cit.*, p. 135).

FIGHTING THE COLD WAR ON THE HOME FRONT:
AMERICA, BRITAIN, AUSTRALIA AND CANADA

Reg Whitaker

'Are you in pain, dear mother?'
'I think there's a pain somewhere in the room', said Mrs. Gradgrind, 'but I couldn't positively say that I have got it.'

Dickens, *Hard Times*

The decade following World War II was the formative period of post-war alignment in international relations, the point of congealment for the Cold War. There is a vast literature on the international aspects of the events of this decade. Yet one of the striking characteristics of this era was domestic: 'a tightening of controls within the capitalist and communist camps, a construction of military blocs, a repression of those suspected of sympathies for the other side (persecution of Titoists in Eastern Europe, McCarthyism in the USA)'.[1] This process of internal political repression was an element in the primordial division of the post-war world into two armed and relatively disciplined camps. It also had profound implications for the politics of the countries involved. The sharpening of ideological conflict and the deployment of coercion to consolidate a quasi-wartime national 'consensus' could not leave unmarked the practice of pluralist and competitive politics in capitalist democracies. It was in the United States, the leader and organiser of the Western bloc, where the impact of McCarthyism on liberal democratic practices was most evident. As a consequence, there is a large literature, often of high quality, on the domestic impact of the Cold War on the USA. There is, however, very little written about the domestic impact on the other English-speaking countries, where the lesser public impression of McCarthyism has generally been taken as notice of its absence. Yet the Cold War was launched in other Western nations allied to the US. The domestic implantation of the Cold War obviously differs according to the specific conditions of individual countries. The American variant—McCarthyism—has no privileged status as a model by which other countries must be judged.

There is a spectrum of domestic responses to the Cold War which requires some specification. Here I will offer an interpretation of the significance of the American experience, followed by a survey, based mainly on secondary sources, of Britain and Australia, and a summary of my own findings, based on extensive research in archival sources, docu-

23

ments obtained under Access to Information and interviews, of the Canadian experience.[2]

In analysing the national experiences of Cold War repression, I wish to make a distinction at the outset between *state repression* and *political repression*. By 'state' repression is meant forms of coercive control exercised through the official state apparatus—the 'legitimate' use of force in the classic Weberian definition. 'Legitimate' of course refers only to the existing legislative and constitutional framework and to actions sanctioned by state authority. 'Political' repression on the other hand, refers to the exercise of coercion outside the state system proper, but originating in the wider political system (parties, pressure groups, private associations). McCarthyism as a generic term describes the spread of repression outside the state system to the political system (e.g., a public smear of an individual by a politician leading to sanctions against that individual such as dismissal by an employer or informal harassment in the community, or the purge of left-wing trade unionists carried out not by the state but by the unions themselves). Although it was McCarthyism in its highly visible American form which raised the most concern among liberals, it is important to realise that state repression was, and is, an integral part of the domestic implantation and reproduction of the Cold War in all Western countries. The greater concentration among America's allies on the repressive apparatus of the state has misled many observers into the false conclusion that domestic repression was a peculiarly American aspect of the Cold War.

Any discussion of the excesses of political repression in the capitalist democracies must begin with a clear disclaimer. The same period marked by McCarthyism in the West, the late 1940s and early 1950s, were also the years of intensified purges and repression in the Soviet bloc. Strictly speaking, from the point of view of political violence, there is scarcely any comparison between the blocs: the communist purges were far more extensive, brutal and bloody, than anything contemplated by the most extreme witch-hunters of the West. It has been estimated that in Eastern Europe alone, over one and a half million Communist Party members were purged; in some countries, top leaders were shot. At the same time in the Soviet Union, Stalin was whipping up anti-semitism, anti-intellectualism, anti-cosmopolitanism, as themes in a purge which 'had Stalin survived. . . would most likely have assumed the horrendous proportions of the ones in 1936–38'.[3]

Yet however much the two blocs differed in their political practices, it is striking how the tempo of repression (if not the intensity) rose and fell as if orchestrated under the common baton of Cold War discipline. Stalin's passing and Senator McCarthy's political demise in the early 1950s were symbolic watersheds marking both a renewed willingness of both camps to negotiate differences and a declining level of domestic discipline and repression. Even at the height of repression, there are haunting similarities: the American discovery of an ubiquitous Red menace within, a 'conspiracy so immense, an infamy so black', was matched on the other side by the discovery of the ubiquity of the Titoist enemy: 'as is characteristic of such operations, the purges transcended any conscious or half-rational purpose of weeding out the anti-Russian or even potentially intransigent elements'.[4] In both camps, repression was *irrational*, uncontrolled, and eventually threatened internal stability. Even if self-destructive and thus self-limiting, repression was also functional to the Cold War, defining in sharply constricted fashion the limits of political dissent and permissible levels of conflict within the two blocs. If the renewal of Cold War competition in the late 1970s and early 1980s has not been marked by a level of repression equivalent to that of the earlier period (again, quite unevenly as between the two blocs), this may only indicate that the first Cold War repression served to congeal domestic political practices in forms appropriate enough that renewed waves of repression are scarcely necessary.

The United States

The main lines of the post-war repression in America are familiar. Coincident with the emergent commitment to global confrontation with the Soviet Union in the late 1940s, a conservative anti-New Deal trend became evident in domestic politics. Republican control of Congress in the 1946 elections was only the tip of the conservative iceberg. A major counterattack against the post-war upsurge in labour militancy was capped by the repressive anti-labour Taft–Hartley Act in 1947. The same year saw the declaration by the Democratic administration of the Loyalty–Security Programme, the basis for a purge of alleged left-wing civil servants; the federal example was followed in turn by state and municipal jurisdictions. By the mid-1950s, tens of thousands of public employees had been fired or resigned under fear of being fired. 1948 saw the publication of the Attorney-General's list of 'subversive' organisations—in effect a public proscription of free association which was updated and expanded from year to year. 1948 also witnessed the public spectacle of the Alger Hiss–Whittaker Chambers confrontation, and the circus-like proceedings of the House Committee on Un-American Activities (HUAC) in Hollywood. The upset re-election of Harry Truman the same year did nothing to quell the fires of right-wing repression, which grew ominously along with the deterioration of the American position in the Cold War, with the Soviet takeovers in Eastern Europe, the Berlin blockade, the 1949 victory of the Communists in China, and the testing of the first Soviet atomic bomb.

By the early 1950s, with American ground forces in action in Korea, the pattern of internal repression was clear. The federal government led the way, with its internal purge, its widespread use of the FBI to carry out domestic spying and undercover operations, its across-the-board use of immigration and passport regulations to control the movements of its own citizens, deport 'undesirables', and to keep out of the country visitors judged dangerous. The atmosphere of suspicion spread downwards through the structures of civil society. Universities and schools were swept by purges, censorship and enforced loyalty oaths. The media were cleansed of dissenting opinions. Persons suspected of disloyalty were fired from jobs far removed from the state, or from classified information. Above all, a distinctive American form of repression became familiar: the Congressional Investigation Committee which hauled witnesses before the television cameras, accused them of treason and disloyalty, and demanded as the price of forgiveness that they publicly recant and 'name names', which is to say, turn public informer on their friends and associates. Those who failed to do so were often jailed, and almost always blacklisted from their professions or employment. The image of the 'witch-hunt' has been often applied to this process, and the name of the most politically successful practitioner of the technique, Senator Joseph McCarthy, became an identifying label: McCarthyism.

The spectacular demagogic talents of McCarthy having lent the entire period the epithet of the 'McCarthy era', has led to a tendency to focus too exclusively on the Senator and his personal phenomenon. The process of internal political repression began well before McCarthy even appeared on the scene, and must be explained in broader terms than the career of one man alone. By and large, however, it did not really survive the political demise of McCarthy in 1954. McCarthy stretched the limits of political intolerance further than anyone else, and when his demagoguery finally consumed itself by attacking a Republican president and the US Army, there followed an apparent exhaustion of the repressive drive, in its highly politicised aspect, at least.[5]

The first, contemporaneous, attempts to explain the repression tended to be limited by two factors. First, McCarthy overshadowed the larger phenomenon of repression; second, explanations of McCarthyism came mainly from American liberals who were themselves deeply implicated in the emergent Cold War consensus. Part of the post-war reformulation of liberal ideology was the delegitimation of Marxism (tolerated to an extent on the margins of the New Deal in the 1930s and war years), and the identification of 'Communists' as beyond the protection of liberal freedoms. Given the near pervasive acceptance of a selectively illiberal consensus on freedom of expression, freedom of association and freedom of thought, Cold War liberalism reacted with considerable revulsion, but also with much intellectual and political confusion, when repression was taken up by right-wing anti-New Deal Republicans like McCarthy as a blunt instrument against liberals.[6] The problem was formulated as being 'McCarthyism' rather than Cold War repression, and explanations were as much expression of the ideological and intellectual crisis of American liberalism at the end of its New Deal hegemony as they were scientific analyses of the phenomenon of repression.

The Cold War liberal response was summed up in a collection by liberal 'stars' of political sociology, edited by Daniel Bell.[7] Bell's stable of academic liberals, ranging from Talcott Parsons to Seymour Martin Lipset, provided weighty and elaborate deployment of some then fashionable themes. McCarthyism was not a product of economic or class forces, nor even of ideology. Instead it reflected status anxieties in mass society. Indeed, it represented the dark side of democracy first revealed by de Tocqueville, the illiberal face of populism. American liberals who in their New Deal days had seen themselves in direct continuity with the Jacksonian and Populist movements of the past, now saw themselves as an embattled and privileged elite under attack by the authoritarian and intolerant masses led by a demagogic tribune of the people.[8]

This explanation, with various nuances, stood more or less unassailed for a number of years. By the late 1960s, however, the decline of Cold War liberalism in the wake of the Kennedy–Johnson fiasco in Vietnam, led to some rethinking of the first Cold War experience. Michael Paul Rogin's *The Intellectuals and McCarthy: the Radical Specter* brilliantly demolished much of the earlier argument.[9] By detailed empirical analysis, Rogin showed that McCarthyism had no links with earlier agrarian and radical populist movements, as the mass society theorists had claimed. An earlier study by political scientist Nelson Polsby had attempted to measure mass support for McCarthy and found it concentrated in areas of traditional Republican strength; McCarthy, Polsby suggested, was 'more dependent on his party, and personally less effective at the grass roots, than has been commonly supposed.'[10] Rogin noted Polsby's findings that the party was the variable most strongly associated with support for McCarthy, and took it further: McCarthy had mobilised one wing, the small town mid-west isolationists, in a divided Republican party. His campaign was enlivened in the context of the Cold War: the 'loss' of China, the inability to win in Korea, and the consequent search for scapegoats within reach, as well as resurgent anti-New Deal sentiments. But rather than representing radicalism, McCarthy reached as far as he did through the manipulation of traditional political institutions and the failure of the Democratic and liberal elites to confront him. This was really a failure of liberal will in the Cold War era. McCarthy lost his purchase on influence when he took on a Republican president, the Senate, and the US Army. In short, 'as McCarthy became "radical", he lost his hold on American politics'.[11]

One of the extraordinary observations to be drawn from the empirical data on public attitudes during the McCarthy era is not the generalised evidence of illiberalism elicited by leading questions—which in any event remains remarkably level over time, both before and after McCarthy—but rather the lack of effect on the public of the highly publicised themes of subversion and fifth column threats. When asked an open-ended question in the summer of 1954 about what worried them most personally, less than one percent of a national sample of Americans mentioned communism (or civil liberties). The first massive quantitative study of voting behaviour in an American national election, in 1952, yielded the surprising finding that despite 'the enormous furore over internal subversion', the issue 'appealed so little to the public that it was scarcely mentioned to our interviewers—indeed, it was of less salience to the decision to vote Republican than the fact that Democratic presidential candidate Adlai Stevenson had been divorced![12] There was nothing approaching a mass mobilisation around extreme anti-communist demands. The idea that McCarthy might have constituted an American Hitler nipped in the bud is a paranoid fantasy; there were no American mass politics of the extreme right. There were, however, extreme right politics played out in the leading institutions of American government, which is a somewhat different matter.

It is important to recognise the specific issue at hand here. Theorising about 'the authoritarian personality' or 'working-class authoritarianism' fails to indicate why the anti-communist issue erupted in the political arena at the particular conjuncture of the late 1940s, and why it died down again in the mid-1950s. This is even more the case with the sort of 'national character' explanations of an anthropological type proffered by cultural critics. It is not that such explanations are necessarily wrong, or lacking in interest. It is simply that by explaining everything, in general, they explain nothing, in particular.[13]

The bias of liberal explanations is further elucidated by recent revisionist history of the origins of political repression in the Cold War era. Kenneth O'Riley has shown in well documented detail that it was, in fact, an agency of the United States government, J. Edgar Hoover's FBI, which beginning in 1946 masterminded a vast anti-communist drive throughout government and the media. The FBI fed the House Committee on Un-American Activities, McCarthy and other congressional witch-hunters with the information without which they would have been unable to operate.[14] This was a bureaucratic, top-down operation. Other work, particularly that of Athan Theoharis, has demonstrated the crucial role played by the Truman administration in bringing on the repression. It was the Democrats who instituted the Loyalty–Security Programme to root out Communists and 'disloyal' employees from the government: state and municipal jurisdictions followed later. It was the Democrats whose Attorney-General raised the rhetorical level concerning the threat of subversion and first published the infamous Attorney-General's List of subversive organisations. It was the Democrats who perfected the art of the Red smear and guilt-by-association in their violent attack on

Henry Wallace's Progressive Party campaign in 1948. Even as late as 1954, after the Democrats' loss of the White House and at the zenith of McCarthyism, it was the liberal Democrat Hubert Humphrey who was instrumental in the passage through Congress of the Communist Control Act, in intention one of the most repressive of all the McCarthy-era laws.[15]

It has sometimes been argued that the Democrats were merely responding to intense right-wing pressure by attempting to appease, and thus pre-empt it.[16] Yet it must be kept in mind that the Truman administration was itself part of the source for the rightward pressures. The Cold War began under Democratic auspices. The Republicans were the party associated with isolationism and fiscal conservatism. With the Truman Doctrine, a peacetime rearmament programme, the Marshall Plan, the creation of NATO, and finally the commitment of American ground forces to combat in Korea, a Democratic president was moving America into permanent military, political and economic intervention on a world scale, at enormous cost. The consolidation of the home front meant the securing of a bipartisan consensus on foreign and defence policy. Early on, especially with the Republican-controlled Congress in 1947–48, there was some difficulty in gaining spending approval. Republican Senator Arthur Vandenberg, a key Truman ally in Congress representing the old isolationist wing, had advised the President to 'scare hell out of the American people'. His advice was taken. The early history of the Cold War commitments of the United States abroad was punctuated by the orchestration of the Red scare at home. This served not only to bring Republican isolationists and penny-pinchers inside, but also to undermine and discredit potential left-wing dissent from within the old Roosevelt Democratic coalition. The latter succeeded with the expulsion of the Henry Wallace wing into the political wilderness, and the Cold War within the CIO against the elements of a labour Left associated with the Communist Party.

The Truman administration did not of course invent the demons of right-wing repression which rose up in the leading institutions of American life. But by pandering to them, by encouraging them, it gave credence to the idea that there were 'Communists' in high places wreaking havoc with the national interest. In short, it lent legitimacy to an issue which could only advantage the Democrats' opponents. The Truman administration believed its pre-emptive repression had worked when Truman was re-elected in the face of a Republican–Dixiecrat–Progressive challenge in the 1948 election. But this was only a brief pause, as the fires of the witch-hunt quickly flared yet higher. With the appearance of McCarthy on the scene in 1950, the vultures came home to roost with a vengeance. Some leading figures from the New Deal civil service were consumed. The State Department, that centre-piece of Truman's new 'internationalism', became a special target of the witch-hunters, particularly after the 'loss' of China. Athan Theoharis has ably summarised the connections between the external and internal Cold Wars under the Democrats:

> The Cold War did not merely influence US foreign policy; it also created a climate that influenced domestic legislation and politics. McCarthyism was not an aberration. It dramatized the acceptance of an anti-Communist rhetoric basic to the Cold War and the shift in focus and tactics of those partisan or conservative Republicans bitterly opposed to the New Deal. Foreign policy gave those Republicans an opportunity to discredit the progressive ideas of the New Deal and a challenge to assail the extended, complex international responsibilities basic to the Truman Administration's containment policy.[17]

What emerges then is a picture of a national government moving to commit America to a permanent 'peacetime' war footing and exploiting the alleged domestic communist threat as a means both of eliminating enemies to its left and gaining the assent of the Right. The issue of internal subversion and the need for repression was then transformed by the Republicans into an instrument of partisan attack on the Democrats. As such, it was largely wielded by the mid-west isolationist wing but tolerated by the Eastern internationalist wing so long as it seemed an effective partisan tactic. Thus there was a period within which the Cold War strategy of the state combined with the dynamics of the party system to foster domestic political repression. When the repression began to turn on the Democrats themselves, they were singularly defenceless against it given that they shared in its fundamental assumptions. Finally, the repression, in the person of McCarthy, threatened to turn on the Republicans, now established in state office. It had become counter-productive, and the major conservative institutions of American government, such as the Senate, the Presidency, and the Republican party itself, rejected McCarthy. The media followed, and the Senator was henceforth excluded from public attention. Repression was taken out of the public political arena and returned to its traditional place in the state system. The McCarthy era came to an end.

Although the period was marked by political, as opposed to state repression, there is, as I have noted, very little evidence of a mass politics. The peculiarities of the American political system, with its division of powers, lack of party discipline, and the diffusion of power and influence across a quasi-feudal complex of committees, subcommittees, chairmanships, bureaux and agencies, etc., obviously provided an institutional framework conducive to the exploitation of the Red scare as a political issue. In such a system, the mobilisation of mass movements may count for a great deal less than the mobilisation of key elites and interest groups. The inattention and apparent indifference of the general public to the issue of communist subversion may have provided the background for the dissipation of the issue following the counter-attack of the Republican establishment, but they did nothing to prevent the freelance witch-hunters of Congress, and those who aped them at the state and local levels, from wheeling and dealing on the basis of political capital essentially drawn from the internal resources of the political system and the political elites themselves.

To be sure, despite its complexity, American politics is democratic in the narrow sense that politicians must get themselves elected, and operate on some sort of popular bases. The question of which specific 'public' offered support has been one which has inspired the considerable efforts of American political scientists. Traditional Republican supporters, especially of the more conservative, isolationist and small town type, seem to have formed the backbone of sympathy for McCarthy in the electorate. The partisan concentration had, at the same time, distinct drawbacks. Two elements of the electorate in particular, Roman Catholics and Southerners, might have been expected to have shown exceptionally high support for McCarthyism. Catholics, responding not only to McCarthy's own Irish Catholicism, but also to the fierce anti-communist ideology then prevalent throughout the Catholic church worldwide, did support McCarthy more than Protestants, by about 8–10 per cent on average. However, this was countered by other factors, most importantly party factors: Catholics predominantly supported the Democrats, and partisan identification undermined a potential mass Catholic base.[18] Southerners tended to display attitudes generally appropriate to the McCarthyite ideology, and Southern politicians were consistently among the most bellicose Cold Warriors and repressive reactionaries on issues of civil liberties. Here again, party intervened—in this case dramatically. McCarthy was especially unpopular in the South, which was solidly, even monolithically Democratic.[19]

There is one further 'public' which warrants examination. What was the response of the working class to McCarthyism, given the prevalence of 'working-class authoritarianism' and the 'revolt of the masses' in standard liberal explanations? Here the answer must be nuanced. Unionized workers tended to show lower than average support for McCarthy and in McCarthy's own state they voted against him more strongly than they voted Democrat. The AFL tended to neutrality, with some unions pro-McCarthy but more being hostile. The CIO unions were anti-McCarthy perhaps more out of Democratic partisanship than because they viewed the Senator as a threat to American institutions.[20]

Working-class or union support for McCarthy, as such, is a much less interesting question than how the issue of anti-communism and the Cold War was played out *within* working-class life. American labour had emerged from the war with pent-up demands for foregone wage increases further encouraged by high post-war inflation. A strike wave followed.

The rightward trend exemplified by resurgent Republicanism was especially virulent in its anti-unionism. The Taft–Hartley Act was one prong of state intervention in labour relations and in the internal affairs of unions; another was the extension of the government's Loyalty–Security programme to industries holding defence contracts; a third were Red-hunting congressional investigations of labour.

The unions were by no means passive victims of attack by the state and the employers. In some cases, right-wing unions actively called in state intervention to assault their more left-wing rivals. The CIO willingly carried out a virulent internal purge. The attack on such unions as the United Electrical Workers, Mine, Mill and Smelter, and the Fur and Leather Workers was successful in drastically depleting their strength. Moreover, large numbers of left-wing officials in other unions were purged. The Communists had never been a crucial element in American labour, but the importation of the Cold War into the heart of the labour movement not only weakened labour unity at an important juncture, but had measurable effect on the blunting of new initiatives of unionization into non-union sectors (white collar occupations and the South) and contributed to the deunionization of sectors where the purges were most concentrated (electrical and textile trades).[21]

There is a broader context yet within which to situate labour. The Cold War was in itself a massive Keynesian programme of spending of which labour was a beneficiary. The Truman administration paid off its union supporters by trading full employment for relatively low wage levels guaranteed by the defence budget. The unions themselves acted as willing conduits of anti-communist ideological hegemony. Lacking autonomous working-class institutions encouraging class consciousness, the American workers were especially vulnerable to the penetration of nationalist, chauvinist, and authoritarian values: values which commended themselves by their association with a system which seemed to pay off. This may be the most significant element in the overall triumph of Cold War anti-communism in America, much more so than the better publicised ravages of McCarthyism among the ranks of intellectuals, civil servants, and other middle-class groups. The Cold War penetrated directly into working-class life and its organisation, and it did so by a combination of selective coercion and material incentives. Ideologically, the effect was devastating for progressive politics in America.

This raises a further question concerning the source of political repression against left-wing unions and unionists. Was this a power play by American capital, a pre-emptive strike against militant working-class demands? Leaving aside controversies about the sources and origins of the Cold War itself and the role of American business in the global confrontation with the Soviet Union, there is actually very little convincing evidence that the internal Cold War was planned and executed in the

boardrooms of corporate America. Indeed, big business executives appeared uncomfortable with the demagogic excesses of McCarthy and the
other witch-hunters.[22] Small business was another matter, as were the
organised local voices of small business such as Chambers of Commerce,
the American Legion, service clubs and the like, which often did function
as agents of repression. But small business could not on its own master-
mind a concerted and successful assault on the American labour movement. Corporate capital on the whole appeared willing to deal with
'responsible' labour leaders, and to the extent that the responsible leaders
were willing to purge their own ranks of radical and unreliable elements,
a moderate level of repressive pressure from the state and investigative
politicians served its purpose. McCarthyite excesses of repression were
more a product of the dynamics of the political system and the partisan
needs of right-wing Republicans.

Britain

In his massive study of the anti-communist repression in Americs, aptly
called *The Great Fear,* David Caute notes that 'Britain also committed
itself to a political and military alliance against the Soviet Union, but
without the corollary of domestic Red-baiting and witch-hunting.' He
also writes that 'American liberalism failed to sustain the authentically
liberal values and standards of tolerance that persisted in Britain despite
that country's. . . general posture of confrontation with Russia. The
British of the Attlee era, unlike the British of the Pitt era or of
the sixteenth-century confrontation with Catholic Spain, kept their
heads. . .'[23] Caute is here expressing the conventional wisdom. So pervasive is this wisdom that there is no study of the domestic impact of
the Cold War on British politics, as such; the picture has to be pieced
together from fragmentary information from disparate sources. The
conventional wisdom may not be wrong. Certainly among the four
countries examined in this study, there can be no doubt that the British
experience is the furthest removed from that of the Americans. But it
should come as no surprise that Britain is another country which does
things differently from the Americans. More to the point are the specific
effects of the Cold War on Britain itself. Here, the experience may turn
out to be more significant than the conventional wisdom allows.

It is well known how Britain emerged from the war as a second-rank
power. In the crucible of the post-war realignment of the world, Britain,
caught between the two superpowers and constricted by severe economic
decline, opted for an alliance with America which not only ensured
subordinate status in diplomacy and defence but also tied British
economic recovery to American dollar aid and meant the subordination
of British capital to the American plan for post-war economic reconstruction under the hegemony of American capital.[24] There were alternatives to

this strategy, mainly issuing from the left-wing of the Labour Party. That they were marginal and easily defeated, and that there was no Gaullist-style national capitalist strategy issuing from the right-wing of the Tory Party, are themselves indications of how profoundly the fundamental ideological assumptions of the Cold War penetrated the central institutions of British politics. On the other hand Britain was a principal power only recently evicted from her imperial residence and perhaps not fully aware of her changed circumstances. It would be an exaggeration to suggest that Britain did not contribute directly to the international policies which led the wartime Allies into the great fissure which was the Cold War; indeed, in a certain sense the British government was at least as determined, perhaps initially more determined, than the Americans to confront the Soviet Union and put the worst face on Soviet interests and intentions, at least in the early phases of the developing Cold War.[25] That this took place under a Labour government with a massive electoral mandate for domestic reforms, is of crucial significance in understanding the internal impact of the Cold War on Britain.

Part of this impact, and the most difficult to document, is the inter-penetration of the American state with key sectors of the British state apparatus. At the military level, even the Labour government made an attempt to maintain autonomy through the development of the British nuclear deterrent. This was not welcomed in Washington, which had tried to undercut Britain's capacity to become a nuclear power through control of strategic materials, but in any event, the specific application of the British bomb to the day-to-day practice of diplomacy was dubious at best.[26] The most important American influence was through the security-intelligence apparatus which America was building on a global scale. To be sure, MI5 needed no American cousins to instill an anti-communist passion so strong as to be turned against even elected governments: the case of the notorious forged 'Zinoviev letter' used to defeat the first Labour government in 1924 is illustration enough of the British security service's impeccable anti-communist lineage. There were specific treaty obligations which further linked Britain directly into the American security-intelligence network, most particularly the UKUSA Agreement, under which the USA, Britain, Canada, Australia and New Zealand integrated their electronic surveillance and cryptological capacities world-wide. This still secret treaty of 1947 brought in its wake not only US access to electronic surveillance *within* the signatory countries, as well as to the Soviet bloc, but it also brought with it a level of integration so close that the right-wing journalist and MI5 mouthpiece Chapman Pincher averred that 'dependence is so great and cooperation so close that I am convinced security chiefs would go to any length to protect the link-up'.[27]

State repression took official form within Britain early in 1948 when

Clement Attlee announced his government's intention to introduce a British version of the Truman Loyalty–Security programme in the civil service. Inspired in part by the Gouzenko spy affair in Canada (see below), and in part by American pressure, the British purge was on a considerably lesser scale than the American and marked by a less savage attitude toward offending employees (from 1948 to 1955 almost two-thirds of 135 permanent civil servants named as security risks were apparently given transfers to positions without security requirements; the remainder were dismissed or resigned). Non-judicial appeal procedures were developed so that it was possible, although very unlikely, that an employee wrongly declared a risk could be reinstated. This system was extended by the introduction of 'positive vetting' in 1952 under a UK–US–France agreement, whereby some 10,000 posts would require an extensive field investigation of 'the whole background of the officer concerned'. The security screening process was also extended to employees of companies with defence contract work, who could face dismissal or the termination of the company's contract were they not to satisfy the security service.[28]

If the British purge does seem mild compared to the American orgy, the principle involved is, at the same time, of considerable significance. Communism as a set of beliefs, and association with known Communists or alleged communist organisations were made criteria for dismissal from public posts. As late as 1956 a special study of security by a Conference of Privy Councillors concluded that 'chief risks are presented by Communists and by persons who for one reason or another are subject to communist influence. The communist faith overrides a man's normal loyalties to his country'. They added that the risk extended to 'sympathisers with communism'. 'Character defects' such as drunkenness, drug addiction, homosexuality, or 'any loose living' were also to be sought out by the security service as grounds for risk. An employee against whom damaging allegations had been made, never had recourse to the courts and the actual appeal procedures did not allow a person to be accompanied by counsel or to cross-examine sources of damaging information, or even to know on what particulars the case against them was built. One scholar suggests that the British purge procedure 'is, in truth, only a faint approximation to the long-recognised procedural form of natural justice', while another writer asks 'why should a person charged with treason be allowed to confront his accusers, and yet a person about to be dismissed because he is likely to commit treason be denied these minimum judicial rights?' These important questions of illiberal procedure mask another, perhaps more crucial, question.

The purge was in fact not all that effective, nor apparently is it now, even taking it on its own terms. As Harold Macmillan told the House of Commons in 1961 after the disclosure of yet another spy scandal, 'such cases. . . by reason of their very nature. . . are very difficult to detect or prevent by any security procedures. No such procedures can guarantee to catch a man who changes his allegiance and skilfully conceals his conversion'. Yet the purge went on. Might we not conclude that the ideological functions of the purge were at least as important as the possibility of detecting a potential espionage agent? What the purge did accomplish was the official proscription of certain political beliefs and political associations, as a 'legitimate' exercise of liberal democracy. The state was setting an example, *pour encourager les autres.* The actual numbers affected are not then so important as the public notice that certain ideas and associations are no longer considered legitimate. The politicised excesses of McCarthyism are only ugly and unnecessary excrescenses on this system. The British establishment had no need of them.[30]

Nor was there any lack of support within Labour ranks for Attlee's civil service purge. Over forty Labour MPs resolved that the purge was 'regrettable', but in the event only five actually voted their regret; 31 Labour members formally congratulated the Prime Minister. The Trade Union Congress approved the move. Like the Truman Democrats in the US, Labour was presiding over an official proscription of certain left-wing tendencies, and with few apparent misgivings.[31]

Inevitably, state repression spread out beyond the civil service and defence industries. The Special Branch, the internal intelligence agency whose business was described by the Metropolitan Commissioner of Police as keeping 'a watch on any body of people. . . whose activities seem likely to result sooner or later in open acts of sedition or disorder', set about under Home Office order in 1946 to compile and collate lists of communist and 'front' supporters—even to enlisting corner newsagents to provide names and addresses of persons ordering the *Morning Star.* Special Branch agents also infiltrated trade unions. A notorious example occurred during the dock strikes in Merseyside and London in the late 1940s when agents secretly recorded the discussions of an *ad hoc* organising committee and passed details on to Arthur Deakin, the right-wing General Secretary of the Transport and General Workers Union (TGWU) who promptly expelled the organisers. In 1951 seven dockers went on trial under a wartime act forbidding incitement to strike: 'the bulk of the evidence against them was speeches recorded by Special Branch officers'. Ian Taylor notes that after the severe political reverses of 1947, the Labour government began to rely on the police 'politically' at the very moment that the removal of controls and the retreat from planning was taking place.[32]

There could, however, be no equivalent in Britain of Taft–Hartley or political assaults from the outside on 'Communist' trade unionists. The working class was too strong, the unions too united, and their political expression, the Labour Party, too popular. State repression of left-wing unionism was not absent, as the above example indicates, but it was not the main focus. Instead, attempts at political repression were made through the trade unions themselves, and through the political mechanism of the Labour Party by appeals to social democratic solidarity.

The Communists did have some strength in the unions, certainly more strength than the Party ever demonstrated in the electoral arena. In the high tide of the British–Soviet wartime alliance, the TUC had been forced to withdraw its 'Black Circular' of 1934 which forebade Communists being accepted as delegates to trades councils. Communists had then consolidated old strongholds (Scottish and Welsh miners' unions), and made new breakthroughs into the Fire Brigades Union, the Amalgamated Engineering Union (AEU), the Electrical Trades Union (ETU) and the TGWU. 'It is no exaggeration', Pelling remarks—with considerable exaggeration—'to say that they were very nearly in charge of the trade union movement.' The facts scarcely suggested anything like communist control of a movement firmly attached as a whole to the Labour Party. However, as the Cold War deepened in the late 1940s, there were elements within the movement which sought to expunge whatever communist influence did exist.[33]

The major offensive was opened up at the end of 1947 when the Labour Party Secretary, Mr Morgan Phillips, issued a circular calling on trade unions to sack all communist officials. Warnings of 'a campaign of sabotage', the fomenting of discontent in the factories and 'destroying the labour movement from within' struck all the right Cold War notes. The government's own civil service purge quickly followed. Arthur Deakin hastened to bring the TGWU into line by issuing his own call for the rank and file to carry out local purges. Apart from the worsening international situation and the fissures opening up during 1947 between Western social democratic parties and the Soviet-line CPs, another motive has been suggested for the anit-communist offensive launched at this time. The government was moving toward a policy of wage restraint and the attack on 'communism' has been construed as an attack on militant opposition from the unions. As Panitch suggests, however, the CP had not been opponents of a national wages policy from 1945 to 1947. Before the White Paper of 1947 the Communist-led ETU had supported such a policy on the TUC General Council. Coincidental with the government's new turn to restraint, however, was the CP switch to militant Cold War opposition. From then on, communist unionists became the most vociferous enemies of restraint. The anti-communist offensive may have been more ideological than material in its origins, but once underway it also served to undermine what had now become the major source of anti-government opposition within the unions. Yet the ideological blinkers of the Cold War were such that the right-wing leadership may have un-wittingly magnified the extent of communist influence by tending to identify all militant opposition after 1947 as being Red—a considerable simplification of reality. A final irony is that strike activity in Britain was at its height when the Communists were in their cooperative phase and then fell sharply after the CP went militant.[34]

The TGWU finally passed a formal exclusion of Communists at its 1949 conference, its campaign to rouse rank and file anti-communism having failed. The National Union of Municipal and Government Workers passed a similar expulsion. Others, such as the ETU and the AEU, rejected such moves. Cracks in international trade union solidarity widened with the 'political' opposition of the CGT unions in France to the Marshall Plan, and finally in early 1948 the TUC, in concert with the AFL and the American State Department, pulled out of the World Federation of Trade Unions, later to form the CIA-backed Confederation of Free Trade Unions.[35]

The record of anti-communism in the British trade unions is spotty at best. It is clear that most of the battles were largely elite manipulations by union bureaucrats. Little shop floor enthusiasm for purging Communists could be roused; by the same token, little enthusiasm for communist issues was apparently generated among the rank and file of unions allegedly under communist influence.[36] The TUC as a whole was in fact able to maintain its strong links with the Labour government, even in the face of austerity and wage restraint, and the British trade union movement was lined up behind the broad Cold War foreign and defence policies of the American alliance. On the other hand, there is no sense in which it can be said that the Cold War was a device for integrating the British working class into the capitalist state as one can say about the American experience. If America's new imperial role could pay off the American working class, Britain was divesting itself of its old imperial role precisely on the grounds of penury. The American alliance could not offer the British working class a real material pay-off, apart from the prevention of outright national bankruptcy. The Cold War thus had limited ideological purchase over the British working class.

The Labour Party did have a direct stake in using the Cold War to discredit opinion and activity on its Left. As a government it wished to encourage working-class solidarity behind its projects, as a party it hoped to kill off its historical rival for working-class support, and as the architect of the anti-Soviet American alliance it wished to maintain as much national unity and consensus behind its defence and foreign policies as possible. In the process, the Party sometimes lent itself to activities not without effects on the practice of liberal democracy.

As a political rival the British CP seemed insubstantial enough. In the great Labour landslide of 1945, and following four years of pro-Soviet official wartime propaganda, the CP managed to elect only two MPs under its name (there were perhaps a handful of 'crypto' Communists who sneaked in under Labour colours—itself a sign of weakness). In 1950 both communist MPs were defeated; within that five year period the Party suffered heavy losses in membership.[37]

In the Labour Party Conference of 1945 a communist request for affiliation (in the spirit of the wartime popular front) was defeated, but quite narrowly. The Labour Party executive was unhappy with the degree of pro-communist sentiment. In 1946 Harold Laski published *The Secret Battalion*, a strong attack on the CP as illiberal, authoritarian and subversive of all freedoms. Communists, Laski argued, could not be taken at their word but were secret, disciplined conspirators seeking to undermine and destroy the Labour Party. The same year the Party Conference turned back another affiliation bid, this time by a heavy majority. However understandable its refusal to allow a rival party to exist within its own structures, it was not content with simple exclusion of the CP but went to more questionable lengths. Since the 1920s Labour had maintained a list of proscribed organisations, membership in which could be grounds for expulsion from the Party. This list, constantly expanded and amended, was in fact a kind of party version of the infamous US Attorney General's List. Given the hegemony of the Labour Party over the British Left and the trade union movement, the proscription list usually prevented the organisations named as communist fronts from gaining any significant membership. This had specific political consequences. In the years before the rise of the CND, peace organisations were banned by the Labour Party as Soviet fronts. Thus at the very moment when a Labour government was making the fateful decision not only to support the American nuclear 'deterrent' but to build a British nuclear threat under British control, popular mobilisation against nuclear weapons from within the ranks of Labour supporters was made more difficult by active repression of the peace councils, the main organisational focus of peace campaigns in this period. When the Labour Party abandoned the list in 1973, Chapman Pincher reported that the event, accelerating Labour's 'lurch to the Left', 'horrified the security authorities'. Well it might, for as long as it lasted and was effective, the list accomplished a great deal of what might otherwise have had to be undertaken by direct state repression.[38]

The uses of anti-communism were particularly evident to the Labour leadership on the matter of party support for Bevin's Cold War foreign policies. Although Labour's ardour for confronting the Soviet Union was characterised by considerably less ideological passion than the evangelical anti-communism of American policymakers, the party leadership, and Bevin in particular, were never loath to invoke the Red smear to undermine opposition. As a series of sketchy, fragmented and sometimes excessively idealist alternatives—a 'socialist foreign policy', the 'third force', and finally 'Bevanism'—flickered uncertainly across the Party stage in the first years of the Cold War, Bevin treated every vote at party conferences on foreign policy implicitly as one of confidence, warning of those who would stab him in the back. Again and again the executive won, and by 1949 Bevinite foreign policy had been overwhelmingly endorsed, its broad lines not to be challenged again while Labour remained in office. What is more surprising in retrospect is the ease with which the executive and the right-wing trade union leaders invoked the threat of communism as lurking behind the various efforts of the Labour Left to articulate an alternative foreign policy. The maintenance of Cold War unity under explicitly anti-communist rhetoric no doubt helped assure suspicious American congress-men that British socialists were safe, albeit eccentric, but the rhetoric had its uses domestically as well.[39]

Opposition which in the view of the leadership went too far—which was not perhaps so far at all—could be met with quite savagely. Such was the experience of certain MPs who were actually expelled from the Party for challenging Cabinet foreign policy. One left-wing MP was expelled for his part in sending a telegram of support to Pietro Nenni, the Italian Socialist leader who refused to adopt the blanket anti-communism being forced upon the non-communist Left in Italy by the Americans in 1948. Among the grounds for expulsion were the MP's membership in the proscribed British–Soviet Friendship Society. The opposition to NATO led by MP Konni Zilliacus, a left-winger but certainly not a CP fellow traveller, was tacitly supported by the abstention in Parliament of over 100 Labour members. Only Zilliacus and one other Labour MP actually voted against the NATO motion, and both were expelled and not allowed to address the 1949 Party Conference. The Zilliacus insurgency, tiny, isolated, and ineffective as it was, was treated by the party as a subversive Fifth Column to be smashed.[40]

The Korean War under the erratic and belligerent auspices of the American military began to drive a wedge into Anglo–American Cold War solidarity, but this did not really penetrate the Labour Party until after it was returned to opposition. Aneurin Bevan's resignation in 1951 over National Health charges to pay for rearmament highlighted just how far the Labour government had gone down the Cold War road: indeed, the government had actually committed itself to a possible war with China over Korea, without prior consultation with Party or Parliament. Yet Bevanism itself as Howell comments, was 'not an alternative to official policy. . . Bevanism was rather a symptom of the tensions produced within the Party by its acceptance, in practice, of existing economic relations'. Bevan's own erratic later course from criticism of the nuclear deterrent to becoming the executives's chief spokesman against unilateral nuclear disarmament, is evidence enough of the lack of coherence in Bevanism.[41]

The weakness of the successive Left challenges to Labour foreign policy should not be allowed to obscure the significance of the triumph of Cold War social democracy. The defeat of the Labour Left meant much more than a short term resolution of factionalism. The dread charge of 'fellow travelling' in the tense and brittle atmosphere of the time served to discredit left-wing socialism in general. Bevin believed standing up to Russia was necessary to preserve social democracy; he succeeded in establishing Britain as part of the American sphere of influence, where American credit and American conditions pre-empted a distinctive social democratic policy at home. As Hinton writes: 'Without a fundamental break from Bevin's foreign policy there could be no sustained socialist offensive at home.' Yet as Miliband suggests, 'what above all caused the retreat of the Labour Left was the exacerbation of the Cold War'. It was a classic vicious circle. Jones notes the symbolic significance of Orwell's *1984* whose publication Orwell naively believed would strengthen social democracy, but was instead used as a right-wing bludgeon by Cold Warriors: 'The reason was partly that socialism and Russia *were* interrelated ideas and the discrediting of one damaged the other, and partly that Cold War reactions to Soviet pressure strengthened the Right and weakened social democracy all over the world.' The discrediting of left-wing socialism was evident in the 'rethinking' of Labour policy in the 1950s which was dominated by the right-wing of the Party (the Healeys, Gaitskells and Daltons). The anti-communist onslaught of the early Cold War years left a truncated Party and an intellectual vacuum on the Left for a decade at least.[42]

If anti-communism had definite effects on the Labour Party, its wider ramifications within British society were much less obvious than they were in McCarthy's America. There is little evidence of widespread political repression. The dismissal of a lecturer at the London School of Slavonic Studies on political grounds, the declaration by a local council that Communists would be banned from teaching—such examples are not lacking, but they are very few in number. Indeed, it is not unreasonable to suggest that more Britons suffered the invidious workings of the US McCarran Act when attempting to visit America in the early 1950s than they ever suffered any form of political repression at home.[43]

To understand why the Cold War repression was limited in the way it was, the role of the Tory Party must be examined. There were a number of elements present in the Britain of the late 1940s which might have suggested a McCarthyite strategy to the Tories. Britain was under a Labour government committed to a socialist-reform programme bitterly resented by British business which was mounting a concerted anti-socialist campaign. Labour was presiding over the beginnings of the dissolution of the Empire, communism was sweeping over Central Europe and the Far East, and by 1951, with the defection of Burgess and Maclean, it was known that there were high level Soviet agents operating within the civil service.

Why not a campaign to blame Britain's decline on a communist fifth column aided and abetted by a pink Labour Party rife with fellow travellers and dupes of Stalin? Certainly the Tories had been happy to connive with the Foreign Office, the secret service, and the Tory press in 1924 to drive the first Labour government out of office in a Red scare created by the forged Zinoviev letter. On occasion, right-wing Tory candidates were not adverse to a spot of Red baiting in constituency contests, and there were sometimes calls at Tory conferences for outlawing communism, but on the whole the Conservatives did surprisingly little with the issue. Anti-communism was the Tory dog that never barked.[44]

Indeed, it is a startling irony that it was Churchill who in 1950 suggested a summit conference with the Soviets to avert the dangers of war, while the Labour government dismissed the idea and publicly worried that the Tories might upset the American allies. If anything, the Tories showed more flexibility on relations with the Soviet bloc and slightly more critical distance from the American policies. The Tory leadership had its own good reasons for discouraging the right-wing of the party. In his infamous 'Gestapo' election speech of 1945, Churchill himself had set the very worst example. His crude attempt to link socialism with totalitarianism was a 'pivotal event' in the election, according to Messrs. McCallum and Readman—but not at all in the manner intended. Instead, Attlee capitalised on it to divest Sir Winston of his wartime image of *national* leadership. The Tories compounded their error by attempting to Red bait Harold Laski, a tactic which 'left the great mass of the electorate surprisingly uninterested'. The popular tide for Labour and the degree of working-class consciousness were simply too high for the Tories to make any Zinoviev-style points. Churchill never forgot this lesson and made sure that Red scare tactics were kept well muffled. Moreover, there could be no question of the Tories charging Labour with harbouring traitors in the government service. The 'traitors' were largely from the same class milieu in which the Tories themselves were situated; the Kim Philbys were protected not by Labour but by upper-class solidarity. Finally, the highly centralised and disciplined nature of parties under the parliamentary system ensured that the Tory leadership could easily control the potential excesses of their right-wingers, unlike the Republican leadership's difficulties with its McCarthy wing.[45]

There was another, deeper, force at work as well. The very strength of the Labour victory in 1945 had impressed the Tories so profoundly that they themselves quickly adopted many of the goals of 1945. What became known as 'Butskellism' was a compound of welfare state assumptions with an emphasis on the liberty of the individual. While one side of Butskellism was a fundamental national consensus behind the American alliance and the Cold War abroad, the other side was the reluctance of the Tories to attack Labour on grounds of disloyalty at home. All the more so when

British middle-class opinion became aroused by the excesses of McCarthy-ism in America, which by the early 1950s became a safe way to vent resentments of American domination, traditional feelings of cultural superiority, and mild British patriotism, without in any sense unsettling any of the basic links which bound Britain to the American empire. The Tories pitched much of their appeal in 1950–51 to this 'liberal and inde-pendent opinion'. Later the Campaign for the Limitation of Secret Police Powers, which sought out and condemned British examples of McCarthy-ite injustice, featured a number of prominent Tories as well as Labour and Liberal members among its sponsors. Given the convergence of the parties, then, it comes as no surprise that Churchill should have found the 1950 election campaign 'demure', nor that this same campaign should have begun with a church service attended by leaders of all the parties where the Archbishop of Canterbury delivered a sermon setting 'the amicable conflict of the election in the shadow of the deeper world conflict of Christianity and materialism'.[46]

Britain then lined up behind the Cold War under social democratic auspices. It would be an exaggeration to say that this process was un-accompanied by domestic repression, certainly at the state level, and—particularly within the Labour Party itself and the trade unions—at the political level as well: yet by comparison with America, the repression was relatively mild. The dynamics of the party system in the post-war conjuncture had much to do with this result. And behind the party system lay the balance of class forces, and the momentary power of the British working class.

Australia

Australia stands between Britain and America on a continuum of domestic repression. 'In Australia', according to one recent account, 'as in America, the Cold War provided the backdrop for a virulent anti-communist crusade that damaged the nation's free institutions and the careers of many innocent individuals. Ironically, the ugly and excessive example of the hysterical anti-communist crusade in America provided the main check on similar tendencies in Australia.'[47]

Australia was in the process of being brusquely drawn into the Cold War as a strategically significant piece of real estate for American military and intelligence operations in the Far East. One imperial connection gave way to another during the late 1940s and early 1950s. Not surprisingly, this realignment along the lines of the great East–West fissure could not take place without profound domestic repercussions. As Robin Gollan writes:[48]

What happened in Australia in these years. . . cannot be understood except in the context of the world contest. Every great issue in society, whether of political policy, ideological stance, or cultural commitment, was measured and judged, in some degree, by its relation to the issues raised by the world-wide conflict. Reactionaries and communists were prepared to be so involved. The rest of the community, who were the majority, were involved whether they liked it or not.'

Like Britain, Australia was governed by a Labour government during the formative period of the Cold War. As in Britain, social democracy presided over the defence, security and intelligence sharing and integration with the Americans which came with the Cold War. As in Britain, the Australian Labor Party (ALP) soon went into the political wilderness— for almost a decade longer in fact than British Labour. But in Australia, the Cold War came home with much more of a vengeance and with more lasting damage to social democracy, both within the ALP and within the labour movement. The ALP government was in fact significantly weaker domestically than Labour in Britain, while the Australian Right was both stronger and less inclined toward compromise on socialism and the welfare state than the British Conservatives. This mix, under conditions of the burgeoning Cold War, encouraged considerable recourse to the Red scare as a political tactic of the Right and, as a result, much confusion and disarray within the ALP and the unions.

Connell and Irving speak of the late 1940s as a 'ruling-class mobilisation' of white collar, ununionised middle class and the self-employed against socialism. As it turned out, this mobilisation was also accompanied by a split within the unions and within the ALP itself on the communist issue. The Labor government tried briefly for a post-war reconstruction policy of full employment by asking the voters in a 1944 referendum for a permanent transfer of powers over prices, production and employment from the states to the Commonwealth (powers exercised during the wartime emergency) Labor lost the referendum and went into retreat, a retreat which turned into a rout when an aroused business community successfully mobilised a mass propaganda campaign to defeat proposed bank nationalisations, and the doctors masterminded a campaign to undermine and destroy 'socialised' health care. These campaigns successfully mobilised mass support behind the new conservatism, and the Red scare was an integral part of the ideological appeal.[49]

Beset on the Right, the Labor government found itself attacked from the Left as well, and at the same time the Australian Communist Party went into the hard-left Cold War line of the late 1940s. A devastating coal strike in 1949 was widely portrayed as a communist conspiracy coinciding with the fall of China. Although communist union officials were not necessarily the most militant, the Labor government accepted the right-wing interpretation and broke the strike by arresting its leaders and freezing union funds. 1949 also saw a series of prosecutions against leading Communists for sedition. The Party Leader went to prison for three years for stating that Australian workers would welcome Soviet troops as liberators. Another leading member followed him, and then a series of prosecutions, especially of communist trade unionists, took place amid 'considerable protest' over 'trumped up charges' and clear threats to freedom of speech. A Victoria Communist defected, sold his story to the sensationalist press, and inspired a state Royal Commission on Communist Subversion. The Labor government responded much as the Truman Democrats did at the same time, by joining in the pack of Red hunters to deflect criticism of their own softness. They were no more successful, not least because the Red scare appealed to isolationist and racist elements within the Australian working class: once encouraged, they set loose divisions which caused long term harm.[50]

The Liberal and Country Parties were eager to smear the ALP as communist dupes. Even before the end of the war, Robert Menzies, the Liberal leader, moved a resolution in Parliament censuring the Labor government for its 'encouragement of communist activities in Australia'. On the eve of the 1946 election, an opposition newspaper told its readers that 'a vote for Labor is a vote for communism'. And in a joint statement in 1949, the leaders of the Liberal and Country Parties promised that if elected they would declare the Communists an illegal party, give the Attorney General the power to declare any associations communist and thus illegal,. and ban Communists from trade union office. They then proceeded to closely identify Labor with communism in the successful election campaign which followed.[51]

When the Menzies government came to office in 1949, it was already stepping into a situation in which McCarthyism had made considerable inroads. As early as 1946 an attack had begun on the Council for Scientific and Industrial Research for allegedly harbouring communist and pro-Soviet scientists. Questions were raised by the Americans and other allies over Australian 'reliability' with regard to atomic research and other classified information. Right-wing ALP members were much in the forefront of the smears, and when the Labor government reorganised the Council, its distinguished head, who had defended the body and warned against the 'sinister' campaign to destroy freedom of inquiry, quit. The Approved Defence Projects Act in 1947 imposed penalties of up to a year's imprisonment on anyone 'who by speech or writing advocates or encourages the prevention, hindrance or obstruction' of any improved defence project.[52]

The Menzies government was as good as its word, introducing in 1950 the Communist Dissolution Bill which, among other things gave the state the right to 'declare' persons or associations communist, and place the onus on the accused to prove their innocence. The idea of dissolving the CP was not seen as effective, even by some cabinet ministers—in the sense of actually getting rid of a party which could go underground, as it had during a period of illegality during the Nazi–Soviet pact of 1939–41. It was, however, seen as electorally effective, and as a brilliant device to divide the ALP. Initially, it did just that. The Labor Executive wanted the main thrust of the legislation accepted. The caucus in the House was divided, but after various amendments had been rejected by the government, a majority was found against acceptance—and was then overruled by the Executive, which had an eye on polls showing two-thirds of Australians favouring the Bill.

The unions were aghast at the powers for state intervention. Menzies on introducing the Bill had 'named' some 40 trade unionists as Communists. At least half a dozen of these names were so blatantly incorrect that Menzies later had to retract them. Ten unions and the Communist Party contested the constitutionality of the Bill in the courts, and secured the services of leading ALP politician Herbert Evatt to argue their case before the High Court. Evatt won, and the Bill was declared outside the powers of the Commonwealth. Shortly thereafter, Evatt succeeded to the leadership of the ALP. With a man considered by the government as a virtual fellow traveller now leading Labor, Menzies secured a double dissolution of both houses of Parliament in 1951 and ran on a Cold War, anti-communist campaign. Despite marginal losses in the House, the governing coalition won control of the Senate. Menzies thereupon called a referendum to amend the constitution to give the Commonwealth 'powers to deal with Communists and communism'. Australians thus had an opportunity unique to the English-speaking countries during the Cold War—they could democratically pass judgment directly upon a repressive piece of anti-communist legislation.[53]

A pamphlet was distributed to all voters laying out the case for a 'yes' vote in the government's words ('the chief instrument' of communist aggression against Australia was the 'fifth column' of secret agents who had wormed their way into 'key places') and the case for the 'no' vote contributed by the ALP, which began by declaring that Labor was 'utterly opposed to communism' and ready to take 'effective action to combat communism in Australia', but was just as opposed to the Menzies proposals which were 'unnecessary, unjust and totalitarian'. At the outset of the campaign, polls showed 80 per cent support for the 'yes' side, which was almost unanimously supported by the newspapers. Dr Evatt threw himself wholeheartedly into the campaign against official McCarthyism, even cooperating with Communists on occasion. Yet despite the repressive atmosphere of the time, deepened by the fact that Australian troops were battling Communists in Korea, the passionate anti-McCarthyite leadership of Labor found resonance in the working class and liberal middle-class opinion. The tide was dramatically reversed by voting day when 51 per cent voted 'no'. True, the Australian electorate has historically shown great caution in accepting constitutional amendments, yet at the same time it was also the case that the 'no' vote ran ahead of Labor support in the general election earlier the same year. One possible interpretation of this result is that had Labor been consistently willing to take a leading position against the repressive excesses of the Cold War, instead of attempting to pre-empt the Right, the overall picture of Cold War Australia might have been less sorry than it in fact was.[54]

Defeat of · the Communist Dissolution Bill was a victory for civil liberties, yet it was in many ways a merely symbolic victory. The machinery of repression was well in place under existing legislation—and had already been used to effect by Labor. The Australian Security and Intelligence Organisation (ASIO) had been set up in 1949 under Labor auspices. ASIO was an important conduit for the integration of Australian security and intelligence into the wider Cold War network—initially set up with the close assistance of MI5, it later developed intimate linkages with the CIA. At the core of ASIO was a small self-constituted elite intelligence group with a mission to save the nation from the irresponsible excesses of democracy and politics. The 'gnomes of Melbourne' as they were dubbed by Dr John Burton (the Secretary of the Department of External Affairs under Evatt, who attempted to pursue an independent foreign policy and drew the wrath of the Right), took full charge when the chief gnome, Sir Charles Spry, was put in charge of ASIO by Menzies in 1950. From this point on, military intelligence was in charge of civilian security, with strong views on foreign and defence policy and machinery at their disposal to ensure that governments acceptable to them were elected. ASIO's controversial if shadowy interventions in politics have continued to be a matter of concern. State Special Branches were co-ordinated with ASIO as subsidiary Red squads which compiled voluminous files on the political opinions and political activities of private citizens. The FBI were direct mentors of the Special Branches, encouraging them to target Labor supporters and engage in fishing operations among even moderately progressive bureaucrats and politicians, precisely along American witch-hunt lines. As a later judicial inquiry found, 'like the Maginot line, all defence against anticipated subversions, real or imagined, were built on one side'. Another mechanism for linking Australia into the American security-intelligence network were the UKUSA secret agreements of 1947 to which Australia was a junior party. These were the wedge for a vast array of American electronic surveillance installations built on Australian territory but largely under American control, with considerable potential for American snooping into domestic Australian politics (and for sharing of this information with the 'safe' network of ASIO and the Special Branch, although not necessarily with elected governments).[55]

McCarthyite attacks on alleged communist subversion in the civil service and fears that America would consider Australia an unreliable ally led the Labor government in 1948 to direct security checks of public servants with access to classified information. Alarm was expressed by the Chairman of the Public Service Board to the Prime Minister about the standards of judgment used, citing adverse reports on 'sympathisers' who discussed 'foreign affairs' or 'left-wing ideologies'. Undaunted, the Prime Minister actually widened the scope of the security screening. With the arrival of Menzies in office, the scope was 'dramatically' widened yet further to include all applicants for positions within the public service, whether classified or not. In 1953, a cabinet directive insisted that no one about whom ASIO had 'some doubts' should have access to classified material. 'Doubts' were garnered by recourse to the voluminous files of ASIO and the Special Branch on political activities and beliefs of citizens, association with organisations considered 'subversive' by the police (apparently including the Council for Civil Liberties), affiliations of relatives and friends, and other information amassed by a network of spies, informers, paid agents, and other such. There was no appeal procedure for persons whose careers might be adversely affected, no recourse to the courts, no opportunity to confront and cross-examine sources of adverse information. Above all, the right-wing political bias of the security service was in effect given official sanction and enforced upon the public service, and on anyone who might wish to serve in the bureaucracy.[56]

Another major area for state repression was in immigration controls. Apparently, the fear of security risks among the displaced persons from Europe who began arriving in Australia in the wake of the war was one of the major reasons for the establishment of ASIO. Under the Menzies government in the 1950s ASIO became a 'virtual foreign service operating under the cover of the Immigration Department' eventually extending to sixteen countries. Liaison was maintained with local security forces to detect and bar 'Communists' among applicants for immigration. As Hall comments, 'leaving aside the question of possible injustice to individuals, the sinister aspect of the operation is how it linked ASIO with the Secret Police of other countries', including exchange of information with some very repressive and undemocratic regimes (of the Right, needless to say). The Menzies government also tried to impose passport restrictions on its own citizens who travelled to countries which the government did not like (Soviet bloc, that is), including on the wife of the Chief of Justice of New South Wales who was active in the Australian Peace Council. This proved difficult to enforce, however, and following the defeat of the Communist Dissolution referendum, the attempt was largely abandoned.[57]

Apart from the Communist Party itself, the main target of the state's repressive apparatus in the early Cold War years was the Australian Peace Council, founded in 1949, and labelled a communist front, not only by ASIO, the police, and the Liberal–Country Party government, but by the ALP leadership as well. Legitimate fears of nuclear war among the population inspired considerable public support for the Peace Council, which was the only organisation mobilising a disarmament campaign at this time. Menzies, during his attempt at banning communism, assiduously whipped up war hysteria around Korea, publicly praising General MacArthur's call for an invasion of China and the use of nuclear weapons against North Korea. In this context, the Peace Council was a rallying point for opposition to war. Alastair Davidson, in his careful and fair study of the Australian Communist Party, notes that while Communists had been influential at the founding of the Peace Council, by the 1950s it 'had become a genuine mass movement in which various Christian denominations were also prominent' and that 'it was not controlled by the Party as much as the Party would have liked'. The security service made no such fine distinctions, and local Peace Councils were infiltrated by spies and agents, their supporters harrassed, their motives denounced. The ALP in opposition joined enthusiastically in the witch-hunt, proscribing membership for party faithful, and withdrawing endorsement of Dr John Burton as an ALP candidate after he attended a peace conference in Peking. A conference in Australia in 1953 organised by ten churchmen was condemned not only by Menzies, but by Evatt as well, on a guilt-by-association basis. Passport harrassments were used against Council members. The effects of this repression in truncating and distorting the debate within Australia on the central question of the threat of nuclear catastrophe in the Cold War and of the implications of Australia's foreign and defence role for war and peace should be obvious.[58]

Undoubtedly the greatest coup for the Liberal–Country government/ASIO nexus was the Petrov affair of 1954. Induced by an ASIO secret undercover agent, a cipher clerk in the Soviet Embassy defected with alleged 'secrets' of widespread Soviet espionage linked to Australian Communists. The dramatic 'rescue' of his wife from the clutches of two KGB heavies on a plane back to Russia was played out in the fullest possible glare of publicity. As Whitlam and Stubbs in their book-length analysis of the affair conclude, the government 'had superbly stage-managed the Petrovs' defection as a Cold War extravaganza'. There are shadowy elements concerning ASIO's collaboration with the government of the day on the very eve of an election, and on the timing of the defection. A Royal Commission was called, sat for three days to air sensational charges of Australian traitors spying for the Soviets, then promptly adjourned until after the election. The ALP had been standing at 52 per cent in the polls; ten days after Mrs Petrov's 'rescue' the Menzies government had shot up to 57 per cent. In the ensuing election, Labor fell victim to a concerted Red baiting campaign in which the press fully participated. Whitlam and Stubbs conclude that a 'strong reason for the return of the government was the communist scare, a scare created by the government itself'. This became clear when the Commission resumed its inquiries. In the end there was very little substance indeed, but much

McCarthyite Red smearing and widely publicised damage to reputations and careers. The Commission was openly partisan, setting the ALP and, in particular, Dr Evatt, as its target as much as communism.[59]

If the Petrov affair represented McCarthyism in close collaboration with the state, some of the most bitter battles of the Cold War in Australia were fought almost entirely outside the state, within the trade unions and the ALP. Well organised and determined movements of anti-communist political repression were launched under the ideological and sectarian banner of Roman Catholicism. Although connections were undoubtedly made with the state security forces, it must be emphasised that the Catholic anti-communist movement was very much a self-directed force with a mass base.

The Australian trade union movement had harboured for some time two divergent and perhaps irreconcilable forces within its bosom. Communists, never successful in any way in electoral politics in Australia, did experience considerable success in the unions, especially during the war. Estimates vary, but perhaps somewhere between a quarter and a half of Australian trade unions were under CP direction by the end of the war. At the same time, the closely-knit Catholic minority in Australia, largely of Irish origin, was 'under-represented in the most esteemed suburbs and occupations' and over-represented in the working class and among ALP voters (in 1954, Catholics accounted for 16 per cent of the Australian electorate, but almost one-third of ALP votes). A small, upwardly mobile new middle class gave ideological leadership to Catholic workers whose class consciousness was often combined with a strong religious identification of an expressly anti-communist definition. During the Spanish Civil War, echoes of the right-wing role of the Church were strongly felt in the Australian Catholic community. A zealous Catholic lay activist with the unlikely, if fitting, name of Bartholomew Augustine Santamaria became a leading figure in Catholic Action and the Catholic Social Movement, or simply, the Movement, which went into high gear in the Cold War era. Like its communist enemies, the Movement was secretive, organised on a cell basis, and exercised tight control and discipline over its members. Parish priests contributed to the climate of fear among Catholics with tales of imminent Red takeovers, and the Movement organised everything from combat training to surveillance and 'exposure' of alleged undercover Communists.[60]

It was in the unions that the militant Catholics made their greatest gains. Under the name of the 'Industrial Groups', or commonly, 'Groupers', they set out to destroy communist influence by, to all intents and purposes, following communist-style tactics for taking over and emphasising zeal above labour unity. At first the ALP leadership seemed content to use the Groupers as battering rams against the Communists, but eventually they became a threat to the ALP itself and were denounced by Dr Evatt. For one thing, certain Catholic ALP members of Parliament were by the early 1950s emerging as rabid and reckless McCarthyites (one charged that the Australian National University was a 'nest of Communists') who played directly into the hands of the Liberal–Country government. Divisions were opening up publicly and embarrassingly within the caucus. For another, the union movement was being split asunder. Once the ALP intervened against the Groupers, it was inevitable that the divisions would extend into the ALP itself. In Victoria, a strong Catholic movement within the ALP had backed the Menzies side in the referendum on Communist Dissolution and this formed the nucleus of a breakaway Anti-communist Labor Party which contested the state elections of 1955. Finally in 1957 the Democratic Labor Party was formed as a rival to the ALP. This has not been a very successful alternative to Labor, although it undoubtedly assisted in keeping the Liberal–Country coalition in power for a generation. In the end, Catholic anti-communism was self-limiting and self-defeating. As Ormonde comments, many Catholic workers were never attracted to the Movement, and others ultimately rejected it because its leaders 'abandoned their radical criticism of the capitalist economic system to concentrate all their physical and intellectual energies on the communist problem'. Anti-communism could not in the last analysis serve as a substitute for working class consciousness. But its destructiveness in the labour movement, in working-class politics, and in the practice of liberal democracy in Australia, should not be underestimated.[61]

In summary, then, Australia came close to America in terms of state and political repression. The two factors which seem most important in explaining this experience were the willingness of the Australian Right and its political expressions in the Liberal and Country Parties to adopt anti-communism as a club with which to beat their social democratic opposition, and the deep divisions within the ALP and the labour movement over the issue and the inability of the leadership to consistently confront the strategy of the Right. In the event, Australia was firmly drawn into a subordinate position under American hegemony, and the Australian Left suffered a devastating defeat and long exile into the political wilderness.

Canada

Canada entered the Cold War early and with as much apparent enthusiasm in official circles as was evident in America and Britain. The late 1940s witnessed a series of steps such as US–Canada defence sharing agreements, security-intelligence agreements and liaison (UKUSA Agreements, FBI–RCMP links), diplomatic and military pacts (NATO and later NORAD), economic arrangements (sharing in the Marshall Plan), and the encouragement of large-scale direct capital investment in Canada by American business, which had the net effect of moving Canada firmly and apparently irrevocably into the American economic, military and diplomatic orbit. The ideology of anti-communism and the defence of free enterprise and the free world figured strongly in the public rhetoric of the period, as did more emotionally restrained opinions of Canada's realistic options and the limitations of autonomous action in the private discussions of the politicians and bureaucrats making the key decisions. There was some early debate within the Department of External Affairs over the question of whether Canada should pursue a hard or conciliatory line toward the USSR. The doves were routed early on, however, as external events closed off conciliatory options. Canada's close allies, Britain and America, in effect determined the narrow limits on Canadian action. At the same time, Canadian policy makers shared in the dominant assumptions of their allies. Ironically, it was the Soviet Union itself which set the seal on official Canadian anti-Sovietism, as early as 1945-46.[62]

The event which had so much to do with sweeping Canada up into the centre of the Cold War maelstrom was also one which defined the Cold War as one fought on both the external and domestic fronts. The defection of the cypher clerk Igor Gouzenko from the Soviet Embassy in Ottawa in the autumn of 1945 with documents implicating Canadian Communists and communist sympathisers in a Soviet espionage network was an international sensation when made public early the next year. It was, in a certain sense, the first public shot fired in the Cold War (private manoeuvrings among the wartime Allies were, of course, rife). The lessons drawn by the Canadian government were that the USSR was an unfriendly power, and that its unfriendliness extended into controlling a disloyal fifth column within Canada. The cry of treason, soon to be brandished about the political stage of America with rough abandon, was in fact first heard in Canada. How it was handled is itself an interesting study in the differences between Canada and the United States.

Close consultation with the British and American governments (much of which remains classified information today) and with elements of the British and American security and intelligence apparatuses led to an elaborate three-country counter-espionage operation. An atomic scientist, Nunn May, was arrested in Britain and eventually sentenced to ten years under the Official Secrets Act. In Canada, a secret order in council empowered the RCMP to arrest a number of Canadian suspects under the War Measures Act. This extremely repressive piece of emergency legislation, still in place after the end of the war, allowed arrest without charge, without counsel, and without habeas corpus. Interrogated at length in the RCMP barracks with no idea of what was happening to them, the suspects were then hauled before a Royal Commission and questioned about their activities in government employment, their past associations, and their political beliefs. The Royal Commission then published its findings, naming eighteen Canadians as Soviet espionage agents, including the Communist Member of Parliament, Fred Rose.[63]

The fact that in subsequent criminal proceedings about half the persons charged were acquitted has led to considerable speculation over the years. There can, however, be no doubt that Soviet espionage operations were taking place in Canada and that Canadians ideologically sympathetic to communism were indeed being utilised. This is hardly surprising, of course, but what is important is the *use* to which these facts were put. First, the readiness of the Canadian government to use extraordinary war powers in peacetime and to dispense altogether with the civil liberties of the individuals suspected of espionage, set the tone for subsequent Cold War practice of state repression. Secondly, although the Canadian government hastened to maintain proper, if cool, diplomatic relations with the USSR, it made no secret of its intention to exploit the Gouzenko affair to the full for its domestic political value. The point was made clearly in the Royal Commission Report, in the statements of government officials, and in the media, that the ideology of communism was at the root of disloyalty to Canada. The Communist Party had been declared an illegal entity during the war, and about a hundred of its supporters interned as enemies of the war effort. Even after the Soviet Union had become an ally after the Nazi invasion in 1941, official protestations of approval of the gallant Red Army were matched by continued hostility on the part of the state and the police towards Canadian Communists. Gouzenko was the signal that the era of 'popular front' alliance (the CPC had supported the Liberals in the 1945 election against the social democrats) was definitely over. That this point was being made in the midst of a post-war strike wave, in which communist trade unionists were prominent, may be only a coincidence—but from the point of view of both the state and capital it was a very happy coincidence.[64]

Gouzenko himself became the first of a series of post-war defectors who were built up by the media as exemplars of courage who chose 'freedom' over totalitarianism (ironically, the mirror-image of the communist traitor who betrayed his country to the USSR). Everything from a best-selling autobiography to a Hollywood movie (improbably starring the dapper Dana Andrews as the squat Gouzenko) publicised the image, as did Gouzenko's elaborate procedures to avoid alleged Soviet assassination squads (the bag over the head in public appearances being the most notable). Interestingly, recent documents acquired under the Access to Information Act indicate that Gouzenko himself advised the Canadian government at a very early stage after his defection about selling a glamourous and highly ideological image of himself through the media. There is no doubt, in short, that the Gouzenko affair was employed deliberately and effectively to launch the Cold War *in* Canada.[65]

The initial reaction of public and politicians was mixed. There were protests against the methods of the Royal Commission (some of those who protested later found themselves in difficulty with 'security' problems), and there were also calls for witch-hunts and cleaning out the traitors by any and all methods. The response of the Canadian government to this situation was to establish a far reaching and elaborate security screening system within the federal government. Beginning in 1946 a system under the supervision of a Security Panel of senior civil servants employing the RCMP security branch as an investigative agency, 'vetted' tens of thousands of civil servants and applicants for posts in the public service each year. Extensive RCMP Red lists, dating back to the time of the Winnipeg General Strike in 1919 and based upon information from agents and informers, were employed as were extensive inquiries among neighbours and associates. Adverse findings, including not only political information, but also 'character defects' such as alcoholism, homosexuality, or socially aberrant habits, would be fatal to a civil servant's career advancement, and perhaps to his or her job. There would, however, be no appeal procedures allowed, no opportunity for a person affected to confront hostile sources of information, or even to know what the case against him or her was. The demands for security screening were so insistent that the RCMP were chronically unable to keep up with the flow. The political implications were clear for public sector workers: as a cabinet directive of 1952 (in force until 1963) put it, 'a person who is a member of the Communist Party, or who by his words or actions shows himself to believe in Marxism–Leninism, or any other ideology which advocates the overthrow of government by force, should not be permitted to enter the public service'.[66]

The ideological uses of security screening were particularly evident in the witch-hunt at the National Film Board. Here American pressures emanating both from the repressive apparatus of the state (FBI and defence intelligence) and from the Hollywood film industry, seeking to crush a small rival in a branch plant market, combined with Canadian Cold War hawks (particularly the Defence Department, willing conduits for American demands) and private sector branch plant capital, to destroy the political independence of an innovative and creative group of documentary film-makers. Built up by the progressive Scottish film-maker John Grierson during the war, the NFB had gained a considerable international reputation. Grierson himself was peripherally smeared in the Gouzenko investigation and banned from the United States by J. Edgar Hoover. The NFB was attacked as harbouring Communists (as many as thirty to forty persons were claimed to be Reds), the liberal head of the Board was forced to resign, and three permanent employees dismissed as security risks, along with many others who fled rather than be fired. Artists and creative persons were put on clear notice that progressive views were no longer safe. It was the Canadian version of the Hollywood inquisition by the Un-American Activities Committee, but it took place within the state sector itself.[67]

The security system extended outside the state sector. The RCMP were called in to vet the political reliability of persons employed by private companies with defence contracts, and workers who failed the test were to be removed from work of a classified nature. Soon private security units attached to defence industries began their own screenings. More bizarre was the extension of screening to seamen on the Great Lakes. This was at the direct insistence of the Americans who were terrified lest Red seamen might infiltrate American ports on weekend leave. It was also at the insistence of the Seafarers International Union (SIU), a gangster American union imported to crush the communist Canadian Seamens Union (CSU). In fact the CSU had already been destroyed by the time the Great Lakes security regulations came into force, and in any event the SIU's control over hiring halls rendered the state's security apparatus superfluous. Eventually, when American McCarthyite paranoia waned, the Canadian authorities dropped this cumbersome and unnecessary intervention into the private sector.[68]

Another prime area for the security apparatus was in immigration. The post-war era saw not only the arrival of large numbers of refugees and displaced persons from Europe, but a more prolonged period of large-scale immigration into Canada of relatively cheap labour which helped fuel the great post-war boom. Identifying and barring 'security risks' among this vast flow of uprooted humanity became a prime concern for state security officials. Working entirely behind the scenes amid elaborate secrecy, plans were drawn up and implemented for screening out possible Communists and other left-wingers (former Nazis and Italian fascists were included as well, but the political thrust was unmistakable). RCMP agents posing as immigration officials were placed in all Canadian visa offices abroad and liaison was established with local security forces and police, as well as with the international operations of the CBI and British security, for access to political and criminal files. Applications rejected on security grounds were never to be told why, nor were sponsoring relatives in Canada, and there was no appeal. Perhaps most important for the RCMP were the invaluable links estbalished with security forces in numerous countries (including those of regimes such as fascist Spain and the Portuguese and Turkish dictatorships).

There were some peculiar distortions created by this security underside to immigration, including the cloaking of anti-semitism and other racial prejudices under the guise of 'national security'. Certain countries were treated unequally due to the existence of large indigenous Communist Parties (France and Italy for example). Perhaps the most peculiar distortion, however, was with regard to prospective immigrants from Soviet bloc countries. Instead of encouraging anti-communist refugees to swell the ranks of right-wing ethnic organisations within Canada, the RCMP (reflecting the then current wisdom of American intelligence) opposed all such immigration on the grounds that anyone who was let out of these regimes must be a Soviet agent. It was only with the Hungarian refugees of 1956–57 when the government itself stepped in and overrode security objections, that the flow from Eastern Europe began to step up, thus ending what can only be described as a bizarre extreme of Cold War irrationality.[69]

The other side of immigration security was the exercise of passport controls against Canadians, which were tried with intermittent success, and the revocation of citizenship for previously naturalised citizens who offended Cold War rules of behaviour. The latter was the case for a large number of Yugoslav–Canadians who emigrated back to their homeland to help in socialist reconstruction under the Tito regime. As in the United States, special controls were exercised to bar temporary visitors from abroad judged to be engaged in politically suspect activities—under this rubric, visiting speakers for left-wing and disarmament meetings were routinely barred, and 'look-out lists' were maintained at ports of entry (some of these read like a who's-who of world celebrities in the arts and sciences, from Sartre to Picasso). The United States and Canada co-operated in barring at the border temporary working visits by organisers and officials from what were believed to be communist-led international unions: a curious mutual exclusion of 'outside agitators'.[70]

As the security mania of the Cold War developed, so did the role and the influence of the RCMP. Anomalously both a state security agency and a regular police force, the RCMP was of course the beneficiary of the semi-mythological prestige of the Mounties. At the same time, like ASIO in Australia, the RCMP security branch was very much a junior partner to their American and British counterparts. The crude right-wing bias typical of all Western security forces was in this case deepened by the RCMP's close relationship with the McCarthy-era FBI and US State Department. State Department documents reveal, for instance, that the RCMP routinely provided American diplomatic and consular representatives in Canada with voluminous material from their files on Canadian 'subversives', access to which was denied Canadian cabinet ministers. Special files were compiled on civil servants and politicians believed to be potentially suspect. In short, the RCMP acted in many ways as an instrument of American Cold War policy, and was an arm for the American security-intelligence apparatus in a peripheral, but not un-important, country on America's border. There were other sinister aspects to the RCMP's files on subversives. Emergency planning for war in this period included plans for concentration camps for immediate internment of persons considered dangerous, including Labour leaders. This had been done during World War II, but now the lists seemed much longer and more comprehensive.[71]

It was a characteristic of state repression in Canada that it was generally exercised with the utmost secrecy. For example, no public indication was given, even in parliament, of the effects of the security screening in the civil service. Questions about security risks were met with an unbending silence. The immigration and passport screening was wrapped in impenetrable bureaucratic fog. All this was in sharp contrast to the American scene, where every effort was apparently made to maximise public exposure of security matters, to publicise, in headlines, even on live television, the names and numbers of 'security risks' fired from state positions. Indeed, the Canadian government even discouraged the dismissal of permanent civil servants on security grounds and favoured their transfer to non-sensitive positions (although numerous temporary positions were terminated), largely out of fear of publicity surrounding such firings. There were fledgling McCarthys, including the leader of the official Opposition in Parliament, who did attempt to politicise the security issue, but the government simply invoked ministerial privilege and the national interest, and weathered the storm in silence. This was a Canadian style of state repression, not unlike that of Britain in the same period, and is certainly important in assessing the Canadian experience.

The party system provides a key to understanding the Canadian experience. With social democracy a relatively underdeveloped third party strain in Canada (lacking institutional links with the weak and fragmented labour movement), Canadian federal politics were dominated by the Liberals, in uninterrupted office from 1935 to 1957, and in symbiotic relationship with the powerful senior civil service and the major centres of corporate power in Canada. The Liberals, as well entrenched as they were, were quite unprepared to allow the communist issue to be used against them by their right-wing opponents, the Conservatives. In this way they may in historical retrospect appear more perceptive and intelligent in their own self-interest than the Truman Democrats in the same period: they survived the domestic repression of the Cold War while the Democrats were consumed in the fires which they themselves had stoked. At the same time, it must be pointed out that the Liberals did not face the necessity of persuading a Republican Congress of the need to vote for huge sums for a global military, diplomatic and economic commitment. Moreover, they held a crucial trump card over their Conservative opponents: near complete political domination over the province of Quebec, and French Canada in general. Catholicism was a strong basis for anti-communist ideology in America and Australia, and Canada was the most Catholic of all three countries. The province of Quebec was under a reactionary, and very repressively anti-communist regime, and French Catholics were generally a political force favouring a McCarthyite stance. Yet for historical reasons, they were prisoners of the Liberal party in national politics. The Conservatives, on the other hand, were based in anti-Catholic and anti-French Protestant Ontario. No national right-wing anti-communist alliance was possible, and the Liberals, under a Quebec Catholic Prime Minister, were able to steer Canada into the Cold War American alliance while maintaining repression for the most part within the secrecy-shrouded bounds of the state—and at the same time preserving their own skins from the potential right-wing backlash, which did erupt in America and Australia.

Although there was, and is, a great deal of self-congratulation in Canada about the more 'liberal' and 'tolerant' political culture as contrasted to the United States, this seems dubious on a number of counts. First, there is the uncomfortable fact that public opinion data show Canadians to be no more tolerant, and no less authoritarian in their attitudes than Americans. If McCarthyism was, as argued earlier, not a mass phenomenon but an elite and party dynamic, then it was a different conjuncture of elites and parties which made the difference in Canada. Nor does it make much more sense to attribute greater attachment to liberal values to the Canadian elites, who in the past had shown considerable intolerance of dissent and great illiberality in dealing with radicalism.[72] Enlightened self-interest might better describe their motives in the Cold War era. Finally, it should not be forgotten that the zealous attempt by governmental and bureaucratic elites to monopolise the means of repression may be no evidence at all of liberality. On the contrary, the exercise of state repression in Canada, and in particular the activities of the RCMP security service, have been continuing sources of controversy and complaint since the beginnings of the Cold War.[73]

Nor would it be fair to suggest that McCarthyite political repression was absent in Canada, even if it never reached the levels of McCarthy's America, or Menzies' Australia. One clear example, with its origins in the state but ramifying into the political system, was the campaign to discredit and destroy the Canadian Peace Congress. Affiliated to the World Peace Council, and under the charismatic leadership of Dr James Endicott, a former church minister and missionary in China who had espoused the cause of the Communists in the Chinese Revolution, the Congress achieved some remarkable successes in mobilising Canadian opinion against the threat of nuclear war in the late forties and early fifties. The Canadian government, busy enlisting Canada in NATO and offering troops for Korea, and integrating beefed-up Canadian forces into continental defence under American direction, was in no mood to allow a free debate among Canadian citizens on the merits of the nuclear balance of terror. The state came down hard on the Congress in what amounted to an officially-inspired McCarthyite attack on the legitimacy of a private association of citizens. The Minister of External Affairs, and later recipient of the Nobel Peace Prize, Lester Pearson, castigated Dr Endicott in public speeches as a disloyal agent of communist totalitarianism. The media took up the cry and soon individual members of the Congress were suffering harrassment, mass meetings were attacked physically by gangs of organised thugs (virtually cheered on by Pearson), Endicott's home was bombed, halls were denied: in short, the full panoply of political repression unfolded. When Endicott travelled to China and gave support to the claims of American germ warfare in Korea and Southern China, the Cabinet actually discussed at length laying charges of treason against him. Ministers were dissuaded only by the enormity of the penalty—death. The real comment on Canada in the Cold War era is that the Cabinet actually discussed treason charges against a Canadian for statements made not about Canada but about the United States! The campaign to discredit the Peace Congress did largely succeed in its objective of amputating the peace movement from the body politic, at least for a few years. Thus it can be said that the Canadian state, when faced with a potentially popular movement of dissent from Cold War policy, was ready to encourage political repression when state repression seemed insufficient.[74]

The uses of political repression were particularly evident in the impact of the Cold War on the Canadian labour movement. The Liberal government, with a long history of attempted co-optation of trade union bureaucrats (and the largest share of the working-class vote across the country), had no intention of carrying out aggressive legislative interventions into union matters (á la Taft–Hartley in the US). The ingredients were there— a minority of militant communist trade union organisers and a few unions under communist leadership, along with a post-war strike wave and pent-up demands for wages and union recognition—but the Liberal government preferred to let the unions purge themselves of radical elements. In this they could rely on the fundamental conservatism of much of the trade union leadership, on American anti-communist influence through the mechanism of the international unions, and also on the dawning recognition among some elements of the trade union leadership that the Canadian working class could be a beneficiary of rearmament and the high employment offered by participation in the warfare state (even if at a lesser level than the Americans). They could also rely upon the influence of the social democratic supporters of the CCF party to carry on a struggle with the Communists which they had been waging since the 1930s.

Despite social democratic imprecations, Communists were often effective, dedicated organisers who helped advance the movement significantly (and sometimes let their political line get in the way, as between 1939 and 1941). The CCF and its union supporters were already pioneering Cold War social democracy by the late 1930s and the war years, particularly in the CCL (Canadian Congress of Labour) where Communists were active organisers. Communists were purged from the United Steel Workers and later the United Auto Workers. Also paralleling American post-war purges, the Fur and Leather Workers were purged of their strong communist leadership. The Mine, Mill and Smelter Workers resisted the purge and were raided in a long struggle for decertification which left only one, albeit large, local branch of Mine, Mill and Smelter Workers in operation. A particularly concerted attack by the CCL, the CCF, the international headquarters, and the American state on the Communist leadership of the International Woodworkers of America in British Columbia in the late 1940s succeeded completely. The United Electrical Workers, on the other hand, under particularly able communist leadership, survived expulsion from the CCL and outlasted a rival union created by its enemies. This was the exception.[75]

In the rival Trades and Labour Congress (TLC) with stronger craft union components, anti-communist purges also were the order of the day by the late 1940s and early 1950s. The most violent and bloody of all the purges was the warfare on the waterfront which finally crushed the Canadian Seamens Union. The apparent collusion of the Canadian state in granting citizenship to the notorious American labour thug, Hal Banks (who much later had to flee back to the US to avoid criminal prosecution), was only one of the questions raised concerning the state's complicity in the armed destruction of the CSU, although the tactical and strategic mistakes of the CSU itself cannot be underestimated. The state gave sanction to the affair when a Labour Relations Board ruled that the CSU could not be considered a legal union since it was Communist controlled.[76]

The great loser in all this was of course the unity, already derisive in Canada, of the labour movement. Militant trade unionism became suspect, loyalty was valued over ability, the movement went into a period of relative quiescence only to be broken in the 1960s. The social democrats won in the long run, as the adherence of the Canadian Labour Congress (representing the merger of the CCL and the TLC) to the CCF's successor, the NDP, in 1961 demonstrated. But in Canada, as well as in Britain and Australia, the self-destructive limitations of Cold War social democracy were every bit as apparent as the limitations of Cold War liberalism in America. Tarred with the indiscriminate brush of guilt-by-association and the reactionary atmosphere of the times, the CCF itself fell victim to the Cold War which it had so enthusiastically assisted, and was virtually paralysed as a political party. The Liberals were the winners, as of course were the employers.

Nor did the incidents of political repression end with the trade union purges. Canada in this era witnessed numerous incidents of McCarthyism in the professions, in schools, in local communities. It was not uncommon for local school boards to bar 'Communists' from teaching; a leading physicist of progressive views was hounded out of the country, and later stripped of citizenship, for spending a sabbatical in Poland; a graduate of law school in British Columbia was refused admission to the bar on the sole grounds that he was a communist supporter (a decision upheld by the Supreme Court of the province); a number of musicians in the Toronto Symphony Orchestra were dismissed because US Immigration officials had barred them from a US engagement on the grounds that they were 'security risks'. The examples could be multiplied. Yet the fact remains that Canada was different from the United States: political repression never became a partisan issue of any significance, and no politician at the national level was able to make a career on Red baiting.

The final act of the McCarthyite phase of the Cold War was played out for Canadians in 1957 in far away Cairo. Here the Canadian ambassador to Egypt, the distinguished Marxist scholar of Japanese history Herbert Norman, committed suicide after old and discredited Red baiting charges were resurrected once again by a US Senate committee. Official Ottawa was deeply angered; Canadian public opinion was outraged; even conservative newspapers expressed deep bitterness against the Americans. Relations between Canada and the US were at their 'all time low', according to the diary of the Canadian ambassador to Washington. Norman's death shocked the Canadian establishment, and defined for many Canadians the ugly excesses of McCarthyism. Yet at the same time, the identification of McCarthyism with America masked the extent that Canada too had travelled down the same road. The strengthened apparatus of state repression would remain as the legacy of the Cold War in Canada.[77]

Conclusion

All four of the countries examined here lined up against the Soviet Union and espoused enthusiastic Cold War ideology on the international front; all four locked themselves into warfare economies and closely integrated defence and security-intelligence networks. American hegemony over the Western alliance ought not to obscure the very considerable degree to which Britain, Canada and Australia willingly chose sides and maintained them.

The Cold War was clearly seen by all participants as a war on two fronts: abroad and at home. All four stepped up their internal controls over dissent, especially dissent from the political and military logic of the Cold War itself. All purged their state apparatus of 'security risks' of doubtful 'loyalty'. By decisively targeting left-wing opinion and activities as 'subversive' and potentially connected to the enemy abroad, all four states intervened in a very specific way into their domestic political communities, delegitimating certain ideas while strengthening others. All four states encouraged, either actively or passively, the extension of state repression into the political realm, especially in the key sector of the trade unions, where anti-communist purges were attempted by unionists themselves.

Political repression outside the state system was most characteristic of America, and to a lesser extent of Australia, with Canada and Britain following at a greater distance. The extent of political repression was most crucially a function of the party system and of the balance of class forces which underlay the party system. Where the working class was weakest and both social democracy and communism virtually non-existent, the anti-communist witch-hunt reached its most feverish intensity; where the working class was strongest and social democracy most hegemonic the sway of anti-communist hysteria seemed most restricted. On the other hand, the ideological bias of the Cold War cut one way, and social democracy itself suffered considerable damage from its attempts to ride the anti-communist tide, as did the liberal New Deal wing of the Democratic Party in America.

A striking feature of all four countries is the relative lack of mass enthusiasm for the Cold War crusade undertaken by national leaders, although that must be balanced against an equivalent lack of mass opposition as well. The domestic battles of the Cold War were battles fought largely by and for competing elites. Given the assumptions of the Cold War it was always obvious which elites would come out on top. Those who tried to pursue anti-communism as a single-minded ideological crusade themselves became destabilising elements in the end and were suppressed. But by the mid-1950s, all four countries were governed by conservative Cold War regimes no longer in need of excessive domestic repression because backed by extensive state apparatuses with considerable control over internal political dissent and with the major forces on the Left blunted and confused by the Cold War itself. That was the legacy of the first decade of the Cold War.

NOTES

1. Fred Halliday, *The Making of the Second Cold War*, (London 1983), p. 8.
2. This project will issue in a book, tentatively titled 'The Cold War in Canada, 1945-1955', in collaboration with Gary Marcuse. Time and expenses involved in this project were provided by grants from the Social Sciences and Humanities Research Council.
3. Zbigniew Brzezinski, *The Soviet bloc: unity and conflict*, (NY 1961), p. 91-97; Roy Medvedev, *Let History judge: the origins and consequences of Stalinism*, (NY 1972), p. 484-97; Adam Ulam, *Expansion and Coexistence*, (NY 1974), p. 466.
4. *Ibid.*, p. 467-8.
5. By 1968, even Republican vice-presidential candidate Spiro Agnew could react with horror when accused of McCarthyism. If he had only known, said Agnew, that his remarks 'would in some way cast me as the Joe McCarthy of 1968, I would have turned five somersaults to avoid saying it'. Quoted in Richard M. Fried, *Men against McCarthy*, (NY 1976), p. 345.
6. Mary Sperling McAuliffe, *Crisis on the Left: Cold War Politics and American liberals 1947-1954*, (Amherst, Mass. 1978), is the best account of the development of Cold War liberalism. For contemporary expressions of the new orthodoxy see Arthur Schlesinger, Jr., *The Vital Center*, (Boston 1949), and for how

far in the direction of repression even ex-Marxist liberals could go, see Sidney Hook, *Heresy, Yes—Conspiracy, No,* (NY 1953), and *Common Sense and the Fifth Amendment,* (NY 1957). An anti-McCarthy tract by James Rorty and Moshe Decter, *McCarthy and the Communists,* (Boston 1954) was sponsored by the American Congress for Cultural Freedom, a largely liberal organisation later revealed to be a CIA front.

7. Daniel Bell, ed., *The New American Right,* (NY 1955), revised and updated as *The Radical Right,* (Garden City, NY 1964).

8. One of the contributors to the Bell collection, Richard Hofstadter, went on to write a long essay on *Anti-intellectualism in American Life,* (NY 1963) to explain the deep cultural roots of McCarthyism.

9. Cambridge, Mass. 1967.

10. 'Towards an explanation of McCarthyism', *Political Studies* 8, (October 1960), p. 268.

11. Rogin, p. 260.

12. Sam Stouffer, *Communism, Conformity and Civil Liberties,* (NY 1955), p. 59, 88. Angus Campbell, *et al., The American Voter,* (NY 1960), p. 50-51. Stouffer also found that at the height of the nationally televised Army–McCarthy hearings two-thirds of the American public could not name a single Senator or Congressman who had been investigating communism (88).

13. On working class authoritarianism see S.M. Lipset, *Political Man,* (Garden City, NY 1963), p. 87-182.

14. *Hoover and the Un-Americans* (Philadelphia 1983). See also Athan Theoharis, *Beyond the Hiss Case: the FBI, Congress and the Cold War,* (Philadelphia 1982).

15. Theoharis, *Seeds of Repression,* (Chicago 1971), and Richard M. Freeland, *The Truman Doctrine and the Origins of McCarthyism,* (NY 1972). An early statement of this view, focussing on McCarthy's own political origins in Wisconsin is John Steinke and James Weinstein, 'McCarthy and the liberals', *Studies on the Left* 2:3 (Summer 1962), reprinted in James Weinstein and David Eakins, ed., *For a New America,* (NY 1970), p. 180-196.

16. Fried, *op. cit.,* 28 ff.

17. Athan Theoharis, *The Yalta Myth,* (Columbia, Mo. 1970), p. 4.

18. D.F. Crosby, *God, Church and Flag,* p. 228-51.

19. Stouffer, *op. cit.,* p. 116-117. Fried, *op. cit.,* p. 311 fn. David Oshinsky, *A Conspiracy So Immense,* (NY 1983), p. 498. Ironically, Southern politicians discovered the communist issue in the late 1950s after it had been largely discredited on the national scene. McCarthy tried to build bridges to the Southerners by championing a states rights position, but what might have been a powerful reactionary alliance in the early 1950s was a non-starter in the latter half of the decade.

20. David Oshinsky, *Senator Joseph McCarthy and the American Labor Movement,* (Columbia, Mo. 1976), p. 108-9.

21. See Mike Davis, 'The barren marriage of American labour and the Democratic party', *New Left Review* 124 (November–December 1980), p. 43-84.

22. A survey by *Fortune* of 253 top executives in 1954 showed a strong majority opposed to McCarthy and little positive support. Charles J.V. Murphy, 'McCarthy and the businessman', *Fortune,* (April 1954), p. 156-92.

23. Caute, p. 30, 20.

24. The most decisive statement of this interpretation is in Joyce and Gabriel Kolko, *The Limits of Power,* (NY 1972), p. 11-90.

25. It may be argued that it was precisely the combination of expanded British commitments abroad and inability to pay for these commitments which contri-

buted to the sudden rush of American dollars and power into the European
and Third World theatres at the end of the war. See Joyce and Gabriel Kolko,
op. cit.; M.R. Gordon, *Conflict and Consensus in Labour's Foreign Policy*,
(Stanford 1969); Alan Bullock, *Ernest Bevin: Foreign Secretary, 1945-1951*,
(London 1983). Elisabeth Barker, *The British Between the Superpowers 1945-
50*, (Toronto 1983); F.S. Northedge and Audrey Wells, *Britain and Soviet
Communism*, (London 1982), p. 103-136.

26. On atomic 'co-operation' see Gregg Herken, *The Winning Weapon*, (NY 1982).
27. Pincher, *Inside Story*, (NY 1979), p. 38. The best account of US–UK co-
    operation in this area is James Bamford, *The Puzzle Palace*, (NY 1983), p. 392–
    425.
28. The purge is discussed in David Williams, *Not in the Public Interest*, (London
    1965) and in H. Street, *Freedom, the Individual and the Law*, (Harmonds-
    worth 1977) and Tony Bunyan, *The History and Practice of the Political
    Police in Britain*, (London 1977).
29. Williams, p. 170-1, 197; Street, p. 246.
30. *Ibid.*, p. 154.
31. David Childs, *Britain Since 1945*, (London 1979), p. 36; Bob Jones, *The Russia
    Complex*, (Manchester 1977), p. 183-4.
32. Bunyan, *Political Police*, p. 123-7; Taylor, *Law and Order*, (London 1981),
    p. 68-9.
33. Pelling, *The British Communist Party*, (London 1958), p. 137.
34. J. Goldstein, *The Government of British Trade Unions*, (London 1952), p. 259-
    60; Jones, p. 198-9; Pelling, p. 153-9; M. Harrison, *Trade Unions and the
    British Labour Party Since 194 *, (London 1960), p. 132-3, 143-5, 153-5,
    182-6. Harrison also notes that the Association of Scientific Workers managed
    to remain unaffiliated with the Labour Party during the Cold War era despite
    criticism of its 'fellow travelling' executive often voiced by the rank and file
    (327). Similar left-wing scientific workers unions in Canada and Australia were
    broken by the atom spy scare and state and political repression in the late
    1940s.
35. During the anti-communist drive in the unions, Britain produced at least one
    example of the ex-communist expose of the Red menace: C.H. 'Bob' Darke's
    The Communist Technique in Britain, (London 1953) written by a lapsed
    Communist busman in London, gave the predictable picture of the Soviet
    octopus, although in rather less lurid tones than some of the American examples
    of this genre.
36. Pelling, *op. cit.*
37. Pelling, *op. cit.*, p. 131-2.
38. Childs, p. 2-9; Harrison, p. 215-16; Laski, *The Secret Battalion*, (London
    1946); Pelling, p. 146-7; Pincher, *Their Trade is Treachery*, (NY 1982), p. 256.
    At times, right-wing Labour leaders could sound almost McCarthyite in their
    intolerant denunciations of all internal opposition as 'Communist'. After the
    1952 Conference Hugh Gaitskell told the *Times* he was disturbed by the number
    of resolutions which were 'Communist-inspired'. He went on to estimate that
    one out of six constituency delegates were Communist or Communist-inspired.
    Even if the proportion were merely one in twenty, Gaitskell opined, 'it is a most
    shocking state of affairs to which the National Executive should give immediate
    attention': Ralph Miliband, *Parliamentary Socialism*, (London 1973), p. 326.
39. Jones, *Russia Complex*, makes the perceptive point that Bevinite 'realism'
    refused to recognise the legitimate interests in security which the USSR required
    in Eastern Europe, while simultaneously using evidence of Soviet power politics
    to buttress its anti-Soviet policies. To the idealists of the 'socialist foreign

policy' school, on the other hand, Soviet policy had ironic lessons to teach: 'the foreign policy of the Soviet Union itself conformed so closely to the principles of the realist school that, it is ironic to reflect, the best mentor of the Labour left in this subject was probably Stalin himself'. (190). Elisabeth Barker, *The British Between the Superpowers*, recounts instances when the Foreign Office and later the Defence Chiefs put forward plans for waging the Cold War as a highly ideological anti-communist crusade on all fronts; Bevin apparently was unimpressed (47, 177–78). On the struggle between the leadership and dissidents within the party see M.R. Gordon, *Conflict and Consensus in Labour's Foreign Policy*, (Stanford 1969), p. 102–64; Harrison, p. 217–8; D. Howell, *British Social Democracy*, (London 1976), p. 140–159; D. Coates, *The Labour Party and the Struggle for Socialism*, (London 1975), p. 68–9.

40. Miliband, *op. cit.*, p. 306; Jones, *Ibid.*, p. 183, 202–5; R.J. Jackson, *Rebels and Whips*, (London 1968), p. 65–71, 203–11.
41. Miliband, *Ibid.*, p. 312–3, 329–36; Howell, p. 187–90; Childs, p. 63–64.
42. Hinton, p. 174–5; Miliband, *op. cit.*, p. 306; Jones, p. 216. Colin Leys notes another long term legacy of anti-communism. The Labour Party adopted a blanket opposition to the political use of industrial action which the Communists advocated after 1947. This greatly strengthened the parliamentarism of Labour. *Politics in Britain*, (Toronto 1983), p. 182.
43. Pelling, *op. cit.*, p. 161–2.
44. L. Chester, S. Fay and H. Young, *The Zinoviev Letter*, (London 1967). H.G. Nicholas, *The British General Election of 1950*, London 1951), p. 222; D.E. Butler, *The British General Election of 1951*, (London 1952), p. 120–21, 199.
45. Gordon, p. 151–2; Northedge and Wells, p. 125–9; R.B. McCallum and A. Readman, *The British General Election of 1945*, (London 1947), p. 142–9.
46. Andrew Gamble, *The Conservative Nation*, (London 1974), ch. 3; Miliband, *Parliamentary Socialism*, p. 308–9; Leon Epstein, *Britain—Uneasy Ally*, (Chicago 1954), p. 182–3; Henry Pelling, *America and the British Left*, (London 1956), p. 153–4; Nicholas, p. 90; Bunyan, p. 166–7; Williams, p. 172–9.
47. Dennis Phillips, *Cold War Two and Australia*, (Sydney 1983), p. 31–2.
48. Gollan, *Revolutionaries and Reformists*, (Canberra 1975), p. 206.
49. R.W. Connell and T.H. Irving, *Class Structure in Australian History*, (1980), ch. 5; Gollan, p. 214–222; Nixon Apple, 'The rise and fall of full employment capitalism', in *Studies in Political Economy* 4, (Autumn 1980), p. 17–8.
50. Gollan, p. 244–8; Kylie Tennant, *Evatt: Politics and Justice*, (Sydney 1970), p. 248–53; Alastair Davidson, *The Communist Party of Australia*, (Stanford 1969). p. 108–10; Enid Campbell and Harry Whitmore, *Freedon in Australia*, (Sydney 1973), p. 327. A maverick ALP anti-communist crusader in Parliament, Jack Lang, combined anti-semitism, isolationism, and opposition to immigration with Red scare hysteria, asserting for instance that the arrival of Jewish refugees from Europe was a plot by the Communist International to dump its agents in Australia. Noting that anti-communism drew on 'indirectly related attitudes, prejudices and fears' typical of the labour movement, one writer rather perversely suggests that Labour's pre-emption of the issue 'occurred too slowly and too reticently': John Iremonger, 'Cold War Warrior' in Heather Radi and Peter Spearritt, eds., *Jack Lang*, (Neutral Bay NSW 1977), p. 229.
51. Gollan, *Ibid.*, p. 178, 152; Davidson, *ibid.*, p. 110–11.
52. Brian Fitzpatrick, *The Australian Commonwealth*, (Melbourne 1956), p. 236–8; Richard Hall, *The Secret State*, (197), p. 41; Davidson, p. 107–8.
53. Phillips, p. 39–41; Hall, p. 50; Leicester Webb, *Communism and Democracy in Australia*, (Melbourne 1954).

54. Webb, p. 127–56, 178–85.
55. Nicholas Whitlam and John Stubbs, *Nest of Traitors,* (Brisbane 1974), p. 13–28; Hall, p. 42–57; Desmond Ball, *A Suitable Piece of Real Estate,* (Sydney 1980). ASIO was given formal legal basis in the Australian Security Intelligence Organisation Act of 1956, which defines 'security' as the 'protection of the Commonwealth and the Territories of the Commonwealth from acts of espionage, sabotage, or subversion, whether directed from or intended to be committed, within the Commonwealth or not': Campbell and Whitmore, p. 334.
56. Phillips, p. 38; Hall, p. 58–64; Campbell and Whitmore, p. 337–8.
57. Fitzpatrick, p. 126–7; Hall, p. 67. Information on Australian passport controls was found in diplomatic dispatches of the Canadian High Commission in Australia: Public Archives of Canada, Ottawa, Privy Council Office Records 1952, file C-22-1.
58. Hall, p. 45; Davidson, p. 104–6; Gollan, p. 260–78.
59. Whitlam and Stubbs, p. 94, 168 and *passim.* Hall suggests that the Petrov Affair was a 'watershed' in relations between Labor and ASIO; Labor believed that ASIO had at best 'connived' with Menzies, and at worst 'conspired to rig documents'—in any event, relations were henceforth adversarial. (50). On Evatt's role see Tennant, *Evatt.*
60. Davidson, p. 126; K.S. Inglis, 'The Australian Catholic Community' in Henry Mayer, ed., *Catholics and the Free Society,* (Melbourne 1961), p. 8; R.N. Spann, 'The Catholic Vote in Australia' in *ibid.,* p. 117; Gollan, p. 174–5; Paul Ormonde, *The Movement,* (Melbourne 1972).
61. Robert Murray, *The Split,* (Melbourne 1970); D.W. Rawson, *Unions and Unionists in Australia,* (Sydney 1978), p. 80–122; P.L. Reynolds, *The Democratic Labor Party,* (Milton Queensland 1974); Louise Overacker, *Australian Parties in a Changing Society,* (Melbourne 1968); Ormonde, p. 66. Even during the referendum on Communist Dissolution, it was apparent that class and party could to an extent override the anti-communist ideology of Catholicism: in a poll on voting intentions Catholics split down the middle while other religious denominations showed majorities in favour of a 'yes' vote; on the other hand, Catholics voted in much higher numbers for the ALP in the 1949 and 1951 elections than they voted for the 'no' side in the referendum (Webb, p. 96–9). One factor which certainly slowed the progress of the Groupers in ousting Communists from union leadership was the simple fact that communist unionists were generally perceived by the rank and file as good militant trade unionists. Even the Victoria Royal Commission on Communism of 1949-50 was forced to conclude that 'where strikes have occurred under communist leadership or influence, the purpose has been really, in the first place, to gain the advantages sought in the men's demands' (quoted in Gollan, p. 257). Catholic ideology could go only so far in the face of this.
62. See for instance Don Page and Don Munton, 'Canadian images of the Cold War 1946-47' in *International Journal* 33, (Summer 1977).
63. Merrily Weisbord, *The Strangest Dream,* (Toronto 1973) contains many interesting interviews with the Communists implicated in the affair.
64. The Report of the Royal Commission to Investigate Certain Facts, etc. (Ottawa 1946); Robert Bothwell and J.L. Granatstein, eds., *The Gouzenko Transcripts,* (1982). I am still in the process of trying to have certain key documents in the case declassified, almost forty years later.
65. The Gouzenko reference is to reports on interviews with Gouzenko in 1945-46 recently released from the Department of External Affairs under the Access to Information Act.
66. Reg Whitaker, 'Origins of the Canadian government's internal security system

1946-1952', in *Canadian Historical Review* 65:2 (1984).

67. Whitaker, 'Origins', p. 171-3.
68. Documents relating to Great Lakes security were found in the records of the Privy Council Office and the Department of Transport and Labour, Public Archives of Canada.
69. Information based mainly on documents from the records of the Departments of Immigration, Labour and the Privy Council Office.
70. Social democratic politicians and right-wing trade unionists sometimes quietly supported the state's intervention against communist trade union organisers through immigration controls.
71. American consular and embassy correspondence, Department of State records, US National Archives. On the RCMP in general, see John Sawatsky, *Men in the Shadows*, (Toronto 1980), and *For Services Rendered*, (Toronto 1982).
72. This includes the prosecution of radicals under the draconian section 98 of the Criminal Code in the 1930s, mass deportations of radicals and labour organisers in the same decade, and the internments and police harrassment of Communists and other dissenters during World War II.
73. See for example the furore which led to the McDonald Royal Commission on RCMP 'wrongdoing'.
74. Stephen Endicott, *James G. Endicott: Rebel Out of China*, (Toronto 1980). I have also been given access to the Endicott Papers by Dr. Endicott, which include much material on the Peace Congress.
75. Irving Abella, *Nationalism, Communism and Canadian Labour*, (Toronto 1973).
76. TLC material based on research by Gary Marcuse for our joint study of the Cold War in Canada (see note 2, above).
77. Norman is the subject of Roger Bowen's forthcoming *E.H. Norman, His Life and Scholarship*, (Toronto 1984).

ERNEST BEVIN AND THE COLD WAR 1945-1950

John Saville

The social legislation of the Labour governments after 1945—the creation of the welfare state as it is commonly thought of—has become an important mythology for the working-class political movement in Britain. The exaggerated claims made at the time by many of Labour's intellectuals— that Britain by 1950 had entered upon a post-capitalist phase of development[1] —have, of course, long been discarded but the general consciousness among a majority of the politically committed that the years after the end of the Second World War somehow represented a qualitative breakthrough are still widely current. In 1983 a marxist could write—in an article devoted to a much too uncritical account of Maynard Keynes:

> Keynes died in 1946, while the postwar Labour government was just beginning its work: the programme of reforms which were to provide an agreed framework for government for the next 25 years and which can be seen as inaugurating the 'Keynesian era'. The successes of that government—in institutional change, in what seemed decisive and irreversible social advance, in economic management— became a model for socialist practice.[2]

Most of these statements are untrue or, incorrect in their implications. It is certainly correct that the social legislation introduced after 1945 was in advance, considerably in advance in most cases, of practice in capitalist democracies elsewhere but within two decades the levels of social provision in France, Germany and the Scandinavian countries were already higher than in Britain; and what is now widely appreciated is that the Attlee governments made remarkably little change to the institutional structure of Britain. The pronounced mal-distribution of wealth and property remained and there were no attempts to modify the economic inequalities that were both built into the system and were continuously being generated by the normal processes of capitalist development. There was no wealth tax; and towards the political institutions of the country— the civil service, the management structures of nationalised industries, the conservative and traditional practices of central and local government—the post-war labour administrations showed a notable caution and respect. Moreover Labour, from the mid sixties, was confronted with increasingly powerful vested interests which had built themselves up after the years of war and which offered continuous resistance to further advances. When the right-wing administration of Thatcher began the piece-meal dismantling of social welfare services from 1979 on there were notably few defences that could be mobilised.

The demolition of national social provision has in some ways sharpened the contrast between what is happening today and what was done after 1945, and the illusions live on as to what exactly was accomplished by the Attlee government. But what has never been seriously questioned is the other part, and the more important part, of the post-war government's policies in the area of foreign affairs; and the connection between the foreign commitments entered into by Attlee and Ernest Bevin, his Foreign Secretary, and the domestic policies of the Labour government have remained confused and little understood. The past four decades have been the only period in the history of the British labour movement—the First World War being an exception—when there has not been a substantial minority opinion in sharp opposition to the dominant conservative attitude and policy in foreign affairs. There have always been some minority views, of course, and the current strong trend against nuclear weapons may well prove a new departure; but the collapse of CND in the early sixties exhibited how tenacious was the consensus established in the years immediately after the ending of the war. The central theme has been anti-Sovietism, and all other issues have been subordinated to the maintenance of the alliance between America and Western Europe—and now including Japan—in furtherance of the anti-Soviet policies directed and coordinated by Washington. Towards the establishment of the relationship between America and Europe in the early post-war years, Attlee and especially Bevin, the leaders of the most powerful but dis-integrating world imperialism, were of crucial importance.

Ernest Bevin was born in 1881 but his political career came only in the last ten years of his life. It was his trade union experience that shaped him beyond any possibility of change, and even here he developed slowly. Not until the years between 1905 and 1908 did he begin to shift his main interests from the chapel to politics; he first became a trade unionist at the age of twenty nine and in the spring of the following year he was appointed a full-time official of the Docker's Union: to remain a trade union official until his appointment as Minister of Labour in 1940.

His long apprenticeship in the Baptist chapel and the Adult school movement marked him intellectually all his life. He was self-taught, with the strengths and weaknesses of that tradition. He came tardily to a recognition of social injustice: a loitering conversion from the politically ignorant 'commonsense' of the ordinary working man to some degree of appreciation of the class nature of society; a matter of political compre-hension that owed almost nothing to theoretical insights and almost everything to the assimilation of practical experience. Bevin was a product of the labourist tradition of nineteenth century Britain and he was to be hardly touched by the twentieth century transition to the labour socialism of mainstream Labour Party activists: labourism with a socialist rhetoric.

Bevin had certain strongly marked personal characteristics. 'After his trade union experience' writes his major biographer in the third and last volume of Bevin's life and times, 'he found it hard to believe in the disinterestedness of those who disagreed with him. . .'[3] There is, of course, nothing in the trade union experience which automatically encourages such attitudes in its practitioners. In spite of his overweening self-confidence in public Bevin was extraordinarily sensitive to criticism, and any opposition he inevitably cast in personal terms. Since he was also thoroughly prejudiced in his views of individuals, criticism became treasonable: the stab in the back was the phrase he must have used dozens of times in his public career. His antipathy to Herbert Morrison, and the bitterness with which that antipathy was expressed, was only one of the most striking illustrations of Bevin's prejudices; and Morrison, it must be noted, was basically on Bevin's side. For those movements, such as the British Communist Party or the Labour Left for which Bevin had a total aversion, there could be no accommodation at any point.

Political and social change, in the theory and practice of labourism, were practicable and possible within the existing system. Parliamentary democracy offered these possibilities. This was the central labourist creed. There were immensely powerful vested interests to be opposed; many narrow-minded individuals to be convinced, in one way or another; the inertia of the system to be overcome. But always social reform was achievable, and with the slow expansion of political democracy in the closing years of the nineteenth century, at local as well as at national levels, the opportunities for change began to widen. The political strength of those who combated change encouraged a reciprocal toughness of stance among working people and especially among those who were trade unionists, for it was they upon whom the struggle largely devolved; and there developed among them a stubborn insistence upon bargaining rights and economic improvement. It also encouraged a view of political action that became inextricably woven into working-class experience in Britain: the understanding that electoral power would provide the necessary leverage for amelioration by legislation. Bevin and his generation, consciously, more often implicitly, had an appreciation of the State that was common to the Fabians and most British socialists of the twentieth century: that the whole apparatus of State power was at the disposal of those who won a parliamentary majority. C.R. Attlee stated the matter in terms to which Bevin undoubtedly gave whole-hearted assent and which certainly informed all his own political beliefs. In *The Labour Party in Perspective*, published in 1937, Attlee emphasised the practicality of the British movement:

It has never consisted of a body of theorists or of revolutionaries who were so absorbed in Utopian dreams that they were unwilling to deal with the actualities of everyday life. From the first, British socialists have taken their share wherever possible in the responsibility of Government. The British system of local government has proved to be an excellent training ground. Long before there were more than a handful of Labour members in Parliament, Socialists had won their way on to local councils and were influencing administration. By showing what could be done in a small sphere they were able to convert many sceptical workers who would only believe what they saw in being.[4]

Attlee was influenced in some small degree by the events of the 1930s; but Bevin not at all. In no way does Bevin appear to have been to the slightest extent radicalised by the events of the inter-war years. The General Strike pushed him into a more not less moderate position: it did also, of course, many of his leading colleagues. And in foreign affairs in the years after Hitler came to power, his comprehension and understanding were outside the progressive tradition which became further radicalised by appeasement and the Spanish experience. In his younger days Bevin had attended a Baptist chapel whose pastor, the Rev. James Moffat Logan, took a courageous stand against the Boer war; but what Bevin's attitude was does not seem to be known. In the First World War he adopted what can only be described as a trade union approach: one which was neither jingoistic nor in political opposition. He was certainly contemptuous of the political pacifism of the ILP as represented by MacDonald and Snowden. The most important international issues of the years between the wars, for the labour movement in Britain, were the Soviet Union, India and the Spanish civil war. About the last, which was such a formative influence upon so many, Bevin was never very interested. He defended non-intervention at the TUC in September 1936 and the bloc vote gave him an overwhelming majority. Throughout the three years of the Spanish war he withheld any effective support for the Republic: no doubt in considerable part because of the communist influence. What was typical of Bevin in the 1930s was the offer which he and Citrine made in February 1937 to Baldwin, then Prime Minister, to help with the difficulties of the rearmament programme in return for an official committee to enquire into holidays with pay. The Amulree committee on which Bevin himself served, recommended one week's paid holiday, instead of the two weeks the TUC asked for, and it passed into law in 1938.

The importance of paid holidays for working people is not denied; but rearmament was a political issue of major importance and to trade it off for the paid holidays issue was entirely typical of the narrow economistic view of their responsibilities adopted by both Citrine and Bevin. But Bevin in these years went beyond Citrine in accepting a more political stance. His position in the TUC made this necessary. He was an early advocate of rearmament against German fascism, and his reasons were those of national interest: not very different from those put forward by Churchill. Bevin was also, in this decade, the foremost advocate in the trade union movement of consultation with employers and government: a policy which developed consciously in the aftermath of the General Strike and which continued and expanded in the following decade. Soon after he became chairman of the General Council of the TUC in 1936 he noted the differences between the reports of the two periods and the extension of the TUC's responsibilities and involvement with both employers and government. 'Most of these things' he commented to his own executive council, 'were to them [in the twenties] propaganda points. Those were the days of advocacy. Ours is the day of administration.'[5]

This growth of corporatism reached new heights during the Second World War, and for Bevin the experience was crucial. The Ministry of Labour had steadily become more important since 1914 and Bevin appreciated the further possibilities in a second wartime situation. This was why, against the advice of some very close to him, like Arthur Deakin, he accepted the Labour department rather than Supply or Economic Warfare. He was right, of course. His very successful tenure of the office, and his considerable contribution to the planning of national resources placed the Ministry of Labour at the centre of decision-making on the domestic front. His personal contribution to the success of his Ministry was crucial to the further consolidation of his basic ideas about the nature of society, the nature and character of the state, and the ways of administration. He became immensely powerful in the War Cabinet and Bullock notes, although with considerable under-emphasis, the impact of power upon his general ideas. It was wartime experience that confirmed for him the central proposition of labourism: the achievement of national recognition and the responsibility for the national interest. The crucial difference for Bevin in the years after 1945, Bullock writes, lay in the fact:

> that the Labour Party was no longer a party of protest but accepted as the con-
> stitutional government of the country, and the working class and trade union
> movement which he represented were no longer excluded from the concept of
> the national interest but entrusted with the responsibility for its maintenance. His
> anger and resentment at this exclusion and the unfitness for responsibility which
> it implied had been one of the most powerful springs of his political activity and
> had led him to attack the Baldwin and Chamberlain administrations as class
> governments. Once the exclusion was removed, he found it natural to take a
> national rather than a class view of his responsibilities.[6]

This is the undiluted statement of the theory and practice of labourism, and Bevin's conception of what constituted 'national interest' simply expressed his fundamentally liberal-labour approach to the analysis and understanding of society. What did Bevin mean by 'national interest'? 'In general terms' replied Bullock, 'the security of the United Kingdom and its overseas possessions against external attack; the continued financial and economic as well as political independence of Britain; the right of its people to trade freely with the rest of the world, their right to maintain a policy of full employment and a decent standard of living.'[7] These were sentiments which any progressively-minded Tory could and did express in these years immediately following the ending of the war; and it is further necessary to emphasise how much the business of wartime administration had deepened Bevin's bias towards corporatism. The more obvious manifestations of class conflict had been considerably muted, and the sharp cleavages of the inter-war years had been blunted and softened. Corporate bias was always implicit in labourism, and Bevin's practical experience of the use of the state machine to mobilise men and resources confirmed his already firm belief in its essentially political neutrality.

Labourism was one central strand in Bevin's thinking; the other was anti-communism which he had exhibited from the early days of the Russian revolution. He played a part in the national movement against intervention in 1919 and 1920, although certainly not the major role that he himself often claimed and which his biographer accepts un-critically.[8] In common with most of the leading trade union and political personalities of the labour movement, but with rather more intensity in his case, he had an animosity towards the British Communist Party which became more pronounced through the years of the thirties, not least because of the success of the Communist Party in the encouragement of rank and file movements in trades organised by Bevin's union. He was with the mainstream of British labour when he pointed to the absence of civil liberty in the Soviet Union; he was certainly the object of a con-tinuous invective against him by the communist and the non-communist Left. In Bevin's case, however, his anti-communism was to be carried over into international affairs, and the common gibe during his period of office as Foreign Secretary that he approached Soviet Russia rather as a communist-inspired breakaway union was not without substance. Dalton reported Bevin saying in September 1946 that Molotov was like a Com-munist in a local Labour Party: if you treated him badly, he made the most of the grievance and if you treated him well, he put up the price next day and abused you. Dalton finished his account of this discussion by writing in his diary about Bevin: 'Full of bright ideas, as well as earthy sense, but dangerously obsessed with Communists.'[9]

It was not ability that Bevin lacked: his capacity for mastering a brief is constantly remarked upon by Bullock, quoting the comments of Bevin's senior officials. What was lacking was any serious intellectual equipment that would have allowed him to evaluate the application of the concept of 'national interest' as interpreted by the traditionally-minded Foreign Office. The United Kingdom was the largest imperialist power in the world, and no appreciation of Britain's position in the world—before 1939 or after 1945—could be realistic without an understanding of what imperialism meant for the dominant power and for those who were dominated. The radical wing of the labour movement in Britain—represented at its most generous by H.N. Brailsford—had developed a theory of imperialism, not least around the case of India, that had widespread currency during the inter-war years and which had encouraged a genuine sense of internationalism. This was a tradition which went back a long way for its earliest beginnings. It was a non-Marxist trend although inevitably after 1917 there was an important influence coming from communist sources. But none of this affected Bevin in any way that can be discerned. Indeed, by 1938 his ideas had crystallised around a liberal approach to international economic problems and in particular to the problems of Empire. He had talked on the question of international economic questions at the Labour Party Conference in 1937 and early in 1938 he wrote an article for his union journal in which he developed his ideas:

> The great colonial powers of Europe should pool their colonial territories and link them up with a European Commonwealth, instead of being limited British, French, Dutch or Belgian concessions as is now the case. Such a European Commonwealth, established on an economic foundation, would give us greater security than we get by trying to maintain the old balance of power. . .[10]

He was further encouraged in these naiveties by his attendance at an unofficial Commonwealth conference in Australia in the autumn of 1938. The leader of the British delegation was Lord Lothian, a vigorous supporter of appeasement, and among the other British delegates was Lionel Curtis, the most woolly of all the 'high-minded Imperialists'[11] associated with the *Round Table,* and the one with the most grossly inflated reputation. The delegates came from the four older Dominions together with those from India, Ireland and the United Kingdom; and most were academics. Bevin returned with neo-imperialist ideas about the extension of the Ottawa agreements beyond the existing Commonwealth countries, and full of suggestions for the better administration of the colonial Empire. 'Our crime isn't exploitation, it's neglect'[12] and there is no evidence that he got beyond these simple untruths by the time he became Foreign Secretary.

His deficiencies as Foreign Secretary were two: first, his lack of practical experience of foreign affairs, and second, the vacuum in his mind of what a Labour, let alone a socialist, foreign policy should involve. He had been privy, of course, to all the foreign policy discussions in the War Cabinet, and he was not ignorant of the range of problems he would be confronted with when he took office. But the political approach he brought to office was compounded of his vigorous anti-communism and anti-Sovietism with a marked conservative view of what the 'national interest' involved.

Bullock is therefore correct to emphasise, as he does on a number of occasions, the fundamental continuity of foreign policy established by the Churchill coalition government with that carried on by Bevin on behalf of the new Labour administration. The permanent under-secretary at the Foreign Office, Sir Alec Cadogan, waiting for Attlee and Bevin to arrive for the resumed Postdam conference, wrote with pleasant frankness in his diary:

> I think we may do better with Bevin than with any other of the Labourites. I think he's broadminded and sensible, honest and courageous. But whether he's an inspired Foreign Minister or not I don't know. He's the heavyweight of the Cabinet and will get his own way with them, so if he can be put on the right line, that may be all right.[13]

The right line was the continuation of the existing line. In the first foreign policy debate of the Labour Government, in August 1945, Anthony Eden recalled the years with Bevin in the War Cabinet:

> Eden: During that period there were many discussions on foreign affairs I cannot recall one single occasion when there was a difference between us. I hope I do not embarrass the Foreign Secretary when I say that.
> Bevin: No.
> Eden: There was no difference on any important issues of foreign policy.[14]

Nor was there to be in the years which followed. Hugh Gaitskell was quoted as saying in October 1954 that he doubted whether foreign policy would play an important part in the next election 'not because it is not important, but because Mr Eden has, in fact, mostly carried on our policy as developed by Ernest Bevin, in some cases against the views of rank and file Tories'.[15] So we get the succession: Churchill and Eden; Bevin; Eden: each following the other and bequeathing their legacy to the Foreign Secretaries who came later. It took, apparently, a few months before Bevin felt himself completely at home with his officials in the Foreign Office as he had with those at the Ministry of Labour. It was largely, it may be surmised, as Bullock does himself suggest, a matter of awkwardness of finding himself in a job he was supposed not to have wanted and surrounded by the social and political elite of the civil service who, whatever their deficiencies, were very clever men. Bevin, for all his blustering arrogance, was by no means always at ease with the imperious smoothness that is the manner of the educated upper class in Britain; and like so many self-made men, he could be easily charmed and flattered, as Lady Diana Cooper, among others, relates in her autobiography.[16] There is an exceedingly instructive story which Gladwyn Jebb tells in his memoirs of his first interview with Bevin:

> In fact he said nothing for a few moments and simply looked me over in my chair. Finally he observed 'Must be kinda queer for a chap like you to see a

chap like me sitting in a chair like this?' Slightly nonplussed, I thought it better not to take up the challenge. So I just shrugged my shoulders and smiled. Bevin was rather nettled. 'Ain't never 'appened before in 'istory,' he remarked, scowling ferociously.[17]

And Jebb told him he was wrong; that Thomas Wolsey 'incidentally, not unlike you physically' was a butcher's son from Ipswich. Bullock adds that whether historically accurate or not 'the comparison visibly impressed Bevin and secured Jebb a permanent place in his good books'.[18]

It was not difficult for the Foreign Office to put Bevin 'on the right line' as Cadogan had written. Attlee left foreign affairs to Bevin, and Bevin got his way in the Cabinet. When there were differences between Attlee and Bevin, the Prime Minister never seems to have insisted upon his particular point of view. Their close relationship—the only one that either man had within the group of leading Ministers—was a source of enormous strength to the officials of the Foreign Office. Bevin was on good terms with the Chiefs of Staff; he had an intimate knowledge of the workings of the Whitehall machine; and he could always rely on the necessary majority at the annual conferences of the Labour Party and the TUC. This was important since Bevin's critics came from within the labour movement. In the House of Commons Tory opposition was largely nominal; it was on his own back benches that Bevin found bitter hostility.

The story of Bevin as Foreign Minister, from the summer of 1945 to his forced resignation, for reasons of ill-health, in early March 1951, has been told by Alan Bullock in the third volume of his very large-scale biography in something over 850 pages. Bullock's analysis is predicated upon certain basic assumptions: given their validity, then the policies Bevin followed were reasonable, sensible and politically desirable. The first was that

> there was a real danger of the Soviet Union and other Communists taking advantage of the weakness of Western Europe to extend their power. We know that this did not follow, but nobody knew it at the time. This was a generation for whom war and occupation were not remote hypotheses but recent and terrible experiences. The fear of another war, the fear of a Russian occupation, haunted Europe in those years and were constantly revived—by the Communist coup in Czechoslovakia, by the Berlin blockade, and by the outbreak of war in Korea which produced near-panic in France and Germany. It is unhistorical to dismiss these fears as groundless because the war and occupation did not occur (p. 845).

The second assumption is 'that there were substantial reasons, accepted by a Labour government which had already begun on the processes of withdrawal in Asia and the Commonwealth, for not pushing it further until the dangerous instability after the war had been replaced by a new balance of power' (p. 847). The third strand in Bevin's policy was to accept a permanent relationship—Bullock calls it an alliance—with North America and Western Europe on the understanding that in the world struggle between the Soviet Union and communism—the two were interchangeable for Bevin—on the one side, and capitalism on the other, Britain could no longer go it alone but was forced to recognise the over-riding strength, and leadership, of the United States. In this respect Bullock is correct in noting the break with traditional policy, but more important, as Bullock also emphasises many times, was the continuity between Labour's foreign policy and that pursued by the Coalition government during the years of war to 1945.

An essay of the present length cannot analyse the range of foreign policy decisions entered upon by Bevin and the Attlee government. What follows is a selection of events and issues which illustrates certain of the leading strands of decision-making and illuminates the general course pursued by the Labour government. Palestine, Malaya and Germany are among the countries excluded from consideration.

An instructive case history was that of Indo-China, one of the issues of colonialism that confronted Bevin very early in his tenure of office; and which exemplifies Bullock's comment about the need to be cautious in the 'withdrawal' from Asia as well as offering a specific illustration of the absence of anything approaching socialist principles in the making of the foreign policy of the Attlee administration.

A further reason for looking, however briefly, at the post-war history of Indo-China is that Bullock dismissed what happened in a couple of sentences; and it clearly did not represent for him anything of importance.[19] If you have a mid-twentieth century Western liberal view of world relationships it can presumably be taken for granted that former colonial powers—in this case, the French—have a moral right to resume their domination; especially if the nationalist movement contained an important if not central component of Communists in the leadership. The story of Indo-China and imperialism goes much further back than the capitulation of the Japanese army in August–September 1945. The Americans, in the early days of the war, had been exceedingly hostile to the European imperialist powers and had been stating their opposition to a return, after the war, to the status quo ante. By 1944 however, what an English historian has called 'the brave days of 1942-3', when the USA was talking about specific dates for the achievement of colonial independence for various countries, were passed and the general attitudes inside the Washington administration were beginning to change. There were many reasons, including the ambitions of the Americans themselves in the Pacific, the growing strength of the French position, and the unyielding attitude of the British on these colonial questions.[20] The British Foreign Office recognised the importance of France in the post-war period —despite Churchill's personal hostility towards de Gaulle, and as Sir Alexander Cadogan wrote to Churchill in November 1944: 'In view of the

well-known American attitude towards the restoration of colonies generally, there is much to be said for the colonial powers sticking together in
the Far East.'[21] How they stuck together was never better illustrated than
in Indo-China between September 1945 and the early months of 1946.

Indo-China began to be an area of growing interest in the second half
of 1944 when post-war problems were being increasingly considered. On
November 15th, 1944 General Wedemeyer, commanding the American
forces in China, reported that British, French and Dutch interests were
making intensive efforts to prepare for the recovery of their possessions
in the Far East.[22] The Americans had already been considering the ideas
of trusteeship but these suggestions were fading rapidly during 1945 and
after Roosevelt's death were never again seriously considered. At Potsdam
the American suggestion that Indo-China should be split at the 16th
parallel was accepted, with the southern half coming within Mountbatten's
command and the northern within the control of Wedemeyer. At the time
the decision was taken it was not expected that the Japanese would
capitulate so quickly and the pro-colonial campaign which the British
had waged on behalf of the French was soon to be tested in political,
rather than in military, terms.

The Vietminh took power in Hanoi in the middle of August and at the
end of the same month the Committee of the South, largely dominated by
Communists, took power in Saigon. The nationalist liberation movement
was much weaker in the south than it was in the north, but it was understood by the Vietnamese everywhere that they were going to work with
the Allies and not with the hated French. Meanwhile, after the capitulation of Japan Mountbatten was beginning to receive orders concerning
Vietnam based upon discussions between the French and the British
Foreign Office: orders with which Mountbatten had some important disagreements although the final text was not communicated to him until the
9 October when the crucial events were over. Before that he had been told
to proceed in accordance with drafts sent to him in early September, the
main points of which were that British troops were to be used to ensure
the disarming of the Japanese, and the release of Allied prisoners but that
responsibility for civil administration rested solely with the French. 'The
general tenor of the agreements' wrote the official historian of British
military administration in the Far East, 'was to safeguard French
sovereignty from avoidable encroachment by Allied Commanders'.[23]

During the early days of September, before the British arrived, the
Vietminh, whose strength in the south was now growing rapidly, continued to argue for cooperation with the Allies. What may, from other
continents and other communist parties, be called the spirit of Teheran
still led the Vietminh to believe that the Allies would support the movement for independence. Among other issues, they denounced the slogan—
used by Trotskyists and certain other nationalist groups—of 'arms for the

people' and they opposed the seizure of land by the peasants.[24] The provisional government in France had already issued a statement on the future of Indo-China on 24 March 1945. While a considerable advance on anything that had gone before—it could, after all, hardly preach a straight return to colonialism—it fell very short of genuine independence. For one thing, Cochin China, Tonkin and Annam were to continue as separate states whereas they were now considered by the nationalists as integral parts of the Republic of Vietnam. The French governor appointed in August 1945 was Admiral Georges Thierry d'Argenlieu, as un-compromising as de Gaulle himself about the inviolability of the French Empire in the post-war world. The French in Indo-China, it hardly needs to be remarked, exhibited all the usual characteristics of colonial over-seers. As Tom Driberg commented in the House of Commons on 28 January 1946, the French administration during the war 'was extremely oppressive and corrupt, and ninety-five per cent pro-Vichy'.[25]

The nucleus of the British forces allocated to Saigon was the 20th Indian Division, commanded by General Douglas D. Gracey, who was later commander-in-chief of the Pakistan Army. The total number of troops who entered Vietnam were around 26,000, very effective and highly disciplined and with a formidable record in the 14th Army. The Indian army, it should be noted, was to the greater part of Asian national-ists, the symbol of imperialist oppression. Advanced groups began flying into Saigon in early September; the main body began to arrive on the 11th September and Gracey landed at Saigon on the 13th, to find the airfield manned by Japanese troops with their generals waiting to pay their respects. The Japanese were to play an interesting role in the weeks to come. There were not enough British troops—mostly Indians or Gurkhas—to go round and the French, already on the way with General Leclerc as GOC, were not to arrive until towards the end of the year. In the interim the Japanese in certain areas, including parts of Saigon, were relied upon to maintain order. Order, as the situation deteriorated, meant fighting and from late September the Japanese were engaged in operations against the local populations. 'Their discipline' said an English Brigadier, 'was excellent'.[26] Some who had been disarmed were brought back into military duty and one consequence, noted at the time, was that Brtish, Indian and French casualties were significantly reduced. An American eye witness reported that 'the British were delighted with the discipline shown by their late enemy and were often warmly admiring, in the best playing-field tradition, of their fine military qualities. It was all very comradely'.[27]

These things came about because the people of south Vietnam did not want a return to French colonial rule and because the commander of the British forces, sent in with specific instructions as to what he could and could not do, took it upon himself to go beyond his brief. There is evidence that Gracey had made up his mind before he arrived in Saigon that Indo-China was going to remain French. His own instructions were clear: to carry through the disarming of the Japanese, to release all Allied prisoners and arrange for their repatriation, and not to become involved in the local political situation. But Gracey's own inclinations are only part of the story: to have remained genuinely neutral would have meant serious negotiation with the Committee of the South and the French being kept at arm's length. The political decision to facilitate the return of the French had already been taken before Gracey and his troops arrived in Saigon, so while Mountbatten was undoubtedly unhappy at what was being done below the 16th parallel—as were many other people including most of the American press, many Labour MPs and curious fellow travellers (sic) such as General Douglas MacArthur—the War Office and the Foreign Office in London were agreed in principle that Gracey must be supported. Mountbatten was instructed accordingly.

The crisis began in earnest on September 21st, a week after Gracey had landed in Saigon. On that day he issued Proclamation No 1 which in effect was a declaration of martial law. It had been under consideration almost since the day of the British arrival. It forbad meetings and demonstrations, and continued the curfew. On the day following the posting of the proclamation, early in the morning, the British took over the Saigon jail from the Vietnamese and allowed French representatives to select over one thousand from among the French prisoners of war who had been interned by the Japanese since 9 March, and gave them arms. On the following morning, the 23 September, these released French soldiers together with paratroopers newly arrived, took over all the buildings of Saigon before the Vietnamese were aware of what was happening. The French had returned, and henceforth there was no possibility of a negotiated settlement between the Vietnamese and the French. This was Gracey's momentous contribution to the post-war history of South East Asia for which the final responsibility rested with the Foreign Office in London. The seeds had now been sown whereby the bloody conflicts between the Western imperialists and the people of Vietnam were to grow steadily, culminating in the full-scale American intervention. Without British military action in the early autumn of 1945 the independence movement in Vietnam would have been successful. Without the British action in September and October—before the build up of French forces—there would have been no chance of the French re-imposing their colonial regime upon the Vietnamese people. If Bevin and the Labour Government had nothing else to their discredit, this counter-revolutionary action against the legitimate national aspirations of a people who had already suffered grievously under French rule, would remain a major national shame of the British people. This is not rhetoric: what the British did in Indo-China in the autumn of 1945 was the prelude to decades of war, butchery and devastation inflicted upon the bodies and the homes and patterns of living of the poverty stricken people of Vietnam. On the 28 January 1946 Noel Baker replied for the Foreign Office in the House of Commons on the casualties in the Indo-China campaign: the British forces were about to withdraw. Some 126 Allied dead had been counted, of which 3 were British and 37 Indian. There was no precise information about the 'Annamites and Tonkinites who opposed our troops: it has been estimated that about 2,700 have been killed'.[28] It was, in the light of what was to follow in the next three decades, a modest enough beginning.

It was not to be expected that Indo-China would merit much attention in London. It was, after all, a far away country in a world large parts of which had just emerged from years of war. Press reports were few and were overshadowed by the news of the similar action in Indonesia, which was on a larger and bloodier scale than in Indo-China, although the pattern was the same: British troops and Japanese slaughtered Indonesian national-ists in the interests of the restoration of western imperialism. It was chance that a British member of parliament was in Vietnam in the late summer and early autumn of 1945. This was Tom Driberg whose questioning in the House of Commons and articles in *Reynolds News* provided most of what publicity there was. Harold Laski, at the time chairman of the Labour Party, remained faithful to his socialist principles. He wrote on the Vietnam and Indonesian events in damning terms. On Indo-China he naturally disputed the French claim to repossess their former colony. 'What may appear to us no more than an enlarged police situation is to the people concerned the destruction of hope.'[29] Bevin and Noel Baker had no difficulty in the House of Commons in evading questions or utter-ing untruths; and there were so many other problems in which inter-national mayhem was being committed that Vietnam could easily be dismissed and forgotten.

The international problem that occasioned most debate in Britain in the last six months of the war and during the early period of Bevin's Foreign Secretaryship was Greece; and it was in connection with Greece, before the war ended, that Bevin's reactionary attitudes on foreign affairs most clearly exhibited themselves.

Greece before 1939 was traditionally reckoned to be within the British sphere of influence. Its geographical position in the Mediterranean was regarded as vitally important for the sea communications between Britain and the Far East as well as for the oil supplies of the Middle East. There were links of great historical significance between the two countries. Churchill during the war years, dominated by his vivid imperialist sense of history, was conscious always of the importance of Greece in the context of Middle East strategy. As would be expected, he was a fervent supporter of the Greek Monarchy; indeed, George II, who had actively

supported the Metaxas dictatorship in the late thirties, was warmly regarded by establishment circles in Britain.[30] It is interesting, and significant,
how differently Churchill approached Yugoslavia—a country with much
less strategic importance for Britain—but which also had a monarchy
and, like Greece, a government in exile in London during the war years.
Churchill, who was always a slippery politician, capable of disguising
contradictory policies in high sounding language, muted his fundamental
anti-communism in respect of Yugoslavia while allowing it full play in
the case of Greece.[31] He was, for example, single-minded to the point of
fanaticism about the restoration of the monarchy in Greece after the war
was over, and anything or anyone who undermined the prestige or the
position of the monarchy aroused immediate hostility in London. One
result was that the Foreign Office always depreciated the importance of
the resistance inside Greece which was outside the control of the
monarchists, and there developed in consequence a bitter conflict between
the Foreign Office in London and the SOE (Special Operations Executive)
in Cairo which was responsible for internal military developments inside
Greece.

The Greek crisis of the war and post-war years has been analysed in
immense detail by British and Greek participants in the Greek struggle,
and by British and Greek historians.[32] Much of the important documentation is to be found in the files of the Public Record Office in London. In
the context of this present review of Bevin and the Labour Government
after 1945 only certain salient points require to be emphasised. The first
is an extension of a matter already referred to: the constant denigration
of EAM, the national resistance movement, and ELAS, its military wing.
Orme Sargent, who was to become deputy permanent secretary in 1947
in succession to Alexander Cadogan, minuted in January 1943:

> The achievements of SOE are sadly out of proportion with the vast sums of
> money which, during the last year and a half, have been spent in Greece; chiefly
> on subsidising communist organisations in opposition to the Greek government,
> which we are supporting.[33]

and a year later, on 23 January 1944, when there was abundant confirmation of the extent of EAM's dominating position inside Greece, Orme
Sargent repeated his earlier observation, notwithstanding the irrefutable
evidence that was reaching Cairo and London:

> The truth, of course, is that the whole guerrilla movement has been largely fiction
> created by SOE to justify a vast expenditure of money and raw material in that
> country.[34]

These comments by Orme Sargent were circulated only within the government machine; but they surfaced in a dramatic way in public discussion

during the most critical period of the counter-revolution which Britain initiated at the end of 1944. In a major House of Commons speech on the 18 January 1945—the first part of which was entirely devoted to Greece 'the most controversial matter of the hour in British policy', said Churchill, and he went on:

> I have been told that I made a mistake in under-rating the power of the communist-dominated ELAS. I must admit that I judged them on their form against the Germans. I do not wish to do them any military injustice. Of course, it was not against the Germans they were trying to fight to any great extent. They were simply taking our arms, lying low and awaiting the moment when they could seize power in the capital by force, or intrigue, and make Greece a Communist state with the totalitarian liquidation of all opponents. I was misled by the little use they were against the Germans, especially once the general victory of the Allies became probable, in spite of the arms we gave to them. I certainly underrated them as a fighting force. . .
>
> While the British were busy distributing the food and endeavouring to keep things steady, the EAM and Communist Ministers, who were eventually increased to seven in the Papandreou Cabinet, were playing a different game. They were playing the game of the ELAS bands and their Communist directors. . .[35]

Churchill was lying. He may, perhaps, have been so besotted by his commitment to the Greek monarchy, or so blinded by his anti-communism that he failed to comprehend the meaning of the flood of reports that had come out of Greece; but these things are unlikely. Churchill had been preparing the counter-revolution in Greece from at least 1943. He himself had insisted on the military operations in early December 1944 as a result of which Greece was returned to the reactionaries and the fascists; and he no doubt felt it necessary that a full-blooded public justification was required. That such a justification involved him in untruths, falsehoods and gross misrepresentation was of course beside the point.

There was no disagreement among those who were either directly engaged in the resistance or who have assessed the evidence later that EAM and ELAS were the dominant political and military forces in Greece at the time of the German withdrawal. In the same debate from which the Churchill quotation above was taken Sir Richard Acland, in an impressively documented speech, named the political committee of EAM and listed their political affiliations as evidence of its broad popular character.[36] In 1952 Stavrianos emphasised that 'to a very considerable degree the EAM became a national liberation front in fact as well as name',[37] and he estimated that towards the end of the occupation period EAM was 'governing the two-thirds of Greece which it had freed'. The 1979 history of Greece by Richard Clogg accepted that EAM 'did clearly enjoy genuine mass support' and that it 'controlled by far the largest armed formations in Greece' (p. 150).

It is important to underline that the aims Churchill was setting himself in foreign and imperialist affairs were throughout the war analysed and understood by the Left in Britain. Churchill, it must always be recalled, was consistently supported, in private and in public, by Attlee and Bevin, members of the War Cabinet. But for the Left there was no 'betrayal' since they always appreciated the reactionary, indeed the counter-revolutionary, policies consistently pursued by Churchill and his colleagues. The most perceptive and the most knowledgeable expert on the British Left was Konni Zilliacus—often quite incorrectly characterised as a communist fellow-traveller—who had from his long service in the League of Nations an unrivalled knowledge of European politics. His predictions were to be proved remarkably accurate. Zilliacus was not alone: Seymour Cocks who was in the House of Commons during the war was another specialist, and Nye Bevan was often the Left's most effective speaker from the back benches. The publications of the Union of Democratic Control were highly informative and the *New Statesman* had access to many sources critical of the Coalition Government's policies round the world. In August–September 1943 Zilliacus wrote a private report for a Fabian Study group on the future international situation as it was developing.[38] He quoted at length from the war of intervention against the young Soviet Republic from 1918; underlined the argument that since 1917 world affairs had been dominated by the necessity to contain the forces of social revolution; and he identified the areas in which major conflict could be expected in Europe once the war against fascism was over. On Greece he emphasised Churchill's 'open partisanship on behalf of the Greek King, who has a black record of hostility to democracy and of pro-fascism'. His memorandum was remarkably prescient in its analysis of future developments and in its more simplified versions these were the ideas of the Left in general.

By the summer of 1944 Churchill was becoming seriously concerned with what was likely to follow in Greece after a German collapse. It was essential, Churchill wrote in his memoirs, from which most of the quotations which follow are taken, 'that there should be no political vacuum in Greece. As I minuted on August 29, "It is most desirable to strike out of the blue without any preliminary crisis. It is the best way to forestall the EAM" ' (Vol. VI, pp. 247-8). The Germans were 'tardy'—the phrase is Churchills—in withdrawing from Athens but this allowed the British to consolidate their political plans. The Caserta agreement of 26 September, which the EAM signed, placed all the guerrilla forces under British command, and early in October the first British forces landed in Greece and Athens was occupied by paratroopers under the British C-in-C, General Scobie, on October 14. The main bulk of troops followed together with the Greek Government and Rex Leeper, the British Ambassador.

'The testing time for our arrangements had now come', Churchill continued in his memoirs. 'At the Moscow conference I had obtained

Russian abstention at a heavy price' (*ibid.*, p. 249). What Churchill was referring to was recorded fifty pages back in the same volume of memoirs: his visit to Moscow in early October 1944, and the agreement with Stalin over spheres of influence in the Balkans. On the first evening (9 October) Churchill set down on a single sheet of paper the percentage influence allotted to the two powers, Russia and Britain. Roumania was to be 90 per cent Russian; Bulgaria 70 per cent Russian; Yugoslavia and Hungary 50 per cent each; and Greece 90 per cent British. Churchill then passed the sheet over to Stalin. 'There was a slight pause. Then he took his blue pencil and made a large tick upon it, and passed it back to us' (p. 198). There was than a long silence, Churchill went on, and Churchill at length proposed that the agreement having been reached the paper should be burnt. 'No, you keep it', Stalin is reported as saying.

As all commentators, then and since, have acknowledged, Stalin kept his word; and he made no attempt to intervene against the British counter-revolution in Greece. It is, however, improbable that the Kremlin did not take full note of the ruthlessness of British actions, and appreciate their implications for their own position in Eastern Europe. It is necessary to underline the point which is mostly forgotten in the analysis of post-war Europe that the British were the first to engage in clearly defined self-interested military action in a country that had been occupied by the Germans; and this, let it be further emphasised, before the war with the Nazis was over.

General Scobie had a very firm idea of what was expected of him and between the date of the arrival of British troops and early December, the internal situation steadily deteriorated. By mid-November, according to his memoirs Churchill was ordering Scobie to make counter-preparations to a military coup by the EAM. The fact of a proposed coup was untrue but the crisis was precipitated on 3 December by the police firing on an unarmed demonstration in the middle of Athens; and from then on the fragile consensus fell apart. Churchill, as ever, was deeply implicated and two days after the Athens firing he intervened directly with orders to Scobie: 'Do not however hesitate to act as if you were in a conquered city where a local rebellion is in progress' (p. 252). And Churchill, in the next paragraph of his memoirs, has a most revealing story which reveals so clearly how these imperialists approach their problems and how, as so often, the experience in one colonial situation helps to confirm or throw light upon another. 'I had in my mind', Churchill wrote after giving the full text of his telegram to Scobie, 'Arthur Balfour's celebrated telegram in the eighties to the British authorities in Ireland: "Don't hesitate to shoot. . ." The setting of the scene was now entirely different. Nevertheless "Don't hesitate to shoot" hung in my mind as a prompter from those far-off days' (*ibid.*).

The civil war that the events of early December precipitated was brought to an uneasy end by first an armistice and then by the Varkiza agreement of 12 February 1945: as a result of which the Left began to be overwhelmed. 'In the months that followed the Varkiza agreement', writes Heinz Richter, 'a counter-revolutionary tide hit Greece, sweeping away everything the Resistance had built up, and brought back to the surface the old structures that still trouble Greece.'[39]

Without the intervention of the British the story of post-war Greece would have been very different. The counter-revolution initiated by Churchill was the major factor in the development of Greek politics after 1945. From the first days of the intervention, there was vociferous criticism at all levels of the British labour movement against the Coalition's Greek policies; but at every stage the Labour Party ministers insisted upon their collective responsibility with their Conservative colleagues. At all points there was unequivocal support for Churchill's approach. Churchill was, of course, being thoroughly consistent with the political attitudes he had always exhibited. He had been a leading figure in the war of intervention against the newly established Bolshevik regime in Russia during and after the First World War; he led the reactionary wing of the Conservative Party against moderate concessions to Indian nationalism in the 1930s; and his record during the Second World War was consistent with his firm imperialist views and with the cardinal necessity of defending Britain's imperialist interests as he understood them. His support for the Greek monarchy stemmed from a recognition both of the strategic importance of Greece across British lines of communication with the East and of the need to support those forces in Greek politics which could resist the growing movement of the Left. Bevin never deviated from his support of Churchill's policies. A fortnight after the bloodshed in Athens' Constitutional Square there was convened a special one day conference of the Labour Party. This was on the 18 December in London. It was Bevin's first major statement of the war years on foreign policy issues, and he vigorously defended the British intervention in Greece. Those replying were allowed five minutes only. Nye Bevan said:

> Mr Bevin has described what is happening in Greece. I have no time to answer him. But there is one complete answer. Only three bodies of public opinion in the world have gone on record in his support, namely Fascist Spain, Fascist Portugal and the majority of Tories in the House of Commons.

and Bevan went on to describe Bevin's account as 'garbled and inadequate where it was not unveracious'.[40] Bevin's account was certainly garbled, but it was an approach that he continued without any alteration when he became Foreign Secretary. Bullock notes that Greece was one of the countries where Bevin's policies came in for most criticism during the first two years of office; but that he never wavered in his support of his officials of the Foreign Office. There were three main reasons for Bevin's continuation of Churchill's policies. The first is that his specialist advisers were not changed and they included, especially at the top level, some notably reactionary personalities. Second, there was Bevin's pervasive anti-communism. He must have believed, as does his biographer, that Churchill intervened in December 1944 in order 'to prevent a communist seizure of power in Athens'.[41] But Bevin's steadfast anti-communist attitude in respect of Greece merged into his general approach to the Middle East. He stated his position very early in office. In a paper circulated to the Cabinet—which now included Nye Bevan, his former critic— dated 11 August 1945, Bevin insisted that

> We must maintain our position in Greece as a part of our Middle East policy, and that unless it is asserted and settled it may have a bad effect on the whole of our Middle East position.

And that position was maintained in spite of a continuous flood of criticism from observers in Europe and in America that the monarchist, conservative and neo-fascist elements in Greece were steadily conducting war against the Left. Bevin, who by his general policy, did nothing to stem this right-wing offensive, made one further decision that was to lead to the renewal of civil war. Britain, against the opinion and advice of all the Greek political groups except those which were monarchist, insisted on the elections of 31 March 1946. Left and Centre in both Britain and Greece were clear that monarchist control of electoral procedures could only give a wholly distorted result. In the event EAM, the Svolos socialists and three other small non-communist groups boycotted the elections, which the monarchists won, inevitably and overwhelmingly. During the spring and summer of 1946 some thousands of armed men began to find their way back to the mountains. On September 1st 1946 a national plebiscite on the return of the monarchy went in favour of George II. The leader of the Populist movement, Constantine Tsaldaris, continued the terror against the Left and the winter of 1946-7 saw a full-scale civil war get under way. By the end of 1949 the Left was beaten: the policies of Churchill and Bevin, with the Americans now in full control, had succeeded. And by this date, too, the Labour Left had been quietened, a story that requires its own telling.[42]

There is one story, however, set out by Bullock in some detail that has not hitherto received the attention it has deserved. It concerns Attlee and his considerable misgivings over Bevin's Middle East policy and not least over what was being done in Greece. Attlee's own biographer, Kenneth Harris, largely missed the significance of what Attlee was trying to do. The story is illuminating, not only because it exhibits Attlee in a more realistic mood but it also illustrates the limitations imposed on the

Prime Minister by his dependence upon the most powerful man in the Cabinet. It further demonstrates the effectiveness of both the Foreign Office and the political weight of the Chiefs of Staff. Hugh Dalton, whose third volume of memoirs was published in 1962, first indicated the misgivings that Attlee was beginning to articulate; but it was not until the thirty year rule on official papers came round to the period of the Labour government that the full detail was revealed. On 2 March 1946 Attlee circulated a paper to the Defence Committee. It was, Bullock writes, among the most radical produced by a British Prime Minister. Attlee summarised the arguments he had put to Dalton in February 1946: that we could no longer expect in time of war to keep open the Mediterranean and we could therefore withdraw troops now from Egypt and the rest of the Middle East including Greece. The future, especially with an independent India, did not lie through the Mediterranean. Attlee concluded his March 2nd paper;

> We must not for sentimental reasons based on the past give hostages to fortune. It may be that we shall have to consider the British Isles as an eastern extension of a strategic area the centre of which is the American continent rather than as a power looking eastwards through the Mediterranean to India and the East.[43]

The discussion on these crucial matters occupied several meetings of the Defence committee but no clear decisions were reached. Bevin had circulated a Foreign Office comment which totally denied Attlee's arguments. In July 1946 the Chiefs of Staff reiterated their belief on the importance of the Mediterranean for oil supplies and as a focus for world communications. Bevin gave little away in the matter of the call-up to the Forces, arguing that there must be sufficient military power to make British foreign policy credible; and the whole discussion and debate petered out. It was however re-opened by Attlee later in the year. On 1st December 1946 Attlee typed a personal letter to Bevin who was in New York in which he raised again, and sharply, the same arguments of his March memorandum: 'The Middle East position is only an outpost position. I am beginning to doubt whether the Greek game is worth the candle.'[44] Early in 1947 Attlee produced a further memorandum in which he first subjected the Chiefs of Staff position to radical criticism and then went on to ask for a serious consideration of the whole Middle East strategy. It produced a very strong impression. In their replies Bevin and the Foreign Office concentrated on the political aspects, and the Chiefs of Staff on the strategic. Bevin's document, drafted by one of his senior officials, ended with this conclusion:

> Your proposal would involve leading from weakness. Our economic and military position is now as bad as it ever will be. When we have consolidated our economy, when the economic revival of Europe has made progress, when it has finally

become clear to the Russians that they cannot drive a wedge between the Americans and ourselves, we shall be in a position to negotiate with Stalin from strength. There is no hurry. Everything suggests that the Russians are now drawing in their horns and have no immediate aggressive intentions. Let us wait until our strength is restored and let us meanwhile, with US help as necessary, hold on to essential positions and concentrate on building up UNO.

And there, the matter ended. Attlee, Bevin and Alexander had a discussion on 9 January 1947, after which Bevin dictated a note to the effect that his general policy was to continue and that no British troops were to be withdrawn save those already agreed upon.[45]

It could not have been within the area of historical possibility for Attlee to have altered in such a dramatic way the course of British foreign policy. The vested interests against him were too powerful, including and not least the Chiefs of Staff whose political activities deserve much more documentation than they have so far received. Bevin himself, as noted above, was the crucial prop for Attlee in the Cabinet and without Bevin it is possible that Attlee would not have remained Prime Minister. There were other reasons, however: among them the decision to manufacture an independent British atom bomb, the discussions on which were taking place at the same time as the review of foreign policy strategy set out above. On the 26 October 1946 there was a meeting of the Cabinet's atomic committee, General 75, to decide whether a gaseous diffusion plant should be built for the production of uranium 235. This would be a necessary preliminary to the production of a British atomic bomb. Cripps and Dalton were opposed on the grounds of cost and it was Bevin's intervention, which Attlee supported on all future occasions, that ensured the independent bomb for Britain. Bevin's words on this occasion, as reported by one who was present, are worth remarking upon, in terms both of what he said and the tone that comes through. They are an authentic reflection of his essential illiteracy on so many issues of foreign affairs. He arrived late at the meeting, having, so he said, fallen asleep after a good lunch; and he is recorded making his opposition in this way:

That won't do at all, we've got to have this. . . I don't mind for myself, but I don't want any other Foreign Secretary of this country to be talked at or by a Secretary of State in the United States as I have just had in my discussion with Mr. Byrnes. We have got to have this thing over here whatever it costs. . . We've got to have the bloody Union Jack flying on top of it.[46]

This was the decisive intervention on the independent British bomb. Attlee fixed the rest of the proceedings. The substantive decision had still to be taken, but that appears to have been almost a formality. On 10 January 1947 General 75 was reconvened as a new Committee, General 163, from which Dalton and Cripps were excluded. Those present were Attlee, Bevin, Morrison, Alexander, Addison and Wilmot. The decision to manufacture the Bomb was not reported to the Cabinet nor to Parliament; and according to Attlee's biographer, Attlee manipulated the financial estimates to conceal the first £100 million expenditure on the Bomb. The secrecy on the Bomb lasted for the rest of his administration. The only politician outside the small inner group of the Cabinet who knew in detail what was taking place in this field of atomic research and production was Sir John Anderson, the Tory chairman of the Advisory Committee which Attlee had established.[47]

The central thrust of Labour's foreign policy, as conducted by Bevin with an undeviating support from Attlee, was pivoted upon a total opposition to the Soviet Union and to all those radical movements, in Europe and elsewhere in which Communists played, or were thought to be playing, an important part. There were, of course, other strands to Britain's foreign strategy but the overriding consideration was what was felt to be the communist threat to established orders. In this crucial regard, Labour was no different from the Conservatives. There was no Labour foreign policy: there was a British policy which continued that which had been elaborated by Churchill and agreed by his colleagues in the War Cabinet. This is not to ignore the genuine differences of opinion within the ruling group during wartime or to fail to appreciate that were some issues in the post-war world which the Conservative Party would have approached differently from the policies followed by Labour. India is the obvious case in point. Indian independence solved itself in the sense that there was no alternative and this regardless of the firm commitment to Indian independence that the British labour movement had always expressed. No doubt under Churchill what would have been offered would have been something short of independence; and in the long run, if independence was nor forthcoming, the result would have been Northern Ireland on a continental scale. But in other colonial countries, whether controlled by the British or by other Europeans, the Labour Government followed a policy indistinguishable from that which the Conservatives could have been expected to implement.

There were, however, two new factors in the post-war world which severely restricted the operations of British foreign policy. One was the absolute and relative decline of Britain as a world power of the first rank compared with either America or the Soviet Union. The second was the overwhelming power of the United States within the capitalist world. The Americans themselves were conscious of the decline of Britain from the early days of the war, and they were increasingly aware of the much weakened part which Britain would play in the post-war world. The American attitude was clear-sighted and ruthless. Lend-lease was ended a few days after the capitulation of Japan in August 1945 in order to pressure the British into the explicit acceptance of the terms of Bretton

Woods, and it was the absence of an appreciation of the new situation in Washington after Roosevelt's death that led to Maynard Keynes' spectacular failure in the negotiations over the American loan in the autumn of 1945. The Americans were determined to end the British system of Imperial preference and the discriminatory aspects of the sterling bloc. But at the same time the US State Department was aware of the importance of Britain in a world which had just come through a devastating war, and of the need which America would have of Britain's cooperation. There were a variety of areas in which British assistance would be crucial; and it was therefore necessary to keep Britain neither too weak nor too strong. Hence the care with which the Americans administered Lend-lease during the war: in ways which maintained the British reserves of gold and dollars at a figure reckoned to be about the minimum necessary for reasonable functioning. It is the American historians such as Gabriel Kolko and Fred Block who have developed the argument that there was a general understanding within the American administration that Britain should be kept neither too weak nor too strong.[48] At the same time there were marked differences of opinion regarding policy towards the Soviet Union within the United States in the closing months of the war and in the immediate post-war period; and Roosevelt's death did not lead to a complete change about but only, in the first months, to a general hardening of attitudes. At this time both Attlee and Bevin, and this must also have been true of many of their senior officials, thought the Americans inexperienced and naive, especially in relation to the Soviet Union. Attlee in early 1946 was reported by Dalton as referring to the 'little men' nominally in charge of the American administration; when Churchill made his strident Fulton speech in March 1946 Attlee was secretly delighted since, according to his biographer, he still considered the Americans to be 'naive in their attitude to Stalin'.[49] There is an interesting passage in Bullock—the context is late 1946, in which Bullock sums up Bevin's general approach to the Americans:

> Bevin was as anxious to have the Americans take a greater share of responsibility for maintaining the independence of Greece as he was in Turkey, Iran and throughout the Middle East. But he had a better understanding than his colleagues in London of the difficulty Americans had—in the country, in Congress, and even in the Administration—in adjusting themselves to the world role they were now called upon to play. From this he continued to draw the same conclusion as he had throughout 1946: that it was essential to give them time, be patient and not to try to force the pace. In his judgment, the risks were too great, the American Government's new-found sense of purpose too brittle, American opinion too unsettled for Britain to surrender her own independence of action into American hands.[50]

No American historian familiar with these years could possibly write in the terms just quoted. The Americans certainly had their problems in terms of their future role as leaders of world anti-communism; and Britain was undoubtedly helpful in that Attlee and Bevin were much more committed to their anti-communism than most of the senior politicians or officials in the United States for many months before the war ended. The Americans needed Britain but it was a very different kind of need from that which afflicted Britain in relation to America. Britain was bankrupted by the war; and Britain's insistence upon pursuing her imperialist role in the Far East and in Europe dramatically weakened her economic position in the world. 'By the end of February 1947', an American historian wrote in 1981, 'the United Kingdom lay naked before the world, stripped of its status, its aspirations, and much of its pride'. The exaggerations are only slight, and it was to be American dollars that rescued the bankrupt.[51]

These comments can be illustrated by an examination of one of the political landmarks of the post-war world: the origins and implementation of the Marshall Plan in the second half of 1947 and through subsequent years. The Marshall Plan has had a very favourable press, both at the time and subsequently by historians, especially British historians. As Bevin himself said in 1949: 'It seemed to bring hope where there was none. The generosity of it was beyond our belief'; and this emphasis upon American magnanimity has always been one of the enduring myths of contemporary history. Another, especially in Britain, is the role played by Britain and by Bevin in particular. Bullock follows a common line of argument when he writes that 'it was Bevin's imagination in seeing what could be made of it [the Marshall Plan] and his boldness in taking the initiative which gave Marshall's remarks the resonance they needed to become effective'.[52] To read some popular British texts it might be thought that Bevin was largely responsible single handed for the Marshall Plan and its implementation; that without Bevin's 'imagination' Western Europe would not have made the economic recovery it achieved and the military interdependence in NATO that was its concomitant. Even K.O. Morgan, who is a good deal more realistic in his appraisal of Labour's foreign policy than is Bullock, writes of the 'extraordinary saga of achievement by Ernest Bevin' between the date of Marshall's Harvard speech and the establishment of NATO in April 1949.[53] In one crucial respect, all the commentators who argue in these terms are correct: Bevin was Washington's man and he accomplished all they hoped for when they planned aid on a massive scale to Western Europe. But their motives were calculated and wholly self-interested and Bevin only did what *they* wanted done. It was the beginning of their role as the dynamic centre of world anti-communism. The Truman doctrine of the spring of 1947 had been limited to Greece and Turkey although its general propositions were easily extended; and it was the development of the basic policies which produced the Truman doctrine that led to the Marshall speech at Harvard on 5 June 1947.

There are several factors in the making of the Marshall Plan that need to be emphasised. There had always been those who prophesied that the aftermath of war would bring a recession of the kind that followed World War One, and during 1947 fears of a serious downturn in the economy of the United States worsened, reaching a peak of disquiet in the middle months of the year. Early in 1947 a meeting of the high level State–Navy–War Coordinating committee gave its estimate that 'the world will not be able to continue to buy US exports at the 1946-7 rate beyond another 12-18 months'. The enormous increase in productive capacity during the war years had made American business highly conscious and deeply concerned about export surpluses. Between the years 1945–47 foreign aid financed about one-third of American exports and with the economic plight of Europe making an increasing impression upon American planners, diplomats and politicians, the time was coming for a serious evaluation of future policies. This chimed in with the increasing anti-communism of the Administration. In May 1947 George Kennan left the National War College to become director of the Policy Planning Staff which had been established by Marshall when he had become Secretary of State earlier in the year. Kennan was unusual among the top officials in Washington in having had first hand experience of Soviet affairs. It was Kennan, of course, who wrote the famous article in *Foreign Affairs* 'The Sources of Soviet Conduct'[54] and although there were many strands of opinion and interest that went to the making of the Marshall Plan, certain of Kennan's ideas became an integral part of American policy. He was, for example, convinced that the announcement of large scale American economic assistance would do much to restore self-confidence in Western Europe; he was equally emphatic that only if the political leaders of Western Europe were willing to seize the opportunity would success follow. It was this aspect of the Marshall speech that Bevin grasped and that has been made so much of by the Bevin idolators. But Kennan later noted that leaving things to European initiative did not mean abdication of a general American responsibility. In a lecture Kennan gave on 18 December 1947 to the National War College he offered a sample of the Tablets in the homely style he sometimes used: 'It doesn't work if you just send the stuff over and relax. It has to be played politically, when it gets over. It has to be dangled, sometimes withdrawn, sometimes extended. It has to be a skillful operation.'[55] As a statement of American magnanimity in the world after 1945, it will not be bettered.

Aid under the original propositions advanced by Marshall was offered to the Soviet Union and its East European satellites as well as to the countries of Western Europe. Kennan was greatly in favour of such an offer being made. If the Russians rejected the offer, as was expected, then the division of Europe could be said to be their responsibility; on the other hand, if in the unlikely event of their acceptance then aid should be used in ways that would undermine Soviet domination of the national economies of the

Eastern bloc. The British were firmly against Soviet acceptance although naturally Bevin went through the motions of a conference in Paris with Molotov and Bidault. When the conference had more or less broken down Bevin told the American ambassador that it was an outcome he had 'anticipated and even wished for given my certainty that Molotov had come to Paris to sabotage our efforts' (Bullock, p. 421). There is one important episode during these early days that is extraordinarily illuminating for the attitudes of both American and British administrations. Just before the meeting in Paris with Molotov and Bidault there were three days of talks between the Americans and the British in London. Attlee, Dalton and Cripps were present as well as Bevin but it was the latter, and his advisers, who dominated the British side. On the first day Bevin in the morning and top level officials in the afternoon tried to persuade the Americans to recognise Britain as a special partner in whatever emerged from the Marshall discussions. Britain, Bevin argued, was on a different basis from other European countries and should not be 'lumped in' as just one more country. Bevin, supported by Attlee and his colleagues, did his best: he played the anti-Soviet card for all it was worth:

> If the UK was considered just another European country, this would fit in with Russian strategy, namely, that the US would encounter a slump and withdraw from Europe; the UK would be helpless and out of dollars, and as merely another European country, the Russians, in command of the Continent, could deal with Britain in due course.

If this was a fair example of the debating ability of Bevin in top level discussions he was not likely to get very far with anyone whom he was not able to bully; but mostly, of course, the sophisticated reactionaries who serviced him from the Foreign Office wrote his briefs. In the present case neither Bevin and the British politicians nor the Civil Servants made any impression on Will Clayton, the Under-Secretary of State in the State Department, and the special relationship was firmly and unambiguously ruled out. Clayton made one or two concessions, notably that American dollars under the aid programme need not necessarily be used for purchases in the United States but could be allocated for food supplies from Canada and Latin America; and he encouraged Bevin to continue in the leadership of the West European movement. But that was all.[56]

The Marshall Plan, with the institutional developments that came into being in order to implement its proposals, confirmed the division of Europe into East and West. By the autumn of 1947 the administrative structures for West European cooperation were rapidly being created. In April 1948 Truman signed the Economic Cooperation Act and this was followed by the establishment in Paris of the new permanent OEEC (Organisation for European Economic Cooperation). The recipients of dollar aid—some 4,000 million was allocated for the first fifteen months—were Britain, France and the Benelux countries with Italy being added later. In all, 12,000 million dollars were allotted to Europe down to January 1951.

The military equivalent to economic aid was the establishment of NATO in April 1949. The establishment of NATO was the inevitable consequence of economic cooperation and it was confirmed, if not hastened, by a number of serious crises between Russia and the West, of which the Berlin blockade was the most spectacular. Certainly for the majority of public opinion in Western Europe the Berlin crisis greatly encouraged anti-Soviet attitudes and in Britain helped to achieve a notable consensus for Bevin's foreign policy which had not been present in the first two years or so of his tenure of the office of Secretary of State. Nye Bevan, for example, was sufficiently moved by the Berlin blockade to recommend sending tanks across the Soviet zone to back up the airlift.[57] The new political support, especially from large parts of the Labour Left, for Bevin's policies in Europe, must be briefly commented upon for it indicated changes of considerable importance for future political attitudes. As already noted there had been severe and continuous criticism of many parts of Bevin's general policy between the assumption of power by the Labour government in the summer of 1945 and for the next two years. The most publicised challenge was probably the debate on foreign policy in November 1946 when the demand for a 'socialist alternative' to existing policies was widely supported. R.H.S. Crossman, one of Bevin's most vociferous critics, made a vigorous attack (18 November 1946) on the government's 'drift into the American camp'; and in the voting on several amendments about 120 Labour MPs were not accounted for. Within a few months the 'Keep Left' was officially formed, mostly of members of what would later be called the *Tribune* group. Their aim in foreign policy was to work for a third force between the two superpowers and independent of both blocs.[58] It was Marshall's speech of 5 June 1947, followed by the political initiatives discussed above, and against the background of a rising level of diplomatic conflict between the Soviet Union and the West, that began to alter quite dramatically the politics of the Left within the Parliamentary Labour Party, and outside in the wider movement. By January 1948 Crossman was announcing in the Commons his conversion from total opposition to Bevin's policies and his support for the American initiatives;[59] and in the American liberal weekly *The Nation* he condemned Russian hostility to Britain in Iran and again called for a third force with the socialist parties of Western Europe. Crossman, too, was foremost among those who changed their minds about the Truman administration and it was during this year, 1948, that Harry Truman began to be seen as America's version of Clement Attlee. His re-election in the autumn of the year was greeted by many of the Parliamentary Left with enthusiasm; and *Tribune* in particular became more anti-Soviet than at any time since the early period of the war. There was a much smaller group of Labour MPs—some like Zilliacus, a genuinely independent social-ist—who remained totally opposed to Bevin and his policies; but in 1948 and 1949 most of the serious critics of Labour's approach to foreign affairs were expelled from the Labour Party.[60]

With the establishment of NATO Bevin's most important contributions to the shaping of Britain's post-war foreign policies were ended. His health was poor throughout his period of office. Indeed, already in 1943, when the man who was to become his personal physician first examined Bevin, he found, so Bullock writes, 'not a sound organ in his body, apart from his feet. He later described Bevin, comprehensively, as suffering from angina pectoris, cardiac failure, arterio-sclerosis, sinusitis, enlarged liver, damaged kidneys and high blood pressure. He was overweight, smoked and drank more than was good for him, took no exercise and was a poor sleeper'.[61] It was said by Lord Franks that Bevin's intellectual powers did not seem to be seriously affected until the last few months before his death.[62] That may be. Bevin hung on to office until the very last and then had to be pushed out by a very reluctant and no doubt embarrassed Attlee. In late January 1951 Bevin was in hospital with pneumonia; he returned to the Foreign Office at the beginning of March and tried to resume work. One of the consultants who examined him at this time commented that, 'He was still alright as far down as his neck.'[63] It was on his 70th birthday that Bevin was told by Attlee that he would have to replace him, and all Bevin could say to his wife when he got home was, 'I've got the sack'. In spite of his undoubted toughness there was always a whining streak in Bevin. He died just over a month later on 14 April 1951.

There are some general comments to be made by way of conclusion. What needs again to be emphasised, since it is missed from most British writing on foreign affairs, is the hostility towards the Soviet Union that Attlee and Bevin brought to their new offices in the summer of 1945, and which for at least the next twelve months made them in certain quite crucial respects the front runners in world anti-communism; before the full implications of American superpower were understood by Congress and the Administration. With Bevin in particular anti-communism was always mixed with his acceptance of traditional imperialist ideology and practice: hence his support for the French in Indo-China, the Dutch in Indonesia and vigorious British military action in Malaya. But Bevin was not alone in his acceptance of an imperialist attitude: it was common to all the Labour leadership as Morrison showed so clearly when he followed Bevin as Foreign Secretary in 1951.

The second point that needs to be stressed, since again it is most commonly omitted by British historians, is the developing subservience of Britain to the United States during the period of the Attlee administration. The Americans imposed strict conditions on the American loan which Keynes negotiated in December 1945: *that* was crucial for Anglo-American relations. Sterling convertibility—a central condition of the loan—was implemented during the summer of 1947, with disastrous effects upon the British reserves; and the financial crisis which followed was itself a very strong argument for the acceptance of the detailed terms of the Marshall Plan. British financial weakness in the post-war years—much assisted by the imperialist role that the Labour government insisted on pursuing—made the path of the American negotiators on any project considerably easier than it otherwise might have been; and although Bevin huffed and puffed on many an occasion—and naturally usually won some concessions—the Americans never had serious difficulty in persuading the British of the way to go. American historians, of all shades of opinion, are clear on the reliability, on basic issues, of the British in international affairs and above all in the unshakeable support for America's confrontation with the Soviet bloc. The siting of American B 29 long-range bombers in East Anglia in mid 1948 was not widely publicised, but the so-called special relationship which first developed during the Attlee administration and which has much enlarged itself since, has increasingly consisted of the use by the United States of the island of Britain as the main American bomber base in Europe, its listening post and in our own day its missile site. American control has always been accepted, and until the most recent years the natives have not shown themselves to be unduly restless. When Attlee wrote in his Defence memorandum of 2 March 1946: 'It may be we shall have to consider the British Isles as an eastern extension of a strategic area the centre of which is the American continent. . .' he was making a remarkable prophecy which has now come to pass.[64]

The alternative to acceptance of the American loan of December 1945 would have been a much greater degree of austerity; the sharp reduction of overseas military expenditures and a much faster rate of demobilisation; the construction of something approaching a siege economy. A tough British response to the ending of American aid might have brought a positive response from the Americans: at least one that did not carry with it the subordination that was to exist. By the medium run the economy might have been in better shape. But the alternatives were never seriously considered. The acceptance of a greater austerity could only have been achieved had the Labour government been prepared to mobilise the British people on a popular and wide ranging democratic basis and, at the same time, have been willing to meet head on the full force of established property interests. It is historically inconceivable that the leading ministers, shaped and moulded by the labourist tradition, could ever have envisaged themselves in these roles. They were cautious men, deferential to the conservative traditions of the country, respectful of property rights; and they were offered a way out. Dollars from America allowed living standards to be slowly improved and the world boom of the 1950s accelerated the change. The implementation of social welfare measures in the immediate post-war years was made possible by the large cushion of American aid; and the same dollars allowed both living standards to rise and a very high level of defence expenditure to be retained. These matters were not understood at the time, nor have they been since. The myths of the welfare state have been allowed to accumulate alongside the widening status of client to the United States, especially unrecognised by the greater part of the British people.

Ernest Bevin did not have to be converted to the traditional ways of Foreign Office thinking for they were already part of his political and emotional perceptions: the belief in the great power thesis; the acceptance of British imperialist rule wherever that was possible; a lack of realism in international economic affairs; and a comprehensive and all-embracing hostility towards the Soviet Union and all its works. Bevin's legacy to his successors included the problems of Aden, Kenya, British Guyana, Cyprus and Suez in the 1950s; the continued burden of a very heavy armament expenditure which was one of the causes of the relative decline of the British economy in the next thirty years; and the subordination of Britain within the military alliance directed by the United States. All the basic postulates of British foreign policy were agreed during Bevin's tenure of office—the entry into the Common Market being the only important new factor in the years which followed. Britain became an island on which American military technology came to be the overriding military presence. With the invasion of Grenada in 1983, and the siting of Cruise missiles in 1984, with no dual control key, the finger on the British trigger is now American.[65]

NOTES

1. Examples are given in J. Saville, 'Labour and Income Distribution', *Socialist Register* (1965), pp. 147–162.
2. J. Grahl, 'The Liberal Revolution', *Marxism Today,* (June, 1983), p. 20.
3. A. Bullock, *Ernest Bevin. Foreign Secretary 1945–1951,* (1983), p. 86. Henceforth referred to as Bullock, vol. 3.
4. C.R. Attlee, *The Labour Party in Perspective,* (1937), pp. 30–1.
5. A. Bullock, *The Life and Times of Ernest Bevin. Vol. 1. Trade Union Leader 1881–1940,* (1960), p. 600.
6. Bullock, vol. 3, p. 109.
7. *Ibid.*
8. Bullock, vol. 1, p. 133 ff. discusses Bevin's role in the movement against intervention. For a more balanced account, S.R. Graubard, *British Labour and the Russian Revolution,* (OUP, 1956), esp. Chs. 4 and 5.
9. H. Dalton, *High Tide and After. Memoirs 1945–1960,* (1962), p. 157.
10. *TGWU Record,* January 1938, p. 154; quoted Bullock, vol. 1, p. 623.

11. 'the high-minded imperialism of the *Round Table*' is Bullock's phrase, vol. 1, p. 627. High-minded imperialists differ from the more earthy imperialists, who are concerned only with money, by concentrating upon high-minded words.

12. Bullock, vol. 1, p. 631, quoting Francis Williams, *Ernest Bevin*, (1952), p. 209.

13. Quoted Bullock, vol. 3, p. 96.

14. *Hansard*, August, 1945.

15. Quoted R. Miliband, *Parliamentary Socialism*, (1961), p. 333, n. 1.

16. Diana Cooper, *Trumpets from the Steep*, (Penguin, 1964), p. 205 ff.

17. Quoted Bullock, vol. 3, p. 97 from *The Memoirs of Lord Gladwyn*, (1972), pp. 175-6.

18. Bullock, vol. 3, p. 97.

19. Bullock, vol. 3, p. 32: 'The British found themselves caught in the crossfire and denounced by both sides and their sympathisers. In Indo-China this was for only a limited time and the British handed over with relief to the French in the spring of 1946.'

20. C. Thorne, 'Indo-China and Anglo-American Relations, 1942-1945', *Pacific Historical Review*, XLV, No. 1, (February, 1976), esp. p. 91 ff. For a somewhat different emphasis upon certain questions, W. LaFeber, 'Roosevelt, Churchill and Indo-China 1942-45', *American Historical Review*, LXXX (1975), pp. 1277-1295.

21. F.O. 371, PREM 3, 1800, quoted in Thorne, 'Indo-China and Anglo-American Relations, 1942-1945', p. 84.

22. G. Rosie, *The British in Vietnam. How the Twenty-Five Year War Began*, (1970), p. 37.

23. F.S.V. Donnison, *British Military Administration in the Far East*, (HMSO, 1956), p. 406.

24. Ellen J. Hammer, *The Struggle for Indo-China 1940-1955*, (Stanford, 1966), Ch. 6.

25. *Hansard*, 25 January 1946, col. 527.

26. Quoted in Rosie, *The British in Vietnam*, p. 92.

27. Harold Isaacs, an American journalist, quoted *ibid.*

28. *Hansard*, 28 January, 1946, col. 527.

29. For the reactions of some of the British Left, see Rosie, *The British in Vietnam*, Ch. 8; and see also Tom Driberg, *Ruling Passions*, (1978), pp. 225-6 where he gives a very casual account of a period during which he was a passionate critic of British intervention.

30. This emerges from most accounts of Anglo-Greek relations in this period: see, among the voluminous literature, R. Clogg, *A Short History of Modern Greece*, (Cambridge, 1979), Ch. 6; and Churchill in August 1944: 'The British nation felt friendly and chivalrous towards him [the Greek King] for his conduct at a difficult moment in both our histories', *The Second World War*, vol. VI, p. 100.

31. See the extraordinary statement by Fitzroy Maclean in *British Policy Towards Wartime Resistance in Yugoslavia and Greece*, (ed. P. Auty and R. Clogg, 1975), pp. 221-228; and much else in this important volume.

32. There is a select bibliography in the Auty and Clogg volume, quoted above in note 31; and see also a later volume, *Greece: From Resistance to Civil War*, ed. M. Sarafis, (Spokesman Books, 1980).

33. R. Clogg, ' "Pearls from Swine', the Foreign Office Papers, SOE and the Greek Resistance', in Auty and Clogg (eds), *op. cit.*, p. 174.

34. *Ibid.*, pp. 173-4.

35. *Hansard*, 18 January, 1945.

36. *Hansard*, 19 January, 1945.

37. L.S. Stavrianos, 'The Greek Liberation Front (EAM): A Study in Resistance,

Organisation and Administration', *Journal Modern History*, XXIV, No. 1, (March, 1952), p. 54 quoted by T. Gittin, 'Counter-Insurgency: Myth and Reality in Greece', *Containment and Revolution*, (1967), pp. 140–181. See also the important volume by Dominique Eudes, *The Kapetanios. Partisans and Civil War* (1972).

38. K. Zilliacus, *I Choose Peace*, (Penguin Special, 1949). The greater part of the memorandum quote in the text is reprinted, pp. 72–80.

39. H. Richter, 'The Battle of Athens and the Role of the British', in M. Sarafis (ed.) *Greece: From Resistance to Civil War*, (1980), p. 78.

40. M. Foot, *Aneurin Bevan. vol. 1: 1897–1945*, (1962), pp. 486–7.

41. Bullock, vol. 3, p. 160.

42. Not all the Labour Left, as is discussed below.

43. Bullock, vol. 3, p. 242.

44. *Ibid.*, p. 340.

45. *Ibid.*, pp. 348–50.

46. *Ibid.*, p. 352.

47. K. Harris, *Attlee*, (1982), p. 286 ff; and J. Saville, 'C.R. Attlee: An Assessment', *Socialist Register* (1983), pp. 161–163.

48. G. Kolko, *The Politics of War*, (New York, 1968); idem, *America and the Crisis of World Capitalism*, (Boston, 1974); Fred L. Block, *The Origins of international Economic Disorder*, (1977).

49. K. Harris, *Attlee*, (1982), p. 298.

50. Bullock, vol. 3, p. 399.

51. The analysis by American historians of British policy is very differently present-ed. The literature is voluminous: see, for example, in addition to the books by Kolko and Block already quoted, J.L. Gaddis, *Strategies of Containment*, (OUP, 1982) with a very full bibliography.

52. Bullock, vol. 3, p. 405.

53. K.O. Morgan, *Labour in Power, 1945–1951*, (Oxford, 1984), p. 275.

54. In *Foreign Affairs*, XXV, (July, 1947), pp. 566–582.

55. Gaddis, *Strategies of Containment*, pp. 37–8.

56. Bullock, vol. 3, Ch. 10.

57. Morgan, *Labour in Power*, p. 277.

58. *Ibid.*, Ch. 6, passim.

59. *Ibid.*, pp. 276–7.

60. *Ibid.*, p. 238.

61. Bullock, vol. 3, p. 288.

62. *Ibid.*, pp. 727–8.

63. *Ibid.*, p. 833.

64. *Ibid.*, p. 242.

65. The most exhaustive study of United States' bases in the United Kingdom is Duncan Campbell, *The Unsinkable Aircraft Carrier. American Military Power in Britain*, (1984). A summary of his conclusions, with a complete list of US military bases and facilities in Britain was published in the CND monthly *Sanity*, No. 5, (May, 1984).

ANTI-COMMUNISM AND AMERICAN INTERVENTION IN GREECE*

Martin Eve

Any survey of anti-Communism must include an account of the Greek experience. It was in Greece that the British first used military force against their former allies of World War Two—one of the more shameful incidents in recent British history—and it was in Greece that the USA most decisively extended its empire. The techniques of neo-colonial rule, first worked out in Greece were a blueprint for intervention in the rest of the world.

While this process was in its outline clearly visible to the world at the time, the story has now been told from the inside, by the careful sifting of State Department documents and other sources. This new evidence gives chapter and verse for what could only previously be surmised, confirms the general picture of US domination but in some important respects causes us to revise earlier assumptions.

Greece was no stranger to being the object of neo-colonial manipulation; from the beginnings of modern Greece the parties had reflected the interests—and even the names—of the great powers of the time: France, Britain and Russia. More recently British hegemony has been established and traditionally was operated through the person of the king—a possibility in a country where there was a royalist regime, flimsily disguised as a constitutional monarchy. This relationship had survived the Metaxas' dictatorship's flirtation with Italian and German fascism and the king continued to act as a British puppet, or 'loyal ally'.

The relations between Britain and Greece entered a new phase with the retreat of the German army in October 1944. This is not the place to relate the means by which the British restored their rule (many aspects of which are dealt with elsewhere in this volume, in John Saville's study of Ernest Bevin). What is relevant here is the way in which that rule was effected. The old pre-war method of controlling Greece through the king, or since this proved for the time being politically impossible, through the Regent, was the method favoured by Churchill. This avoided the necessity for Britain to concern itself with and assume responsibility for

* *American Intervention in Greece 1943–1949* by Lawrence Wittner (Columbia University Press, New York, 1982). The quotations are all taken from this work, where full references can be found. I am greatly indebted to Marion Sarafis for her help in preparing this review.

101

detailed aspects of Greek life. Britain would determine the political leadership (on British orders two prime ministers were dismissed, and a third was refused leave to resign) and work through them. This traditional view of how things should be done was at variance with that of the shrewd Minister Resident, Harold Macmillan, who devised a detailed plan by which every Greek minister would have a British 'adviser' whose advice he would be compelled to take. In addition a British Military Mission would actually nominate for all posts in the armed forces and police. This plan, put forward with some determination in 1945 (but not referred to in its author's Memoirs) was rejected for a number of reasons, including the improbability of finding a Greek politician who would humiliate himself and his country by signing such an agreement. Instead the British Ambassador in Athens would become a sort of de facto High Commissioner and would form a link in the chain of command with the Regent and Prime Minister of Greece.

This system, which had worked so well in the inter-war years, was not a conspicuous success. Two years later, the country was in the grip of a right-wing terror, prisons and concentration camps were full to overflowing with former resistance fighters, the Greek economy was in chaos and increasingly dependent on foreign aid, while in the mountains of the north a civil war had begun.

The executants of British policy, now a Labour cabinet, who had presided over the emerging situation, now wished to wash their hands of it. Not that there was significant support in the cabinet for any effective curb on the excesses of the Right; but that the Chancellor, Hugh Dalton, was gaining more and more support for his contention that Britain could no longer afford the cost of being the Protecting Power. It was in these circumstances that in February 1947 Britain despatched to the USA an ultimatum; Britain would quit Greece at the end of March if the USA did not take over their burden from them.

The suddenness of this threat—soon realised to be a bluff—caused a flurry in the State Department. Within five days a consensus had emerged as to how to take on the assignment; the question of *whether* to take it on was virtually unasked. While detailed planning went on, it was remembered that the request for aid had not come, as it happened, from Greece at all. This was soon put right; the State Department drafted a suitable request which was handed to the Greek Ambassador in Washington, and in due course transmitted from Athens. There were now two subjects of discussion: first, how the new American hegemony would be operated and secondly, how the American involvement would be 'sold' to Congress and the American people.

On the first question, there was little disagreement; the Americans would operate their version of the Macmillan plan, though it is doubtful if they knew of its existence, and appoint 'advisers' for every ministry; a military mission of up to 40 officers would offer 'strategic' advice to the Greek Army. This modest figure of '10–40' was later to grow, but it should be remembered that British plans for pulling out of Greece did not involve the removal either of their military mission (1,400 men) or of their regular troops (14,000). Though both of these figures were to be reduced, there were always more British military advisers than American, and some troops remained until 1954.

Over the second question there was more room for argument. The problems faced by the Truman administration in early 1947 were by no means the same as those of a few years later. In Congress the biggest obstacle was not opposition from liberal New Dealers chary of backing a fascistic regime, but of old-fashioned Isolationists still occupying their traditional Southern and mid-Western seats in the Senate; Byrd, Vandenberg, Talmadge, etc. were still a powerful force in Washington. For this opposition, the arguments were hastily assembled. Under the cover of anti-Communism the State Department spokesmen wheeled out a strange mixture of threats; Soviet expansion, the Communist threat to freedom, and when the ageing senators were still reluctant to move as fast as was required of them, an even starker alternative. There were two systems in the world, the capitalist and the communist; it was them or us. With the spectre of the spread of a collectivist economy to Virginia even Senator Byrd was won over. But another argument was being quietly used, and less quietly in business circles. And this line of thinking appears to be much closer to the real thoughts of the men in the State Department.

In the days when the Isolationists held sway in America, the USA had been one of the main sources of oil in the world and a net exporter. This was no longer the case. America was now increasingly dependent on the oil fields of Saudi Arabia, where the Aramco consortium had recently acquired its monopoly position, and on the other oil fields of the Gulf where a number of US oil companies were moving into a traditionally British area. The Soviet pressures on Iran and Turkey, it was argued, and the Communist threat to Greece were all part of a concerted move to cut off the USA from her vital oil supply.

This was not, however, the argument publicly advanced for the Greek involvement. Nor, after some discussion and agonising, was the anti-Communist argument the one deployed for the public, in general. The State Department had conducted its own survey and concluded that 70 per cent of the population were opposed to a 'get tough with Russia' policy. Two years after the GIs and the Red Army had embraced one another on the Elbe, the American public were not disposed to respond to the call of anti-Communism. Public opinion and the press had been widely critical of the British record in Greece, and one of the problems facing the British had been US newspapermen, whose reporting had been subjected to British military censorship. For the people of America the emphasis was placed on support for democracy, and the rehabilitation of a small friendly country. According to the State Department official who wrote the final draft

> The administration recognized that taking a stand against Soviet expansion might touch off a jingoistic crusade. At least partly for that reason the President's message avoided mention of the Soviet Union and pitched United States policy on a pro-freedom rather than an anti-Communist plane.

The emphasis of the Truman doctrine was rather on the extension of the US sphere of influence to Greece and Turkey, than a landmark in anti-Soviet rhetoric like Churchill's Fulton speech the previous year.

Although the British ultimatum had come out of the blue, the US had already experienced some foretaste of dealing with the Greek political leaders. More than one delegation had been sent to ask for money, and had shown a shocking lack of realism in the amounts they expected to receive.

The executives of the new imperial power, the American Mission for Aid to Greece (AMAG), hastily brought together under the leadership of Dwight Griswold, were none too pleased with what they found in Greece. Griswold reported that the Greek government was corrupt, inefficient and should be replaced. In Washington, Secretary of State Marshall and Dean Rusk agreed with him, but counselled a more careful approach, as the latter put it, 'to avoid charges of imperialism'. Although little attention was paid to this, there were problems for the Greeks in the abrupt change-over. Politicians like Tsaldaris, the Populist leader, who had become accustomed to working with the British suddenly found themselves putting their signature to a request for American aid. Soon they were expressing their gratitude:

> The hearts of the Greek people are profoundly touched by the generosity and good will of the American people and by the benevolent interest of a great and friendly nation in the welfare of Greece.

Again, the message had been composed in the State Department.

In the event it took all of six months to reconstruct the government, and the result—a Liberal–Populist coalition headed by the 84-year old Sofoulis—was not entirely satisfactory to the Americans. AMAG meanwhile had been getting to work, their advisers active in every ministry. This activity can best be described under four headings: 1) the economy; 2) the trade union movement; 3) civil liberties and 4) the military dimension.

The economy

The Greek economy had suffered more than most during the war; the German occupiers had never looked to Greece as a source of industrial material, and before their total withdrawal their occupation had been confined to the larger towns. Greece's only chrome mine had been sabotaged by its miners and was out of action; the large urban populations of Athens and Salonica were dependent on United Nations Relief & Rehabilitation for their survival; British rule had not succeeded in generating any investment or getting the remains of industry going again. Even UNRRA and other aid found its way into the hands of the black-marketeers and speculators, and the only market that flourished was that in gold sovereigns. Inflation was out of control and nullified all attempts to revive the economy. Greece's only significant asset, her shipping fleet, brought little or no profit to her; the gains were made by the shipping magnates and salted away in America.

The American economic advisers who arrived in March 1947 took no time to weigh up the situation and decide what to do; indeed they knew what to do before they set foot in Greece. In a refrain familiar in the monetarist 'eighties, they laid down the new laws. Greeks must stop looking to the rest of the world to feed them; they should forget their dreams of limitless dollar credits from the USA and of vast reparations from Germany and Italy. As an AMAG memorandum noted:

Greece is not only a poor country. . . but is likely to continue a poor country.

Initially some attempts were made to control the import of luxury foreign goods and to tax the ostentatious wealth of the rich; these half-hearted initiatives were soon abandoned. AMAG rejected rationing and price-controls; such war-time controls as existed on imports or on the export of capital were dismantled. A wage freeze was imposed: attempts to collect income tax were abandoned in favour of indirect taxation; against much protesting from a normally compliant government, the subsidy on bread was withdrawn, increasing the price by 75 per cent. No measures were taken to secure any revenue from shipping, so that the benefits that arose from the receipt of a gift of one hundred surplus Liberty ships were experienced only by the Greek ship owners. Budget cuts were made in the modest relief and reconstruction programmes, and the government was required to add to the problems of poverty and unemployment by sacking 20,000 civil servants. As the American member of the Currency Committee of the Bank of Greece expressed it:

The primary task was to lower the socially acceptable standard of living.

In this aim AMAG were undoubtedly successful; less successful was any revival of the Greek economy. Only in 1950 did industrial production reach its pre-war (1938) level; Greece was still dependent on foreign aid for 47 per cent of its expenditure. Unemployment was high, and so was inflation, though it was an undoubted achievement of AMAG to have brought this down from the runaway figures of 1947. Possibly connected with the military situation was the only other success that AMAG could claim—a road improvements programme. The endemic problems of the Greek economy remained what they had been before the Americans arrived.

The trade union movement
This harsh economic policy, in particular the wage-freeze introduced in 1947 could not be implemented without a confrontation with the trade union movement. Greece had never fully achieved free democratic unions; there was a tradition of government control and interference which the Metaxas dictatorship had done nothing to modify. On the other hand both before the war and later, the influence of the Communist Party (KKE) was noticeable in the Tobacco Workers and Maritime unions in particular and in 1947 the prestige of the KKE was high throughout the working class. When the Americans arrived however, the trade unions were still negotiating to be allowed to elect their leadership. The general cycle of events was this: a British Trade Union delegation would arrive, negotiate a compromise deal between the Left and the other factions, which would then be sabotaged in one way or another by the government and the Right. One thing all were agreed on, if there were elections the Left would win them overwhelmingly. Some of the so-called trade union leaders of the Right had no basis of support at all, one of them, who came close to becoming the Secretary of the Greek TUC being actually a former Minister of Labour under Metaxas. This certainly accounted for why the Left was prepared to agree to the various compromises, confident that they would quickly regain their position once elections were held. Although AMAG introduced the American Federation of Labour expert Irving Brown, they were content to begin with to allow the British to continue to exercise their role as trade union advisers. Vincent Tewson, therefore, was sent for once again to negotiate a settlement so that the long-awaited elections could proceed. This time the Left (ERGAS) agreed to only six seats on an executive of twenty-one, but the deal ran into difficulties with the Americans. A difference of approach, or perhaps of aim, began to emerge between Britain and America.

> We must make an effort [Vincent Tewson suggested] to convince the British labour movement we tried our best.

For the Americans

Mr Keeley actually argued that if free elections would produce a Communist executive it would be better to have none.

The US Embassy now demanded total exclusion of the Communists from the executive. This, British readers may be surprised to learn, drew strong protests from Bevin, as a result of which the Americans made a tactical withdrawal. Without in any way abandoning their aim of purging the Greek labour movement of all communist leaders, they returned to negotiating something like the Tewson formula. However, they undermined this compromise later by insisting that the Greeks disaffiliate from the World Federation (to which incidentally the British TUC was affiliated at the time)—knowing that this would be totally unacceptable to the Left. Finally all hope for settlement was finished off by the arrest of three of the six communist representatives. These arrests were the first of many, and not only Communists but many liberal trade union leaders were imprisoned or exiled. By the end of 1947, ERGAS itself was declared illegal—an action characterised by Tewson as 'indefensible'. Even less defensible was the introduction of the death penalty for striking, urged on Tsaldaris by Griswold's deputy. This was too much for world opinion, and even the AFL joined with the CIO in strong protests. AMAG now went into reverse to persuade the Greek government to repeal the law. Sofoulis and Tsaldaris resisted this counter-order, which was not carried out for a number of weeks.

The Greek trade union movement now became the arena for a squalid struggle between corrupt right-wing operators, while the government moved against the last stronghold of the Left, the Maritime Union. Ten of its leaders were executed and others (like Tony Ambatielos) were to lie in gaol under sentence of death for many years. Greek trade unions have yet to recover from the effects of this legacy.

Civil liberties

There were two central questions in the evolution of post-war Greek political life. The first was whether the hope for a democratic evolution widespread at the time of Liberation could still be realised; or whether there would be a return to the traditions of pre-war Greece and the Metaxas dictatorship. The other related to the civil war; was there to be conciliation and an attempt to find a peaceful solution, or was it to be regarded as a fight to the finish?

In regard to the first question, the American advisers had encouraged the Greek government in the destruction of the trade union movement. As with the trade unions, the government needed no encouragement to take drastic measures against its opponents. As the Minister of Public Order Zervas said to the US military chief, General Livesay:

> No matter what the operations of the army, the main thing is to kill the communists in the towns.

When the Americans took over in Greece there were some 17,000 Leftists in gaol in circumstances which require some explanation. After the fighting in Athens in December 1944, there had been negotiated, first a cease-fire and then the Varkiza Agreement, signed by the organisation of the Resistance movement, EAM, and by the Greek government. EAM had tried to negotiate a full amnesty, but were forced to agree the following amnesty clause:

> An amnesty for political crimes committed between the 3 December and the publication of the law establishing the amnesty. From this amnesty shall be excluded common law crimes against life and property which were not absolutely necessary to the achievement of the political crime concerned.

The questions: what was a common law crime and what was 'absolutely necessary' were therefore going to be decided by the judges in the courts. There had been no purge of the judiciary, and these were therefore the same judges who had sat dispensing fascist justice on behalf of the Greek Quisling government throughout the occupation. Thus every member of ELAS who had taken part in a military operation could be, and thousands were, accused of the 'common-law' crime of murder, frequently being accused of 'murder of persons unknown' so that there was little difficulty in securing convictions after the most perfunctory hearings. In fact the situation was worse than Wittner represents it; the Greek courts held that the provisions of the Varkiza Agreement only referred to the 'December events' and that there was no amnesty for the crime of armed resistance prior to that date. This was a threat to the liberty—and life—of every member of ELAS, thousands of whom were imprisoned for long sentences, and many executed. Along with the unrestrained reign of terror in the countryside, originated by General Grivas' 'X'-ites and other armed bands, and joined by the gendarmerie, these facts explain why so many former ELAS members went into hiding or took to the mountains, long before there was any question of a civil war.

Against this background, the Greek government in July 1947 sounded out Ambassador MacVeagh to obtain approval for further arrests, and through him Secretary of State Marshall, who replied that

> we should not interpose objections.

A week later a wave of arrests began, more than 14,000 people were rounded up and exiled to the islands. This measure drew protests even from British officials, including the Ambassador; but the US showed no inclination to stop the flow of Greeks to Makronisos and the other concentration camps.

Griswold, the head of AMAG, publicly defended Makronisos, claiming that the inmates were 'well-treated' and receiving 'indoctrination courses'. In fact the reaction of the Americans to the growing legal and illegal terror was not to attempt to mitigate it in any way, but to improve public relations so that it would not receive such a bad press throughout the world. The Greek government was urged to issue communiqués explaining the executions. Criticism of widespread arrests and executions was

a political weapon of the Communists. . . to smear the Greek state.

Despite rumours to the contrary the US Embassy

had never requested the Greek government to suspend the execution of traitors.

The policy of executing their political opponents came to a climax in early 1948 when the Minister of Justice, Ladas, planned to execute 2,961 prisoners. Most of these had been in prison since the Liberation and their crime was participation in the Resistance. Ladas prepared a secret plan for the executions to avoid unfavourable publicity, but after the assassination of Ladas these were carried out openly as a 'reprisal'. This produced an international outcry; in Britain Bevin protested strongly and even Churchill privately expressed his disapproval of the practice of shooting prisoners. Faced with these pressures, Ladas' successor at the Ministry began to back down. In this he was bitterly opposed by the US chargé. There now began an argument between the Americans on the spot who were encouraging the Greek government to murder their opponents, and the State Department which was feeling the blast of foreign disapproval. Ambassador Grady (successor to MacVeagh) continued to defend the death sentences, including those on Manolis Glezos (who had achieved international fame by tearing down the Nazi swastika from the Acropolis in 1941) and on a number of Jehovah's Witnesses who had refused call-up. In the outcome a hundred prisoners were executed not the three thousand proposed, but this owed everything to world opinion and nothing to the 'advisers' of the Greek government.

These were not the only attacks on civil liberties; measures were taken to purge the Church (the Bishop of Kozani who had figured in the Resistance was defrocked), and there was a wholesale purge of Leftists in government service. The illegal harassment of the left-wing press gave way to a full-scale assault. So much so that Sofoulis complained about these 'fascist measures'—measures which he, as Prime Minister, was powerless to prevent.

On the second question—that of conciliation and attempts to end the civil war by agreement—the American record was the same. In the early stages it is true that the US were urging an 'amnesty' policy on the Greek government. But this proposal for individual unconditional surrender was taken seriously by no-one, least of all by the soldiers of the Democratic Army who knew how the government forces treated their prisoners. As the American Porter wrote, the programme

> looked plausible on paper. . . The appointment of General Zervas as Minister of Public Order completely destroyed anyone's inclination to take it seriously.

The point, however, was not amnesty but the conducting of negotiations for a settlement, and for this there was beginning to be a groundswell of international opinion. The men and women of the Democratic Army had not taken to the hills in order to overthrow the government in Athens, but first, to avoid being arrested or murdered and secondly to claim a legitimate place within political society, similar to that enjoyed by their French or Italian comrades. This should have been clear, not only because Marcos, the Commander of the Democratic Army, constantly reiterated it in a series of peace initiatives from the mountains, but from other indications besides. The Americans noted that the Democratic Army imposed on itself, or had imposed on it, a man-power ceiling; they knew, but ignored the fact that the Democratic Army was receiving no aid whatsoever from the Soviet Union, in contrast with the vast amounts of aid they were giving to the government side. They also ignored the signs that Moscow was distancing itself from Yugoslavia, the chief backers of the Democratic Army; and when, in June 1948 this came to an open rift, they still ignored the diplomatic possibilities and continued with the war relentlessly. As George Kennan said:

> The problem in Greece is merely one of cessation of aggression and does not call for discussion or negotiation of any kind.

This was not the view taken by the world community, and among other initiatives through the UN was a particularly promising one from Australia. This called for an end to the fighting and for internationally supervised free elections with other guarantees. Supported by several countries, this was made public in late 1948. The US, having failed to stifle the initiative privately, did succeed in crushing it publicly. General Marcos' serious proposals for a settlement (July 1947, September 1947, April 1948), a peace feeler from Moscow to Tsaldaris—these moves from the other side were ignored; while those in Athens who were in favour of conciliation, Tsouderos, Sofianopoulos and others, were actively discouraged. So the war dragged on.

Military involvement

When the British had demanded that the US take over responsibility for Greece, it was essentially an economic burden that they had in mind. The civil war was seen primarily as an additional drain on resources which it was beyond Britain's ability to meet. At first, therefore, the American plan was to hand over to the Greek Army large quantities of weapons and supplies and leave them to get on with the job of putting down the rebels. Two years after the end of the Second World War, the US held enormous stocks of surplus weapons and supplies which could be handed over at a fraction of their original cost, thus ensuring a modest budget to get through Congress. A suspicious Congress had been assured that the number of US personnel would be minimal—an advisory mission of 10–40 under General Livesay. At this time the Greek Army (GNA), swollen with the recruitment of the collaborating Security Batallions, was already a force of 120,000 men facing a rebel army of only a few thousands. Not only this but the British, while sloughing off their financial commitments, had not withdrawn their large military mission and substantial number of troops.

It soon became clear that the first-stage strategy was not working; rebel activity was spreading to all parts of Greece. The Greek government was asking for an increase in their army—i.e. for more money to pay for an additional 20,000 troops. General Livesay turned this down and pointed out that what was required was not more troops but more effective use of the existing numbers. As the first American commander reported

there is nothing wrong with Greece that time, forceful US guidance and American dollars will not correct.

The dollars were already flowing, it was the turn of the forceful guidance. The '10–40' military advisers began to grow in numbers and in activity; in September 1947 another 150 were requested and the question was raised of American 'operational advice'. By the end of 1947 this had been agreed, Livesay was replaced by the more aggressive General Van Fleet, and the Greek Army was now, in fact, being led down to divisional level by American officers. This army was swollen to the enormous number of a quarter of a million troops, not counting the right-wing armed groups in the villages; but despite this more than ten-to-one superiority over the Democratic Army, not to mention their superiority in weaponry, the military situation showed no sign of improvement. Behind the scenes two discussions were taking place. One concerned the possible deployment of American fighting troops, and this came very close to being implemented. The other, more discreet, discussion concerned contingency plans if the civil war should be lost.

The pattern which was to become familiar elsewhere in the world was here drawn out in blueprint; heavy dollar support, a foreign army being armed, trained and led into battle under American direction. The basic difficulty faced in Greece was soon recognised—the reluctance of the GNA to engage the enemy. During 1948 and 1949 the GNA was re-organised to replace the rifle with artillery and combat planes. The enemy could now be engaged at longer range. But these methods did not, during 1948, bring the desired result; to American dismay

> the operations of the Greek armed forces. . . have not resulted in any substantial reduction of the guerilla threat.

Van Fleet acknowledged that anything that had been accomplished had been 'done by air and artillery'. The Americans, in Washington or in Athens had no new recipe for changing the situation in their favour; a more draconian regime in the GNA was instituted under General Papagos, with dismissal of many officers and increased use of firing squads. New weapons were deployed, including for the first time anywhere, Napalm.

The situation changed dramatically in August 1949. What had been a few months earlier a critical situation for the Greek government became a total defeat for the Democratic Army, the remains of which withdrew across the Albanian frontier. The Americans were able to claim that their massive resources, their weaponry and their leadership—and without the participation of American troops—had brought victory, and this was the lesson they learned for the future. The reality, as was realised by less blinkered observers at the time, was otherwise. The US policy makers seem to have ignored the consequences of the break between the Soviet Union and Yugoslavia. As this rift widened, the fate of the Democratic Army became more precarious. Contrary to the general belief, Yugoslav aid had been measured and restrained; for instance, many Slav-speaking refugees from Macedonia and others were being held in Yugoslavia, and conspicuously *not* being armed and sent back across the frontier. Yugoslavia, in dispute with the British over Trieste, now found itself totally isolated by Soviet hostility. It could not be expected that in these circumstances the involvement on the Greek frontier would be long continued. (Still less so when Zachariades and the leadership of KKE came out strongly in support of the Cominform). On the other hand, Stalin had never shown any enthusiasm for a civil war in Greece, which conflicted with his plans for the division of the Balkans into spheres of influence. The Albanians and Bulgars were accordingly called into line, a line which was now almost exclusively preoccupied with bringing down Tito. For this policy the civil war was an embarrassment, and Stalin ordered its winding up.

In Greece the USA had inherited a neo-colony from Britain; the mechanisms of control were already in existence, and were taken over and used without restraint. Lawrence Wittner shows how the techniques of remote control over Greek political development, over the economy and in the military sphere were perfected—in parallel with the techniques of managing Congress and manipulating the media in the US itself. Using the documents available he has built up a devastating case against his country's rulers. These documents do not include any of the reports relating to the CIA's activities, all of which have been 'weeded' from the public record. The picture that he paints is thus only of the respectable or clean area of US policy. One can only surmise how the dirty end will appear when that story is ultimately told.

Despite its manifest importance, Wittner's work has received not a single review in Britain, and has been badly underestimated in the USA where it was published. It is a book not just for the Greek specialist (for whom, incidentally, it is invaluable) but for anyone attempting to understand the nature of Cold War politics and how under the cover of anti-Communism the USA imposes its control over its clients. The apparent success of the American intervention in Greece led to the same methods being applied in Guatemala, El Salvador and, with disastrous results, in Vietnam.

ANTI-COMMUNIST ACTIVISM IN BELGIUM, 1930-1944[1]

Rudi Van Doorslaar

Wollweber

Anyone who knows Belgium will not be surprised to learn that our story begins in Antwerp, an international port of vital importance to the Belgian economy and a nerve centre where antagonistic social forces meet. On 10 November 1937, the Italian steamer *Boccacio* entered Dock No. 53. Louis Schokkaert, one of the dockers taken on to unload the vessel, contrived to leave a small package on board without being noticed. Some ten days later, the *Boccacio* sank off the coast of Brittany with the loss of one officer. The sabotage was the work of Antwerp-based members of the Wollweber group.[2] Ernst Wollweber, a Communist who had been elected to the Reichstag in 1928, was the head of both Profintern's seamens' section and of the clandestine KPD organisation that smuggled propaganda into Nazi Germany. He had been selected by the Communist International to organise clandestine units to sabotage ships carrying supplies to the Nationalists in Spain. The organisation's European bases were in Germany, the Baltic countries, Scandinavia, Britain, the Netherlands and Belgium. Wollweber had given responsibility for The Netherlands and Belgium to Joop Schaap, who came originally from Rotterdam. His lieutenant in Antwerp was a lorry driver called Alfons Fictels, who succeeded in recruiting a number of dockers to help him in his clandestine work. We will not go into any details about the attempted sabotage in Antwerp when an initial attempt to sabotage a German vessel in September 1937 came to nothing. In November, the action against the *Boccacio* had the desired result. In June 1938, a third attempt against the Japanese cargo vessel *Kasij Maru* was also successful: a large explosion occurred in the Channel and the ship was forced to make for the nearest port.

These illegal activities naturally attracted the attention of the police. According to the charges brought against the Wollweber group by the Volksgerichtshof in Berlin in 1942, 'By 1938, police investigations were going ahead on an international scale.'[3] The Germans had in fact started a major investigation in late 1937; it was carried out by the Gestapo and was headed by Richard Heydrich.[4] In Belgium, investigations were co-ordinated by Georges Block, the superintendent in charge of the Police Judiciaire's [Criminal Investigation Department] political bureau in

114

Antwerp. Given the nature of his position, Block was of course in close contact with the Sûreté Publique and military counter-intelligence.

In Belgium, as in the rest of Europe, a number of different police departments were involved in political issues. The Sûreté de l'Etat, for instance, had originally been responsible for the surveillance of foreigners. The Sûreté Publique was subdivided into the Police des Etrangers, the Commissariat Général aux Délégations Judiciaries and the Sûreté de l'Etat itself, and was responsible to the Minister for Justice. Officially, the Sûreté had no intelligence functions, except in wartime.[5] The Sûreté Militaire and its counter-intelligence section were responsible to the Minister for National Defence; in time of war they became the Third Section of the High Command. The Police Judiciaire also had its own political sections. Although its personnel were employed by the Ministry of Justice, they were directly responsible to the public prosecutor, the Procureurs du Roi and the Procureurs Généraux.[6] Finally, the local police forces had had political sections since the nineteenth century; they were responsible to the Bourgmestre and, indirectly, to the Minister for Justice.

Georges Block used the classic tactics of infiltration to track down those responsible for the sabotage that had taken place in Antwerp. It is unlikely that he had any success before 1938. In August 1936, Julien Lepomme, a docker and former boxer from Antwerp, was arrested after a series of burglaries. Later that year he was sentenced to four years imprisonment, but was released early in 1938. Lepomme, who had been a member of the Communist Party for years, was soon recruited into the clandestine Wollweber organisation by Schaap and Fictels. Block also recruited him as an agent. It has proved impossible to discover from Belgian sources just what the Antwerp Prosecutor's Department knew about the Wollweber group. German sources, on the other hand, tell us a great deal.[7] On 12th July 1938, Gestapo chief Heinrich Muller wrote to Schmidt-Rolke, the German Consul General in Antwerp, and told him that Berlin knew only that a group of Communists connected with Profintern's seamen's section was at work. Six days later Schmidt-Rolke replied, telling Muller that he had learned from the Police Judiciaire in Antwerp that the leaders were Schaap and Fictels. In October, Muller informed the Consul General that on 25th October he would, on Heydrich's orders, be visiting Antwerp, together with Streckenbach, the head of the Gestapo in Hamburg. They wanted to have a meeting with the Police Judiciaire, but no such meeting appears to have taken place. A few weeks later, Streckenbach once more set off for Antwerp, on 'private' business. This time he did succeed in meeting Jozef Celis, the chief superintendent of the Police Judiciaire. The Consul General had done his work well.

An anti-Bolshevik alliance with Germany?

How are we to explain these contacts? The German police had been trying to organise an international campaign against Bolshevism since 1936. Between 30th August and 13th September, representatives of the police forces of fourteen or fifteen countries met in Berlin to exchange ideas.[8] Belgium was represented by officials from the Sûreté Publique. During the Parteitage that took place in Nuremburg after the congress, administrator Robert de Floy was presented with a German decoration. It is difficult to say whether or not the conference had any concrete results. In October, de Floy did receive certain information from Heydrich, but the contents have never been disclosed. On the other hand, what Heydrich and Himmler wanted is perfectly clear: mutual cooperation, both in terms of intelligence and concrete action against any political movement (i.e. of the left) that might threaten the security of any of the contracting states. Any exile who opposed National-Socialism came into that category. It is unlikely that any official treaty was signed, although that was of course what Himmler wanted. It is, therefore, also unlikely that Belgium was represented at the 1938 Berlin Congress. Research into the Wollweber group has shown that no Belgian delegate attended the conference held in Hamburg and Berlin in September 1938. On the other hand, the Police Judiciaire's colleagues in the Netherlands, Denmark and Norway did accept Germany's invitation.[9]

The fact that contacts were established between the German and Belgian police forces is obviously not an isolated incident. On the contrary, it is quite in line with Belgian foreign policy in the late thirties. In 1936, Belgium broke off the military pact that had been signed with France in 1921. The new policy of neutralism and independence reflected the Establishment's reluctance to be drawn into a possible conflict between the Popular Front government in France, which had ties with the Soviet Union, and the Nazi government in Berlin. Moscow and Berlin were already at war in Spain, and the conservatives, backed by the Court, opted for Berlin. The new line on foreign policy was welcomed in Berlin and it was probably in order to strengthen the new spirit of cordiality that the Sûreté's representatives were invited to Berlin. At the same time, contacts between the Belgian Sûreté and the French intelligence services, which had previously been very close, became almost clandestine. Belgium's absence from the 1938 Anti-Bolshevik Conference may have owed something to the country's historical links with its First World War allies and to a reluctance—or inability—to become too closely identified with Germany. It should also be remembered that although the military men in the counter-intelligence service were staunchly anti-communist, they had no illusions as to the Abwehr's plans for Belgium.

Antwerp

To return, however, to Antwerp. Both German and Belgian reactions to the activities of the Wollweber group have to be seen in terms of a broader context. The economic activity of the port was a vital link in the Belgian economy, which was primarily based upon import-export trade. Trade with Germany had increased considerably since 1933. Many anti-fascist emigrés from Germany passed through Antwerp, and the town also had a Jewish population which was mainly concentrated in the diamond trade. Camille Huysmans, the mayor, was the secretary of the Second International and was to become its president in February 1940. He took a strong anti-fascist line and was therefore in an extremely difficult position. As he had little confidence in Block's political bureau, he established his own political police force in April 1937. This was the Dienst der Bijzondere Opdrachten (Special Missions Unit) and its main tasks were to prevent Communist agitation in the docks and to uncover German plots. These were difficult tasks which implied the use of tactics like infiltration and they often brought the Special Missions into conflict with the agents of Block and Celis. Lepomme, for instance, supplied the Special Missions Unit with information about the work he was doing for Block, but there is nothing to prove that he was not also passing on information to Block. The Special Missions also recruited agents from the German emigré groups in order to track down spies working for the Gestapo and Abwehr.

It must also be remembered that when Huysmans was made Bourgmestre of Antwerp in 1933, he came under violent attack from the Right, not least because of the welcome he gave the emigrés. The German Consul took every possible opportunity to use economic pressure and political arguments against him.[10] The information German agents gathered on agitators in the port was passed on to the 'right' newspapers and was used to influence opinions in Brussels. In May 1938, the German Consul General informed his superiors that the Sûreté had decided to use the national Gendarmerie to arrest undesirable aliens rather than the local police forces.[11]

Industry and the Church

For the Special Missions Unit, anti-communism was primarily a means to avoid being attacked by the Right and by the employers' associations. An examination of one of their actions teaches us a great deal about their intentions. It also takes us to the very centre of the anti-communist campaign. In June 1938 the BTB, the transport union which worked with the dockers, plastered Antwerp with posters showing a picture of a certain Noël, a well known Communist militant on the docks. The poster gave his real name as Leon de Ridder and it also gave the number of his SEPES membership card. The Société d'Etudes Politiques, Economiques et Sociales was an organisation specialising in anti-communist intelligence and propaganda and was founded in 1925. It described itself as the Belgian section of the Entente Internationale Contre le Bolchevisme, which had been founded by Théodore Aubert in Geneva in 1924. Its General Secretary was Jean Spiltoir, a former army officer who, in the early twenties, had been the leader of the Union Civique, a para-military strike-breaking organisation. The aim of SEPES was 'to promote the idea of class collaboration, the only principle that can give the country the social peace it requires if it is to go on existing and developing. That is why SEPES is fighting the most active enemy of social peace: communism'.[12] SEPES gathered intelligence on Communists, both at the national and the international level, socialists, trade unions and on separatists (in other words, Flemish nationalists).[13] In ideological terms, it represented the right wing Catholic tradition of Belgian nationalism. Initially, it financed its activities by undertaking intelligence and protection missions for SURCOMIN (Sûreté Commerciale et Industrielle), which had been set up by Spiltoir in 1925. In the early thirties, it began to receive money from the Comité Central Industriel, the most powerful employers' association in Belgium.[14] This new development coincided with an outbreak of spontaneous strikes in the Hainaut coalfield, where the miners had begun to turn against the socialist trade unions. For the first time since its foundation in 1921, the Communist Party had at last found a mass audience. Not even the economic crisis of the previous two years had given it that.

SEPES had some thirty bases throughout Belgium, most of them staffed by ex-officers who had worked in the censorship and intelligence units of the Belgian army during the occupation of Germany. Since at least 1936–37, the strings had been pulled by the director of a company owned by the Société Générale.[15] Marcel de Roover had served as a volunteer with the Force Publique in the Belgian Congo in the First World War. In 1919 he was appointed as Belgium's representative to General Denikin in White Russia. After a diplomatic posting to Sofia in 1920–26, he became a director of SOGECHIM (Société Générale Industrielle et Chimique du Haut Katanga).[16] In 1941 he became a director of BRUFINA, the Banque de Bruxelles's holding company, and thus entered the orbit of Baron Paul de Launoit. De Roover, who in 1966 became Belgium's representative on the World Anti-communist League, played a central role in anti-communist activities in Belgium before, during and after the Second World War.

In 1937, when De Roover began to support Spiltoir, SEPES began to work closely with the Concentration de Propagande Anti-Communiste (COPAC). When COPAC was officially founded in 1938, its president was Vicomte Charles Terlinden. With Terlinden, we enter the world of the far Right. He was a Ligue Nationale sympathiser (the Ligue Nationale was the most important fascist organisation in the country prior to the rise of Rexism), worked with all the Franco support committees and was

President of the Comité d'action pour l'Universalité de Rome, which received support from Mussolini's propaganda services. The leading light in COPAC was Félix André Morlion, the Dominican priest who also ran the Centrale de Presse Catholique. COPAC and SEPES began to cooperate more closely: in 1938 Emile Stappaerts, a former army officer who worked closely with Spiltoir, became both director general of SEPES and treasurer of COPAC. In general, SEPES functioned as an intelligence service, with COPAC working as a huge propaganda machine propelled by Morlion's shock brigades. The coordination and intensification of the anti-communist movement coincided with the major Communist upsurge that occurred in Belgium after the great strike wave of 1936 and the victory of the Popular Front in France.

According to the Reichssicherheitshauptamt in Berlin, SEPES was a *getarntes Büro* (Secret bureau) of the Belgian Sûreté Militaire.[17] There is, however, no proof that this was in fact the case. According to Carl Peters, the co-founder of SEPES and the organisation's head in Antwerp, SEPES had excellent contacts with both the Sûreté de l'Etat and the Antwerp Police Judiciaire,[18] but that does not necessarily imply that information was not also supplied to the military in Brussels. SEPES does not appear to have had direct links with the Gestapo, but in September 1937 it did send a list of Communist agitators, some of whom were German emigrés, to the German Embassy in Brussels. It also called upon the Belgian authorities to deport them.[19]

SEPES's best-documented publication was probably *Le Port d'Anvers et le communisme,* which appeared in July 1938. It dealt at length with the smuggling of propaganda into Germany. It is quite obvious that SEPES could not have acquired this information unless it had contacts in the police or without using infiltration tactics. Which takes us back to Leon de Ridder, alias Leon Noël. He had been a member of the Communist Party since 1929 and was a member of a group working with seamen and dockers. De Ridder made himself so useful that Peters paid him out of SEPES funds and tried to provide him with a cover story by getting a company in the docks to employ him. That cannot have proved difficult, as, according to Special Mission sources, de Ridder often visited the offices of the Centrale des Employeurs du Port d'Anvers. The CEPA had long been pressurising the city council to improve trade relations between Belgium and Germany. De Ridder was eventually unmasked as a double agent by Huysmans's Special Missions Unit and the information was passed on to the BTB. The Special Missions had two aims: making the Communists look ridiculous and discrediting the Right. After all, conservative newspapers like *La Métropole, De Gazet van Antwerpen, Volk en Staat* and *De Nieuwe Stad* regularly published information supplied by SEPES.

The Popular Front and the Phoney War

The examples we have looked at show how the political and social events
of the thirties and especially the rise of Communism after 1936 led to
increasingly savage repression. The repression was organised by a state
apparatus (the political police, whose main task was the surveillance of
the Communist Party) and by a variety of networks organised by militants
from the far Right Nationalist movement and led by individuals from the
world of high finance and from the Catholic Church. Two other events had
a profound influence on anti-communism: the outbreak of civil war in
Spain in 1936 and the signing of the Soviet–German non-aggression pact
in 1939.

It was only natural for those who were fighting Communism to look
for its areas of weakness. After the so-called plot of 1923, fifteen Communist leaders were arrested, but they were released after spending four
months in prison. The trial, which had been meant to destroy the Party
completely, became a propaganda success for the Communists and a defeat
for both the Sûreté and the Public Prosecutor. From that point onwards,
anti-communist action became both more sophisticated and more effective.
The weak point in the campaign the Communists organised in solidarity
with the Spanish Republic was, of course, the recruitment of volunteers
for the International Brigades. In January 1937, the Communist recruiting
organisation was declared illegal, and any volunteers who were found to be
making for Spain were called into the army. A second and equally effective
intervention was organised by SEPES and COPAC. The Communists had
not been very selective in their recruitment of volunteers, and the
conditions in which the shock units had been forced to fight in Spain led
to considerable discontent amongst some of the Brigaders who had returned to Belgium. COPAC and SEPES gladly took the opportunity to give
them financial help—with money from industry—and to organise them.[20]
During the municipal elections of 1938, COPAC mounted a major propaganda campaign around the issue. The campaign was typical of COPAC's
strategy. That almost the entire press was anti-communist was not enough
for COPAC, as the press did not have sufficient impact upon the groups
that were most at risk from Communism, namely the working classes.

The signing of the Soviet–German pact in August 1939 made it perfectly clear that the Communist movement took its orders from Moscow.
Rather than making a frontal attack on the Party, as it did in 1923, the
government decided to close down its press. This, it claimed, was in line
with its policy of neutralism, but it in fact had more to do with Communist
agitation in the mines and in the army. The witch hunt was on.[21] In
March 1940, both houses passed a law providing for the defence of
'national institutions'. A bill to ban the Communist Party was dropped, as
no political party in Belgium has any legal status. The witch hunt
continued throughout the phoney war and ended with the arrest of

several hundred Communists when Germany attacked Belgium on 10 May
1940. Together with the Flemish nationalists, the Rexists and thousands
of German and Austrian political refugees, including many Jews, they
were deported to the south of France.[22]

The Occupation

As a result of the pact with the Soviet Union, the SIPO–SD (Sicherheits-
polizei-Sicherheitsdienst) did not make a direct attack on the Communist
Party when it reached Brussels with the German troops. After some hesitation, it accepted that its presence was legal. The Communist press, however, remained banned. For the German military administration (and its
Belgian secretaries general),[23] the main priorities were economic recovery
and a return to social stability. When, in the last months of 1940, the
Communist Party began to denounce the 'new order's' social demagogy,
militants began to be arrested. In the meantime, the German police began
to make preparations for an intelligence operation. The Gestapo was
already well informed about minor issues like the Wollweber group, the
emigrés and Comintern agents, and the Party's leaders and representatives
were known to everyone. Its image of Belgian Communism as a whole was,
however, somewhat fanciful. The Gestapo therefore needed information
and the obvious place to look for it was in the files held by the Belgian
political police.

In the first week of July 1940, the German Military Administration
ordered the arrest of those responsible for the internments and deportations of 10 May. The Flemish nationalists had already been calling for
such measures. Those arrested included the prosecutor Ganshof van der
Meersch and four officials from the Sûreté de l'Etat. Together with
Georges Block, Robert de Foy and Fernand Louwage, who were respectively the Sûreté Publique's administrator general and its inspector-general,
were taken to Berlin.[24] While Block was in Berlin, the German Police,
armed with lists of what they wanted, visited the Prosecutor's Office in
Antwerp and seized a number of files. Shortly afterwards, a number of
secret files were 'discovered' in the Palais de Justice in Brussels. They too
were forwarded to Berlin. In the meantime, Heydrich informed Reeder,
the head of the German Military Administration in Belgium, that de Foy
was not to be prosecuted for his part in the events of May 1940 because
he had collaborated with the Reichssicherheitshauptamt in the months
leading up to the invasion.[25] The three Belgian police officers remained in
Berlin until 14th August 1940, but it is improbable that that had anything to do with the May arrests. It has to be seen in terms of the long-
standing connections that existed between officials of the German and
Belgian police forces. A number of points seem to support that interpretation. Shortly before the invasion of the Soviet Union, the head of
SIPO–SD in Brussels received a detailed list of Belgian Communists from

Berlin. He was astonished when Muller told him that the information had
been supplied by individuals who had been held by the Belgian police
during the victorious march to the West.[26]

In Antwerp, developments were more concrete. The SIPO used the
Police Judiciaire's files to draw up a voluminous report on the Communist
Party's organisation in Belgium.[27] The author of the report was Max
Gunther, a Gestapo agent whose real name was Emiel Van Thielen, a
native of Antwerp. He had taken German nationality and had already
played an important role in the Wollweber investigation. Together with
Block, he had been responsible for rolling up the Wollweber network by
arresting Fictels in August 1940 and his collaborators in December
1940.[28] Block had introduced his agent Lepomme to Gunther, who in
turn recruited into the service of the Gestapo. Lepomme was killed by
the resistance in August 1942.[29] On 11th November 1942, the Volksgerichtshof in Berlin condemned the Antwerp-based members of the
Wollweber group to death and, with the exception of Alfons Fictels, they
were all executed. Fictels died at Gros-Rosen in March 1942.

The help the Antwerp Police Judiciaire gave the German police in 1940
and 1941 was not an isolated incident. The files of the Police des Etrangers
held no secrets for the German police. In Liège, both the mayor and the
public prosecutor supplied the Germans with lists of local militants.[30] The
evidence we have collected suggests that until the Soviet Union's entry
into the war, the occupying forces could count on considerable help from
Belgian magistrates and from certain police units. The indirect contribution they made by supplying information on militants was quite in keeping
with the prevailing atmosphere in the Belgian administration during the
first year of the occupation. As late as October 1941, a report drawn up
by Colonel Dethise, the Commandant of the Gendarmerie, argued that the
Communist Party, the terrorist groups ('which may be the same thing as
the Party'), the VNV and Rex, all represented a threat to state security.[31]
By deciding to stay at their posts in the administration, the economy,
the magistrature and the police, the leading figures in the Belgian establishment were opting for what they saw as a continuation of the pre-war
policy of neutralism. In other words, they chose 'the lesser evil'. Their
policy of independence and neutralism was not, however, simply an
expression of their desire to take a neutral stance in the international
conflict between Germany, France and Great Britain. It was an ideological
position designed to promote the political, economic and cultural
influence of Germany.[32] As early as 1936, the Belgian establishment had
decided to open the country up to German influence because it thought
that, from an ideological point of view, France was no longer a reliable
ally. This was clearly a class reflex, and the same attitude prevailed during
the first year of the occupation. The 'realist' option of the 'lesser evil' was
based upon the assumption that Germany and Great Britain would reach

a compromise peace and that Belgium would be absorbed into the German sphere of influence. It is important to note that the split between the king and the government (the king insisted on staying with his troops after the surrender, whilst the government wanted to continue the struggle from abroad) helped to reinforce and popularise hostility towards the political parties and parliamentary institutions and a desire for a strong executive personified by the monarch. Attempts to rally political and military forces to the king have to be understood in terms of this reactionary climate.[33]

A description of all the attempts that were made to do this would be beyond the scope of this article. But it is illuminating to look at the political positions of the instigators of the anti-communist activity of the thirties. COPAC's spokesman Vicomte Charles Terlinden issued a long manifesto putting forward his ideas as to what should be done after the departure of the Germans. He argued that the king would be 'the man of the hour' and would have to establish a 'military-style' provisional government. A number of military associations which recruited both men on active service and reservists had been formed, the most important being the Légion Belge. Commander Charles Claser, the founder of the Légion, had originally been thinking in terms of anti-German resistance but joined forces with Terlinden, who became the Légion's political commissar. Terlinden's programme was simplicity itself: a strong regime capable of halting a Communist offensive and with the king there to prevent the politicians returning.[34]

In the autumn of 1940, General Biebuyck called for the formation of a 'Rassemblement National et Social des Anciens Combattants autour du Roi', with the slogans: 'The king will think for us. His will shall be our will and he will lead us to a better future.' The real leader of the Rassemblement was its Secretary General, Marcel de Roover. Thanks to him, links were established between the military associations and far Right political movements like the Mouvement National Royaliste and the Légion Nationale.

De Roover, Terlinden and others like them wanted to turn the military associations into a pro-monarchist authoritarian army, but their ambitions were not to be fulfilled. In the early summer of 1941, the Légion Belge adopted the line taken by the Allies and by the Belgian government in exile in London. In December 1942, it was recognised as the official clandestine army of Belgium. It is better known by the name it used at the Liberation: Armée Secrète.

Despite these later developments, until the summer of 1941, the main preoccupation of these groups was anti-communism. SEPES's Secretary General Jean Speltoir was already in contact with the VNV and in Antwerp the entire right-wing began a concerted anti-communist campaign. Although separatism represented a major threat to the Belgian nationalists, they did not reject the possibility of a tactical anti-communist alliance out of hand. During the occupation, the main problem facing the Légion Belge, which was still thinking in terms of a compromise peace and a German withdrawal, was the neutralisation of the VNV. It was in that context that the head of the Légion's intelligence service in Brabant read a report on the VNV to the Légion's commander.[35] An agreement had already been reached to obtain information from Spiltoir, who 'currently has contacts in Flemish circles'. According to Spiltoir, the VNV leaders were coming to terms with reality and their separatism was now a thing of the past: 'In a Belgian Kingdom, the Flemish will be loyal supporters of the king.' The programme outlined by Spiltoir was not lacking in clarity: 'Flemish nationalism is one of the most resolute and best armed enemies of revolutionary Communism, both in Flanders and in Belgium as a whole. We now have an opportunity to integrate Flemish nationalism into a united Belgium. The threat it represented when it was in opposition will probably vanish.' When asked for his opinion of the report, Marcel de Roover said that he thought Spiltoir was being somewhat optimistic, but added that he had received information suggesting that the VNV was moving in the right political direction. The Légion's political intelligence unit was working closely with 'Zéro', the intelligence service set up by BRUFINA and the Banque de Bruxelles, and it was also collecting information on Communist activities at this time. That was of course completely in line with its earlier activities.[36]

All these preparations had become meaningless by the summer of 1941. Great Britain was still holding out, and in June the Soviet Union entered the war, followed by the United States. The war had become a war for freedom and democracy and a war against oppression and dictatorship. 'Realism', with its profoundly conservative and reactionary connotations and its note of anti-communism, was about to be replaced by resistance and a resurgence of democracy.

Anti-Communism in decline

As Germany attacked the Soviet Union on 22nd June 1941, the German police arrested hundreds of Communist militants and sympathisers in Belgium in an operation known as Summer Solstice. Although Summer Solstice has not been analysed in any detail, it does seem that pre-war activities were the main criteria for arrest.[37] This suggests that the Germans were acting on the basis of information supplied by the Belgian police and had not succeeded in penetrating the clandestine structures established by the Communist Party. The Communists then increased their efforts to liberate the country, beginning an armed struggle and active at the political and trade union levels. During this second phase, the German police sought the active collaboration of the State Prosecutors in their attempts to break up the Party's clandestine organisation, but after

1942 they were faced with an increasingly lax attitude on the part of the Belgian magistrature.

In this context, it is instructive to look at the correspondence exchanged between Armand Tilman, a former officer with the Police Marine who had transferred to the Police Judiciaire at the beginning of the occupation, and a deputy public prosecutor in Brussels.[38] Tilman, whose work in Antwerp had mainly been concerned with Communist activity and who had worked closely with Block and Celis, wanted the courts to take repressive action against the Communists. Until 1941, he was listened to, but after 1942 the public prosecutor changed his tone. The explanation for the change is both political and pragmatic; the Soviet Union was now an ally and there could be no question of using systematic and organised repression against illegal Communist actions against the occupying forces and their Belgian collaborators. Tilman was forced to limit his activities to gathering intelligence; no action could be taken until it was proved that the Communists were going to provoke a civil war in an attempt to seize power.

Although there is no documentary evidence, it seems improbable that the deputy public prosecutor was simply expressing a personal opinion. It is much more likely that his views reflected a general current of opinion within the Belgian establishment, all of whose members had contacts of some kind with the Belgian Government in London. As late as July 1942, that same government was, it should be remembered, still describing Claser's Légion Belge as a para-military fascist organisation whose one aim was the seizure of power and the restoration of the king to the throne. When a major section of the Establishment began to change its attitude, it became much easier for the Communists to establish contacts with groups that had previously been hostile. Despite the savage repression organised by the German police, the Communists had succeeded in extending their activities and their influence was now much greater than it had been before the war. The fact that some police units were headed by German-appointed supporters of the 'new order' and were still hunting down Communists merely served to increase Communist influence. In April 1943, Secretary General Gerard Romsee, who was a former member of the VNV leadership, established a 'Service d'Inspection' inside the Ministry of the Interior. It was headed by Tilman, who had broken off his relations with the magistrature and Block in 1942. Tilman systematically went ahead with his anti-communist activities and collaborated directly with the Gestapo. As a result he was condemned to life imprisonment. In 1948, he himself admitted that his great mistake had been his failure to understand the objective and subjective aspects of anti-communism.[39] He had, in other words, failed to understand that anti-communism was merely one element within a reactionary ideology that had been forced into retreat since 1942.

Conclusions

Anti-communism is older than Communism itself. This apparent paradox conceals an important truth about anti-communism: it is simply a continuation of a policy that was used against the labour movement throughout the latter half of the nineteenth century.

Communism first appeared in organised form after the victory of the Bolshevik Revolution in Russia. The Communist Parties of the Western world were formed as sections of an International. Moscow became the centre of their world.

In both Belgium and other countries, the bourgeois state defended itself against the Communists' self-proclaimed aim of taking power, by force if need be, by simultaneously strengthening its repressive apparatus and by adapting it through the introduction of universal suffrage and social laws. Once the crisis of the First World War was over, those who had had to be forced to accept social and political democratisation against their will saw Communism as the main enemy in their attempts to turn back the tide of history. Professional anti-communists were thus able to use these elements in their struggle against any form of social change. The task mobilised only a small fraction of those who defended reactionary ideas, but the architects of anti-communism were still close to the centre of political, economic and social power.

We have seen how the economic crisis and the subsequent rise of Communism in Belgium led to a reaction on the part of both the state apparatus and the private networks organised by the big industrialists and even sections of the clergy. We have also seen that the connections between the private and public sectors were at times very close indeed.

After 1935, this reaction was only one element within a general anti-democratic shift to the Right that resulted from a serious crisis in a country threatened with economic collapse. The same change, together with the fears of the bourgeoisie, also explains the move towards a policy of so-called neutralism and independence in foreign affairs. The result was 'Finlandisation' at the hands of Germany. The Communists became outlaws in the 'real' Belgium of the bourgeoisie.

The campaign of May 1940 and the occupation, could not alter the balance of power. On the contrary, the climate of 1940 and early 1941 was extremely reactionary and led some people to believe that a 'new order' was about to emerge in Belgium. Their hopes were to be disappointed. By the summer of 1941, the nature of the war had changed. The Belgian establishment had no alternative but to turn to those whose victory now seemed certain. This naturally worked to the advantage of the Communists. For the first time in their existence, they were tolerated and even enjoyed the support of the anti-fascist democratic majority in occupied Belgium.

Anti-communism went into temporary retreat, but after the defeat of

Germany it became even more virulent than it had been before the war. The Cold War led to new heights of anti-communism, both in Belgium and throughout the Western world. Anti-communism became a reflection of the struggle between the two countries which had emerged from the war as superpowers: the Soviet Union and the United States. The new conjuncture gave many anti-communist elements in Belgium a new lease of life and enabled them to return to their old activities. For their part, the Communists left the Government in 1947 and thus returned to the marginal position they had always occupied in Belgian society.

NOTES

1. This article derives from a detailed study of the history of anti-communism in Belgium written in collaboration with Etienne Verhoeyen. Our ambition was to produce a study of Belgian anti-communism during the Cold War, and we hope that it will soon be available in book form. I would like here to express my thanks to my friend Verhoeyen for his invaluable help.
2. For the activities of the Wollweber organisation in Belgium and the Netherlands, see H. Dankaart and R. Van Doorslaer, 'De aktiviteiten van een kommunistische sabotageorganisatie in Antwerpen en Rotterdam. De organisatie Wollweber', *VMT Cahier* 1, Gent 1979.
3. *Oberreischsanwalt beim Volkersgerichtshof, Affaire contre Schokkaert e.a.*, Bundesarchiv Koblenz, R6011, 75.
4. *Internationale scheepssabotage 1936–1940*, Rapport BNV, no. 20, Rapport du Service de Renseignements des Pays-Bas de l'immédiat après-guerre, Cited, H. Dankaart, *Uit het leven van anti-fascisten*, 1982, (unpublished manuscript).
5. It acquired intelligence functions in March 1940, when it became part of the Ministry of Defence.
6. The Police Judiciaire became responsible to the Public Prosecutor in 1919, when Europe was going through a period of serious social agitation.
7. PAB, Pol. Geheim 8, *Sabotageakte auf deutschen Schiffen*, Bonn, Archives Auswärtiges Amt—Wilhelmstrasse, Generalkonsulat Antwerpen.
8. A. de Jonghe, 'De strijd Himmler-Reeder om de benoeming van een HSSPF te Brussel, deel 38', in *Bijdragen tot de geschiedenis van de tweede wereldoorloog*, 5th December 1978. The fifteen countries were Belgium, Bulgaria, Brazil, Denmark, Finland, Greece, Holland, Hungary, Italy, Japan, Poland, Portugal, Switzerland, Uruguay and Yugoslavia.
9. L. de Jongh, *Het Koninkrijk der Nederlanden in de Tweede Wereldoorlog, Deel 1, Voorspel*, The Hague 1969.
10. H. Balthazar, 'Camille Huysmans en Duitsland (1936–1940), in *Bijdragen tot het C. Huysmans-onderzoek*, Antwerp 1971.
11. *Ibid.*
12. *Bulletin de la SEPES*, 8ième année, no. 2, 15th March 1932.
13. The Flemish movement originated as a petty bourgeois reaction against French influence in Flanders. In the nineteenth century French was in effect the dominant language of the Flemish establishment. The movement had members in the traditional Catholic, liberal and socialist parties, but it was not until after the First World War that it developed its own political structures. The maximalist wing of Flemish nationalism, which wanted a 'Groot-Dietsland' (union between the Netherlands and Flanders) was represented by the Vlaamsch Nationaal Verbond (VNV), which was founded in 1933. The VNV developed pro-Nazi

views and enjoyed considerable influence in the second half of the thirties. During the occupation, it became the main collaborationist movement in Flanders.

The right-wing and far Right patriotic Belgian nationalists were obviously opposed to the Flemish separatists who wanted to divide Belgium, even though there were ideological similarities between the two movements.

14. M. José Gotovitch, interview with Carl Peters, 24th March 1972. *Interviews Centre de Recherches et d'Etudes Historiques de la Seconde Guerre Mondiale* (CREHSGM).

15. The Société Générale is so large that its history is virtually that of Belgium itself. It was founded in 1822 and by 1840 its holding company had a controlling interest in most of the country's metallurgical and textile industries. After the First World War, the Société Générale extended its influence to the colonies, gained control over the docks and consolidated its hold on basic industries.

16. 'Biographie de Marcel de Roover par A. Lederer', in *Biographie belge d'outre-mer*, VII, fascicule A, 1972.

17. *Übersicht über die Verwaltung, Polizei, Nachrichtendienste Und Waltanschau-lichen Gegnerkriese in Belgien', n.d.* [1940], Archives GREHSGM.

18. Cf note 11 above.

19. H.E. Tutas, *Nazionalsozialismus und Exil,* Munich and Vienna, 1975.

20. R. Van Doorslaer, 'Les volontaires gantois pour les Brigades Internationales. Motivations du volontariat pour un conflit politico-militaire', *Cahiers d'Histoire de la Seconde Guerre Mondiale,* 6, 1980.

21. R. Van Doorslaer, *De KPB en het Sovjet-Duits Niet-aanvalspakt, 1939–1941,* Brussels 1975.

22. J. Gotovitch and J.G. Libois, *L'An 40. La Belgique occupée,* Brussels 1971; C.H. Valeminck, *Dossier Abbeville. Arrestaties en deportaties in mei 1940,* Louvain 1977.

23. A secretary-general was the highest official in the ministerial administration. In time of war he could replace a minister and had extensive legislative and executive power.

24. Statement made by Eggert Reeder, 14th November 1948. Van Falkenhausen trial, item 113. Archives CREHSGM. *De Roode Vaan,* 28th November 1945.

25. A. De Jonghe, *op. cit.*

26. *Ibid.*

27. *Die kommunistische Organisation in Belgien (III. Internationale).* The document was found in the archives of the Reichssicherheitshauptamt in Berlin in 1945. Author's archives.

28. *De Roode Van,* 28th November 1945.

29. *Het Vrije Woord,* (the Communist Party's clandestine newspaper for Antwerp), September 1942.

30. Boulogne-Destexhe trial, *La Dernière heure,* 25th September 1946.

31. *Rapport de l'Etat Major de la Gendarmerie du 13 octobre 1941.* Author's archives.

32. Dirk Martin, 'De Duitse "vijfde kolonne" in Belgie 1936–1940', *Revue belge d'histoire contemporaine,* XI, 1980, 1–2.

33. F. Balace, 'Psychologie de l'officier belge face à la défaite: juin 1940–automne 1941', *Actes du Colloque d'histoire militaire belge, 1930–1980,* Musée Royale de l'armée et d'histoire militaire, 1981; J. Gotovitch and J.G. Libois, *op. cit.*

34. F. Balace, *op. cit.*

35. *Carnet des comptes-rendus des séances du commandement de la Légion Belge, séance du lier août 1941.* Archives of the author.

36. G. Bastien, *L'Armée secrète,* Mémoire de fin d'études, Ecole Royale Militaire.

37. J. Gotovitch, 'Introduction à l'étude de la déportation. Le convoi du 22 décembre 1941', *Cahiers d'histoire de la deuxieme guerre mondiale*, I, 1967.
38. *Mémoire de défence rédigé par Armand Tilman dans la prison de St Gilles*, 1948. Author's archives.
39. *Ibid.*

Translated by David Macey

ANTI-COMMUNISM AND THE KOREAN WAR
(1950–1953)

Jon Halliday

1. Introduction

On April 16, 1952 the (London) *Daily Worker* carried a small item about a press conference given in Mexico City by the great Mexican painter, Diego Rivera. His latest painting, *Nightmare of War and Dream of Peace,* commissioned by the government, had just been cut down. Its two themes were the collection of signatures (including by Frida Kahlo) for the Five-Power Peace Pact and the exposure of the atrocities of the Korean War. The painting has since disappeared (it is reportedly in Beijing). Even Picasso's *Massacre in Korea* (1951) is rarely reproduced or mentioned. Rather, the Korean War is 'known', indeed *un*-known, to much of the Western world through *M.A.S.H.* This brilliantly resolves the problem of the nature of the Korean War by keeping almost all Koreans well out of sight, and isolating a few GIs in a tent, leaving them to ruminate about sickness, sex and golf.

In its evasion, *M.A.S.H.* reveals a central truth about the Korean War— that it was not just anti-Communist but so anti-*Korean* that the US and its allies, including Britain, not only could not take in who the enemy really was, but even who their Korean allies were. All Koreans became 'gooks' and very soon US pilots were being given orders to strafe, napalm and bomb *any* grouping of Koreans.[1] In Western history and mythology there has been a double elimination: of Korean Communism and of the Korean revolutionary movement, on the one hand, and of the whole history, culture and society of Korea as a nation. The paradoxical paroxysm of this is that although the US and its allies actually occupied North Korea—the only time the US has ever occupied a Communist country, and the only case of effective 'rollback'—this experience is censored out of existence. There is not a single study on a unique event in post-World War II history: the ousting of an established Communist regime and the occupation of its capital and 90 per cent of its territory.

2. Korea: Unknown but Invaded

It is not possible to prove that if the West had known more about Korea it would have behaved any differently—it might even have behaved worse. But ignorance was a factor in the West's scorn for the interests of the Korean people. At the Cairo Conference in 1943 Britain suggested the fatal formula that Korea should be free and independent 'in due course'. In the end, in spite of efforts by the Russians (who were not in Cairo), Korea got the worst treatment of any nation in the whole world as a result of the Second World War. In spite of the fact that it had had absolutely nothing to do with any attack on the Allies, it was occupied in mid-1945 — North of the 38th Parallel by the Russians, South of the Parallel by the Americans. Like Germany, which was an aggressor nation, it was divided. But it got a much worse administration in the South than did Western Germany—in a sense, Korea (South) got the occupation which Japan deserved, or which was designed for Japan.[2]

Korea, which was one of the oldest nations on earth, with a rich culture, was occupied by Japan from 1910 until 1945 and annexed outright to Japan under an extremely harsh administration. The fact that it was occupied by a non-European power and that both its language and that of the colonising country were known by few in the West contributed to the general ignorance of the country. Very little was published in the West about the resistance to Japanese colonialism. Unfortunately, probably the best known fact about Korea was that many Koreans were deployed as guards by the Japanese in POW camps, where their brutality became legendary. After 1945 very few Western correspondents visited Korea. One of the few to do so was Edgar Snow, who spent New Year 1946 with US troops on the 38th Parallel. In what seems to have been his only article on the trip, a little-known short piece in the *Saturday Evening Post*, Snow opened with an important statement: 'When everything has been said about our occupation of Korea, probably the most significant thing is that we stopped a revolution here.'[3] In fact, unbeknownst to most people in the West, the US had actually overthrown the existing nation-wide Korean regime set up in September 1945 and was backing, arming and often participating in a reign of terror which ultimately broke the left-wing movement in much of the South and drove it either underground, into prison, into the North, or to its graves. Mark Gayn was one of the very few people to witness some of the upheavals in the South under the American occupation, which he ranked, justifiably, with the great peasant rebellions of history.[3a] By the time the Korean War erupted in June 1950 probably about 100,000 people had been massacred or killed in guerrilla fighting in the South.

The North

Ignorance about what was really happening in the South, as well as of the history of Korea (including of Korea's lack of responsibility for war against the Allies) was combined with an equally total ignorance of what was happening in the Northern half of the country. Unfortunately, in both cases it was not 'pure' ignorance: lack of knowledge, as often, was fused with false knowledge, prejudice and outright lies.

There have been two major problems for the world left as regards the North Korean regime. First, the nature of the Soviet occupation of the North (1945–48). Second, the background, credentials and policies of the new Korean administration set up in the North after the Japanese surrender. Both of these need excavating. It is as impossible to understand the Korean War without these as it would be to understand the Vietnam War without knowing anything about the Vietnamese revolutionary movement, the history of Ho Chi Minh, etc. Yet, this is exactly how the Korean War has usually been handled—*even on the left.*[4]

The Soviet occupation of North Korea lasted from August 1945 until September 1948 (formal independence; Soviet troops withdrew by the end of 1948). It was *atypical* compared to Russia's role in Eastern Europe. The Russians recognised the local Korean organisations, the People's Committees, and, more surprisingly, accepted a highly decentralised administration and a broad political coalition in the North during the early months. There was *personal* indiscipline in the early months, but no looting of plant and equipment, as there was in Northeast China. On the contrary, the Russians rapidly set about making a major effort to rehabilitate the economy and promoted not just agricultural revival, but renewed industrialisation and high growth.[5] As Cumings sums up in a striking formulation: the Soviet people were disliked but their policies were popular; with the Americans it was the other way round.

Dispute about the nature of the Soviet occupation is inextricably linked to controversy (and ignorance) about the history of the Korean revolutionary movement and the credentials of Kim Il Sung.[6] The main specific of the Korean revolutionary movement is that it had been based mainly *outside* Korea, chiefly among the Korean diaspora in Northeast China, and was at its strongest not in the period immediately preceding liberation (as in Yugoslavia and Albania), but in the late 1930s. Kim was an important guerrilla leader in Northeast China in the 1930s, but seems to have had to lie low (perhaps at Stalin's behest) during the early 1940s in the Soviet Far East. He was by no means, as Seoul and many Western sources still claim, an unknown fraud. Neither was he, as official hagiography claims, the undisputed national leader, much less, as Pyongyang often outrageously suggests, did he lead the liberation of his country. Northern Korea was freed by the Soviet Red Army.

However, under the umbrella of a generally 'hands off' Soviet administration, the new Korean administration in the North set about from early 1946 implementing a series of radical reforms (Land Reform, Equality of the Sexes, etc.) which are demonstrably Korean and there is solid documentary evidence to show that from at least mid-1946 Kim established his own 'Korea-first' line.

The result was not simply the social and economic transformation of the North, but a further boost to the *national* credentials of Kim and the

Korean radical movement. The Korean Communist movement, although divided in the diaspora, had solid credentials, widely recognised, as the force which had consistently fought the Japanese. Although it did not actually liberate Korea, it did immediately thereafter demonstrate its superior claim to represent the nation in several indisputable ways. First, in its energetic elimination of Japanese colonialism (seizure of all Japanese property immediately and punishment of collaborators); second, land reform ('land to the tiller' reform in March 1946—the fastest and most peaceful land reform in Asia, and probably in any socialist country ever); third, formal equality for women (July 1946)—leading to some real advances—within what had been a very traditional patriarchal society;[7] and, last but not least, on policy for a united and independent Korea.

The upshot was a tremendous surge of support throughout the whole of Korea in favour of the North. Cumings has noted that some 350,000–370,000 Koreans in Japan (many originally from the South) chose to return to the North—'probably the largest group of voluntary emigrés to a socialist country on record' (to be followed by many more later).[8] A dispatch to the *New York Post* from Seoul on November 20, 1945 stated: 'it is noteworthy that, whereas a constant stream of Koreans moves south across the border, an even larger stream wends its way slowly into the Russian zone'.[9]

A further strong sign of the North's popularity was the 'demonstration effect' of the reforms in the North.[10] The Americans were also worried that the Russians, in their first occupation-cum-liberation of a Third World country, might come off better than America and that Soviet tutelage might seem more appealing than American to the Third World.

The South

The other side of the coin was what was happening in South Korea. There the US refused to recognise the People's Committees and even, initially, deployed Japanese troops against the Korean patriotic movement (far worse than similar actions in Indochina and Indonesia, given the length and harshness of Japanese colonial rule in Korea). In October 1945 the aged conservative politician, Syngman Rhee returned to Korea. Rhee had been in exile in the USA for 34 years (much more out of touch with his country and much more controlled by his mentors than Kim Il Sung who got called a Russian 'puppet' after fighting the Japanese). Not all is yet clear about Rhee's return, but it seems he returned against the wishes of the State Department, probably with the support of MacArthur and the deputy of the OSS, M. Preston Goodfellow.[11] Rhee himself had not collaborated with the Japanese, and he had a reputation as a well-known old Nationalist. The regime which he soon presided over, however, was made up largely of two groups: former collaborators with the Japanese, especially in the key sectors, army and police; and right-wing American advisers like Goodfellow who in private looked forward to being able to throw the left into 'concentration camps'.[12] Rhee was not only cantankerous, but incipiently senile. He set about eliminating the organized left—and much of the centre and even right-wing opposition (his main Nationalist rival, Kim Koo was assassinated by an army officer in 1948; the main centre-left leader, Yo Un-hyong, was assassinated in July 1947 in broad daylight on a Seoul street in sight of a police box).

Furthermore, the Rhee regime had no policy for economic recovery (it was, in many ways, a 're-tread' of the Yi regime which ruled Korea for five centuries before the Japanese occuaption). There were very large peasant uprisings throughout the South, particularly in 1946.

By 1947, with the People's Committees virtually smashed in the South, but with Rhee and the US unable to establish a viable regime, the US called in the United Nations to try to legitimize the Rhee government, at least in the South—and, if possible, endorse it for the North, too. The history of this incredible fraud has been described elsewhere.[13] The essential points are two. First, the separate election in the South was opposed by every single political leader in the whole of Korea except Rhee and it is a fair estimate that at least 80 per cent of the organized political forces opposed it; all the main Southern leaders, including the very conservative Kim Koo and Kimm Kiu-sic, travelled to the North for two nation-wide concerences to try to stave off the division of their country.[14] (It is difficult to think of such an event in Germany in 1948!) Second, the UN, leaving aside its political will and bias, never had the personnel or the resources to be adequately informed about what was actually happening in the South, and particularly was quite incapable of checking the 1948 election.

It was on the basis of this unilateral move that the Republic of Korea (ROK) was set up, based on Seoul, in August 1948, with Rhee as President. It claimed jurisdiction over the whole nation.

In that same month another poll took place. The North claims that this was a nation-wide election (clandestine in the South) in which 77.52 per cent of the Southern electorate (99.97 per cent in the North) took part—and it is on this poll that the regime established in Pyongyang in September 1948, the Democratic People's Republic of Korea (DPRK), bases its claim to represent the entire nation.[15]

Contrary to Western claims then and now, some sort of poll did indeed take place in some areas of the South, as well as in the North. But Merrill is surely correct to state that DPRK claims are exaggerated.[16] The trouble with the DPRK's claim is that it is inherently unverifiable. The claim simply is not and cannot be recognised widely, either within Korea or abroad. The DPRK has a strong claim to represent the nation, but not on narrow legalistic (and unprovable) criteria. The specific *political* confusion which prevailed on the left (except in the 'down-the-line' Communist movement) when the Korean War erupted in June 1950 is partly explicable by the linked phenomena of: *a*) UN cover for the ROK and *b*) the 'failure'/inability of the DPRK to establish its credentials as not simply a legitimate government for the Northern half of Korea, but as the organised force which had the right, or the best claim to represent the whole Korean nation. In turn, the reasons for this relate to a combination of: 1) 'genuine' ignorance about Korea and its revolutionary movement; 2) assimilation (both thinking and unthinking) of Kim to Stalin and of the DPRK to the USSR: very few in the West could imagine either that Kim was independent of Russia, or that he could be independent in alliance with Russia. The left in the West could locate the DPRK and Korean Workers' [Communist] Party, the KWP neither in their local Korean context nor in their international context.

3. *The Background and Start of the War*
When Gertrude Stein was dying she is reported to have raised herself on her cushions and asked those gathered round her bed: 'What is the answer?' After she had fallen back and all thought she was gone, she lifted herself up once more and said: 'What is the question?', whereupon she died. It is an extraordinary fact that the main question asked about the Korean War is: 'Who started it?' Even on the left, this is usually considered the central issue. But this is a question never asked, for example, about the Vietnam War. The distance is easily demarcated by simply posing the question: 'Who started the Vietnam War?'

The Korean War was essentially a civil war, *delayed* by foreign intervention (in 1945) further complicated by the foreign-imposed division of the country and thus, in the form it took, ultimately caused by that foreign intervention. Without US (and Russian) occupation and division, the left would easily have taken over the whole of Korea, just as it did in Yugoslavia. South Korea was not invaded by North Korea in June 1950, it was invaded by US imperialism in 1945.

The background to the war can be traced to the combination of dual occupation and the establishment of two separate regimes, each claiming jurisdiction over the whole nation. While the USA and USSR formally occupied their respective halves, the uncompleted civil struggle was partly held at bay—partly by repression, and partly by a left/right redistribution into North and South, respectively. Inter alia, of course, this politico-geographic redistribution meant that both regimes were made up of people from both North and South Korea (this was especially important in the case of the ROK army, which was staffed and headed almost entirely by former collaborators with the Japanese, many of them refugees from the North eager to oust the Pyongyang government).

After the proclamation of the DPRK on September 9, 1948, the USSR announced that it would withdraw its armed forces by the end of 1948, which it did. The USA withdrew its forces by mid-1949, leaving behind a substantial advisory group, KMAG.[17]

The proximate background to the war involves two major aspects both of which have been grossly undervalued in the conventional literature. The first is the state of extreme dissension and revolt inside the ROK, including within the ROK state, between its founding in mid-1948 and June 25, 1950. The second is the very heavy cross-border fighting which went on, particularly from mid-1949.

According to the official US military history of the war, the ROK Army 'disintegrated' immediately after June 25, 1950.[18] One reason it did so was that both it and the ROK state had been in a state of some disintegration for quite some time. Immediately after the ROK was set up, the new army was almost torn apart by a series of major mutinies, during which rebel troops seized and held major cities for up to one week. Unknown scores of officers were executed; and major purges carried out. In May 1949 two battalions of troops went over to the DPRK, with their officers.[19] And one navy ship mutinied and went over to the DPRK.

At the same time, a fairly extensive guerrilla movement sprang up, particularly in the mountain areas and on Cheju Island, off the South coast. There were countless skirmishes and killings of the much-hated Rhee police. The US–Rhee campaign against the guerrillas on Cheju Island has been called by Cumings 'one of the most brutal, sustained, and intensive counterinsurgency campaigns in postwar Asia'.[20] Probably about one hundred thousand people were killed in fighting and massacres inside South Korea before the Korean War even began. It may also be noted that this level of violence contrasts markedly with the very low use of violence among Koreans themselves at the time of liberation from the Japanese.

At the top, Rhee's own regime was becoming increasingly isolated. The US Congress began to cut off funds. And in (rigged) elections in May 1950 Rhee and his supporters won only a small minority of the seats in the National Assembly. Once again, Rhee's reaction was violence. His own police force raided the Assembly and arrested 22 Assemblymen: 16 of them received smashed skulls, ribs or broken eardrums. By June 1950, the Rhee regime was reeling.[21]

Throughout this period there were skirmishes around the 38th Parallel. From about mid-1949 these began to escalate. Both the size and the causes of these clashes have been seriously understated in the West. In August 1949 the head of KMAG, Gen. William Roberts, wrote to a friend, Gen. Bolté, about these clashes: 'Each was in our opinion brought on by the presence of a small South Korean salient north of the parallel. Each was characterized by the [ROKA] CO's screaming "invasion, reinforce, ammo!". . . The South Koreans wish to invade the North. . . Most incidents on the parallel are due to needling by opposing local forces.

Both North and South are at fault. No attacks by the North have ever been in serious proportions.'[22] The former Chief of the ROK Navy General Staff, Rear Admiral Lee Young-woon, told me that in August 1949 he launched a totally unprovoked assault on the DPRK Navy at Monggumppo on the orders of Rhee's Minister of Defence, Shin Sin-mo. 'You have to take into account things like that,' Admiral Lee said. Likewise, the former ROK intelligence Brigadier General Choi Duk Shin, told me: 'The first thing you have to remember is that most leaders of the South Korean Army were refugees from the North and hated communism. They had already [i.e., before June 25, 1950] invaded the North several times to a depth of 3–4 miles. . . The fact is that the high-ranking officers in the South needed a war.'[23]

The key question is thus not at all 'Who fired the first shot on the morning of June 25?' The real question is: why did the cross-border fighting erupt *at that moment* into full-scale fighting and what were the political and military factors which decided the DPRK to cross the Parallel in force and push into the South?

The answer lies in a complex combination of domestic and international factors. Conventional Western analyses over-emphasise the international factors at the expense of the local ones and, of course, emphasise Communist conspiracy at the expense of US and right-wing North Pacific intrigues. But the key and simple fact is that Korea was over-ripe for revolution, which the US had blocked in the South. The DPRK's case does not rest on the size of a putative cross-border incursion by the ROK Army on the morning of June 25, but on its credentials to represent the nation (which is the criterion accepted by all parties, in effect).

My own, tentative, view is that the DPRK took a *political* decision, on rather short notice, *on its own,* to cross the Parallel and detonate the collapse of the Rhee regime, in the hope that this could be accomplished without or before a US intervention. This gamble failed—although it very nearly paid off. The Rhee regime did disintegrate well ahead of the arrival of the People's Army (KPA). The population of the South, on the whole, seems to have welcomed liberation from Rhee.[24] The KPA was able to arm large numbers of the local population. But the US was able to hold onto a corner of Southeast Korea, the Pusan Perimeter, and stage a comeback with the Inchon landing in September 1950.

What is most unclear is the role of Rhee and his personal allies in all this. Richard Nixon has written, long after the event, that June 25 was 'a miscalcualtion by them, based upon a misrepresentation by us'.[25] There was feinting, thrusting and skirmishing along the Parallel, with large-scale artillery battles and in August 1949 Admiral Lee's attempt to sink the entire DPRK fleet.

There are two arguments against the DPRK/world communist line that the war was started by Rhee. One is that the ROK army and state apparatus manifestly collapsed immediately after June 25, 1950, and Rhee was almost out of his job and out of Korea for good. The second is that although the US got into the war quite quickly, it equally manifestly was not geared up for an instant assault on the DPRK on June 25, 1950. Both of these arguments have to be tackled.

As for the first one: it does not mean anything at all that the ROK collapsed, except to demonstrate that it was in a rotten condition. If one takes a longer time perspective, it is clear that although Rhee retreated at the beginning, the Korean War saved him. Without it he was finished, as some senior US officials have acknowledged.

No one can dispute the documented historical record that Rhee and his top officials wanted to invade the North, were planning for this and were trying to draw the US in. This is unequivocally on the public record. There are at least two major possibilities along these lines. One is that Rhee, in June 1950, knew, or thought, that US support was forthcoming. The other is that he thought it *might* be, and made a unilateral move *in order* to force the US to come in, even if his initial move did not 'succeed' (in the sense of making a major advance into the North). Since most Western sources agree that the only thing that was holding Rhee back before June 25, 1950, was lack of US support at the top for an invasion of the North, it is necessary to see if anything changed on this front in mid-1950.

The DPRK has made much of a visit by John Foster Dulles to South Korea in mid-June 1950. Dulles visited the 38th Parallel, made a speech to the National Assembly, and met privately with Rhee. On the record, he gave very strong—*and unqualified*—support to Rhee, without any disclaimer about Rhee's stated intentions to invade the North. The DPRK has claimed, with some documentary support, that Dulles went further.[26] These claims have been generally dismissed in the West.

But there is strong evidence that the DPRK was correct to read the Dulles visit as a major shift in US policy. MacArthur actually states in his memoirs that Dulles 'apparently *reversed*' US policy on the question of the commitment to Rhee—exactly one week before the war started.[27] Not enough attention has been paid to the possibility that Rhee interpreted Dulles' statements to mean that he could force US backing by starting a war—or even that he got such backing in advance, perhaps from a *part* of the US regime. This would make sense of Rhee attacking and being hurled back (another possibility, of course, is that he was so demented that he genuinely expected the DPRK to collapse). Western sources have, on the whole, disgracefully underestimated, or even concealed, Rhee's constant bellicosity in trying to invade the DPRK before June 1950, in trying to prevent the war being brought to an end in 1953 and in trying to get US backing to start the war up again in 1953-54.

There is another possibility: that the DPRK, too, read the Dulles pronouncements as meaning that the US would now give a much firmer commitment to Rhee and that therefore *either* he might attack and, if so, the US would come in once it was ready (i.e., very soon, but perhaps not immediately); *or,* that the DPRK's hopes of Rhee being toppled by domestic opposition now only had a very limited time-span. One has to make sense of the fact that the KPA moved, according to US intelligence, on June 25 less than half mobilised—not a normal way to start an offensive war. The US ambassador to Seoul, John Muccio, stated, long after the event: 'I felt that if the Communists were anywhere near as intelligent as we credited them with being, they would not use force because the South had many weaknesses.'[28]

The lack of preparedness of the US can be interpreted in different ways. Several leading US figures have stated that they welcomed the Korean War. US Secretary of State Dean Acheson acknowledged afterwards that 'Korea came along and saved us'.[29] Gen. Van Fleet, commander of the 8th Army, said that 'Korea has been a blessing. There had to be a Korea either here or some place in the world.'[30] So one cannot dismiss the idea that *some* American officials wanted *a* war. The fact that the US was not geared up for an instant counter-attack in Korea (though it was geared up for both instant *political* action and instant military retaliation) is not inconsistent with the possibility that a *part* of the US apparatus looked favourably on a war in Korea.

Anti-communism naturally took the form not merely of attributing malign intentions to the DPRK, but of designating Kim Il Sung as a Russian 'puppet'. This was, after all, the time when Dean Rusk, the man who had actually drawn the line through the middle of Korea in 1945, was calling the People's Republic of China 'a Slavic Manchukuo'. The idea that the DPRK could be taken seriously, that it had its own history and revolutionary experience, that Kim might be a 'Tito', was rarely voiced. Least of all was it stated that Kim and the KPA (Korean People's Army) had much closer ties with China than with Russia, and that his relations with Stalin had historically been rather difficult.

Khrushchev's memoirs, published in the West as *Khrushchev Remembers,* in 1970–71 provide an excellent example of the complexity of the problem of using and evaluating evidence. These contain a very interesting chapter on the Korean War (Vol. I, Part 2, ch. 11). Khrushchev's chapter has been consistently deployed—in a wholly uncritical way—when it not only badly needs evaluation, *but after this evaluation has actually been carried out and it has been found wanting:* not in the sense of whether or not the material is authentic, but as to whether or not the published text reproduces accurately what Khrushchev said on the tapes. John Merrill has shown that this is not the case.[31]

The published version unequivocally describes two visits to Moscow by Kim Il Sung before the Korean War, from which it has been widely concluded that Kim planned the war with Stalin. But where the published text confidently states: 'Kim went home and then returned to Moscow when he had everything worked out' (394), the full transcript reads: 'In my opinion, either the date of his return was set, or he was to inform us as soon as he finished preparing all his ideas. Then, I don't remember in which month *or year* [my italics—JH] Kim Il-sung came and related his plan to Stalin.'

Not even US intelligence picked up any sign of a second visit by Kim, and there is no independent confirmation of it. Reliance on Khrushchev as proof that Kim returned to Moscow to co-ordinate with Stalin the plan for launching the war is severely undermined by the fact that Khrushchev cannot date Kim's *first* visit. Published text: 'About. . . the end of 1949, Kim Il-sung arrived. . . to hold consultations with Stalin.' (393) (In fact, this visit was in March 1949, a full 15 months before the Korean War broke out.) But on the tapes, Khrushchev cannot even get the year right: 'I don't remember which year this corresponds to, but in my opinion, it seems, it was 1950. . .'

So what the original tape amounts to is that Khrushchev gets the *confirmed* visit by Kim out by a whole year (when timing is rather important) and cannot place the alleged second visit to any year at all. Khrushchev *may* be right. But it hardly seems good enough evidence on which to be adamant.

Yet Khrushchev's memoirs in the published version continue to be wheeled out, with no hint of criticism, or even enquiry.

The other text most often cited to buttress the claim that the North planned and executed the start of the war is an article in *Life* by Pawel Monat, usually referred to as 'Polish military attaché in North Korea during the Korean War'. This he was. But Monat did not actually reach Korea until July 1952. He does have an account of how the war started— but it is entirely second-hand, rather long after the event—and suspiciously pat. Most references to his version cite only an article in *Life,* rarely the detailed version in his book, *Spy in the U.S.*[32] Once again, the context of the evidence needs to be taken into account, and the context is a defection to the US.

The standard Western version—that the Russians detonated and sustained the war—also takes a knock from an unexpected source recently released in the British archives: Douglas MacArthur himself.[33] In a report dated November 21, 1950, James (now Sir James) Plimsoll reports that MacArthur had told him that: 'No evidence had been found of any close connection between the Soviet Union and the North Korean aggression. The only possible link was the Russian equipment being used. . .' MacArthur referred to the 'accidental' bombing of the Soviet Union—for which Russia even declined compensation. Nor did the Soviet Union complain when the US hit a power plant in Northeast Korea that supplied the Soviet Far East and cut off the power. Plimsoll goes on: '7. MacArthur thought that, if it had really inspired the North Korean aggression, the

Soviet Union would not have abandoned the North Koreans so completely, giving them no assistance whatever. This would have been the greatest betrayal in history since Judas accepted his thirty pieces of silver.'

The Western line also fails to provide any rational explanation for the behaviour of the USSR at the UN (unless the ultra-Machiavellian thesis that Stalin wanted Kim to stew in his own juice is true, which I doubt). The Russians were absent over the question of recognition of the People's Republic of China. But it seems inconceivable—even as a deep feint—that they would have sustained this stance had they known war was about to erupt.

As a coda to the UN saga, it is worth noting how permeated the entire UN structure then was by anti-Communism and anti-Communists. Two-thirds of the entire UN headquarters staff were American citizens, tightly controlled by FBI screening and subjected to close anti-Communist surveillance.[34] The UN took many of its key decisions on very inadequate information, frequently manipulated by the Secretary General, Trygve Lie, and US officials. Information reaching the UN sometimes came from UN staff in Korea, but some was based on unverified reports by provenly unreliable or downright lying sources like Syngman Rhee, his Minister of Defence and ROK Army officers.

When the war broke out the UN, for the first time in its history, rejected the fundamental principle of hearing both sides of the story. The DPRK was not allowed to present its case. In autumn 1950 the DPRK sent the UN photostatic copies of materials captured in Seoul to back up its case. Some of these documents, which demonstrate that Rhee was planning to invade the North, were authenticated by their authors or recipients (including one US embassy official and one close (US) adviser to Rhee). To my knowledge, none has been *dis*owned by any living first-hand witness. These documents reached the UN and were apparently made available for consultation in early November 1950. They subsequently disappeared.[35]

Quite apart from its shabby treatment of the DPRK, the UN as a body at no time went to the root of the problem, which is that it itself, via US manipulation, had helped to create and give legitimacy to an unrepresentative regime which was itself a threat to peace in Korea and throughout the world. The rather sober complaints of the DPRK on this score before June 1950 were repeatedly brushed aside.

4. The Political Character of the War
Anti-Communism leapt into action in the West to empty the Korean War of all its essential features: rather than a civil war, it was made part of the Cold War; rather than a war with manifest local roots, it was attributed to the hand of the Kremlin and the counterpart of the demotion of the Korean revolutionary movement was the downplaying of the belligerency

of Rhee; rather than a war which had many features of a war of liberation from a hated tyrant, it was presented as an unjustified invasion which visited misery and massacre on the population of the South.

Most of the time it was genuinely impossible or very difficult for an ordinary citizen to find out what the truth was. The US imposed very tight censorship on correspondents in Korea. The newspaper proprietors did the same in England: James Cameron resigned from *Picture Post* over the blocking of his reporting on Rhee's atrocities; Rene Cutforth had his reports on napalm suppressed by the BBC.[36] In the USA Senators McCarran and McCarthy went after domestic dissidents in a well-known witchhunt, which had far more to do with Korea than has generally been recognised (for example, the first charge against Owen Lattimore was connected with Korea).[37]

Anti-communism and a refusal to look at Korean society both played a big role in the treatment of the two determining (and linked) episodes of the war: the occupation/liberation of the South by the KPA and the occupation of the North by the US/UN/Rhee forces.

Reunification I (June–September 1950)
The standard Western version is that the KPA got a hostile reception; that the North imposed an alien Communist occupation regime; and that extensive massacres were carried out.

The DPRK version is that the KPA got a warm welcome; that the People's Committees were re-activated and that the new regime was based largely on Southern Communists; that the new regime armed large numbers of the Southern population; that land reform, equality for women and other reforms were enacted; and that the Rhee regime carried out extensive massacres in the South both immediately ahead of the KPA, in the rear areas and in the areas which Rhee reoccupied immediately after the KPA was driven out in September 1950.[38] But the official DPRK line (since August 1953) is that the new regime based on the People's Committee also committed some murders and atrocities in June–September 1950.[39]

There is not space here to disentangle and weigh all the conflicting evidence on a comprehensive basis. But the main points are:

a) the KPA *was* given a warm welcome; the strongest evidence for this is in the memoirs of US Gen. Dean.[40]

b) The new regime *was* based on the local People's Committee which, although severely reduced by Rhee's repression, had a better claim to be popularly representative than any other bodies.

c) The KPA did arm and recruit very large numbers of the local population; estimates vary between 400–500,000.[41] Some Western critics suggest these were press-ganged. Again, the evidence of Gen. Dean, who can hardly be accused of bias in this direction, contradicts this interpretation.

d) The new regime did carry out very extensive reforms. Its claims to have enacted a major land reform in the short period of liberation have generally been dismissed or ignored. But in 1973 a clearly authorised volume was published in South Korea which reproduces the land reforms figures with only the mildest disclaimer, viz., that there were 'some exaggerated figures'.[42]

e) Strong, if indirect, evidence for support in the South for the new administration comes from the number of people killed by Rhee when he reoccupied the South; Gregory Henderson, a US diplomat who was there at the time, has written that 'probably over 100,000' people were killed without trial in the South immediately after the re-establishment of the Rhee regime in autumn 1950.[43]

Only three Western correspondents, to my knowledge, were personally present at any point during the KPA occupation of the South: Philip Deane of the (London) *Observer* and Maurice Chanteloup of AFP, who witnessed the advent of the KPA and then were taken off to the North as prisoners in July 1950; and the British correspondent, Alan Winnington, of the (London) *Daily Worker*. Winnington states that the ROK killed between 200,000 and 400,000 people as Rhee retreated before the KPA.[44] This claim was widely derided or ignored in the West. But there is evidence to indicate that it merits re-examination. Particularly striking is the testimony of Philip Deane which, although second-hand, is impressive because it provides a rare and explicit bridge over the 'information gap' between conflicting versions. Deane recounts being told by Winnington of a massacre by Rhee's police at Taejon—and just not believing it. A few weeks later, Deane was told about the same incident by a French missionary, Fr. Cadars. Cadars had witnessed with his own eyes the ROK police shooting 1,700 people in one incident near Taejon—with American officers watching.[45] ROK Admiral Lee told me that Rhee had systematically had political prisoners executed on the way South, and attempted to pin these deaths on the KPA and/or the local Communists.[46] Reporters like James Cameron and René Cutforth witnessed repeated, systematic brutality by Rhee's police. René Cutforth described the activity of Rhee's forces (in a later period) as 'plenty of massacres, not much fighting'.[47] British Foreign Office files record numerous atrocities by Rhee's forces in the South. Since Rhee (and the US) officially endorsed killing *anyone* on the grounds of being *suspected* of 'Communism', and since Rhee showed such a flagrant disregard for the lives of his own people,[48] is Winnington's version so implausible after all?

Of course, the case does not rest simply on who did more and worse atrocities. There is solid evidence to show that the local Communists executed numbers of people without trial, mainly in two moments: initially on liberation—mainly police and some landlords; and then right at the end when the People's Committee seems to have panicked after the Inchon landing in September 1950. But, quite apart from any political or moral judgment on who was executed and for what, there are two points worth making.[49] First, it seems out of the question that the Communists killed anything like as many people as the Rhee regime—and quite unfounded allegations to this effect by the British government were and are most dishonest. Secondly, in some ways more important, the systematic cruelty and what Cutforth called the 'horrible brutality' of Rhee's police was quite unparalleled. They used torture routinely, plus death by crucifixion and other gruesome means.[50]

A final—and, to me impressive—piece of evidence about the behaviour of the short-lived left-wing regime, at least in Seoul, comes from the official US Air Force study of Seoul under Communist occupation, *The Reds Take A City*. This is *the* official US study of the occupation of Seoul. It is also the source for much later speculation. In this book of *selected first-hand* accounts of Communist rule, there is not one single eye-witness to an atrocity by the Communists. There is one account of a People's Court, by one Kun-ho Lee, described as 'the author of several widely known volumes on Korean law'.[51] According to Lee, the People's Court 'In effect. . . massacred innocent people.' How does he know? Because he heard this from his 'older aunt' (who, he says, was an eye-witness). Surely, one can ask for better than this in a book of selected first-hand accounts compiled only a few months after the alleged events. The absence of any direct evidence, when it is manifest from the book that it would be there if it could have been found, is most convincing of all to me.

Reunification II (October–December 1950)
Between October 1950 and December 1950 the US, with the aid of Commonwealth (including British) and Turkish troops, occupied 90 per cent of North Korea (territory and population).

For cosmetic reasons, the US decided it would be good if ROK troops led the advance into the North. De facto, the new administration was a US military occupation regime, under which, and under whose authority (sometimes explicit and conscious, sometimes implicit and ignorant, but none the less thereby responsible), there operated a vast rag bag of Rhee police, ROK Army, youth groups, gangs of thugs, and old landlords. Once again, there is little or no agreement about what actually happened. But unlike with the 3-month occupation of the South, there are not really two opposing versions of events. There is one version—and one silence. The DPRK version is that (while the KPA staged a well-organized retreat) the US–Rhee forces carried out extensive massacres, especially of Party cadres, but also of ordinary civilians, women and children.[52] The West says nothing at all about its one and only successful case of rollback. To my knowledge, there is not even a detailed attempt to refute the DPRK version.

The DPRK says 'hundreds of thousands'[53] of people were killed but has never given detailed and comprehensive figures for deaths during the occupation of the North. Soviet figures show that the North lost well over 1 million people between 1949 and 1953.[54] The area which apparently had the highest proportion of people massacred was Sinchon County in South Hwanghae Province, where 35,383 people out of 142,788 reportedly were killed.[55]

The DPRK does not present overall and comprehensive figures. Its case is also weakened by failing to differentiate between actions attributed to US (and other UN) forces, on the one hand, and those of Rhee troops, police and irregulars, on the other, and between responsibility for these actions.

But the DPRK allegations are a lot stronger than is generally acknowledged in the West. Although it is not possible to be sure exactly what happened everywhere, it seems probable that the core of the accusations is true—viz., that the US and Rhee forces slaughtered very large numbers of people during their occupation of the North.

Not only are there the detailed accusations made by the DPRK regime, plus some physical evidence (which is not conclusive, and could be faked); there are also reports of visiting foreign delegations, especially those of the International Federation of Democratic Women in 1951 and the International Association of Democratic Lawyers in 1952, plus those of Wilfred Burchett and Alan Winnington.[56] The dismissal of *all* this evidence under the rubric of anti-communism is not convincing. Least of all when allegations of killings are made by first-hand witnesses like Julian Tunstall. Even an Australian Catholic priest who was a prisoner in the North at the time gives credence to these allegations (in regard to one specific locale where 600 people were reported massacred).[57] British Foreign Office files confirm that major atrocities took place.

It is also necessary to set all this in context, just as with My Lai. First of all, there was the stated intention of Rhee to exterminate Communism and Commun*ists,* even those 'suspected' of Communism, and the verified *active* campaign of his police and army to find suspects; since this was done on a vast scale in the South, it would be illogical to assume it was not done in the North, where many people could reasonably be supposed to be Communists. Second, there was the manifest contempt for Korean life on the part of the US troops, along with orders to kill any potential 'enemy'. The ground troops, too, were operating under a canopy of airborne destruction which created a context of brutalization. By the time the UN forces got into the DPRK, the US had plastered the North with millions of gallons of napalm and other explosives and within five months of the war starting the US officially grounded its bomber force—because there were no more targets to hit (something which never happened in

Vietnam)[58] Quite unsympathetic US military leaders often referred to what had been done in Korea in terms of the worst slaughter ever known.[59] UN ground forces systematically burnt down entire villages and towns, especially on the retreat in late 1950.[60]

'Don't Rock the Boat'

The files recently opened in Britain reveal a shameful performance by the government, Labour as well as Conservative. Most startling is the cabinet discussion over whether or not to prosecute the *Daily Worker—for treason*—for publishing Alan Winnington's pamphlet, *I Saw the Truth in Korea* (which simply exposed crimes by Rhee's government, none of which had been disproved). There seems to be only one reason the cabinet decided not to prosecute—because if the verdict was 'guilty' there was only one sentence possible: death, which was mandatory.[61]

The entire drift of government policy, though by no means nearly as menacing as in the USA, was to try to shut everyone up. One emblematic case involved the United Nations Association (of Britain), which wanted to print in *United Nations News* of January 1951 James Cameron's story on atrocities (by Rhee) which had been banned from *Picture Post* and then leaked to the *Daily Worker*. Mr Judd of *UN News* approached Sir Gladwyn Jebb (then British ambassador to the UN) to write a reply. An internal memo from the Foreign Office dated November 23, 1950, states: 'Mr Judd has a mania for writing to high-ups at the slightest provocation.' But Gladwyn Jebb was no fool. He wisely declined, because, as he wrote to Sir Pierson Dixon at the Foreign Office: 'It would be by no means easy to draft anything which would appear convincing. . .' Dixon concludes: 'I think that Judd is being very misguided in this affair. . . This is only one of several cases where the United Nations Association in this country has got out of step recently.'[62]

When local branches of the United Nations Association, and trade union branches, write to the government about Rhee's atrocities, the Foreign office tries to damp everything down, counselling against publication of the correspondence 'as otherwise all the other branches of the United Nations Association will be tempted to start up correspondence with the F.O. We may then find many of our letters to the branches being published. . .

'The best way to prevent correspondence with the branches seems to be to refer them to their head office.'

When the Labour Party branch at Newcastle-under-Lyme passed a resolution condemning Rhee's brutalities, the government replied by saying that Britain was not fighting for the Rhee regime, but to resist aggression. In other cases it fobs off complaints by saying that it will continue to pay attention to the issue (although in at least one case, the Foreign Office explicitly cut this assurance out of a draft reply to questions in the Commons).

Another technique, despicable in its callousness, was to say 'so what?' On November 7, 1950 the *Daily Mirror* carried a detailed report from its correspondent Don Greenlees describing appalling beatings, people being bashed with rifle butts and executions of women and men. George Thomas (now Lord Tonypandy) was planning to ask a question about this on November 13. The Foreign Office briefing for the minister in the Commons reads: 'If attention is called to the *Daily Mirror* report of the 7th November it might be said that it contains nothing substantially different from earlier reports.'

When Mr Judd wrote to Ernest Bevin, the Foreign Secretary, about Britain and the United Nations doing something about Rhee's behaviour, the Foreign Office ducked out once again and wrote Judd that: 'The United Nations Commission has. . . no legal power. . . to take over the conduct of affairs in the territory already administered by the Government of the Republic.' All the time the government knew of Rhee's brutality. 'It is unfortunate that brutalities have been committed by the South Koreans and that the Administration has at times attempted to impose its will in a manner which has laid it open to some criticism from successive United Nations commissions.' Earlier a covering letter from Britain's man in Korea, Alec Adams, to the Foreign Office spelled things out a bit more: '. . . even by reading between the lines you probably do not guess at the reprisals, police brutality, summary methods, etc. which arise probably nearly as much among the S. Koreans as among the Northern 'red' ones.'[63] The *Times* reported: 'An officer of a United Nations investigation team said that reprisals are as numerous as reports (sic) of Communist atrocities. Most non-Korean members of the United Nations forces are aware of this. . .' (Oct. 25, 1950).

But the essence of the British government position—viz. to be deaf and dumb about the Rhee regime (with a few token enquiries)—is perhaps best summed up by their treatment of a problem in December 1950: British troops had witnessed a mass execution by Rhee forces. The report from Seoul[64] to the F.O. is worried: 'As I understand it, considerable feeling was aroused among British troops both because of the callous way in which the executions were carried out and because they mistook two of those shot for boys (they were in fact women. . . wearing trousers). . . 4. Fearing that there would be an incident if British troops were again subjected [!] to the spectacle of mass executions in their vicinity I represented to the United States embassy yesterday the urgent need to dissuade the Korean authorities from running unnecessary risks [!] " [Rhee's forces were rushing through mass executions in case the KPA returned to Seoul—JH] This execution took place on December 15. On December 17th another mass execution took place. But no problem—British (and US) troops were kept away. J.S.H. Shattock at the F.O. writes to Adams in

Seoul: 'The continuing reports of "atrocities" and "political shootings" (quote marks in original) are, as you know, giving us a lot of trouble. . . we are indeed sorry to have to burden you with these requests for information.' A few days later all is well and a F.O. official writes on the report: 'Public interest in the executions seems to have abated and we do not expect much further trouble.'

James Cameron records that when he sent his dossier on Rhee's atrocities to the British delegation at the UN (then headed by Kenneth Younger) nothing happened.[65]

The old British techniques of isolation and malign neglect were skillfully deployed by the government and the press. The most senior former Foreign Office figure who opposed the war, Sir John Pratt, the distinguished China expert (and Boris Karloff's brother) was crudely attacked and ostracized.[66] Emrys Hughes was refused permission to stage an exhibition of photographs of the bombing of Pyong-yang in the House of Commons.[67] Monica Felton, the British delegate on the Women's delegation to the DPRK in 1951 was sacked from her job as Chairman of Stevenage Development Corporation. The press, with the exception of the *Daily Worker,* ignored the IADL report in 1952. And the report of the 1952 International Scientific Commission on bacterial warfare, made up of eminent scientists, including Britain's Joseph Needham, was dismissed without investigation of its claims. The government called its evidence 'pseudo-scientific' and the report itself 'obviously valueless'.[68]

Although Britain did not descend to the excesses of HUAC, McCarran and McCarthy in the USA, the behaviour of the Labour and Conservative governments and the media proprietors constitutes a shabby and shameful episode in British history, with honourable exceptions, such as S.O. Davies (MP for Merthyr Tydfil) and Emrys Hughes among the politicians, and many among the press corps in Korea.

5. *China Enters the War*

China's entry into the Korean War was widely represented in the West as the ultimate proof of both Communist aggression and of the co-ordination of the Communist camp (this in spite of the fact that the allegedly monolithic socialist bloc had 2 countries, both directly affected, fighting, as against 16 on the other side—and much later, too!). It is hard now to reconstruct the mythology of the time, still perhaps best summed up in Dean Rusk's characterisation of the PRC as a 'Slavic Manchukuo'.

The basic Western portrayal of China at the time was made up of the following elements: *a*) China was a Russian puppet; *b*) it flouted the rules of international law, especially in two ways: (i) it intervened in a war in another country without good reason; (ii) it failed to signal its intentions in a conventional ('honourable'/'civilized') manner. The West's position was summed up in the resolution put through the UN on February 1, 1951 which condemned China as an 'aggressor' nation for entering the Korean War. It need hardly be recalled: 1) that US forces had reached the actual border of China before China intervened; 2) that China had good reason to fear that the UN forces might well carry on across the Yalu.[69]

When China did enter the war in late 1950 little effort was expended on trying to understand its real methods, objectives and general behaviour. The first thing lacking was an appreciation of the very deep ties between the Chinese and Korean revolutionary movements, and especially between the two revolutionary armies, the KPA and the PLA (China). Here propaganda about Kim as a Russian puppet perhaps served to blind the perpetrators of the myth. Few paid attention to the fact that very large numbers of Koreans—perhaps as many as 200,000 (in 1949) had fought with the PLA.[70] One of the senior commanders of the KPA, Mu Jong, had fought on the Long March. Kim Il Sung and most of the top officers in the KPA had fought with the Chinese Communists in Manchuria in the 1930s. The Korean forces had played a major role in helping liberate Northeast China—and were known as the Korean Volunteer Army—a name echoed in the title given the Chinese forces in Korea, the Chinese People's Volunteers (CPVs). When China entered the Korean War it stated that this was not simply in self-defence, but also a blood debt it owed the Korean people.

Shortly after they entered Korea, the CPVs helped bring about the what Dean Acheson called 'the worst defeat of U.S. forces since Bull Run', yet were denigrated as 'hordes' (the title of the first 'scholarly' work on the PLA published in the US was *Red China's Fighting Hordes*).[71] Rare were the observers, like René Cutforth, who noted the way the Chinese tried to fight a 'people's war' in extremely difficult circumstances.[72] Last, but not least, anti-Communist venom was poured on the Chinese for their treatment of POWs, when the record shows a much more nuanced picture than was given at the time—and still widely believed now, even if swept under the rug.

6. Refugees and POWs

Around mid-1951 the war more or less stabilised near the 38th Parallel, where it had started. Truce talks began, and dragged on for two years before an Armistice was signed on July 27, 1953 (South Korea refused to sign the Armistice and Rhee vigorously opposed it before it was signed and afterwards).[73] The US dragged out the war in an attempt to try to legitimate its first full-scale counter-revolutionary war against Communism. Having come in on the side of an unpopular autocrat against what was in effect the 'national liberation movement' embodied in the DPRK/KPA, the US had to work hard to try to make it appear that *its* side (Rhee) was popular and the enemy, the DPRK—and China—unpopular.

The main immediate stumbling block to a peace agreement was one thrown up by the US about the POWs. The generally accepted interpretation of the Geneva Conventions was that prisoners were to be returned to their country of origin. The US insisted on 'voluntary repatriation'. A nice high-sounding phrase. But it did not mean what it seemed to.[74] The essence of the US strategy was to attempt to manufacture a plebiscite out of the only two groups of Koreans (and Chinese) who could be coerced or manipulated into appearing to back the US thesis. The question of the POWs and the manufacture of refugees were part of a linked phenomenon: to try to make the Korean 'people' speak against the DPRK, socialism and the Korean national movement. The US and Rhee therefore not only 'created' refugees, but also *invented* them on a vast scale, denied the reality of contrary movements (cf. re 1945–46), ascribed population loss in the North (much of which was caused by devastating bombing) to people fleeing; refugees and POWs became the centre-piece in the West's presentation of its case.[75]

The POW issue had some of the same characteristics as the refugee question. Here it was necessary to show: 1) that as many as possible POWs in UN hands did not want to go back to 'Communism' and that as few as possible UN POWs in Communist hands wanted to stay on the other side; then 2) if any did, this decision had to be written off to 'Brainwashing', 'menticide'—and torture.

There can be little doubt that the general feeling in the West is that the final verdict on the justice and injustice of the Korean War was based on the answers to two questions: first, 'Who started it?'; second, who and how many (respectively) wanted to stay with/go back to Communism? I think it can equally flatly be stated that the West won a major propaganda victory *in the West*. Most people still believe that Western POWs were brainwashed or coerced. *And* that the UN did not maltreat the POWs it held, at least not on a scale comparable to that alleged with the other side.

There is not space here to disentangle this murky issue as it would merit. But a few points are worth making.

1. The UN side demonstrably exercised large-scale violence against POWs—*and actually killed hundreds of POWs in pitched battles.* Ridgway brought troops and tanks back 200 miles from the front line because, as he himself said: 'I wanted the killing machinery on hand to do a thorough job.'[76] All this while the UN was juggling false statistics about UN POWs dying.

2. The Communist POWs, just like British troops captured by the Germans, did not regard being in captivity as a reason to give up. They carried on the struggle in the camps.[77]

3. The US let Rhee's right-wing thugs rampage through the UN camps, and also imported squads of Kuomintang agents from Taiwan to 'screen' the POWs. The US ambassador Muccio, later referred to these Chiang

troops as 'Gestapos'[78] and one US official described the situation in the camps as 'a reign of terror'. The chief US negotiator at Panmunjom, Admiral Joy, recorded in his diary that when the Nationalist Chinese leaders in the compound asked who wanted to go back to the PRC 'those doing so were either beaten black and blue or killed (sic). . .' (b). Records by two interpreters, available to US officials, estimated that if a fair poll were made, instead of the 85 per cent refusals which the US registered, the real figure would have been 15 per cent. The US felt it particularly important to get a high level of defections among the Chinese. Rhee helped all this along by raiding the camps and forcibly deporting ('releasing') some 27,000 prisoners, including thousands of Chinese to Taiwan. The US did its bit, too, by dishonestly reclassifying detainees as civilians.

But what can not be disputed are two things: a) the UN killed far more prisoners than the Communists did (or allowed to die in captivity); b) the extreme violence used, on a systematic scale, in the POW camps run by the UN invalidates any claim that those refusing repatriation represent a verifiable plebiscite for anti-Communism.

7. Back to Oblivion?

The war finally came to an end with the signing of the Armistice on July 27, 1953. Far more attention has been given to the start of the war than to its end. But Rhee's vigorous opposition to ending the war is itself an element which must be taken into account in characterizing the war politically. The fact is that the DPRK side made active efforts to bring the fighting to a stop and the ROK side took active steps to keep it going. This does not answer the question of who started it all, but it does tell one something about the two Korean sides.

Between early summer 1951 when the front roughly stabilised and the Armistice two years later, the US gradually intensified its bombing of the North. Much discussion in the West has fixed on the question of whether or not the US used bacterial warfare in Korea. But much less attention has been focused on the staggering destruction rained down on the DPRK. More bombs were dropped on the DPRK during the Korean War than were dropped on the whole of Europe (from all sources) in World War II. The US not only burned most of the DPRK to the ground, it incinerated unknown hundreds of thousands of Koreans by napalm, drove much of the rest of the population and industry underground, and finally bombed irrigation dams (last done by the Nazis, and deemed a war crime at Nuremberg). In an interview given in 1954 and embargoed until after his death Douglas MacArthur said: 'I would have dropped between 30 and 50 atomic bombs. . . across the neck of Manchuria.' Later he planned 'to spread. . . from the Sea of Japan to the Yellow Sea [i.e., across the middle of North Korea]. . . a belt of radioactive cobalt. . . It has an active life of between 60 and 120 years.'[79] Gen. Ridgway wanted to use chemical weapons in winter 1950-51 (MacArthur had to remind him that poison gas had been outlawed by the Geneva Convention). The destruction in North Korea was worse even than that in North Vietnam. Recently declassified documents and diaries show that the US was ready to think about doing absolutely anything to North Korea including killing much of the population as well as destroying the country, its agriculture, irrigation and its entire ecology.[80] I think that it is within this general context that discussion of the specific issue of germ warfare needs to be set.

One argument can be easily dismissed: that germ warfare was not used because it was too horrible. The top echelons of the US government and military discussed—and did—things in their way just as horrible. The US regime did not care what happened to the population of the DPRK as such.

The germ warfare issue is extremely contentious and there is not space here to go over it in detail.[81] Several recent texts throw much new light on it. It is still very much an open question whether it was used—and whether on an experimental or a mass basis. During the Korean War the world Communist movement developed a huge campaign, of a co-ordinated kind, on the issue. The West vehemently denied that it had used bacterial weapons—and this was generally believed in the West. But the West lied about some extremely important elements: in particular, they denied that the US had given protection to leading members of the Japanese germ warfare establishment, headed by Gen. Ishii. Communist accusations to this effect were dismissed as propaganda when they were in fact true—and when the US government knew them to be true (Ishii had even been taken to Fort Detrick, Maryland, in 1949, after which his trail goes dead).[82] The DPRK also accused the US of taking in a member of the Nazi germ warfare programme, Gen. Walter Schreiber. This was, to my knowledge, never acknowledged at the time (and still remains a very little known aspect of US policy, of rather more significance than re-employing Klaus Barbie, in its way). Yet, in 1983 it was confirmed that the DPRK accusation was true.[83] All this, of course, does not prove that the US used germ warfare in Korea. But it does show that an important part of the DPRK–Chinese case—which was denied by the US at the time with a vehemence equal to that used to deny the charges of using germ warfare—was true.

The West denigrated the report of the International Scientific Commission in 1952 and at least one of its members was hounded. But the evidence in the ISC Report was never scientifically disproved (nor was it, as the British government so flippantly claimed, 'pseudo-scientific').[84] Some American pilots confessed in captivity to having dropped germ bombs. After their release some of these 'de-confessed'. In the West the original confessions are dismissed as due to coercion. But the recantations are accepted. Yet there is evidence that pressure was exercised to obtain at least some of the recantations.[85]

In fact neither side has really engaged with the arguments and evidence of the other. Claude Bourdet remarked at the time that the generally greater mendacity of the Communist camp imposed upon it the greater obligation to establish its case.[86] And it is true that in the time of Stalin the world Communist movement had a poor record for truth on many questions. It tended to handle issues like the Korean War in 'campaigns', with rigid formulations, manifest evasions and sometimes inventions, many of which still mar the official (and only) DPRK version of events. The West seems prodigal with information, leaks and revelations by contrast. Yet, when all is said and done, on the Korean War, the West lied far more than the other side, and on many of the most fundamental questions.

But unlike with the Vietnam War, the arguments can rarely been settled by a direct appeal to published sources. The Korean War is still buried. It has to be *excavated* even more than analysed.

It also needs to be re-conceptualised. For it was *the* great turning point of the post-1945 world, the transitional war between World War II and all that followed. It was the first time (apart from Greece) the US went to war directly against a Communist revolution, and the only time it engaged in battle directly with a major Communist power (China). It was the only time the US managed to round up a broad coalition of client armies, 16 in all, from all the five continents (Colombia from Latin America; Ethiopia and South Africa from Africa). It conditioned the evolution of the whole modern world. In the USA, it stimulated the witchhunts which go under the misnomer of 'McCarthyism'; the CIA quadrupled in size during the Korean War; US military spending rose sharply. According to Dean Acheson, it also 'destroyed the Truman administration'.[87] Australia was solidified into a pro-US stance. The Korean War in effect brought down the Labour government in 1951—and ultimately thus destroyed the Labour Party in the long term. To help pay for a defence budget in 1951 which accounted for 14 per cent of national income, Labour put a 50 per cent charge on National Health dentures and spectacles. NATO, which had been founded in 1949, was given a colossal boost by the Korean War. Korea also allowed the US to consolidate its alliances with new client armies around the world, like those of Greece, Turkey, the Philippines and Thailand.[88]

It was the Korean War, not the revolution in China, which led to the US decision to keep China divided by blocking off access to Taiwan. It was US hostility to China in the Korean War, not hostility to the Chinese revolution as such, which got China branded an 'aggressor' at the UN in February 1951. And it was the Korean War which caused, or provided the occasion for the US to step up its backing both for the regime in the Philippines against the Huks—and for the French in Indochina.[89] And there is a very strong link between the Korean and Indochina wars. Many of the senior French officers in Indochina like Marshal Juin, travelled up to Korea, and senior US officers like Gen. Collins travelled down to Vietnam. At the end of the Korean War in 1953 a number of KMAG officers moved straight on to Vietnam.[90] In strategic thinking, too, Korea led directly on to 'flexible response' and the new ideas of Maxwell Taylor and John F. Kennedy. The Korean War also had a major effect on China's strategic thinking and on its subsequent diplomatic behaviour.[91]

One reason Korea needs to be re-conceptualized is that it is absent from so much of the discussion of the post-war world. Although it was *the only* war between the West as a bloc and the Communist world, it was fought in and over a society about which the West knew and cared little. Thus, just to take some of the very best texts produced from the left: the Korean revolutionary movement is absent from I.F. Stone's *Hidden History;* the Korean War is absent from what is probably the single most brilliant conceptualisation of the Cold War, by G. Therborn, when it is in fact the *centre* of the Cold War; and the radical transformation of the DPRK receives treatment both scanty and unsympathetic in Schurmann's *The Logic of World Power,* even though the land reform was probably the most peaceful and the most successful ever carried out in a socialist country.[92]

The greatest victory of anti-Communism has been the obliteration of Korea and it was this massive blotting out of an entire nation and its culture which allowed the US to wage such a brutal war. But anti-communism, like everything, has its differentials. Even though it was China which was the main target of US accusations and phobias about 'brainwashing', China is now accepted as an ally of the US (although, interestingly, the 1951 condemnation of China has never been repealed by the UN). But North Korea is still effectively ostracized and little understood: none of the major Western states or Japan recognise it, and over 30 years after the end of the war, the US still maintains its toughest trade embargo against it.

It seems most unlikely that the dangerous situation in the Far East and the tragedy of Korea's division can be resolved without some attempt to come to grips with the past and to understand it. This must involve some minimal understanding of the Korean War. And this in turn demands some effort to pose the war in different terms from those usually deployed. Instead of only talking about the start of the war, one must look at its causes and its origins. Instead of fixating on one entirely 'intra-Western' question like the firing of MacArthur in April 1951, it is necessary to examine the nature and political character of the war, and of the whole ongoing political struggle in Korea. As Gertrude Stein rightly implied, without the right questions one is unlikely to get the right answers.

In conclusion, may I appeal to anyone with first-hand knowledge, whether personal eye-witness information or documents, on the Korean War, to contact me via the *Socialist Register*. Any information would be greatly appreciated and will be treated in confidence. J.H.

NOTES

1. For the 'Gook syndrome' see Reginald Thompson, *Cry Korea*, (London, Macdonald, 1951), p. 44. (Thompson was the *Daily Telegraph* correspondent in Korea during the early part of the war); Julian Tunstall, *I Fought in Korea*, (London, Lawrence & Wishart, 1953), p. 12, where he reports officers' orders to 'Shoot everything in white' (most Korean civilians wore white) and 'Take no prisoners'. Capt. Walter Karig, 'Korea—Tougher to crack than Okinawa', *Collier's*, September 23, 1950, p. 24 (the subtitle of this article is: 'Our Red foe scorns all rules of civilized warfare, hides behind women's skirts and has children play near bombing targets').

2. On this and what follows, the outstanding source is Bruce Cumings' *The Origins of the Korean War: Liberation and the Emergence of Separate Regimes 1945-1947*, (Princeton, Princeton University Press, 1981).

3. Snow, 'We Meet Russia in Korea', *Saturday Evening Post*, March 30, 1946, p. 18. This re-appears, somewhat re-written, in Snow, *Journey to the Beginning*, (London, Gollancz, 1959), pp. 393-398 ('We Stop a Revolution'). Robert Klonsky, '27 Years Ago: A United States Soldier in South Korea', *Korea Focus*, (New York), Vol. 2, no. 1 (Jan.-Feb. 1973), pp. 63-4, says Snow's published text was much watered down.

3a. Mark Gayn, *Japan Diary*, (New York, 1948) has an excellent section of over 100 pages on South Korea in late 1946.

4. For example, I.F. Stone, *The Hidden History of the Korean War*, (New York, Monthly Review Press, 1952; re-issued 1969), is a pioneering, outstanding and courageous exposé of US machinations and deceit—which is all Stone claims to be doing. But the book contains only a single reference to the Korean Workers' [Communist] Party and only two references to Kim Il Sung (p. 224), both in contexts where they could be removed without altering the sense. The trouble is that there are really *two* 'hidden histories': one certainly is the secret history of what the USA was up to in Korea; but the other, without which the former cannot be properly understood, is the history of the Korean left. The US did not just choose to intervene *anywhere*—it chose to go to war for the first time after 1945 on a major scale (apart from Greece) in *and against* a country with a strong revolutionary movement.

5. See Cumings, cit, esp. ch. 11. Interesting observations in Edwin W. Pauley, *Report on Japanese Assets in Soviet-Occupied Korea* to the President of the United States (June 1946), based on a visit to North Korea in May-June 1946 by a US mission headed by Pauley.

6. On Kim's career, see Cumings, cit., esp. pp. 397-403, for a judicious sifting of the evidence.

7. I have discussed these reforms and their long-term impact in two texts: 'The North Korean Enigma', *New Left Review*, no. 127 (1981) and 'The North Korean Model: Gaps and Questions', *World Development*, no. 9/10, 1981.

8. Cumings, p. 562; cf. p. 61.

9. *Amerasia*, December 1945, pp. 324-5. At the time both Seoul and the US were spreading reports of large numbers of people fleeing the Soviet zone and of atrocities there. But Pauley, a staunch anti-Communist, reported to Truman:

'. . . I was present when many returning Koreans were cross-examined and they all (sic—JH) broke down and admitted that what they were reporting were things they had heard and not things they had seen' (Pauley, *Report*, p. 139). It is also interesting that Pauley refers to *'returning'* Koreans: many of those moving from North to South were people returning to their villages who had been displaced by the Japanese to points North—especially Northern Korea and Manchuria; cf. Cumings, cit., p. 425–6.

10.   Cumings, cit., pp. 417–8, 424–6.

11.   For new light on Rhee's career and his return, see Cumings, cit., pp. 188 ff. James Cameron refers to 'the allegedly noble old exile, the extreme reactionary. . . Syngman Rhee', (*Point of Departure*, (London, Panther, 1980), p. 98). By mid-1948 the US political adviser, Joseph E. Jacobs, was writing that 'He [Rhee] is definitely suffering from a messiah complex. . . Some of his own friends say that in the mornings he is usually rational, but by afternoon he is completely "off the beam".' (Cited in Charles M. Dobbs, *The Unwanted Symbol: American Foreign Policy, the Cold War, and Korea, 1945-1950*, (Kent State University Press, 1981), p. 154. (Dobbs' title is typical of a certain whitewashing, 'accidental' school.) Probably the single best text on Rhee is by himself, an interview he gave in *U.S. News and World Report*, August 13, 1954.

12.   Letter from Goodfellow to US General John R. Hodge, Occupation Commander, June 21 1946, cited in Cumings, cit., p. 532.

13.   I have discussed this in 'The United Nations and Korea', in Frank Baldwin, ed., *Without Parallel: The American–Korean Relationship Since 1945*, (New York, Pantheon Books, 1974).

14.   This is dealt with in detail, with references on contentious issues in 'The Korean Revolution' in my pamphlet, *Three Articles on the Korean Revolution*, (London, AREAS, 1972, pp. 12–13) (edited version with the same title in *Socialist Revolution*, (San Francisco), Vol. 1, no. 6, (1970)).

15.   *The US Imperialists Started the Korean War*, (Pyongyang, Foreign Languages Publishing House, 1977), p. 67–8. This is a useful exposition of the DPRK case, with many references to Western sources (many apparently re-translated via Japanese).

16.   John Merrill, 'The Cheju-do Rebellion', *Journal of Korean Studies*, (Seattle), Vol. 2 (1980), pp. 177–8.

17.   Robert K. Sawyer, *Military Advisors in Korea: KMAG in Peace and War*, (Washington, D.C., Department of the Army, Office of the Chief of Military History, 1962), p. 42. KMAG was the (US) Korean Military Advisory Group.

18.   Roy E. Appleman, *South to the Naktong, North to the Yalu*, (Washington, D.C., Department of the Army, Office of the Chief of Military History, 1956), p. 34.

19.   Se-Jin Kim, *The Politics of Military Revolution in Korea*, (Chapel Hill, University of North Carolina Press, 1971), p. 55.

20.   Cumings, cit., p. 349. Merrill, cit., (note 16) is a pioneering study of the rebellion on Cheju Island, off the Southern coast of Korea.

21.   Andrew Roth, 'Korea's Impending Explosion', *The Nation*, August 13, 1949, p. 152. For the weakness of the Rhee regime, see the CIA study, 'Prospects for the Survival of the Republic of Korea', October 28, 1948, cited in John Merrill, 'Internal Warfare in Korea', in Bruce Cumings, ed., *Child of Conflict: The Korean–American Relationship, 1943, 1953*, (Seattle, University of Washington Press, 1983), p. 144.

22.   Roberts to Bolté, August 19, 1949, cited by Merrill, *ibid.*, p. 148.

23.   Author's interviews with Rear Admiral Lee and Brig. Gen. Choi, New York City, April 3, 1977. For the Japanese background of the ROK Army top brass,

see Kim, *The Politics of Military Revolution, cit.* At the beginning of the Korean War every single top commander in the ROK Army except one was a former member of the Japanese Army. The Korean People's Army (KPA) was led entirely by veterans of the anti-Japanese resistance. A reasonable analogy would be the West fielding former members of the Waffen SS against, say, Tito's partisans.

24. '. . . millions of South Koreans welcomed the prospect of unification, even on Communist terms. They had suffered police brutality, intellectual repression and political purge. Few felt much incentive to fight for profiteers or to die for Syngman Rhee. Only 10 per cent of the Seoul population abandoned the city; many troops deserted, and a number of public figures, including Kimm Kiu Sic, joined the North', (Alfred Crofts, 'The Case of Korea: Our Falling Ramparts. . .', *The Nation,* June 25, 1960, p. 547). Rhee and his backers claimed that Southern political figures (including some Assemblymen) who went to the North when the Korean War broke out were killed. But quite recently a man who had known them before June 1950 met one of them and ascertained that he and several others were alive and well as of 1982 (private communication to the author). There is not space to argue out all the issues here; I have attempted to develop the discussion about the start of the war in 'What Happened in Korea?', *Bulletin of Concerned Asian Scholars,* Vol. 5, no. 3, (November 1973) and 'The Korean War: Some Notes on Evidence and Solidarity', *ibid.,* Vol. 11, no. 3 (1979) (henceforth: *BCAS*).

25. Richard Nixon, *The Real War,* (New York, Warner Books, 1980), p. 254, cited by Bruce Cumings, 'Introduction: The Course of Korean-American Relations, 1943-1953', in Cumings, ed., *Child of Conflict,* p. 49.

26. Ministry of Foreign Affairs of the Democratic People's Republic of Korea, *Documents and Materials Exposing the Instigators of the Civil War in Korea: Documents from the archives of the Rhee Syngman Government,* (Pyongyang, 1950), especially Part IV; on this volume see text below. I have discussed the events of June 1950 and the Dulles visit in more detail in 'The Korean War. . .' *BCAS,* XI. 3, 1979, cit.

27. Douglas MacArthur, *Reminiscences,* (New York, Crest paperback ed., 1965), p. 371.

28. John J. Muccio, May 1975, in Francis H. Heller, ed., *The Korean War: A 25-Year Perspective,* (Lawrence, The Regents Press of Kansas, 1977), p. 11.

29. At Princeton Seminars, July 9, 1953, cited in Cumings, 'Introduction', in id., ed., *Child of Conflict,* p. 49.

30. *New York Journal-American,* January 19, 1952, cited in I.F. Stone, *cit.,* p. 348. The possibility that the US wished to try 'rollback' in Korea is made stronger by the fact that the first attempt to topple a Communist regime after World War II, that in Albania, in 1949, had just failed.

31. John Merrill, review of *Khrushchev Remembers, Journal of Korean Studies,* Vol. 3 (1981), pp. 181 ff. Numbers in the text in brackets refer to Vol. I of the (UK) Penguin edition, 1977.

32. Monat's much-cited (but little read?) article is in *Life,* June 27, 1960; a full account is in his book: Pawel Monat, with John Dille, *Spy in the U.S.,* (London, F. Muller, 1964), pp. 193 ff.

33. Public Records Office [henceforth: PRO] (UK), FO371/84075. Plimsoll was chief Australian delegate on UNCURK, the UN Commission for the Reunification and Rehabilitation of Korea.

34. Shirley Hazzard, 'The betrayal of the Charter', *Times Literary Supplement,* (London), September 17, 1982, pp. 967–8, is an excellent exposé and critique of the standard complacent line, exemplified in Evan Luard's, *A History of the*

United Nations, which Hazzard reviews. Some information on Trygve Lie's combination of machination and negligence in my 'The United Nations and Korea'. Excellent analysis in Marie-France Labouz, *L'ONU et la Corée,* (Paris, Presses Universitaires de Paris, 1980).

35. Confirmation that they had reached the UN is contained in a 'Note by the Secretariat', dated 6 November, 1950 (UN document, A/C.1/565/Add. 1). Information about their disappearance: author's telephone conversation with a senior UN official, June 19, 1984, New York. The volume published by the DPRK Foreign Ministry in 1950, *Documents and Materials Exposing. . .* (cited in note 26) may contain some or all of the documents sent in photostatic form to the UN, but I have been unable to confirm this. The volume also contains interesting confessions by senior officials of the Rhee regime who were captured by the KPA.

36. Cameron's account is in his *Point of Departure,* pp. 145 ff; René Cutforth provides lugubrious reflections in *The Listener,* November 11, 1969, pp. 342–3; I had two memorable encounters with the late René Cutforth and owe him for much fascinating information and insight into the Korean War. There is an excellent account of press censorship in Korea in Phillip Knightley, *The First Casualty,* (London, André Deutsch, 1975).

37. Stanley I. Kutler, *The American Inquisition: Justice and Injustice in the Cold War,* (New York, Hill & Wang, 1982) has good chapters on Lattimore and John W. Powell, both with much valuable new information on connections between Korea and the US witchhunts.

38. The DPRK case can be read in *The US Imperialists Started the Korean War.*

39. Immediately after the end of the Korean War the DPRK put on trial and executed a group of key Southern Communist leaders (see BBC, *Summary of World Broadcasts,* Part V (Far East), no. 277 (August 18, 1953), pp. 36–56, for details). I have tried to disentangle this murky affair in 'The Korean War: Notes. . .' in *BCAS,* XI, 3, p. 8. While there is no reason to doubt that there were extensive reprisals, the DPRK case against the Southern Communists as it stands is not persuasive.

40. William F. Dean, *General Dean's Story,* (New York, Viking Press, 1954), especially pp. 67–80.

41. John Gittings, 'Talks, Bombs and Germs: Another Look at the Korean War', *Journal of Contemporary Asia,* Vol. 5, no. 2 (1975), p. 208, gives a figure of 500,000 ROK troops 'believed to have been re-educated and enlisted' in the KPA. Other sources suggest Southern civilians also joined up (or were enrolled) and Gen. Dean implies that this is the case (Dean, *cit.,* p. 68, 78).

42. Kim Chum-kon, *The Korean War,* (Seoul, Kwangmyong Publishing Co., 1973), p. 384. The text of the land reform is available in BBC, *Summary of World Broadcasts,* Far East (Part V), no. 64 (July 11, 1950), pp. 11–12. Details confirmed to the author by six senior KPA officers, interview, Pyongyang, July 26, 1977.

43. Gregory Henderson, *Korea: The Politics of the Vortex,* (Cambridge, Harvard University Press, 1968), p. 167.

44. Alan Winnington, *I saw the truth in Korea,* (London, Daily Worker, 1950), p. 6.

45. Philip Deane, *Captive in Korea,* (London, Hamish Hamilton, 1953), pp. 83–4.

46. Interviews with the author, New York, April 3, 1977; Los Angeles, March 1978.

47. Interview with the author, March 1983. In the *Listener,* Cutforth wrote of 'other sickening sights: the shooting without trial of civilians, designated by the police as "communist". These executions were done. . . on any patch of waste ground where you could dig a trench and line up a row of prisoners in front of it. Then there was the horrible brutality and corruption of Syngman Rhee's

police, among whose chief rackets was the selling of destitute girls from the refugee columns into the city brothels.' (*Listener,* November 11, 1969, p. 343).

48. The largest massacre by Rhee's forces which is undisputed even in Western sources was that at Koch'ang in February 1951 when 'about 600 men and women, young and old, were herded into a narrow valley and mowed down with machine guns', (John Kie-Chiang Oh, *Korea: Democracy on Trial,* (Ithaca, Cornell University Press, 1968), p. 35, 206). The callousness of Rhee's regime also emerges from an event very little discussed in the standard literature: the National Defence Corps scandal. This involved 'South Korean young men, who had been forcibly impressed into the army from refugee camps, starved to death by army leaders who misappropriated their supplies and rations', (Chung Kyungmo, 'The Second Liberation of South Korea and the Democratization of Japan', *The Japan Interpreter,* Vol. 9, no. 2 (1974), p. 194). Chung says 50,000 'reportedly' died. But a source very close to the Seoul government cites, with no disclaimer, a figure of 'over 90,000' (Kim, *The Politics of Military Revolution, cit.,* p. 70). Whether the figure is 50,000 or 90,000 plus, this is surely one of the biggest atrocities of modern times.

49. Gayn, *Japan Diary,* provides excellent background on the origins of the police force, many with Japanese training. An adviser to the US embassy wrote in late June 1950: 'The jails in Seoul are overcrowded with political prisoners. Six weeks ago I inspected a police jail in Inch'on. The prisoners there were living under conditions which I hesitate to describe in this letter. It reminds you of a sense of the Divina Comedia (sic). Goya could have painted what we saw there. What is going to happen to the almost 10,000 political prisoners in case the capital is to be surrendered? It is hard to imagine the acts of vengeance and hatred which the people will commit. . .' (cited in Frank Baldwin, ed., Harold Joyce Noble, *Embassy At War,* (Seattle, University of Washington Press, 1975), p. 255).

50. Crucifixions: Cameron, *Point of Departure,* p. 134; cf. photograph in the *Daily Worker,* October 5, 1950; Winnington, *I Saw the Truth. . .,* passim.

51. John W. Riley, Jr., and Wilbur Schramn, *The Reds Take A City: The Communist Occupation of Seoul, with Eyewitness Accounts,* (Greenwood Press, Westport, Conn., 1973 [reprint of 1951 edition]), p. 46); I have discussed this valuable source at greater length in 'The Korean War: Notes. . .', *BCAS,* XI, 3.

52. *The US Imperialists Started the Korean War, cit.,* pp. 288 ff. I have discussed these events more fully in *BCAS,* XI, 3.

53. *The US Imperialists. . .,* p. 236.

54. V.V. Martynov, *Koreya,* (Moscow, Izdatel'stvo 'Mysl', 1970), p. 59, cited in Robert Ante, 'The Transformation of the Economic Geography of the DPRK', *Korea Focus,* Vol. I, no. 3 (n.d. [1972]), p. 55. These figures show a decline of 11.76 per cent in the population between 1949 and 1953.

55. *The US Imperialists. . .,* pp. 233, 235; during a visit to Sinchon County, I was informed that the Sinchon figure was considerably above the national average (author's interview, July 28, 1977).

56. Monica Felton, a British member of the International Women's delegation, reports on their findings in *That's Why I Went,* (London, Lawrence & Wishart, 1953). International Association of Democratic Lawyers, *Reports on Investigations in Korea and China,* (March-April 1952), (Brussels, IADL, 1952); press conference and article by Jack Gaster, British member of the IADL delegation, in *Daily Worker,* April 23 and May 9, 1952.

57. Philip Crosbie, *Three Winters Cold,* (Dublin, Browne and Nolan, 1955), p. 220; cf. J. Tunstall, *cit.,* p. 39, for first-hand testimony by a British soldier who was in the North; for a first-hand account by a US soldier, Scott D. Oliver, a sergeant-

major in the Marines, see letter by Oliver in *Korea Focus,* Vol. 3, no. 1 (August–September 1974), pp. 40 ff, including mass rape.

58. Major General Emmett O'Donnell, Jnr., testifying to the MacArthur hearings, June 25, 1951 (US Congress, Senate, Committee on Armed Services and Committee on Foreign Relations, *Military Situation in the Far East: Hearings to Conduct an Inquiry into the Military Situation in the Far East and Facts Surrounding the Relief of General of the Army Douglas MacArthur from His Assignments in That Area,* 82nd Congress, 1st Session, 1951, Vol. 4, p. 3063.

59. MacArthur: 'The war in Korea has already almost destroyed that nation. . . I have never seen such devastation. . . I have seen, I guess, as much blood and disaster as any living man, and it just turned my stomach, the last time I was there. After I looked at that wreckage and those thousands of women and children and everything, I vomited. . .' (*MacArthur Hearings,* Vol. 1, p. 82). note that MacArthur was fired one-quarter of the way into the war and this testimony is less than one-third of the way into the war—and before the US greatly increased its bombing of the North.

At the same hearings Senator Stennis asked Gen. O'Donnell: '. . . North Korea has been virtually destroyed, hasn't it?. . .'

Gen. O'Donnell: 'Oh, yes, we did it all later anyhow. . .I would say that the entire, almost the entire Korean Peninsula is just a terrible mess. Everything is destroyed. There is nothing standing worthy of the name. . .' (Vol. 4, p. 3075). Gen. Curtis LeMay, head of Strategic Air Command during the Korean War, later recalled asking the Pentagon for permission to 'burn down' five of the biggest cities in North Korea and being told 'It's too horrible'. But, LeMay observed, 'over a period of three years or so. . . we burned down *every* town in North Korea. . . Now, over a period of three years, that's palatable'. (LeMay oral history in John Foster Dulles papers, Princeton University, cited in Bruce Cumings, 'Korea—the New Nuclear Flashpoint', *The Nation,* April 7, 1984, p. 416). For US bombing of North Korea, including major dams in spring 1953, cf. Gittings, 'Talks, Bombs and Germs. . .', *cit.,* pp. 212–6.

60. 'We burned anything and everything that could be consumed by the raging flames', (Scott Oliver, letter, *cit.,* p. 40 [this is before the UN retreat] ; cf. Tunstall, *I Fought in Korea,* p. 49. (US troops burning Pyongyang on the retreat). All this after the UN had dropped some 7,800,000 gallons of napalm on the DPRK.

61. Cab. 71 (50), November 6, 1950, P.R.O., London.

62. FO 371/84179, PRO; information below from same.

63. FO 371/84055, PRO, London.

64. FO 371/84075, PRO, London.

65. Cameron, *Point of Departure,* p. 145.

66. Pratt wrote a pioneering pamphlet, *Korea: The Lie That Led to War,* (London, British China Friendship Association, 1951).

67. Gittings, 'Talks, Bombs and Germs', p. 214.

68. *Korea,* No. 1 (1953), Cmd. 8793 (London, HMSO, March 1953), p. 11.

69. The documents recently released on Attlee's visit to Washington in early December 1950 are very revealing on this score. Acheson thought the US might actually be thrown right off the Korean peninsula and there was discussion of having to do 'a Dunkirk' or 'a Tobruk' (= holding a redoubt round Seoul). Attlee spent more time trying to persuade Truman not to attack China than on anything to do with the atomic bomb (FO 371/84105, PRO, London).

70. Bruce Cumings, 'The Korean War: Korean Society, American Society', unpublished paper delivered to a seminar on 'War and Society' at the Shelby Cullom Davis Center, Princeton University, October 14, 1983; earlier back-

ground in Cumings, *Origins*, pp. 411 ff. The first Chinese troops moved into Korea on or about October 14, 1950; the major CPV–KPA counter-attack started on November 26.

71. Acheson quote in letter to Truman, July 25, 1955, in Dean Acheson, *Among Friends: Personal Letters of Dean Acheson*, ed., David S. McLellan, (New York, Dodd, Mead & Co., 1980), p. 104, cited in Cumings, 'The Korean War: Korean Society, American Society' (cited in note 70). *Red China's Fighting Hordes* by Lt. Col. Robert B. Rigg, (Harrisburg, Pa., Military Service Publishing Co., 1951).

72. René Cutforth, *Korean Reporter*, (London, Allan Wingate, 1952), pp. 103-4, reports a battle where the Chinese deliberately tried not to kill the ordinary British soldiers, only the officers—at high cost to themselves. This severely unnerved the British officer corps (interview with the author).

73. The US prepared a plan ('Operation Everready') to arrest Rhee and his top associates (see John Kotch, 'The Origins of the American Security Commitment to Korea', in Cumings, ed., *Child of Conflict*, pp. 244 ff). Cf. Mark W. Clark, *From the Danube to the Yalu*, (New York, Harper & Brothers, 1954), ch. 18. Richard Nixon, *The Memoirs of Richard Nixon*, (London, Arrow Books, edition, 1979), pp. 126-9, for Rhee's attempts to persuade Nixon and Eisenhower to re-start the war in late 1953; and Rhee's interview to *US News and World Report*, August 13, 1954. Barton J. Bernstein, 'The Pawn as Rook: The Struggle to End the Korean War', *BCAS*, Vol. 10, no. 1 (1978).

74. Useful discussion of these issues, using many unpublished sources, in Barton J. Bernstein, 'The Struggle over the Korean Armistice: Prisoners of Repatriation?', in Cumings, ed., *Child of Conflict*; US Secretary of State Dean Acheson considered that 'voluntary repatriation' contravened the Geneva Convention (p. 277). Important material in Alan Winnington and Wilfred Burchett, *Plain Perfidy*, (Peking, 1954). The US goal was both *local* (i.e. specific to the Korean War) and more *general*—to attempt to demoralise Communist states everywhere.

75. Harold E. Fey, 'How Refugees Are Made', *Christian Century*, January 23, 1952 (ROK troops forcing people out of their homes—not only to increase the 'head count' but also to facilitate looting, etc.); cf. Cutforth, *Listener, cit.*, p. 343. When refugees got in the way, they were dispensed with: on the second retreat from Seoul in January 1951, the US mortared the Han River just South of the capital to block refugees already on the ice (Cutforth, *Korean Reporter*, 116-7). For grotesque manipulation of figures, see Rhee's interview, *US News*, August 13, 1954.

76. Matthew B. Ridgway, *Soldier: The Memoirs of Matthew B. Ridgway*, (New York, Harper & Brothers, 1956), p. 233. The biggest known massacres were on Koje Island and on Pongam Island, where 85 POWs were killed in one incident (in December 1952). Wilfred Burchett and Alan Winnington, *Koje Unscreened*, (London, Britian-China Friendship Association, n.d. [1953?]), p. 3, says 'some three thousand prisoners of war were killed or wounded. . . up to the end of 1952' according to American official communiques and western news agency reports alone. For overall totals and comparison, cf. Gittings, 'Talks, Bombs and Germs', pp. 210–211; cf. Gavan McCormack, *Cold War Hot War: An Australian perspective on the Korean War*, (Sydney, Hale & Iremonger, 1983), pp. 143 ff., for US invention of figures and propaganda campaign on this issue.

77. As Gen. Collins rather sourly put it, 'their deliberate utilization of prisoners of war to harass their captors and warp world opinion in their favour was an effective tactic. . .' (J. Lawton Collins, *War in Peacetime: The History and Lessons of Korea*, (Boston, Houghton Mifflin, 1969), p. 343). One of Gen. Collins' 'lessons' is that the North Koreans caused the Tonkin Gulf Incident (p. 387). Striking evidence of local popular support for the POWs—200 miles

behind the front line in an area which the KPA never reached—comes from Gen. Mark Clark, who notes that after the big battle on Koje in June 1952, the US 'moved the village that served as a key center in the [DPRK] communications network. . . so that contact between villagers and prisoners was next to impossible'. (Clark, *From the Danube to the Yalu*, p. 65). Another US source has a photograph of the village being 'moved'—by being burned to the ground (Walter G. Hermes, *Truce Tent and Fighting Front*, (Washington, D.C., Government Printing Office, 1966), p. 261.

78. Information from Bernstein, 'The Struggle over the Korean Armistice', pp. 274 ff, esp. 285. Dean Acheson himself acknowledged the dishonest reclassification of prisoners (ib., p. 286). The question of the real allegiances and desires of the POWs is extremely complicated: in the case of the Chinese troops, many, especially among those captured early in the fighting, were soldiers who had until very recently been in the Kuomintang armies; interesting information on this in William C. Bradbury, Samuel M. Meyers and Albert D. Biderman, eds., *Mass Behavior in Battle and Captivity: The Communist Soldier in the Korean War*, (Chicago, University of Chicago Press, 1968), including two chapters co-authored by Jeane J. Kirkpatrick.

79. Cited in Cumings, *The Nation*, April 7, 1984, p. 416; information immediately below from same. Just after MacArthur was dismissed, *Newsweek* wrote: 'You can disregard the talk about "sowing" a radio-active strip across Korea. The Pentagon says this would be unduly expensive. However, placing a band of lingering nerve gas across the peninsula has been under discussion for some time. . .' (April 30, 1951 (Periscope)).

80. Among the most frightening things unearthed is Truman's diary, in which he fantasized privately about dropping atomic bombs on Moscow, Leningrad, Beijing, Shanghai and other cities. He also complained that 'Dealing with communist governments is like an honest man trying to deal with. . . the head of a dope ring'. (Truman diary, entry for January 27, 1952, cited in Bernstein, 'Struggle over the Korean Armistice', pp. 291, 290; cf. Barton J. Bernstein, 'Truman's Secret Thoughts on Ending the Korean War', *Foreign Service Journal*, 57 (November 1980)). On the other hand, some of these papers show how much US leaders loathed Rhee (for Eisenhower on Rhee, see Robert H. Ferrell, ed., *The Eisenhower Diaries*, (New York, W.W. Norton, 1981), pp. 248, 275); of course, Eisenhower did little about this at the time.

81. McCormack, *Cold War Hot War*, ch. 11, is a good summing up, and references there; see also: Stephen L. Endicott, 'Germ Warfare and "Plausible Denial": The Korean War 1950-1953', *Modern China*, Vol. 5, no. 1 (January 1979), and Jaap van Ginneken, 'Bacteriological Warfare', *Journal of Contemporary Asia*, Vol. 7, no. 2 (1977). A recent addition to the literature arguing that germ warfare was not used is Albert E. Cowdrey, ' "Germ Warfare" and Public Health in the Korean Conflict', *Asian Perspective*, (Seoul), Vol. 7, no. 2 (1983).

82. John W. Powell, 'Japan's Germ Warfare: The U.S. Cover-up of a Crime', *BCAS*, Vol. 12, no. 4 (1980) [shorter version in *Bulletin of Atomic Scientists*, October 1981]. On Powell's own case, see Kutler, *The American Inquisition, cit.*, ch. 8; this also discusses the still unresolved mystery of the raid by US Gen. Sams into the Wonsan area in March 1951—a raid which was reported in strange terms in *Newsweek*, April 9, 1951 and then written up in graphic terms in *Collier's*, September 22, 1951 (Peter Kalischer, 'Doctor Commando').

83. *International Herald Tribune*, February 21, 1983 (from Reuters), where it is reported that Schreiber 'helped direct the U.S. Air Force bacteriological warfare program [and had been] convicted in absentia by a Polish tribunal of conducting medical experiments on prisoners at Auschwitz'. The DPRK allega-

tion is reproduced in *The US Imperialists Started the Korean War, cit.,* p. 254; van Ginneken, 'Bacteriological Warfare', p. 135.

84. See note 68.
85. Endicott, *cit.,* particularly on the case of Col. Walker M. Mahurin; Mahurin's recantation contains one very good phrase: 'The confession written for the Chinese was made almost exactly as this one.' (p. 37 of text in UN document A/C.1/L.66; this UN document contains the text of 10 recantations submitted by the US to the UN (in General Assembly, *Official Records,* 1st Committee, 8th Session, Agenda Item 24 (26 October 1953)). This recantation was made aboard a US hospital ship in the Pacific and sworn before one Henry R. Petersen, notorious later in the Watergate affair. Cf. McCormack, *Cold War Hot War,* ch. 11.
86. Claude Bourdet, 'Vérité et Bactéries', *l'Observateur* (Paris), n. 101 (April 17, 1952).
87. Letter of July 25, 1955 to Truman, as cited in note 71.
88. In some ways the most important alliance it consolidated was that with South Korea itself. When the Vietnam war escalated, the US found few allies to help it out (all veterans of Korea, though). By far the most important was the army of South Korea, which altogether rotated 312,000 troops through Indochina (Vietnam and Cambodia). Inter alia, these Korean troops distinguished themselves for their brutality. One of the top ROK officers, who commanded the notorious 'White Horse' brigade in Vietnam, was the current dictator of South Korea, Chon Doo Hwan. These Vietnam veterans were deployed by Chon to put down the big Kwangju uprising in May 1980. The long legacy of the Korean War in the form of client armies is a major phenomenon which might merit the term 'sub-imperialism' if this had not been used to designate a different item.
89. All this is spelled out in Truman's declaration of June 27, 1950, in *Department of State Bulletin,* July 3, 1950.
90. Clark, *From the Danube to the Yalu,* pp. 319, 321-2; Collins, *War in Peacetime,* p. 357.
91. Peng Teh-huai, *A Report on the Chinese People's Volunteers in Korea,* (September 12, 1953), supplement to *People's China,* October 1, 1953. Much later, the Vietnamese claimed that China had advocated 'a Korean-type solution [for] Indochina. . . i.e., cessation of hostilities without any political solution' (Ministry of Foreign Affairs, *The Truth About Vietnam–China Relations Over the Last Thirty Years,* (Hanoi, 1979), p. 19). The Korean War also greatly affected the DPRK's relations with both the USSR and China; and China's relations with the USSR (most of the China's $2 billion debt to the USSR was contracted during the Korean War for arms supplies).
92. I single these texts out only because they are so important; my comments on Stone above (note 4); Göran Therborn, 'From Petrograd to Saigon', *New Left Review,* 48 (1968); Franz Schurmann, *The Logic of World Power,* (New York, Pantheon, 1974); for example: 'Collectivization had aroused considerable peasant discontent, and Kim Il Sung's harsh rule produced much the same type of tensions as in Soviet-dominated countries of Eastern Europea', (p. 239). Collectivization had not yet taken place in the period referred to (before the Korean War); Kim's rule was not comparable to Eastern Europe in many important ways. The Korean War is extremely well integrated into Joyce and Gabriel Kolko's *The Limits of Power: The World and United States Foreign Policy, 1945-1954,* (New York, Harper & Row, 1972).

ANTI-COMMUNISM IN THE FEDERAL REPUBLIC OF GERMANY

William D. Graf

Anti-communism is the most powerful political force in the world. Endowed with an imposing ideology, and a set of vivid images and sacred dogmas, it commands the psychic and material resources of the most potent industrial–military arsenal in the history of mankind. Its forces are deployed on every continent, its influence is felt in every major region, and it is capable of acts which—when ascribed to the communists —are considered violent and venal. Our fear that communism might someday take over most of the world blinds us to the fact that anti-communism already has.

—*Michael Parenti*[1]

The Communists at least talk about the problems. We too often just talk about the Communists.

—*Richard Nixon*[2]

It is scarcely an exaggeration to state that the ideological foundation of the West German partial state has been, and is anti-communism. Although anti-communism in the FRG performs substantially the same social functions as it does in advanced capitalist countries elsewhere—ersatz ideology, social discipline, rationale for class domination—the special conditions prevailing there since 1945 have formed and developed it in specific, distinguishable ways. And like the other elements of class domination, it is dynamic, evolving and hence constantly being reproduced and transformed. It is these special conditions and this dynamic quality (which for now might be summed up as the post-fascist society, the country's position as 'front line' in the Cold War, the 'internalization' of class conflict and the 'successful' capitalist political economy) that lend West German anti-communism its peculiar shape and substance. In what follows, an attempt is made to analyse and comprehend both the 'specificity' and the 'universality' of anti-communism in the FRG.[3]

The context of West German anti-communism

Total defeat following upon total war, devastation and destitution, and four-power occupation produced, in the weeks and months after the capitulation of the Third Reich, a peculiar constellation of forces in Germany which seemed to point to rapid socio-economic change, if not to a *pre-revolutionary situation.* Subjectively, there now developed a popular anti-fascist and hence anti-capitalist mood which penetrated deeply even into the bourgeois classes[4] and which was based on a realisation that the

164

former ruling classes and the pre-war socio-economic system had produced —or at least failed to anticipate, to resist—fascism and war. And objectively, the class power of the National Socialist elite and its class allies had been diminished—temporarily and by outside military power, to be sure. The power of the Junker elites in the East was finally broken by the incorporation of much of their territory into Poland and the Soviet Union and the expropriation and redistribution of their lands in the Soviet occupation zone. Business elites, the captains of industry and finance, found their assets sequestered and their leading members imprisoned. With the collapse of the Nazi state, the judiciary and civil service, to say nothing of the government, were deprived of any institutional power base. And more generally, perhaps two-thirds of the former middle classes had been (again temporarily) proletarianised economically[5] and their ranks were swollen by an influx of declassé refugees and expellees from the East.[6]

Although the popular mood of this period was at least as much one of shock, bewilderment and apathy as of political engagement,[7] and although a mass socialist consciousness had not been developed by a preceding period of galvanising anti-Nazi struggles—a situation reminiscent of the 'ersatz revolution' of 1918—nevertheless the overwhelming majority of politically aware and politically active Germans did advocate a socialist reordering of society and economy. Practically all public discourse, including party programmes and pronouncements, major issues of contention between Germans and occupiers, constitutional debates and the substantial themes in the communications media (though these were subject to direct Allied control until 1947), revolved around proposals for expropriation, socialisation and communal ownership coupled with the protection and extension of civil liberties.

This tendency toward *democratic socialism* was best exemplified by the unified anti-fascist movement (or antifa), a popular, left-wing organisation which arose spontaneously at the local level in all four zones of occupation. The antifa movement was significant for a number of reasons, all of which bear directly on the subsequent development of anti-communist ideology in the FRG. First, it derived its leadership and mass support from the anti-Nazi elite,[8] a category encompassing mainly the Left: leftist Social Democrats, communists, members of radical socialist organisations and trade unionists, including returning exiles and former concentration camp inmates, who had been early and consistent opponents of the Third Reich.9 Second, its central programmatic tenet was the unification of the socialist movement to overcome the old controversy between 'democratic socialism' and 'proletarian dictatorship' that had prevented the KPD and SPD from establishing a common anti-fascist front during the Weimar Republic.10 Third, its ideology was uncompromisingly and irreducibly democratic socialist, with neither of these principles realisable in isolation from the other; not merely politics but society and economy as well would be the objects of democratisation and socialisation.[11] And fourth, the antifas not only championed radical socialist programmes such as the nationalisation of mines, banks, big industries and other key economic sectors,[12] they also began to effect concrete socialist measures like the formation of *Aktionsgemeinschaften* of SPD and KPD members in many centres, occupation of plants belonging to war criminals, cessation of arms-related production, etc.[13]

This mass indigenous movement toward democratic socialism represe-sented a threat to all four occupation powers who in April (in the Western zones) and May (in the Soviet zone) 1945, banned it. In the Soviet case, the main reasons for suppressing the antifas were probably tactical: to enhance the relative strength (and therefore bargaining power) of the KPD before allowing it to merge into a unified socialist party.[14] But in the Western zones—which, under American domination (Marshall Plan aid, relief and rehabilitation of allied countries), would shortly be incorporated into an anti-Soviet Trizone—the threat posed by the antifa movement was of a much more fundamental kind. From the perspective of maintaining and reinvigorating the world capitalist system, 'containing'—and later 'rolling back'—communism on an international scale, and asserting the US arrival as a world power and defender of liberal democracy, the anti-capitalist orientation of the anti-fascist groups was positively dysfunctional. From the outset, American policy was guided by an 'anti-communist impulse' (Parenti) which lay at the centre of the 'range of interests' posited by John Gimbel:

> Besides wanting to denazify, demilitarize, decartelize, democratize and reorient Germans and Germany, Americans were also interested in seeing to their own security, bringing about the economic rehabilitation of Germany and Europe, and guaranteeing the continuance of free enterprise. They wanted to frustrate social-ism, to forestall Communism, to spare American taxpayers' money, to counter-act French plans to dismember Germany, and to contain the Soviet Union in Central Europe.[15]

Thus US Directive JCS 1067 imposed a quarantine on all political activities in the Western zone and dissolved the antifas, prohibited political parties, rejected *Land* constitutional provisions calling for socialisation of key economic sectors and suspended trade union activities including proposals for worker co-determination. When parties and trade unions were readmitted several months later, they were officially licenced and regrouped along pre-1933 party lines, and their leaders appointed by military government at first from the non-Nazi (as well as, in some measure, the non-socialist) elite groups, but as the Cold War intensified, increasingly from among former NSDAP members and others prominent in the Third Reich.

Hence a substantial proportion of the leaders chosen to guide the 'New Germany' were in orientation and outlook much like the pre-war elites. Ideological vindication for this dual process of *restoration* of pre-war elites and *renazification* was also furnished by JCS 1067, which advanced the thesis of collective guilt, an undifferentiated concept that held the entire German people responsible for the crimes and aberrations committed 'in the name of the people' by the ruling classes of the Third Reich. Like its counterpart, 'the sole responsibility of Hitler' (which would be invoked by the restored German elites), this thesis had the effect of exonerating those individuals and classes who had in fact actively collaborated in the Nazi seizure of power and were involved in the formulation and execution of their policies.

Through the interstices of the collective guilt edifice, all but the most flagrant and brutal elites of the Third Reich, in the judiciary, state bureaucracy, educational system, military and, not least of all, business entered into the elite structure of the Second Republic: almost all the representatives of big business labelled as war criminals by the American Kilgore Commission in 1945 were back in their former positions by 1948; and of roghly 53,000 civil servants dismissed on account of their Nazi pasts after 1945, only about 1,000 remained permanently excluded, while the judiciary was almost 100 per cent restored as early as 1946.[16]

Their presence of course contributed, and was intended to contribute to the 'economic offensive' needed to wage the Cold War. Restored capitalism, with its ideologically tenuous anti-communism and its objective need to forestall the imminent 'historical turn' in the FRG, required quick and tangible results in the form of economic improvement. This in turn necessitated the abandonment of the economic conditions of the Yalta and Potsdam agreements, just as renazification signified the negation of its political provisions. Thus (token) decartelisation measures and reparations were halted and replaced by currency reform and Marshall Plan aid. Not only did this policy effectively consign to East Germany the burden of reparations for all Germany—since the devastated Soviet Union, as the chief victim of Nazi aggression, was bent upon exacting the reparations assigned to it by the Potsdam accords—but the shedding of the relatively underdeveloped agrarian areas in the East amounted to a gain for the now more export-oriented West German economy: 'as soon as [West] Germany could find the exports with which to pay for substitute imports of food, she stood to gain by the switch.[17] A grossly undervalued Deutschmark, a reservoir of cheap mobile labour furnished by the mass of unemployed and refugees from the East, and the massive tasks of reconstruction which absorbed total productive capacities completed the formula of the *Wirtschaftswunder*. Without prior socio-economic change, of course, the beneficiaries of post-war economic recovery and development would have to be the restored elites.

Herein lies the source of yet another apologetic myth, namely that German leaders in the post-war period somehow surmounted 'the burden of the past' and 'ideological barriers'; they 'did not agonize over questions of collective guilt, overcoming the past, or the Weimar tradition, but got right to work on building the new state'.[18] Naturally. All this was accomplished *on their behalf* by the Western military governments and rationalised by the 'exigencies of the Cold War' as well as the need to 'contain' the 'communist menace'.

Thus, the context of West German anti-communism was in considerable measure *co*-determined by Allied, particularly American, foreign policy. Military government's initial role was basically passive: to delay popular reforms until 'normal' conditions could be restored. With the intensification of the Cold War, Allied policy was increasingly based on active interventionism which ranged from military threats to restoration and renazification in the unified Western zone.[19] The anti-communist orientation of American policy developed into a multi-front offensive that would involve the subordination of the German people's interests in practically every sphere of social interaction. Militarily, it would require a degree of militancy and willingness to sacrifice on the part of a war-weary population. Politically, it would mean the repression of the pervasive social democratic tendencies and compulsory adherence to a formally liberal democratic system underpinned by a restored capitalist economy. Economically, it appeared to jeopardise the reconstruction and rebuilding programme—though the ensuing *Wirtschaftswunder* and remilitarisation helped to assuage this reservation. Socially, it would mean in essence the reestablishment of class domination despite the new spirit of egalitarianism. And in terms of foreign policy, the anti-communist offensive, given Germany's strategic location and the East–West constellation of interests, would produce national division.

To make this comprehensive violation of (West) German interests palatable, a powerful legitimating and vindicating ideological conception was required. Here anti-communism presented itself as ideally suited to American goals in particular. For it was sufficient merely to 'translate' an already well-developed and proven doctrine into the German idiom; local socio-economic conditions and newly re-emerging interests would provide its direction and momentum. Not surprisingly, therefore, 're-education for democracy', facilitated by military government monopoly over curriculum content, the mass media and all political and social organisations, very quickly became re-education in the spirit of anti-communism.[20]

American appeals to freedom and democracy in the name of militant anti-communism of course corresponded with certain concrete fears and longings abundantly present in post-war Germany. Even prior to the capitulation, the German masses who, on hearing the Allied demand for total surrender, had feared the worst, and who had certainly been at least vaguely aware of the Nazis' crimes against humanity—as witnesses to the brutal round-up of Jews and other 'undesirables', through rumours of genocide, daily contact with forced labourers, etc.—had supported the war effort to the very end. Anti-communism provided a point of common cause with the Western victors and hence, even at this late date, a means of avoiding being called to account for their complicity. Moreover, the Soviet Union—against whom many of the Nazi war crimes had been perpetrated—was actively engaged, as already mentioned, in realising the provisions of the Potsdam agreements, including *inter alia* the fixing of Germany's Eastern boundary at the Oder-Neisse Line, the exaction of reparations, comprehensive dismantlings and the like. Refugees and expellees arriving by their thousands in the Western zones brought with them a variety of resentments and horror stories. An anti-communist alliance with the Western powers thus appeared vastly preferable to having to undergo an accounting for the destruction wrought by the Third Reich.

In any case, anti-communism—unlike, say, liberal rights or even social rights—was already firmly imbedded in German popular thought. It was merely an extension of traditional anti-social democratism which had been pursued, during the Second Reich, with equally traditional German methods: censorship, persecution, political ban and Berufsverbot.[21] And during the Third Reich, anti-communism was of course an integral part of the total Weltanschauung of racism and *Volksgemeinschaft;* indeed it could be argued that anti-communism represented the essential *raison d'être* of National Socialism.[22] Thus, the German people after 1945, subject to the trauma of a (second) lost war accompanied by the unambiguous realisation of total defeat and shared responsibility, conditioned by twelve years of Nazi propaganda under the control of the SS State, and encumbered by an awareness of their complicity in all this, seized the ideological rope of anti-communism extended to them by the Western occupation powers who for their part needed a capitalist, liberal-democratic and anti-communist (West) Germany to complete their new international economic order.

Christian democracy and clerical anti-communism
But here again, a one-sided reading of the role of Western intervention in West Germany can too readily be used to coin a further apology based on the notion of the 'omnipotence of the occupation authorities' which sees Germany as the 'helpless object' of four-power policies[23] or asserts that the occupation relieved the German people of the 'last direct responsibility' for political developments.[24] No doubt, as Rolf Badstubner argues, the presence and intervention of the occupation powers were 'indispensable pre-requisites' to and a 'condition of the success' of the restoration of

capitalism and with it the success of anti-communism. But:

> If the [imperialist bourgeoisie] had not been successful in recreating, through its policies, a mass political base for its political line. . ., then the bayonets of the imperialist occupation powers, however numerous, could not have prevented the historical turn in all Germany for any length of time.[25]

It would be simplistic and rather misleading, however, to regard West German Christian Democracy—the *Christlich-Demokratische Union* or CDU in the North and Southwest, the *Christlich-Soziale Union* or CSU in Bavaria—as a mere agent of the military governments in the Trizone and of the USA in the FRG. True, the Christian Democratic parties, at the head of a bourgeois party coalition, proved most capable of operating within the parameters set by the occupation powers (including militant anti-communism). But the Union was also able to extend and improvise upon the given limitations to transform the West German partial state into one of the leading anti-communist advanced capitalist countries in Europe, and to place its own stamp on it.

In the 1945–1949 period, no political party aspiring to mass support could dispense with a socialist programme. By the same token, every party seeking to derive that mass support from popular elections had to be licenced by the military government and thus had to function within the liberal democratic rules of the game. Not only did this situation preclude a unification of the labour movement, as has been shown, it also prevented any reversion to undemocratic beliefs or practices on the right—with the singular exception of anti-communism. Since capitalism was for the moment utterly discredited, the conservative forces needed other ideological rallying points with which to 'begin again'. Here Christianity presented itself as both amenable to the occupying powers and conducive to 'moderating' and mitigating the radical-socialist programmes of the SPD and KPD.

The surviving churches provided an institutional anchor for Christian Democracy. For, despite their strong involvement in the old authoritarian state as well as in the Third Reich,[26] because they had co-existed with the Nazi regime and indeed, had benefited from it for so long—the well-publicised struggles between church and state had not developed until very late in the Third Reich—they were relatively prosperous and intact in 1945 and surrounded by an aura of anti-fascism which then enabled them to exert a disproportionate influence on politics and society. Their pronounced pre-political appeal and anti-socialist tradition were essential latent qualifiers of such initially necessary CDU/CSU political statements as the 1947 Ahlen Programme which, among other things, demanded the abolition of the capitalist system and championed 'a new social and economic order'.[27]

Christian Democracy, formulated in this period as 'Christian Socialism', represented the provisional ideological foundation of West German conservatism—until it could be replaced by clerical anti-communism, as will be discussed presently. Like much else about the CDU/CSU, the party was no mere updated version of, say, the old Centre Party based on Catholicism. Rather, it was supra-denominational and, in religious matters, entirely undogmatic. Indeed, more than any other West German party, it was a product of its time and conditions. The negative precedent of the fragmentation of the bourgeois camp during the Weimar Republic, the strong apolitical-authoritarian tradition of modern German history and the success of the NSDAP in attracting support from all social classes—albeit disproportionately from the middle classes—surely played an important role in the establishment of the CDU/CSU.

Ideologically, apart from anti-communism and the free West, the party has never committed itself to a single consistent and logical programme after Ahlen, but instead has confined its pronouncements to generalised slogans and adapted its platforms to suit changing socio-economic conditions. In this way, it has managed to gain mass support from all classes: at election time roughly all occupational and income groups vote in more or less equal proportions for the party. In other words, the CDU/CSU, the *Volkspartei* par excellence, 'plays a mediating and integrating role between the social partners which is hardly different from the state itself'.[28] In fact, the coalition sustaining the CDU/CSU has been basically the same as that upon which the Third Reich relied; the difference is that while the latter resorted to enforced 'coordination' of these groups, the former has been able to 'pluralise' them into a paternal conservatism. Dynamic, adaptive, capable of concessions to its 'labour wing' and other distinct social minorities, not predisposed against limited reforms, the CDU/CSU was the first 'aggregate' or 'conglomerate' party in post-war politics in the FRG. And what it, like other modern conservative parties, 'really "aggregates" are the different interests of the dominant classes.'[29]

Consequently, the CDU/CSU has been able to present itself as reformist, progressive, representative of the general will, religious, modern, above-party, anti-communist, or whatever the exigencies of the current situation demanded; and this it could do with some justification, for it was simultaneously all and—with the exception of anti-communist—none of these.

From this mass basis and these ideological propensities, and given the system-immanent function of Christian Democracy, the consolidating dominant classes were able to forge the CDU State[30] as the chief instrument of West German anti-communism. This state had several dimensions. Politically, a strong state was necessary to guide popular opinion away from the prevalent anti-capitalist mood and to contain opposition to the new course. In contrast to the 'dual executive' of the

Weimar Republic, the new government structures provided for a strong executive and entrenched it by immunising it from popular pressures (e.g. 'Five Per Cent Clause' to restrict parliamentary representation of new parties, exclusion of plebiscites and referenda, 'constructive vote of non-confidence' to replace the executive). The socio-economic dimension meant, more than anything else, the *Wirtschaftswunder* whose very successes were tangible reinforcements of the 'free market economy' and 'social partnership' proclaimed by the CDU/CSU. The rapid return to pre-eminence of the business classes, their close collaboration with the CDU State, and the extreme income disparities which the 'miracle' produced served to further the process of restoration and renazification begun under military government.

Thus pending reforms in education, social services, 'morality laws' (abortion, equal rights for illegitimate children, etc.) were deferred or removed from the political agenda, at least partly under pressure from the churches' 'moderating influences'. Thus too, the return of former Nazis to prominent positions in public life: Dr Hans Globke, Adenauer's State Secretary in the Chancellery and close confidant, had not only helped to write the authoritative commentary to the Nuremberg Race Laws, but had been instrumental in drafting these laws in the first place. Indeed, Adenauer's first cabinets were permeated with ex-Nazis: Theodor Oberlander, Minister of Refugees; Gerhard Schroeder, Minister of the Interior; Hans-Christoph Seebohm, Minister of Transportation—a full one-third of Adenauer's first cabinet in all. Many more former National Socialists were absorbed by the diplomatic service, the judiciary (as already discussed), the *Länder* governments, the *Bundeswehr,* at the top levels of business and government service and the educational system.[31] Therefore, in Professor Kühnl's words, since

> . . . important positions of leadership are in the hands of groups who consorted with fascism, who profited from fascism and were intellectually affected by it, it is not surprising that authoritarian and fascist tendencies are at work here in a variety of forms.[32]

Nor is it surprising that during the 1960s even the highest representatives of the Federal Republic, President Lübke and Chancellor Kiesinger, were both nominated by 'groups who had had important functions in the fascist period',[33] and had themselves been closely associated with National Socialism, Kiesinger as party member and functionary in Goebbels' Propaganda Ministry and Lübke as builder and alleged (but not definitively proven) constructor of concentration camps.

And finally, the supra-national dimensions of the CDU State are a crucial factor in explaining the nature of West German anti-communism. For, established on the foundation of an aggressive anti-communist policy, the Western partial state in a sense owed its continued existence to its ability to function as a bulwark against communism. This involved several things. The issue of rearming the Federal Republic first came up in late 1947, in connection with the policy of containment, and gained further impetus with the outbreak of the Korean War. But due to popular opposition, no headway was made until 1955 and 1956 when a series of laws was promulgated providing for voluntary military service, production of war materials and universal conscription. Just as the *Wirtschaftswunder* restored much of the lost prestige of business, so rearmament helped immensely to make the military more respectable again, and encouraged even more active German identification with the 'policy of strength' and the 'rollback of communism'. Moreover, defence spending, as a form of public expenditure without redistribution, tends to produce economic growth favouring the status quo, thus sealing class interaction between business and military elites.

Rearmament also served to harden the front lines of the Cold War and encourage the GDR to remilitarise as well. If until 1956 there had been any prospect for reunification, the rearming of the FRG meant that henceforth national unity could only be achieved by an act of war. Western integration merely reinforced this situation. West German entry into NATO, its membership in the EDC, the OECD, the Customs Union, the ECM, the Council of Europe, the World Bank and the International Monetary Fund—these were all stages toward comprehensive political, economic, social and military interdependence, each another reinforcement of the Cold War and a de facto move away from the officially proclaimed goal of national reunification. The trade-off for West German subordination to the interests of 'the West' was the final return of political sovereignty, a sovereighty which Ekkehard Krippendorff describes as having been attained '. . . by means of the most complete and comprehensive "integration" imaginable for any country in recent history (with only the GDR as its logical counterpart)'.[34]

This (necessarily rather lengthy) analysis of the CDU State in its several dimensions reveals several crucial ideological compulsions built into Christian Democracy's structure of domination. At its very core, CDU/CSU policy was profoundly irrational. It aspired to be nationalist even as it anchored 'its' partial state in the Western alliance. It proclaimed peace while entering into an anti-communist military alliance expressly aimed at revising the post-war status quo in Middle Europe. It presented an image of security and continuity even while precluding any realistic security for a generation or more. Its image of conciliator and aggregator was palpably belied by its restoration of class domination and its preference for business interests.

These contradictions and social antagonisms could only be mediated by strong, socially effective ideological tenets which, paradoxically, would have to be put across in the guise of 'apolitical' truths acceptable to broad sectors and classes[35] —a loose conglomeration of popular resentments, apprehensions and generalised, ritualised beliefs. These ideological elements would have to be asserted in a militant, aggressive form and removed from susceptibility to criticism in proportion to their basic irrationality,[36] not at all unlike the crusader quality of American anti-communism.

What was distinctive about the prevailing ideology of the CDU State can thus be summed up in the formula, *clerical anti-communism:* a combination of politicised religious notions which enter into and shape the dominant ideology to an extent unique among advanced capitalist countries, and an intensive, irrational anti-communism (but with a very rational social function) comparable in style and substance to American McCarthyism—with the important difference that the West German anti-communists were not attempting to expose or undermine the government; they were part of it.

But before considering the import of clerical anti-communism, it is worth recalling that anti-communism in the FRG, in the immediate post-war period, did at least have a rational basis. There existed well grounded reasons for criticism of Soviet policy in occupied Germany as well as the strategy, tactics and beliefs of the KPD and, after February 1946, the SED in the Soviet zone. This point will be developed further in the following section. So long as the other parties—including the Christian Democrats—offered alternative proposals and programmes, the level of inter-party debate was comparatively objective. But with the intensification of the Cold War in 1947 and the establishment of the Western fragment state in 1949, the quality of West German anti-communism, nurtured and fostered by the CDU/CSU, became increasingly emotive and irrational, reaching its apogee in the 1950s. It is argued here that this irrationalisation of anti-communism can be traced to both the *premises* and *social functions* of Christian Democracy.

Concerning these premises, the clerical basis of Christian Democracy, sustained by the relative pre-eminence of the churches already alluded to, in many respects merely revived the old notion of the 'struggle for the West' against the 'anti-christian' forces at work in communism and socialism. For example, the idea of a 'decisive battle' between the 'Christian West' and 'Asiatic Bolshevism' has always been an integral part of the churches' political Weltanschauung. This fixation on 'the West' functioned in part as an ersatz nationalism in the CDU State, a kind of consolation for the national unity that had to be sacrificed to restore capitalism and maintain class domination; whereas rational internationalism would have had an exiguous mass appeal, a cultural-religious invocation of *das Abendland,* Christianity, etc. provided a regressive substitute.

Even when the churches have not actively propagated expressly anti-communist ideas or emotional appeals, the basic ideological predisposition which they have helped to produce has frequently lent itself to application by professional anti-communists. Let one example stand for many: when rightist circles began calling for atomic weapons in 1956, they declared, among other things, that the choice for the atom bomb was more than a military decision, that it was also a Christian decision; the soldiers supporting the policy were said to 'believe that the destruction of physical existence is little against the ravage of the soul and conscience by an absolute ideology. They have already learned how dead one can be while one's body is still alive'.[37] Statements such as these were almost never challenged by the churches; on the contrary, they were the stuff of 'pastoral letters', sermons and the like.

And concerning the social functions of anti-communism, the conversion of West Germany into an extension and instrument of American (anti-communist) foreign policy also necessitated the production of a corresponding mythology. The 'theory' of totalitarianism performed this necessary function with remarkable economy and efficiency and, like much else about Cold War ideology in the FRG, was preformulated and pretested by the major occupation power. In its cruder initial form, the concept of totalitarianism rested on a simplistic notion—first advanced by George Kennan in an influential article in *Foreign Affairs*—of the 'Russian national character' as aggressive and expansionist, thus inevitably leading to 'Soviet imperialism' which the West was bound to resist. By 1949, the thesis was further refined by a joint study group, called together by the American Departments of State and Defense whose mandate was to analyse the implications of Soviet possession of atomic weapons. The results of its deliberations, National Security Council Paper NSC-68, argued that totalitarianism practised domestically in the Soviet Union leads to expansionism abroad. The Soviets, unable to tolerate the existence of free societies elsewhere (which by their very being would undermine Soviet stability), were bound to conquer and subordinate the rest of the world. Hence, 'diplomacy with the Soviet Union was out of the question because they could never choose—their internal character would drive them to expand everywhere'.[38] This view, typically, resonated through official West German thinking throughout the fifties. Returning from a visit to Moscow in 1955, for example, Konrad Adenauer declared:

> I learned at first hand that the Kremlin leaders are firmly convinced that Communism under Moscow leadership will one day rule the world. And. . . although I only travelled a few kilometers through the country, I could see on the faces of the men I met that they had lost their souls. People in Russia can no longer laugh or cry. They are without souls. Such a regime, I am more than ever convinced, is fatal to mankind.[39]

Indeed, Adenauer himself was at the forefront of the anti-communist vanguard. For him, 'the issue is whether Europe will remain Christian or whether it will go heathen'; therefore 'God has endowed Germany with the task of saving Western Europe and Western Christianity'.[40]

Totalitarianism, in its later sophisticated versions, 'successfully'—meaning in terms of its mass effectiveness—posited an identity between fascism and communism and in this way was able to transfer existing popular feelings of anti-Nazism, revulsion at the scope of war crimes and genocide, and other negative attitudes towards the just-defeated enemy onto the newly emerging 'rival' for global influence and hegemony. In order to do so, not only did Stalinism have to be styled as communism *per se,* but the very different starting points, mass bases, social functions and goals of communism and fascism had to be ignored or downplayed[41] while certain temporal, external similarities (purges, single ideology, monopoly over the media and means of coercion, etc.) was absolutised and essentialised, and posited as the 'basic nature' of the two systems.[42] Above all other things, a fundamental antagonism was proclaimed between 'freedom', attainable alone in and through liberal democracy, on the one hand, and 'totalitarian bondage' on the other. The inference is evident: the real line of social choice was said to run between 'liberalism' and 'dictatorship' rather than between social interests and/or social classes. Even as the ideological phenomenon of totalitarianism addressed a deep and justified post-war longing for democratisation and participation, therefore, it negated the socio-economic reforms which would have been pre-requisite to any meaningful exercise of liberal rights and the concretisation of abstract 'freedom'.

The theory of totalitarianism corresponds with the 'totalisation' of the communist 'enemy' into the source and bearer of all evil, the agent of sinister forces and the embodiment of every conceivable negative attribute—entirely analogous to the role of the Jew in National Socialist ideology. The exaggeration of the 'bolshevist threat' or the 'world communist conspiracy' onto a comprehensive emotional plane, beyond the bounds of normal credibility, transformed ideological anti-communism into an article of faith, subject to examination only in terms of total acceptance and commitment—or rejection and thus exclusion from practically every facet of social life. This exclusive quality of anti-communism helps to account for its near-total hegemony, since 'the most powerful ideologies are not those which prevail against all challengers, but those which are never challenged because in their ubiquity they appear more like "the nature of things" '.[43]

How was it possible then, for this 'totalised' or 'reified' anti-communism to emerge so rapidly and thoroughly in less than half a decade? In addition to mass complicity in the excesses of the Third Reich and a general fear of the Soviets' desire to settle accounts, as well as the anti-socialist aspects of the German political culture, already mentioned, post-war anti-communism was in part 'successful' as a result of conscious manipulation by the groups who stood to gain from its acceptance: the elites in government, business, the state bureaucracy including the military, and former Nazis at all levels of society. This has already been alluded to in terms of the legitimation of the Bonn Republic. Indeed, 'official' communist accounts of anti-communism persist in viewing the phenomenon almost exclusively in terms of a conspiracy by the 'most aggressive groups of the imperialist bourgeoisie' who further it by means of 'resurrecting the most reactionary philosophical, ideological and political conceptions'.[44] Although this partial interpretation by and large holds, it fails by itself to account for all the dimensions of the syndrome, namely its mass support and its special appeal. Nevertheless, it can be established, e.g., that the major representatives of West German business, the BDI (League of German Industry) and BDA (Association of German Employers), have consistently been a leading force in the dissemination of anti-communist propaganda. While styling business as the creator and maintainer of the 'liberal market economy' and thus of freedom and democracy as such (and at the same time promoting renazification and restoration, and tenaciously opposing the extension of democracy into the workplace), these associations have mounted an unprecedented anti-communist offensive using the substantial resources available to them. Hence,

> . . . the invocation of the communist peril assumes such a prominent place in the ideologies of the employers' associations because it fulfils two functions at once: because it expresses an agreement with popular views and at the same time serves entrepreneurs' interests, or in short, because it provides universally accepted arguments for the promotion of particularist interests.[45]

Similarly, West German rearmament and renascent militarism, and the huge expenditures of resources and energies they entailed, were rationalised by anti-communism. But once established, the national defence system developed its own ideological corollaries: siege mentality, war readiness, dependence on 'the West'. Whole networks of vested interests, from suppliers and contractors to banks, universities and conservative politicians in this way acquired an interest in the perpetuation of anti-communism.

The manipulative aspect of West German anti-communism is further underlined if one briefly considers its *main techniques* and *domestic functions.*

Apart from the 'ordinary' techniques of anti-communism as practised in most advanced capitalist countries—guilt by association, accusations of being objectively in agreement with communist designs, one-sided polemical defamation, criminalisation or threat of criminalisation, etc.[46]— that of moral discrimination is particularly invidious. To be anti-communist is to be free, Christian, moral; to be 'soft' on communism is to be unfree, atheistic, immoral. Framed in such terms, the dichotomy could not be subjected to rational discussion, since morals are absolutes. In practice, the technique could be made to work against any group or individual who did not support the anti-communism-induced social consensus.

For example, opponents of atomic armaments were accused of an overriding opportunism in so far as they were said to hope that a coming victory of communism would bring them certain advantages. Furthermore, it was immoral to partake of economic prosperity and to attack it at the same time; if one was against the FRG's social order, then one ought to go live in the GDR. The—desired and intended—results of the application of such methods was a great pressure toward social conformity. Accusations of anti-communism needed only to be levelled, not supported; the onus of proof then automatically went over to the accused who, even if s/he could prove his/her innocence, was 'tainted' by the charge. Political proposals or policies were judged not according to their intrinsic merits but by the degree to which they were associated with communist objectives or by the number of 'Eastern contacts' which their proposers were said to have had.

The actual practice of clerical anti-communism, almost incidentally, infringed upon the liberal rights of freedom of information and expression, and upon the ideals of peace and coexistence which it was supposed to be upholding. Freedom tended to be defined negatively, in terms of the state's relationship to communism: the *defence* of 'freedom and democracy' became itself 'freedom'. Similarly, advocating peace and coexistence was equated with supporting communism. According to the extreme rightist *Rotbuch,* 'peace' for the communists meant world revolution, and hence those in the West desiring peace were 'fighters for the world revolution'.

From all this, it is now possible to infer the central domestic function of anti-communism, namely *social discipline.* Clerical anti-communism in the FRG fulfilled, and was intended to fulfil this specific task: what Reiche and Gäng have termed the 'externalisation of the class struggle'[47] or, in the words of the late Werner Hofmann, 'the transposition of the vertical intra-societal conflicts onto the horizontal level'.[48] By means of involving a potent external enemy, actual domestic class conflict is transformed into an ostensibly international one. At the same time, this foreign enemy, who is attempting to sow dissension through its 'agents' in one's own free society, must be combatted with every means. In the US, this syndrome produced the concept of un-American activities. In the FRG it led to the *Alleinvertretungsanspruch* or the claim of the Western state to represent the German nation and the German 'essence'. 'Germany' is thus defined as the area where the traditional social order remains with its old values, norms and modes of behaviour, while 'the Zone' is where foreign powers rule through local agents. Implicitly, therefore, the latter has a certain right or mandate to restore unity by 'liberating' the oppressed fragment and integrating it into its own just, authentic system.[49]

This task of maintaining national integrity requires a massive effort to achieve a unity of purpose. It means, first, persevering with the status quo, since—according to the 'avalanche' myth popularised by the BDA—any social reform, however insignificant, might set off a whole chain of socio-economic change that could work to the advantage of the communists. Second, it means ruthlessly exposing and eliminating all threats to the enforced consensus: war-resisters, Easter Marchers, pacifists, critical intellectuals, mavericks in the established parties and, in particular, alleged communists. And thus, third, it means ideological cohesiveness or a predominant orthodoxy within the framework of which every individual or group is under compulsion to prove itself the best anti-communist; 'orthodoxy magnifies itself into monomania'.[50]

To sum up, the import of this section on the forms, functions and significance of clerical anti-communism can be concretised with a brief discussion of the actual treatment by the CDU State of the German Communist Party.[51]

The KPD of the early 1950s, hampered by an excessive dependence on the GDR as well as being the focus of anti-communist sentiments and discrimination by official laws and government measures, found itself with a very limited mass following. On the other hand, it remained the consistent articulator of a number of popular interests which were not, or not adequately represented by, the major parties. Its continued advocacy of an anti-fascist, socialist front, its opposition to rearmament and atomic weapons, its resistance to authoritarian trends such as restrictions on free speech and emergency laws, and its demands for a greater measure of economic democracy were aims shared by members of a great range of groups, including neglected interests within the established parties. It was evident, in the climate of anti-communism just described, that to discredit or even criminalise the KPD would also be to reduce the appeal of all groups that shared any of its aims. During the first half of 1951, as the Federal Government continued its negotiations toward rearmament over growing opposition, the first legal persecution of communist organisations began, resulting in the banning of the Communist Youth Movement and the Union of Persons Persecuted by the Nazis. In September, decisive moves were made toward the incorporation of the FRG into the EDC, and within a week the government made a formal application for the banning of the party. When subsequently the question of a West German contribution to the European defence system was shelved, so too were proceedings against the KPD. When in 1954 the government moved again toward rearmament and membership in NATO, the trial against the KPD also resumed. In 1956, Adenauer articulated his 'policy of strength' and called for universal conscription; and about the same time repressive measures were taken against a communist-sponsored organisation and several of its members made to stand trial for treason. As the popular St. Paul's Church movement against militarisation acquired mass support, the Federal Constitutional Court decreed the official suspension of the KPD.

The correspondence between the growth of opposition and the promulgation of anti-KPD measures may or may not have been as direct as their temporal sequence seems to suggest. But the ban did bring with it a number of implications for liberal democracy and its concomitant ideology, clerical anti-communism. First, after 1956, KPD party functionaries and members were the victims of a wave of arrests, interrogations and trials. These applied not only to party members but also to their families, so-called substitute organisations and persons or groups suspected of sympathising with communist views. A comprehensive apparatus was developed to undertake surveillance of all these individuals and organisations. Third, the ban of the KPD was also an offensive against the broader socialist Left. Not only did it result in the suppression of criticism aimed at specific government policies (rearmament, Western integration), it virtually precluded any kind of criticism based on a questioning of the capitalist socio-economic order. If the KPD's programmes for socialism and peace were 'criminal', so too were by extension those of the SPD and DGB.

The KPD ban also rehabilitated and vindicated anew the military and bourgeois classes, and opened the way for all manner of traditionalist organisations, military clubs, and neo-Nazi associations. When the 1952 banning of the Social Reich Party, a neo-fascist formation, is cited as evidence that the Federal Government was impartially dealing with 'extremists' on both sides, then it must be recalled that, unlike the KPD, the SRP was permitted to develop successor organisations (e.g. former SS members' clubs, veterans associations) which were not subject to further persecution. And where former Nazis could join other political parties, the very presence of former communists in a party frequently meant that the party was designated as 'communist infiltrated' and therefore subject to legalised persecution and/or counterinsurgency measures.

Social Democratic anti-communism
In a sense, the SPD 'ought to have' been the predominant party in postwar Germany. Not only did it consistently reflect the popular current of the time, democratic socialism, and incorporate by far the majority of proven anti-Nazi individuals and groups from the pre-war era, it also—in a reunited Germany and free from Allied intervention—*would have* secured a majority in nation-wide elections. (In retrospect, one can only speculate about the extent to which this demographic fact contributed to the respective political elites' decisions to create separate states from out of

the Western and Eastern zones.) From this perspective, SPD party policies under Kurt Schumacher were logical and purposeful: reunification before external alliances ('national' socialism), relentless opposition to both occupation powers' attempts to intervene in German politics (national sovereignty and self-determination), indivisibility of socialisn and democracy (*'der Sozialismus wird demokratisch sein, oder er wird gar nicht sein!'*) and therefore no compromises with either 'communist authoritarianism' or 'capitalist reaction' (*'gegen Kommunismus und Kapitalismus mit gleicher Härte'*).

However, what was a viable and competitive programme of democratic socialism for the post-fascist society was transformed, virtually overnight—with the creation of the separate Western state, formation of the bourgeois coalition, West German involvement in the Cold War and onset of the restoration—into a programme of fundamental or categorical opposition. Despite the changed constellation of forces after 1949, the party determined, in its Bad Dürkheim Sixteen Points of August 1949, to pursue an 'as-if' policy: proceeding as if it were about to gain political power, as if reunification was imminent, as if the occupation were ended and Germany entirely independent[52]—and as if the KPD in the Western state were still the rival it had been in the Eastern zone in 1946 when it overwhelmed the SPD and established the SED.

Here, a brief excursus is needed in order to achieve some conceptual clarity for the argument that follows. In an abstract sense, a distinction can be made between *rational* or *irrational anti-communism*. Rational anti-communism bears at least some relation to empirical communist theory and/or practice and therefore is in some measure concerned with the content of its pronouncements or the effects of its acts. Irrational anti-communism, on the other hand, deprives anti-communism of its rational basis (or 'transcends' it) and is more comprehensible in terms of the goals of those propagating it and the psychological traits of those espousing it. Similarly—and this is admittedly rather more tenuous—it is possible to speak of *progressive* and *regressive anti-communism*. The latter's social function is the preservation of a class-divided social formation and the forestalling or negation of socialist reform. Progressive anti-communism, on the other hand, need not be the contradiction in terms that it first appears. There are, after all, a number of dissonances between any consistent theory of democratic socialism and the praxis of state socialism, particularly the GDR after 1945. The UAPD (Independent Labour Party), one of the independent leftist parties which surfaced briefly during the 1950s, suggested some differentiating criteria. Whereas the 'bourgeois combats what is still revolutionary' in communism, independent socialists criticise its non-, or anti-revolutionary aspects: absence of internal democracy, subservience to Soviet interests, ideological opportunism, etc. But 'our main enemy is and remains the capitalist system, and we oppose the KPD only because it is waging the struggle against capitalism on the wrong basis. . .'[53] Similar conclusions can be derived from Crusius and Dutschke's class distinction of anti-communism:

> Whereas the anticommunism of the bourgeoisie is based on its interest in defend-ing its political and economic power positions, the anticommunism of the wage-dependent classes has a different motivation. For them it is a matter of maintaining their higher standard of living, their freedom of opinion, their freedom of move-ment, in short all those things that are results of the struggles of the German labour movement.[54]

Of the Schumacher SPD—to return to the main line of argument—it could be said that its anti-communism was consistently progressive, in the above sense, but frequently irrational in its attacks on the 'Red Fascists' and 'Soviet dupes' against whom it sought to profile itself. Though Schumacherian anti-communism was therefore grounded in a progressive premise, when invoked irrationally it led to a number of *wrong tactics*. Its shrillness, for instance, often matched that of the CDU/CSU and, being indistinguishable from it to the unsophisticated observer, merely rein-forced it. Intransigent opposition directed 'with equal severity' against communism and capitalism, overlooked the salient reality that an anti-communist campaign was already being waged by the resources of the CDU State with the backing of foreign trend-setting powers; the real 'enemy' of democratic socialism, in the Western partial state, was capitalism.

Moreover, even while the federal SPD was practising its fundamental opposition, whole groups of SPD members were entering into elected positions (e.g. the 'mayors' wing' in the major cities) and appointed offices (civil services and other state institutions) at the local and *Land* levels, in part on the strength of an anti-communism that was neither progressive nor rational. A final tactical problematic for the post-1949 SPD arose from an almost Lassallean tendency to equate 'democracy' with parliamentarism (*Nur-Parlamentarismus*), which in time evolved into an inability to envision other than strictly constitutional solutions to the problems—NATO, rearmament, restoration, renazification—which were in part created by 'extraparliamentary' class power and outside intervention, and which the SPD attacked in radically phrased speeches and writings.

After Schumacher's death in 1952, these mounting contradictions produced, *inter alia,* a mediocre leadership, an ossified party structure, a decline in membership and a desperate search for a way out of the '33 per cent ghetto' which the electoral successes of the CDU/CSU—with its absolute majority in 1957—left it mired in. Lacking a collective will to realise a programme of democratic socialism, the party, through several conventions and an extended 'programme debate', increasingly emulated the basic ideology and catch-all nature of Christian Democracy. Anti-communism was seen as the most available and attractive bridge to this policy of 'embracement'. Social Democratic anti-communism, as propagated by its *Ostbüro,* the party organs and the party leaders, was increasingly used to threaten dissident members with expulsion, or actually to expel them—e.g. the left-wing trade unionists around Viktor Agartz or the editors of the radical newspaper, *Die Andere Zeitung*—and to coerce the loyalty of those who remained. In its concern to make the party more acceptable and to open it to the 'new middle classes', the party leaders failed to comprehend that the total, irrational anti-communism they now began to espouse was an ideology formed by and for the CDU State and its beneficiaries and hence worked mainly to the advantage of the SPD's political opponents:

> [The SPD] will never be in a position to represent the interests of big industry more plausibly than big industry itself, to echo the legends of the 'Christian West' and the 'Free West' better than the qualified authors of this ideology, the CDU. It cannot relate anti-bolshevist horror stories in a more gruesome manner than the professional anti-bolshevists of the stamp of Taubert and his consorts from the school of Herr Dr. Geobbels.[55]

The outcome of the programme discussion was the 1959 Bad Godesberg Programme that proclaimed the SPD a *Volkspartei,* rather than a class party, which now addressed the middle class groups previously immune from socialist appeals, accepted the socio-economic order established by the CDU State (including Western integration), abandoned all references to Marx and defined socialism in terms of material benefits and 'anti-totalitarian' freedom. If the Godesberg Programme amounted to the SPD's surrender of an independent domestic policy, Herbert Wehner's 30 June 1960 speech to the Bundestag accomplished the same thing in foreign policy. Henceforth, the Atlantic Alliance, the European Defence Community and the policy of 'reunification on the basis of strength' would characterise the SPD's foreign policy.[56]

Meanwhile, the 'pragmatic' wing of the party—led by Willy Brandt, Fritz Erler and Herbert Wehner—with its image of 'moderate reform' and 'modernity' had gained ascendancy. Under its guidance anti-communism was further developed into an integrating factor in as much as the party could now set itself up as a collection of anti-communist, social democratic and leftist elements, claiming that any party or movement to the left of it was bound to become communist, or at least a communist tool. This being the case, such groups could *a priori* be defamed as just that; the self-fulfilling prophecy nature of anti-communism was re-enacted by the SPD in this way. The principle was further applied to 'leftist deviationists' within the party,[57] which led to another series of expulsions and resignations from the party in the early sixties. The further removed the SPD's praxis became from its former socialist goals, the more prominent became the role of anti-communism as a method of discipline and integration.

This increasingly irrational, regressive anti-communism was quite functional, in terms of the policy of *Angleichung* or the process of disposing of the past, de-emphasising ideology and defining programmatic principles in terms of 'values' rather than goals. It had the twofold purpose of facilitating the SPD leaders' bid for power within the framework of existing state and society, and of integrating the party, its membership and its supporters into this changed social perspective. The absence of binding principles, it is evident, gave the leaders a greater scope or freedom of movement and the ability to alter policies as circumstances changed.[58]

Having thus foregone the goals to which political power had been a means, and forced to rely on anti-communism as an ideological ersatz and instrument of intra-party discipline, the SPD leadership instigated a wave of expulsions of individuals and groups who, for the most part, continued to espouse nothing more than pre-Godesberg party policies. For instance, the Socialist Students' League (SDS), which advocated detente with the East and recognition of the Oder-Neisse Line as Germany's Eastern boundary (an integral part of Willy Brandt's later Ostpolitik!) and public discussion of the 'brown' pasts of highly placed judges, politicians and civil servants (a campaign in part documented with materials originating in 'the East'), was expelled in July 1960.[59] Then the SFG or Society for the Promotion of the SDS, a group of SPD intellectuals and socialists who had come together to assist the SDS' efforts to remain an effective force outside the party, was forced to choose between it and membership in the SPD. Most, e.g. Wolfgang Abendroth, Ossip Flechtheim, Heinz Brakemeier and Fritz Lamn, chose to remain in the SFG and were therefore expelled.[60] Other attempts to form a political grouping to the left of the SPD—for instance the Socialist League (SB) or Union of Independent Socialists (VUS)—were similarly defamed and denied by the SPD.

The first large party founded on the single issue of peace, namely the DFU or German Peace Union—whose supporters happened to include a number of communist or communist-associated individuals—was subject to especially vehement attacks by the SPD. In fact, Social Democracy, as one of the 'pillars' of the CDU State, now had an interest in the elimination of the DFU for many of the same reasons the CDU/CSU had had in banning the KPD in 1956. And it employed many of the same methods, including irrational anti-communism. For the SPD, the DFU was an 'agency of communist infiltration', a 'collection of useful idiots' for the CPSU and SED, and 'the vanguard of communist takeover' tactics.[61] The party executive then declared membership in the DFU incompatible with membership in the SPD.[62]

This analysis of Social Democratic anti-communism, as part of the co-optation process of the labour movement in advanced capitalism, suggests several things. For one, it demonstrates the process by which the SPD, like all other Western social democratic parties, has evolved an ideology of 'labourism' which John Saville defines as 'the theory and practice of class collaboration'.[63] As the social democratic party accepts, and attempts to gain a share in the class hegemony of the capitalist state, it produces a number of conflicts within itself. For instance, while the party leaders are actively collaborating in a 'party cartel' assuming a basic ideological consensus both within the party and among parties—which in the SPD's case was expressed by 'concerted action' as its version of the 'social partnership' thesis—actual economic struggles at the party bases (for higher wages, more codetermination, less armaments, etc.) tended to undermine the strategy of labourism. In the absence of a system-transforming mission or even of a coherent programme of opposition, then, anti-communism appears initially as a highly functional ideology, (1) to rationalise the surrender or 'postponement' of the party's socialist goals, thus preventing an outward drift by the traditionally supportive working classes; (2) to discipline the party left and strengthen the party leadership; and simultaneously (3) to increase the party's attractiveness to the middle classes in whom it sees an extension of its mass base. The assumption underlying this strategy is that the capitalist social system itself has undergone a transformation into some variation of an 'em-bourgeoised society' or a 'levelled-off middle-class society', thus making class struggle obsolete in any case.

To assume this, however, is not to wish away wage disputes, the fact of subordinate work or capitalist relations of production, all of which proceed independently of the SPD's will. Anti-communism can only obscure, not eliminate this fact. To adopt anti-communism in its bourgeois-irrational form—'whose specific quality, in contrast to the relevant leftist critique of the Soviets, is its undifferentiated and total demonisation of socialist structures together with their Leninist and Stalinist deformations'[64]—is to see that anti-communism's essence is that of an interest-motivated ideology of the dominant classes aimed at discrediting *all* class actions and movements, including the 'moderate' and 'reasonable' demands advanced by Social Democracy, who, by espousing it, objectively carries 'labourism' to its outermost, absurd limits.

Ostpolitik and Berufsverbot: A 'double strategy' of anti-communism
It is ironical that even as the SPD was completing its embracement of the CDU State a series of developments not only rendered many of the CDU/CSU's post-war power sources obsolete but also partly vindicated many

of the SPD's now abandoned policies.

Economically, the salient tendency of the early and mid-1960s was the rapid slowing down and increasing crisis-susceptibility of the *Wirtschaftswunder*. The factors making for economic prosperity and expansion—Marshall Plan aid, the Korean War-induced export boom, rearmament, state-subsidised partiality to private enterprise, trade focus on the West—now began to give way to market satiation, production slowdown and less 'social peace'. As this phase of post-war expansion came to an end, important sectors among German business increasingly looked Eastward for new (or, more precisely, the revival of traditional) markets for manufactured goods and sources of raw materials, a trade relationship of vital importance to the export-dependent sectors of German industry, particularly steel. But the anti-communist premises of Adenauer's foreign and domestic policy—which, as has been shown, were both essential for popular support and 'total' and hence immutable—presented a hindrance to trade with the East.

Against what he saw as the 'particularist' interests of certain manufacturing and industrial sectors, Adenauer constantly posited the 'national interest', patriotism and anti-communist solidarity, and this policy was upheld by the powerful BDI. Where irrational political policy opposed economic interests, as far as the exporters (represented by the *Ostausschuss* or Eastern Committee as their main lobby) were concerned, either the 'national interest' had to be redefined or trade with the communist countries had to be 'depoliticised'. This was especially so as other Western European countries (notably Britain and France), affected also by similar economic imperatives, were increasing trade relations with Eastern Europe even as the FRG's share was declining.[65]

Thus, irrational, regressive anti-communism, while still partly functional in domestic politics, became an obstacle to economic development. Foreign policy in turn represented a hindrance to economic policy; but a number of factors were at work to force it to adapt as well—despite the SPD's recent total embracement of it in all its essentials. For one, American foreign policy, which continued to 'guide' and impose the parameters of West German policy, shifted to an emphasis on detente and coexistence under the Kennedy administration, thereby depriving Adenauer of his resolute ally, John Foster Dulles. Pressure was automatically placed on the CDU/CSU to do away with the now most obviously dysfunctional aspects of its foreign policy, e.g. the *Alleinvertretungsanspruch* and Hallstein Doctrine; but to do this would undermine both the class basis and internal unity of Christian Democracy.[66] A temporary solution was sought in the hastily constituted Adenauer–De Gaulle partnership based on hard-line anti-communism, but the Franco–German Friendship Treaty made little impact on a public opinion increasingly in favour of improved relations with communist countries.[67] The erection of the Berlin Wall, as the logical response to the 'policy of strength', demonstrated further the bankruptcy of aggressive foreign policy and indicated that the status quo in Middle Europe was likely to remain fixed for some time. (Incidentally, the 'Anti-Fascist Protective Wall' also put, or should have put paid to the myth of 'communist aggression'; whatever else it might have signified—ideological inadequacies, loss of regime legitimacy—the Wall was aimed at holding on to the status quo, not at external aggression.)

Adenauer and his foreign minister Heinrich von Brentano were more or less compelled to retire in 1963. The Ludwig Erhard government appointed Gerhard Schroeder foreign minister with a mandate to carry out a limited Ostpolitik on the basis of a 'policy of motion'. But apart from the establishment of several trade missions and cultural exchanges with Eastern Europe, the policy was unable to move beyond its anti-communist premises: Hallstein Doctrine and non-recognition of the GDR. The CDU/CSU could not develop a coherent economic or foreign policy toward the communist states so long as the party remained divided between its Eastern and Atlanticist/Gaullist wings.

Beyond this, the CDU/CSU–FDP coalition had attempted since the late 1950s to enact a series of 'emergency laws' which, however, had not managed to obtain the required 2/3 legislative majority. This legislation, which was reminiscent of Article 48 of the Weimar Constitution—press censorship, banning of the opposition, suspension of the right to strike, ambiguous definition of 'state of emergency', etc.[68]—was transparently directed at potential domestic opposition, particularly trade union demands, anti-nuclear groups, leftist anti-system opposition, etc., which might be expected to increase as the economic miracle subsided, for:

> The laws legalise the establishment of a complicated bureaucratic machine whose finely meshed gears can only function if the verbally invoked 'external emergency' and the atomic catastrophe do *not* occur. Patently conceived for 'times of peace', they can only be aimed at securing the social status quo against social crisis.[69]

In this situation, the SPD, which had abandoned in principle its opposition to such emergency measures, declared its solidarity with the CDU/CSU's foreign policy and became more attractive as a possible coalition partner. Moreover, the SPD's willingness to undertake economic planning and state intervention corresponded with big business' plans for economic growth; the Erhardian neo-liberal economic policies were increasingly seen as less adequate than Karl Schiller's concept of 'overall economic guidance' (*gesamtwirtschaftliche Steuerung*).[70] Thus Erhard too, as a remnant of the Adenauer line, had to be dropped and replaced in 1966 by Kurt-Georg Kiesinger before the Union could enter into a Grand Coalition.

The SPD, for its part, was also vitally interested in a Grand Coalition.

Beset by growing intra-party dissent, unable to function even as a 'loyal opposition'—for instance by calling attention to the 'Spiegel Affair' of 1962 or the telephone tapping, Fibag and HS 30 scandals of the early sixties—fixed on a strategy of image-making and poll-chasing, and lacking alternative policies and programmes in all vital areas, the SPD leadership desperately needed a share of power to vindicate its post-Godesberg course and demonstrate its 'responsibility' and 'governing capacity'. This the Grand Coalition of December 1966 provided.

A full accounting of the import of the Grand Coalition cannot be undertaken within the scope of this paper. But in terms of its central focus, anti-communism, several points need to be made. The SPD's participation in the *Grosse Koalition* self-evidently led to an erosion in its traditional working-class support. The economic crisis of the late sixties was mainly overcome, within the framework of Schiller's policy of 'concerted action', by positing business as the driving force of economic recovery, so rationalising the relationship between it and the state (more planning, more coordination, guaranteed profits) and consciously further-ing its capital accumulation by means of more tax write-offs, subsidies and the like. Naturally, the representatives of organised labour, in particular the militant metalworkers' union, found themselves increasingly in con-frontation with the SPD leadership. In all the *Land* elections of 1967 and 1968 the SPD's share of the popular vote declined, in some cases drastically.

Furthermore, the formation of the Grand Coalition can also be seen as the final catalyst for the development of the Extraparliamentary Opposition (APO) from out of the hitherto diffuse groups who no longer saw the state as capable of responding to their needs: the student movement (with the SDS as its centre!), the peace movement, disillusioned and expelled Social Democrats, various single-issue movements from the anti-emergency laws *Notstand der Demokratie* to the Easter Marchers, pacifists, neutralists, more or less radical Marxists, etc. The intensity of the APO's opposition to basic trends in the West German social order—blind anti-communism, emergency laws, Vietnam, militarism, the 'party cartel', anti-abortion legislation, stagnation of political life, etc.—at the very least indicated some of the problems associated with the SPD's policy of unqualified embracement of the Right.

The SPD leadership's reaction to these developments was ambiguous. On the one hand, APO demonstrations and mass rallies merely confirmed the need for the emergency laws that they had collaborated on in passing into law. Anti-communism still functions as an instrument of intra-party discipline, as the expulsion of the Student University League (SHB) in mid-1968, as well of many individuals and entire party constituency organisations, demonstrated. But on the other hand, the party leaders, faced with the problem of declining mass support and fundamental

opposition from the Left, were compelled to search for a means of pro-
filing the party within the coalition and, armed with their new image of
'respectability', to develop an effective electoral appeal. An alternative
foreign policy, which need not entail basic domestic reforms, offered
itself as the most efficient means of accomplishing this. Crucial to the
success of an independent SPD foreign policy would be the support of
business (whose relative pre-eminence, as has just been suggested, had
been considerably enhanced by the SPD's participation in the Grand
Coalition).

True, the Grand Coalition had managed to 'depoliticise' East–West
trade and to work out commercial agreements with some East European
countries, notably with Romania in 1967. But trade was still subordinate
to political considerations. The *conditio sine qua non* of further progress
was recognition of the GDR, which the CDU/CSU could not do, not even
within the coalition, without dismembering itself and renouncing the
ideological foundation on which it rested. It was evident that the CDU/
CSU could not cope with this admixture of business interests and
emotionally charged anti-communism, that is, was incapable of operating
between the extremes of 'export interests and the primacy of foreign
policy, between patriotism and profit'.[71]

But the Social Democrats could. For in the conservative, irrational,
anti-communist climate of the FRG under the CDU State, merely to
advocate a foreign policy that corresponded with popular opinion and
economic necessity—even while tenaciously opposing radical change—was
to acquire an image which accorded with the party's post-Godesberg
'moderate reformism' profile. But before Ostpolitik could be made the
basis of an SPD bid for electoral power, several conditions and concessions
were necessary.

First, the Social Democrats would need a coalition partner. Despite the
party's total focus on system-immanence and respectability, its share of
the popular vote, in the 1961 and 1965 elections, had not risen beyond
what *Genosse Trend* (a combination of demographics and social change)
probably would have produced in any case. And, as just suggested, the
party's participation in the Grand Coalition was actually causing considerable 'voter drift'. At this juncture, a coalition with the Free Democrats
appeared most attractive. The FDP, like the SPD, was not encumbered
with a hard core of 'cold warriors', clerical anti-communists and other
groups with a vested interest in the old-style anti-communism. (It did
contain a small expellee faction as well as many anti-clerical former Nazis;
but these could be dispensed with and 'equalised' with the expected new
'liberal' voters defecting from the other parties.) The FDP was also not
committed to any working class constituency and was thus entirely free to
champion middle class interests, the same interests that the SPD also
sought to attract. Although since 1949 the FDP had been the CDU/CSU's

more or less constant coalition partner, as the more 'pure' representative of business, its policies had always been more rationally and clearly in favour of the 'modern' sectors of the capitalist economy.

A second precondition for the SPD's Ostpolitik was the removal of the ban on the KPD. After all, a policy of suppressing and demonising communists domestically does not accord with 'normal' trade and political relations with foreign communist states. In any case, a decriminalised communist party, after years of persecution, represented no threat to the basic constitutional order; on the contrary its existence could be displayed as evidence of a new tolerance. Even within the framework of the Grand Coalition, the SPD was able to effect the relegalisation of German Communism, reconstituted in 1968 as the DKP (German Communist Party).

Third, business support was essential, not merely from the *Ostausschuss* and manufacturing sectors, but beyond these, the 'progressive' elements of the financial and productive sectors as well. This was obtained in part by a calculated appeal to the long-range interests of business as a whole, an appeal which can be summed up in the notion of *Modell Deutschland*.[72] The *Modell Deutschland* advocates took seriously Franz-Josef Strauss' current aphorism about West Germany having been too long an economic giant yet still a political dwarf. The FRG had now advanced to the rank of the world's second or third greatest capitalist power, but in foreign policy was subordinate to the interests of the other Western powers. Now, however, the FRG had to prepare for its 'world-political responsibilities', which would involve accepting international realities—Oder-Neisse Line, national division—and adopting a more flexible foreign policy. Business' cooperation would be crucial here. Since the export sector had historically been the motor of economic development, its well-being—ensured by a more amenable international climate—would develop the economy as a whole. State and business would complement each other, and their collaboration would underpin the FRG's enhanced position in the world society and economy. Integration into the 'open' and 'free' international economy would replace 'economic nationalism' and immobilism. Keynesian public planning and spending, predicated on continuous economic growth, would provide optimal conditions for accumulation. The SPD/FDP bias toward technology and modern management would enhance the FRG's export capacities. At the same time, labour peace would be guaranteed by the presence of the SPD—who, better than the CDU/CSU, could 'moderate' and contain worker demands—while at the same time 'socialist excesses' could be averted by the corrective presence of the FDP. In any case, the 'humane side' of the new coalition would work to labour's advantage: continued economic growth would bring larger welfare benefits while normal relations with the GDR would ease tensions and reunite families.

Fourth, finally, a mass electoral basis had to be ensured and fundamental opposition reduced on both right and left. This involved a dual strategy. On the one hand, Ostpolitik, and all the developments associated with it, had to address a wide range of interests: to the Right it offered enhanced national power and prosperity and to the Left it held out a more rational foreign policy, dialogue with the East, and a promise of ultimate detente and peace; for the Right Karl Schiller embodied technocratic efficiency, social partnership and state support of business interests, while for the Left Willy Brandt was the symbol of peace, liberalisation and compassion. In Ostpolitik, therefore, the 'non-material' interests of politically separated families and friends combined with the 'post-material' interests of the peace and anti-nuclear movements to constitute a mass basis for the very 'materialist' interests of the more 'dynamic' sectors of West German business.

The Small Coalition, assembled in 1969, was remarkably successful in ensuring the latter: intersystem trade between East and West more than doubled between 1955 and 1973,[73] the FRG's trade surplus with Eastern Europe went from DM 0.7 bn in 1970 to almost DM 8 bn in 1975,[74] and West German exports of DM 1.6 bn in 1971 to the Soviet Union amounted to DM 4.8 bn by 1974.[75] Despite virulent anti-communism-founded attacks from the CDU/CSU—freed now, by being thrust into opposition, of its intra-party tensions between the Atlanticists and the Easterners—the Social–Liberal coalition was able, between 1969 and 1972, rapidly to 'normalise' relations with the East through binding treaties with the Soviet Union, Poland, Czechoslovakia, etc., as well as regularise intra-German relations by recognising the GDR and the Oder-Neisse Line. For this the Small Coalition realised a significant electoral victory in 1972 and Chancellor Willy Brandt was accorded a Nobel Peace Prize in 1973.

Although this section so far has emphasised the objective and subjective factors tending to *transform* clerical anti-communism, this should not be taken to mean that anti-communism as such was *reduced* or done away with by Ostpolitik (though in a sense it did deprive it of its rational basis). On the contrary, its essential social functions remained, even as the faces of its main beneficiaries in the political realm changed. To begin with, the disparate groups, whose support was required for these dramatically shifting foreign policy orientations, needed a common and non-specific ideological cohesive force. Once in power, the first Social–Liberal coalition rested on a bare and unreliable majority that was subject to a virulent anti-communist campaign from the Right: not only the CDU/CSU but also their allied mass media, interest associations, many of the state agencies, and a number of business sectors. And within both SPD and FDP, vocal minorities continued to oppose this or that aspect of Ostpolitik. Domestically, therefore, anti-communism was still essential to counter the opposition, enforce social cohesion and maintain intra-party discipline in both SPD and FDP. For these reasons,

> . . . the architects of Ostpolitik felt compelled to emphasize over and over again that international cooperation with communist regimes did in no way imply a weakening of the resistance offered to communist groups at home. That is how Ostpolitik rhymes with Berufsverbot. [76]

What was needed, was a new *form* of anti-communism, more differentiated and sophisticated than clerical anti-communism, to be sure, but nevertheless consistent and potent. This was accomplished by the Berufsverbot.

Although as a result of Amnesty International Reports, the findings of the Russell Tribunal and a multiplicity of petitions, protests and the like by various national organisations concerned with civil liberties, the basic features of the Berufsverbot are well known, it is worth briefly reconsidering them here in order later to relate them to their anti-communist functions. In popular usage, Berufsverbot refers to the Anti-Radical Decree of 28 January 1972,[77] a joint declaration by the Federal Chancellor and the *Länder* premiers banning from public service, at the federal, *Land* or local level, persons defined as 'extremists', 'radicals' or 'anti-democrats', whether on the left or right. It was signed into law, at the peak of the Ostpolitik 'offensive' and shortly before the (crucial) 1972 elections by Chancellor Brandt (who later admitted that it had been a mistake[78]). And since then it

> . . . has had the active support of a legislature that provides a broad network of legislation authorizing political repression, of a judiciary that is frighteningly cooperative and pliant, and, most alarming, of a trade union movement that with only few exceptions collaborates to the point of—admitted and documented—'cooperation' with the Special Branch. [79]

Etymologically, the term Berufsverbot (ban on practising one's occupation) alludes to the fact that, in a nation where well over one-tenth of the working force are public servants—from railway workers to university professors—to be barred from the public service is *de facto* to be excluded from one's profession, particularly in the case of teachers, administrators and others who cannot expect to find a post outside the state agencies. Probably about 1.5 million Germans have been exposed to investigations in the years since its inception and perhaps two thousand have lost their jobs or not been hired as a result.

Critics of the Berufsverbot have rightly made much of its continuity with the *Obrigkeitsstaat* tradition in Germany. Bismarck's Anti-Socialist Law, the Nazi complex of political justice and Adenauer's 1960 Anti-Radical Law are all self-evident precedents. The comparison with National Socialism is particularly instructive. For then as now anti-communism was depersonalised and bureaucratised thus in a sense dehumanising individuals affected by it and facilitating the repressive measures taken against them.

(Though the parallel cannot be taken too far, it is noteworthy that the system of concentration camps and mass genocide had to be thoroughly bureaucratised and depersonalised to be effective,[80] a phenomenon most succinctly captured by Hannah Arendt's coinage, 'the banality of evil'.[81]) Conceptual, even linguistic continuities abound. For instance, the 1933 Law Respecting the Restoration of the Professional Civil Service, in its 1937 version, stated that 'the civil servant must at all times and without reservation serve the National Socialist State' (loyalty to the state principle), while today's Federal Civil Service Law requires public employees 'to provide an absolute guarantee of their loyalty to the free democratic principles in accordance with the Basic Law' (loyalty to the constitution principle).[82]

In the ambiguity of terms like 'loyalty to the state' and 'loyalty to the constitution'—as well as the whole gamut of West German anti-communist legalese, such as unconstitutional activities, guilt by association, crimes against the constitution, libelling the state, contacts with persons accused of any of the above, etc.—is revealed the special 'genius' of the Berufsverbot. On the one hand, obviously political issues and problems are ostensibly depoliticised and objectivised by their removal from the narrowly political arena of legislatures and political parties and their transposition into the legal system where they are treated 'dispassionately' by 'experts'. By 'legal system' is meant not only the entire court structure, from local to federal level, but the whole range of secret service and enforcement agencies, the several levels of the Office for Constitutional Protection, the Special Branch, Military Intelligence, the police force, etc. These agencies may interview individuals, gather information about them at their discretion, consult experts, requisition credit or personnel records, and so forth.

But on the other hand, the veneer of objectivity is belied in a number of ways. Without exception, all the agencies of the 'legal system' (as just defined) are shot through with former National Socialists, though nowadays, due to attrition, less than ten and twenty years ago. As Franz Hegmann writes:

> Considering the fact that the 'Neo-Nazi' network includes or has included at various times high ranking government officials in the Office of the Federal Presidency, the Federal Administrative Court and even the Federal Bureau for the Protection of the Constitution (the West-German FBI). . . incidents of political bias become somewhat more plausible. The Nazi network within the ranks of the civil service is complemented by the members of the old Nazi elite in private industry, who disappeared more or less from the open political scene only to acquire a substantial foothold in the upper economic-industrial power complex.

He adds that:

It is somewhat intriguing in this context that former servants of the Nazi state and active members of the largest 'terror organization' in human history are now engaged in the prosecution of so-called student radicals.[83]

The 'incidents of political bias' to which he refers relate to the consistent use of Berufsverbot against the Left in stark contrast to the law's favourable treatment of neo-fascist organisations. This observation points to the extreme subjectivity and arbitrariness with which it can and has been applied, which in turn demonstrates the role of 'the legal system' in generating and enforcing anti-communism. For instance, constitutional interpretation, in the hands of ex-Nazi legal experts, has increasingly been (re-)oriented to its Hegelian and authoritarian antecedents. Thus Theodor Maunz—the same constitutional expert who once wrote the definitive commentary on the National Socialist legal system and who now does the same for the FRG, in a work approaching its 22nd edition—has carried on the struggle against 'legal positivism' and 'parliamentary absolutism' which he would replace by a 'state in itself' whose 'servants owe it a 'state-consciousness'.[84] At the same time, the constitutional-protection agencies have expanded the list of 'reasons for doubt', i.e. pretexts for undertaking an investigation into an applicant's or civil servant's loyalty to the constitution.[85] And the latter concept, nowhere codified, is left to judicial discretion.

Not only has the Berufsverbot affected pre-eminently the Left, therefore, but the definition of (leftist) 'hostility to the constitution' has been steadily extended to include not only communists (a legal party since 1968) and their sympathisers, but also pacifists, Greens, practitioners of alternative lifestyles, members of GDR-oriented groups, militant trade unionists, radical journalists, critical teachers, and so on. Even SPD members and supporters have been affected, as will be discussed in the next section. If necessary, exceptional legal sophistry can be used to rationalise this anti-Left bias. For example, the Federal Administrative Court—'two of whose members were active in the service of the Third Reich'[86]—ruled that the neo-fascist NPD was a legally constituted party according to Article 21 of the Basic Law and that membership in it was not grounds for rejection or dismissal from the civil service. Yet the same principle did not apply to DKP members since their party was anti-constitutional (verfassungswidrig) even though not actually hostile to the constitution (verfassungsfeindlich) as stipulated by law as a pre-requisite to imposing a formal ban.[87]

In any case—and this too is part of Berufsverbot's 'genius'—the ban is directed at *individuals* rather than organisations as such. In this way, it has been able to penetrate through 'formal' legal safeguards and remove individuals from public employment even while upholding the right of their party or association to exist. This in a way dismembers and atomises the collective goals of the party/association and reduces them to individuals' problems: 'the big cauldron of hostility to the constitution was replaced by thousands of little cauldrons of constitutional hostility'.[88] As such it is an ersatz ban on the affected (constitutionally protected) parties/associations by means of 'administering' away their key members. More important, the Berufsverbot thus acts as a deterrent to potential recruits and supporters of oppositional movements or even to those who might consider signing a petition or attending a rally sponsored by such a group.

This represents a stage beyond the old clerical anti-communism which 'merely' blacklisted identifiable organisations according to specified criteria (before proceeding to persecute all manner of persons remotely associated with such groups). Henceforth, individuals from the whole spectrum of leftist opposition could at any time be declared hostile to the constitution and deprived of their livelihood. And the definition of hostility to the constitution, it has just been shown, is set by the Right. Thus despite the apparent constitutionalism in which the Berufsverbot is ensconced, it is subject to certain 'higher' or 'overriding' norms. CDU/CSU Chancellor candidate Rainer Barzel addressed his parliamentary party in 1973 with these words:

> If existing legal bases are not sufficient to exclude DKP members from public service, the CDU/CSU is prepared, together with the other democratic parties, to create this legal basis. In the process, an amendment to the Basic Law must be taken into consideration.[89]

The anti-communism embodied by the Berufsverbot and the complex of constitutional deformations surrounding it distinguishes West Germany not only from its Weimar predecessor but also from other capitalist liberal democracies. What is specifically and qualitatively new about all this, as summarised by Friedhelm Hase, is

> . . . that [today, unlike in the Weimar Republic] the West German state lays claim, and this claim is based on the law, to the competence politically to eliminate certain political currents in general, to ban them once and for all from the political stage. Political repression has here pushed aside the aspects of situation and occasion, which characterised it in the past; it has cut itself free from the concrete circumstances and risks of specific, changing situations and is largely independent of determinate dangers and any political evaluation of them, quite different from normal states of emergency, exceptional situations and police-defined dangers. The 'free democratic basic order' legitimates its acts of repression not with certain situations and circumstances, but at a universal, ideological level.[90]

Once again, therefore, the *defence* of the 'free democratic basic order' overrides the civil rights anchored in that order, from freedom of speech and association to the freedom to choose one's profession. Coining the term *Gesinnungsschnüffelei* (nosing into people's thinking), Herbert Wehner, himself a major formulator of SPD policies in this period, said of the Berufsverbot: 'I don't see any point in wanting to protect the free democratic basic order by taking a first step toward doing away with it.'[91] The concept of militant democracy—developed for compelling historical reasons—becomes militant defence of the existing socio-economic order. Protection of a set of norms and rules to guide political life becomes protection and enforcement of the ruling ideology. What is being defended and enforced, therefore, is advanced capitalism whose major justification remains anti-communism, but an anti-communism elevated now to a legal norm and practical imperative.

Ersatz anti-communism: law and order

So far, the concept of ersatz has figured prominently in this analysis of anti-communism in the FRG: clerical anti-communism as ersatz ideology, Social Democratic anti-communism ersatz for socialist policies and goals, Berufsverbot as ersatz ban on oppositional politics, the 'legal system' as ersatz for political controversy. This section will add a final substitute-metaphor: law and order as ersatz anti-communism.

The Berufsverbot in fact represents an initial attempt to make the law a substitute for more explicitly political anti-communism, as the preceding section has argued. Nevertheless, the Berufsverbot in itself was not sufficient to prevent—though it did help to turn around—anti-communist-grounded defamation campaigns against the SPD from the Right. Once West German relations with Eastern Europe had been normalised and rationalised—and it had become apparent that Ostpolitik could not progress beyond the regularisation of East–West relations to develop, e.g. a separate all-European identity or present an alternative to the arms race—there was a real possibility of a conservative reaction to these rapid changes in foreign policy, despite the Small Coalition's increasingly repressive domestic measures. This reaction was facilitated by the SPD's continuing strategy, developed for purposes of intra-party discipline, of insisting that 'illegality' or 'criminal' politics begins to the immediate left of the party, or indeed at the extreme left within the party itself. Not only does this strategy deprive Social Democracy of a political buffer for apologetic purposes, it actually reinforces what the Christian Democrats had claimed all along, namely that the SPD, however well-intentioned, borders on the criminal, anti-constitutional forces, and even harbours many of them in its own ranks; the true guardian of the constitution and the most reliable safeguard of law and order is therefore the CDU/CSU.

For these reasons, it has frequently been possible for the Berufsverbot to be turned against its formulators. In several CDU/CSU-governed *Länder,* it has been deployed against Social Democrats already in, or seeking entry to the civil service,[92] and (less frequently) against Free Democrats as well.[93] Indeed, among the salient 'reasons for doubt' (as described above) in deciding whether to investigate a civil servant or applicant were often participation in demonstrations on behalf of the SPD's Ostpolitik, belonging to the SPD youth organisations SHB and Jusos, and—at least in Bavaria —trade union membership. Social Democratic scholars of international reputation were denied, or dismissed from, university posts not only because they advocated a union of the Left (sociologist Horst Holzer) but also because they had taken part in the anti-emergency laws campaign and the peace movement (mainstream SPD member and political scientist Wolf-Dieter Narr).[94] Many SPD school teachers, public administrators and other state employees were similarly affected.

The SPD leadership, in this situation—lacking the will to effect the kinds of political reforms that might have deprived the Berufsverbot of its social functions—was forced to operate between two increasingly antagonistic constituencies: *progressive intra-party forces* and the party's perceived *sources of mass support,* particularly 'its' new groups among the middle classes and dynamic sectors of business.

(1) The comparatively small, but highly visible and articulate inner-party anti-Berufsverbot grouping—made up largely of feminists, jurists, left trade unionists, Jusos, remaining SHB members—did manage to pass resolutions as early as the 1973 Party Convention in Hanover, reinforced at the 1974 Munich Convention, to the effect that an individual's membership in a legal political party ought not to affect his/her employment opportunities in the civil service and that reasons for denial of employment should be stated in writing and must not be based on the testimony of anonymous witnesses. That these resolutions were framed so comparatively modestly is a reflection of the leadership's successful strategy of formulating the issues innocuously and proceeding cautiously. But at the same time, intra-party discipline was invoked to prevent members from consorting with (legal but) 'anti-constitutional' organisations and from becoming involved in extra-parliamentary actions.

> The Presidium of the SPD repeats, for good reason, its urgent recommendation to all party members not to take part in the transparent campaign against ostensible 'Berufsverbote' and to stay away from events where there is a pressing suspicion that they are guided by the DKP or largely influenced by it.[95]

Violations of this intra-party anti-communist and 'moderate' consensus were then penalised all the more severely. The increasingly radicalised Jusos, for instance, though too large and important a grouping to be disciplined en masse, saw many of their members ostracised and expelled during the 1970s. Particularly threatening, from the party leadership's perspective, was the 'stamocap wing' within the Young Socialists whose core theoretical concern evoked the concept of state monopoly capitalism which was said to have originated in the East. The party leaders therefore expelled the leading stamocap representatives and distanced themselves from their doctrines. In 1977, for example, Klaus-Uwe Benneter was deprived of his party membership for writing that:

> The SPD, on account of its tradition and its programme, is obliged to regard the party system as a class-specific spectrum. From this viewpoint, the CDU and CSU are the parties of the class opponents, while the Communists, who are our political opponents, are not the class enemy.[96]

Thus, the Berufsverbot which, though hazardous, remains functional, has never been repealed nor repudiated by the SPD. It has only been allowed to wither partially away. In 1975, the Federal Government presented a bill, based on the 1973 and 1974 party resolutions, which would have made membership in a 'radical organisation' alone insufficient grounds for removal from the civil service; but the legislation was vetoed by the CDU/CSU dominated Bundesrat. In May 1976, the Federal Government issued directives, in substance identical to the 1975 bill, which however applied only to the Federal civil service. By the late seventies, some SPD *Land* governments (Bremen, Berlin, Hesse) did away with automatic checks on applicants, and in 1979 the Saar, as the first CDU *Land* government, also abolished such checks. The Federal Government did the same. Nevertheless, the substance of the Berufsverbot remains, in as much as applicants and officials can still be investigated and rejected 'for cause', thus retaining its 'deterrent' effect. And its social function— pressures toward conformity and social discipline—has not changed at all. A major reason why the most contentious techniques of the Berufsverbot could be gradually mitigated, was related to the growing importance, during the seventies, of another form of anti-communism—counter-insurgency or anti-terrorism—a motif which will be examined presently.

(2) To return to the main line of argument, the SPD leadership, whose power rested on its ability to integrate the party into the advanced capitalist society and political economy, could not simply dispense with the Berufsverbot if it wished to hold together the mass voting base of workers, new middle classes and dynamic business sectors that kept it in power. On the contrary, developments reinforced the objective need for social discipline and ersatz ideology. For by now it was evident that Ostpolitik had run its course and that the constantly growing economy—the foundation and key assumption of the Keynsian social partnership theory of *Modell Deutschland*—was more and more susceptible to crisis.

With the signing of the treaties with the Soviet Union and its allies, as well as agreement with the GDR on the formula 'two German states in one German nation', the limits of Ostpolitik—namely those imposed by the existing world order—were reached. Far from overcoming the tension between two hostile political and ideological blocs, Ostpolitik had in fact presupposed a prior 'Westpolitik' involving a retrenchment and fortification of the Western Alliance with its anti-communist raison d'être. Ostpolitik, having formalised the East–West status quo and facilitated an upsurge in intersystem trade, therefore list its momentum as the front lines of the Cold War rapidly reossified, particularly after the Reagan administration assumed office in the USA in 1980.

Immobilism in foreign policy more or less coincided with the series of economic reverses and crises said to have been precipitated by the formation of OPEC as the first successful producers' cartel of Southern states. Social tensions rose as the FRG experienced strike waves in 1971 and 1973, while at the same time promised reforms in parity codetermination, education, tax law, abortion laws, etc. were deferred, diluted or done away with. To be sure, the SPD could point to the FDP's 'countervailing power' within the Small Coalition, to the CDU/CSU's pre-eminence in the Bundesrat, or to the conservative bias of the courts and civil service, to exculpate itself in some measure from its failure to 'deliver' on the reforms. But its policies and measures clearly aimed at triggering economic recovery by exacting 'restraint' and 'temporary sacrifices' on the part of the party's traditional supporters in the blue collar classes rather than its 'new' voters. Among these policies and measures were wage freezes or if necessary wage rollbacks, cutbacks in social security programmes, petrol rationing (not however coupled with measures to combat profiteering by the big concerns), new incentives for business, especially the export sectors (which had produced one-fourth of total GNP and demand for which now declined by 10 per cent),[97] revaluations of the Deutschmark, etc.

Changes in the leadership of the Small Coalition facilitated the shift from (system-immanent) reformism to crisis-management and efficiency. Helmut Schmidt, a central figure on the SPD Right and Schiller's apparent successor as the party's special friend of business, replaced Willy Brandt (who, however, remained party chairman) on the latter's resignation following the 1974 'Guillaume Affair'; while Hans-Dietrich Genscher became FDP leader when Walter Scheel moved into the Federal President's office. The Schmidt–Genscher government, not so closely identified with reformism and detente, had a freer hand to deal, 'pragmatically' and with 'no nonsense', with the escalating problems of the West German state. The new leadership 'team' was well placed to call for unity and solidarity to overcome labour unrest or intra-party conflicts over defence spending, nuclear power uses, arms sales to Saudi Arabia, and the like, while at the same time developing more direct ties to business and the conservative parties.

'Law and order' here appeared as an opportune ideological tenet to assert the 'unity' and 'solidarity' of this resurrected *Volksgemeinschaft* (or at least *Interessengemeinschaft*), even as economic reverses and political ossification were producing both 'material' (strikes, lock-outs) and 'non-material' (peace demonstrations, citizens' initiatives, opposition to nuclear generator sites, ecology movement, anti-Berufsverbot actions) class conflict. Of course the Berufsverbot itself represented an initial campaign to reduce political issues to apparently legal ones, and, on the strength of the reduct-ion, to criminalise, ban and delegitimate all political opposition. The previous section has demonstrated this.

These methods, and the great apparatus of the 'legal system' that had been put in place to carry them out, could then be applied, *mutatis mutandis,* to the emergent ideology and praxis of *counter-insurgency* and *anti-terrorism.*

To be sure, individual acts of terrorism did take place in the FRG throughout the 1970s which collectively furnished the necessary pretext for an anti-terrorist law-and-order campaign. From the early actions of the 'Baader-Meinhof Gang' at the start of the decade, to the 1972 Munich Olympics tragedy and the 1975 kidnapping of Peter Lorenz by the 2nd June 1967 Movement, to the mid-1970s 'executions' of BDA President Hanns-Martin Schleyer, Federal Prosecutor Friedrich Buback and banker Jürgen Ponto, up to the freeing of 93 hostages from the Lufthansa air-craft held in Mogadishu, the well-publicised actions of the 'terrorists' and the state's draconic counter-measures eclipsed practically all other popular political dialogue. The subjective feeling of 'a nation at bay' was rein-forced by the international wave of similar incidents (activities of the Italian Red Brigades, the Vienna kidnappings of OPEC officials, repeated aircraft hijackings, attempts on the lives of Ronald Reagan and Pope John-Paul II) which evoked a mood of 'the West under siege'.

Like a number of governments of other advanced capitalist societies, the ruling coalition of the FRG found in the terrorism issue an oppor-tunity to restore much of its declining legitimacy. It recognised early the 'peculiarly obscene, evocative meaning'[98] that terrorism triggered in popular thinking and dwelt on this image to style terrorists as irrational, bloodthirsty crazies and misfits bent on sublimating their individual neuroses and pathologies through sabotaging society as a whole and 'its' state.

Anti-terrorism, when used as an ideology ersatz to marshal public support and justify social discipline, requires, like anti-communism, a 'total' undifferentiated version such as this individual-psychological inter-pretation. If the concept's propagators are successful in this, as they have been in the FRG, then two domestically 'destabilising' aspects of the terrorist phenomenon can be excluded. First, the demands and programmes of the terrorist organisations can be rendered irrelevant by ignoring or denying them. Few West Germans knew that, for instance, the 2nd June 1967 Movement arose in reaction to the police murder of a Berlin student demonstrator on that day and gained impetus from the attempted assassination of Rudi Dutschke by a young rightist who had gained his inspiration from reading *Bild-Zeitung,* a conservative-extremist tabloid published by the quasi-monopolist Springer Press. Fewer still were aware of the Red Army Faction's critique of the 'party cartel' in the FRG, of escalating armaments, of fading detente, of law-and-order politics, of the Berufsverbot and of advanced capitalism in general. Seldom was the symbolic significance of the terrorists' targets considered: Buback as the zealous administrator of anti-constitutionally defined crimes and political justice aimed at the Left, Ponto as a powerful and conservative banker, Schleyer (a former Nazi) as the head of the most powerful, consistently anti-communist interest association of West German business. Even where individual terrorist ideas were publicised, this was in the form of caricature or *a priori* rejection, so that they were discredited in any case.

Second, terrorism is treated as a strictly isolated phenomenon. Nothing is said about its socio-economic context. No distinction is made, for instance, between 'state terrorism' and 'individual terrorism',[99] for if it were, it would be revealed that the former normally precedes the latter.[100] Hence the professional anti-insurgents need not confront the *administrative terror* of a Berufsverbot which, lacking any objective criteria of 'hostility to the constitution', devoid of constitutional safeguards against its abuse, and governed by an entirely arbitrary procedure, potentially affects all aspiring civil servants and hence terrorises them.[101] There is no discussion of the *structural terror,* integral to capitalism, of inadequate diet, poor housing or greatly reduced life-chances for the poor, handicapped or disadvantaged. No mention is made of *police/military terror* in general that not merely forcibly suppresses demonstrations and occasionally causes the death or injury of participants, but also, as a presence, inhibits non-conformist social action.

Rather, individual terrorists, decried by the media, all the government parties—who try to outdo each other in intensity and vehemence—and state agencies, become the vilified, dehumanised outgroup and all the rest of society the injured, attacked group. The siege mentality is transformed, via the manipulation of people's fears, into a revenge mentality, which in turn not only prepares the population for a more repressive state, but leads them to advocate it.[102] Thus, from 1970–74, police expenditures rose from DM 2.56 bn to DM 5.16 bn, while the budget for the Criminal Investigation Department grew sixfold; at the same time the police forces were reorganised and centralised.[103] The technological, modernising orientation of *Modell Deutschland* was extended to the fields of national security, counter-insurgency and anti-terrorist techniques. At least in part for this reason, the state of siege did not produce any updated version of the *Freikorps* or *Geheimbündler*—or for that matter any vigilante groups or death squads. Anti-terrorist actions could be contained and developed entirely within the systemised and computerised state agencies.[104] Indeed, by the late seventies the West German security system had become one of the world's most observed, admired and emulated such systems.

All these developments—hard line against terrorists, irrationalisation of the object of resentment, inflation of state repressive apparatus, etc.—are in substance not much different from those occurring in similarly situated capitalist democracies (though the thoroughness and comprehensiveness with which they have been carried out are in themselves typical of the FRG). But what is 'specifically German' about the anti-terrorist campaign is its use as a starting point for much further-reaching measures, ensconced in and legitimated by law, extended again (like the communist ban and Berufsverbot) to encompass any and all opposition to the dominant socio-economic order, whether actual or latent.

The 'legal system' is deployed in two main ways to effect the criminalisation of politics and to enforce law and order as a means of social discipline. Existing laws are interpreted broadly and 'with licence' by the politically responsive agents of law enforcement and adjudication. Any publicly expressed reservations about, e.g., official versions of events surrounding the Baader-Meinhof actions, are penalised as 'defamation of the state'. Indeed, so intense had official paranoia become that the federal law enforcers decided to run checks of all 1,500 mourners at the funeral of Ensslin, Baader and Raspe who, it will be recalled, ostensibly committed suicide in Stuttgart-Stammheim prison.[105] Moreover,

> in trials of demonstrators, squatters and occupiers of building sites, in charges of 'defamation of the state' or 'breach of the peace', in Berufsverbote or action to preserve 'industrial' or 'communal' peace—resistance is labelled terror. Criticism, information and protest are punished as 'subversion' and publicity if necessary reduced to what is officially published.[106]

Then, as the next stage, further-reaching laws—in most cases prepared long beforehand—are passed and executed with haste and zeal. The Law for the Protection of Communal Peace, promulgated unanimously by the Bundestag in January 1976, goes beyond penalising actual 'criminal' acts to define individual motives and attitudes as criteria for sentencing offend-ers. Persons guilty of 'giving support and approval to violence' in any manner likely to 'disturb the public peace' are liable to lengthy jail terms.[106] 'Threatening, rewarding or approving criminal acts' as criteria mean that guilt can be established if an accused expresses (even the most vague and artificially construed) agreement with what subsequently are determined to be 'terrorist acts'. Even to advocate violence in any way, for any reason, can render an individual culpable, since such statements are 'socially harmful and dangerous to the community'. However:

> Obviously there will be no action, nor is any intended, if a police chief or interior minister explains why it was 'necessary and unavoidable' for his officers to move against pickets to clear the way into a factory for strike-breakers.

Obviously there should be no action when the Federal Chancellor 'welcomes in the name of the Free World' the US army's 'defence' of 'our freedom' in Vietnam or elsewhere with genocide.

Obviously no case will be brought if a mayor tries to explain to his fellow citizens why a speculator has the right to have his house cleared by the police, the tenants put out on the street, and the house then demolished to make way for a lavish office block.[107]

As interpreted by the High Court, 'guilt' arises not only from thinking in similar categories as 'terrorists', it is also present if one 'approves' 'crimes' committed abroad, by foreigners, which in no way affect the FRG. For such approval can be construed as 'contributing to the growth of general readiness for criminal activity at home'.[108]

Similarly, the complex of regulations that make up Section 129 of the Penal Code is formally directed at 'terrorism', but in reality affects the entire left spectrum. (The law is rarely applied against the Right—since 'dog won't eat dog'[109]—not even against expressly violent neo-fascist organisations who are by and large treated as basically right-thinking but impatient individuals who merely need time to cool down.) The Left, for the law-makers and law-adjudicators, is engaged in a broad, sinister conspiracy based on an ingenious division of labour. Thus, the High Court pronounced that:

One participant practices an activity whose anti-constitutional character is immediately obvious, while another carries on agitation disguised in general political aims and a third engages in tasks of a purely technical nature.[110]

It is almost superfluous to add that, on the basis of a court judgment such as this, huge numbers of people can and have been investigated, interviewed, scrutinised—indeed terrorised—not because of their acts, their writings, their contacts (though these count as well) but because of the ideas they are presumed to hold or the passages they might be inclined to write, or even the general predisposition they might have.

By way of summary, then, one need only reiterate the premise of this section: law and order, in the sense depicted here, has become an ersatz for anti-communism in the FRG. With Sebastian Cobler, we can state that the courts have become organs of justification rather than justice,[111] and that the police-militarist values of conformity, *Ordnung* and obedience have come to prevail as leitmotifs in the dominant ideology of the Federal Republic. The *Rechtsstaat*, mediated by the 'legal system', increasingly proximates the *Polizeistaat;* and where the two converge, the *Obrigkeitsstaat* is their necessary product.

Conclusions: Anti-communism in ideology and praxis in the FRG
It was always somewhat incongruous that the SPD should have emerged

as the party of law and order and the apparent main beneficiary of anti-communism. To be sure, in order to do so it had to abandon every vestige of socialism—save, perhaps, a residual social orientation which however was coupled with a much more consistent business orientation—and adapt to a post-war social, economic and political constellation shaped by American foreign policy interests and developed by Christian Democracy. In this sense, the occasionally conjured 'SPD State' is nothing more than an extended and rationalised CDU State. This is especially evident if the composition and orientation of all the other state institutions is recalled, in particular the continued CDU/CSU domination of the Bundesrat, many *Länder* and hundreds of municipalities. The more Social Democracy emulated and 'modernised' the CDU State, therefore, the longer it was able to stay in power. Anti-communism, together with its several ersatz variants, was the ideological vehicle of this *Angleichung.* Yet anti-communism—meaning here anti-socialism, anti-reformism, indeed anti-democratisation—amounts to an acceptance of the ground rules laid down by the most conservative interests in society, enacting political competition/conflict on their terms and hence ultimately working to the advantage of the Right.

True, even after the waning of Ostpolitik and the shattering of the Keynesian equation of business prosperity and worker welfare by the post-1973 economic crisis, the Small Coalition was able to maintain a tenuous hold on federal political power. But this was due in part to its willingness and capacity to propagate anti-communism and anti-terrorism more virulently and systematically than the Right. (Would the CDU/CSU have been capable of enacting a Berufsverbot or a Law for the Protection of Communal Peace?) Anti-communism enabled the SPD to govern without having to face the socialist policy implications on the basis of which it had been elected by the working classes, and it provided ideological vindication for abandoning its original anti-capitalism. Further, it smoothed the way to collaboration with business interests and the wooing of middle class voters. But at the same time, the competition between Christian Democracy and Social Democracy to outdo one another—in proposing legislation, making speeches, influencing the public—in the direction and intensity of anti-communism undoubtedly produced a more durable and intense anti-communism than would have occurred in, say, a CDU/CSU led state. In any case the SPD, like the CDU before it, ceased to be a consciousness-producing party and was transformed into an opinion-reflecting one; beyond a broad resistance to change, it, again like the CDU/CSU, cannot be said to have a clear direction or raison d'être, not even after its 1983 electoral reverse.

The Small Coalition also owed some of its staying power to Christian Democracy's tardiness in coming to grips with the changing, 'modernising' environment of political life in the FRG. For the many voting-research studies carried out over the past three decades clearly demonstrate a well-established mass sense of 'regime legitimacy' and 'system legitimacy'.[112] Crude, undifferentiated anti-communism no longer quasi-automatically deters potential SPD supporters. Whereas the SPD took the lead in refining and adapting anti-communism—e.g. by combining Ostpolitik and Berufs-verbot—the CDU/CSU persevered, throughout the 1970s, in essentially Adenauerian anti-communism. Having unsuccessfully attempted to wage the 1972 campaign by defaming Ostpolitik and all those 'tainted' by it, the Christian Democrats, inspired by the then Party Secretary Kurt Bieden-kopf, adopted a strategy of even less sophisticated anti-communism suggesting that the SPD, like the Communists, was bent on a 'collectivist society' and a 'total state' which would destroy initiative and liberty.[113] Translated into electoral slogans for 1976, the strategy was formulated as *Freiheit statt Sozialismus* (CDU) and *Freiheit oder Sozialismus* (CSU).[114] The old 'all roads of socialism lead to Moscow' argument was basically revived in an explicit equation of the SPD with 'actually existing social-ism'. In the words of now Federal Chancellor Helmut Kohl:

> Socialism is by no means merely a condition prevailing in the Soviet Unior or the GDR. Socialism occurs everywhere where the state, ostensibly seeking the well-being of all, takes more and more rights unto itself thus pre-empting the citizen. In this connection, Max Weber has painted the monstrous picture of the totalitarian welfare state as 'the comfortable dwelling of obedience'. Socialism—that is not only Communist dictatorship, the Wall and the Gulag Archipelago. Socialism—that is also the creeping dismantling of liberal society by means of tax laws, economic policies hostile to private property, collective school system, etc., etc. So-called democratic socialism is creating, in innumerable individual spheres, the very dependent society which must then re-elect it. Many countries in the Free West are already on the road to this obedient society. We in Germany must resist its beginnings.[115]

In 1980, the Christian Democrats chose Franz-Josef Strauss, the spokes-man for the most conservative elements, the most implacable anti-communists in the party, as their chancellor candidate. His invocation of an imminent communist takeover was also unsuccessful with the (marginally) more sophisticated electorate.

Despite the CDU/CSU's belated adaptation to popular sentiments, the SPD, in its role of 'manager' of the CDU State and vanguard of anti-communism, was increasingly debilitated by mounting contradictions on the left, right and centre.

The party's centre—the trade union contingent and its working class supporters—has been gradually defecting since the Grand Coalition. As already suggested, in a situation of limited growth where public spending could not ensure both business profits and higher wages, the basis of the social partnership has crumbled. The SPD consistently directed its measures aimed at recovery towards business prosperity, which to some extent was achieved, but without higher wages and full employment. Although limited reforms have been registered—notably in education, unemployment insurance, rent control, legalisation of abortion—these have been halted at the point where they came up against the interests of business and the wishes of the middle classes, i.e. delayed and diluted.

On the right, even the most dynamic sectors of business have increasingly moved away from the notion of a social partnership toward a more frank acceptance of social conflict and an indifference toward the once highly touted 'entrepreneurial social conscience'. Analogous developments have produced Reaganism in the US and Thatcherism in the UK. In the FRG it initially led to a fundamental cleavage with the Small Coalition. The FDP saw a monetarist economic policy, a reduced state role in the economy and a more direct reliance on market forces as the solution to stagflation and economic immobility. But the SPD party conventions continued to advocate more public spending (to stimulate business activity, not to ameliorate the workers' situation), while the top leadership emphasised austerity and wage restraints. This was opposed by both centre and left.

From the left, the critique of the SPD has been bitter and protracted, mainly over the issues of nuclear energy and disarmament. Disoriented by the conflict between (1) the need to placate its supporters on the right, the party accepted the (anti-communist-grounded) NATO logic of deterrence, thus permitting the stationing of US medium-range missiles on German territory and increasing the West German contribution to the Western Alliance; and (2) the desire to forestall growing opposition on the party left as well as the rapid rise in support for the anti-nuclear Green Party, it surrounded these actions with considerable rhetoric about the need for peace, detente, etc. Calling the SPD 'the party of moderate exterminism', Rudolf Bahro saw it as 'trying to master the difficult feat of harmonizing its faith in a deterrent with its own credibility as a party of peace'.[116] And members of the SPD left, demonstrating in front of the 1982 Party Convention, summed up a decade of the party's peace policy development, as they chanted:

SPD 1972—mehr Demokratie wagen
SPD 1982—mehr Panzerwagen

At some point, therefore, all the contradictions of the Social Liberal coalition, resting as it did on the (updated) post-war anti-communist consensus, had to crystallise and induce a fresh 'Wende' in the politics of the FRG. The coalition's advantages to the conservative forces—ability to coopt the trade unions, creation of conditions for East–West trade, maintenance of labour peace, technological and managerial innovativeness—declined in importance with the re-intensification of the Cold War, the growth of fundamental opposition (the Greens), the rise of social in-discipline (protests, demonstrations in favour of peace, disarmament, social justice), and above all the shrinking national economy (wages versus profits). Under the circumstances, the CDU/CSU appeared as the more adequate instrument of confrontational, class conscious politics: a more reliable ally in the Western Alliance, more willing to hold the line on labour demands (e.g. the 35 hour week), more expressly monetarist in fiscal policy, more willing to cut back the welfare state, and now more able to foster the anti-communist ideology that will be needed in coming years to make permanent structural employment palatable, to induce the population to accept lesser social benefits, and to overcome popular resistance to nuclear reactors and growing arms arsenals. It is the mandate of the Christian Democratic/Free Democratic coalition, negotiated in 1982 and electorally legitimated in 1983, to do just that. The SPD, having played out its role in the evolution of West German anti-communism, has been thrust, internally divided and ideologically confused, back on to the periphery of political life.

An analysis of anti-communism in the FRG, as in other advanced capitalist states, demonstrates anew the ideological paucity, the absence of vision that characterises these societies. It reveals liberal democracy to be a new and militant orthodoxy. It panders to, dredges up and manipulates the basest fears and resentments in the population and canalises them into an irrational, aggressive apology for the status quo. Indeed, it deprives people of their very hopes and their futures: 'the place that would be occupied in public opinion by a better future order, is today occupied by a negative image, the apparition of communism'.[117] In particular, anti-communism, as a largely self-fulfilling prophecy, undermines hopes for disarmament and peace. Its logical end is war.

NOTES

1. Michael Parenti, *The Anti-communist Impulse*, (New York, 1967), pp. 3–4.
2. From a speech delivered to the New York Economics Club in May 1984, here quoted from *Sunday Star*, (Toronto), 27 May, 1984.
3. In preparing this study, I have relied in part—particularly in the first three sub-sections—on research carried out for and concepts developed in my *The German Left Since 1945: Socialism and Social Democracy in the German Federal Republic*, (Cambridge, UK and New York, 1976).
4. Gerhard Stuby, 'Bürgerliche Demokratietheorien in der Bundesrepublik', in Reinhard Kühnl (ed.), *Der bürgerliche Staat der Gegenwart. Formen bürgerlicher Herrschaft II*, (Reinbek bei Hamburg, 1972), p. 91.
5. Thomas Wellmann, 'Die soziologische Lage der Bundesrepublik', in *Deutsche Rundschau*, LXXXIX (1953), p. 591.
6. By contrast, the church hierarchy had emerged relatively unscathed (the implications of which will be discussed presently) and, due to the decimation and levelling of the middle classes, the owners of industrial machinery and real

property—though temporarily in disarray—were now in a relatively better position than they had been during the Third Reich, at least in the Western occupation zones.

7. In March 1946, one-third of the respondents to a poll said they were no longer interested in politics and felt it safer to stay out, while three quarters had no intention of joining a political party. (Lewis J. Edinger, *Kurt Schumacher: A Study in Personality and Political Behaviour,* (Stanford, 1965), p. 76). Seventy per cent of the respondents to an OMGUS (i.e. Office of the Military Government of the United States) poll of October 1947 said they would refuse to assume responsible political office (*OMGUS Public Opinion Survey,* Series I, No. 88); and between February 1947 and August 1949 six in ten Germans said they would choose a government offering economic security in preference to one guaranteeing civil liberties (*OMGUS Public Opinion Survey,* Series I, No. 175, 6). In November 1945, 80 per cent declared themselves not personally interested in political affairs and preferred to leave them to others; by January 1949, however, this figure had declined to 60 per cent (*OMGUS Public Opinion Survey,* Series I, Nos. 100 and 175).

8. A term coined by Gabriel A. Almond, 'The Social Composition of the German Resistance', in G. Almond and W. Kraus (eds.), *The Struggle for Democracy in Germany,* (Chapel Hill, N.C., 1949), p. 107.

9. 'Apart from a few prominent writers and intellectuals. . . exiles not belonging to the left-wing groups played a very minor role in the anti-Nazi exile movement. . . The political life of the anti-Nazi movement thus revolved primarily around the various left-wing groups', (Lewis J. Edinger, *German Exile Politics,* (Berkeley, 1956), p. xi). At least 90 per cent of all prison sentences handed down for political reasons between 1933 and the outbreak of WW II were to supporters of the labour movement (Wolfgang Abendroth, *Sozialgeschichte der europäischen Arbeiterbewegung,* (Frankfurt, 1965), p. 176).

10. See Albrecht Kaden, *Einheit oder Freiheit? Die Wiedergründung der SPD 1945/46,* (Hanover, 1964), p. 46.

11. See, e.g., the 'Buchenwald Manifesto' reproduced in Hermann Brill, *Gegen den Strom,* (Offenbach, 1946).

12. *Dokumente und Materialien zur Geschichte der Deutschen Arbeiterbewegung,* Series III, Vol. 1, (E. Berlin, 1956), p. 267.

13. *Ibid.,* also see Rolf Badstubner, *Restauration in Westdeutschland 1945-1949,* (E. Berlin, 1969), p. 118; and G. Mannschatz and J. Seider, *Zum Kampf der KPD im Ruhrgebiet für die Einigung der Arbeiterklasse und die Entmachtung der Monopolherren 1945-1947,* (E. Berlin, 1962), pp. 57-58.

14. Abendroth, *op. cit.,* p. 176.

15. John Gimbel, *The American Occupation of Germany. Politics and the Military 1945-1949,* (Stanford, 1968), p. xiii.

16. Arnold Brecht, 'Personnel Management', in Edward H. Lichtfield (ed.), *Governing Post-war Germany,* (Ithica, New York, 1963), p. 264.

17. Michael Balfour, *Four-Power Control in Germany and Austria 1945-1946, I. Germany,* (London, 1956), p. 175.

18. A myth perpetuated by David P. Conradt, *The German Polity,* (New York and London, 1982), p. 88, following a well established tradition in West German social science.

19. Although this is not the place to assign 'responsibility' for the Cold War, it is worth mentioning that all the important measures which made irreversible the division of Germany were initiated by the Western occupation powers, particularly the American military government. This is as true of the formation of the Bi- and Tri-zones, the imposition of currency reform and the propagation of

anti-communism as it is of the establishment of a Western separate state and the NATO alliance.

20. On this, see H.-J. Brauns, U. Jaeggi, K.P. Kisker, A. Zerdick, B. Zimmermann, *SPD in der Krise. Die deutsche Sozialdemokratie seit 1945*, (Frankfurt, 1976), p. 39.

21. And anti-social democratism in turn can be traced back to reactionary anti-republicanism as the German feudalist answer to the French Revolution; see R. Crusius and M. Wilke, 'Der Antikommunismus als Legitimationsproblem der deutschen Linken', in R. Dutschke and M. Wilke (eds.), *Die Sowjetunion, Solschenizyn und die westliche Linke*, (Reinbek bei Hamburg, 1975), p. 73.

22. If, that is, one places the analysis of fascism in the context of an analysis of capitalism. This is done, e.g., in Francois Chatelet *et. al., Elements pour une Analyse du Fascisme*, (Paris, 1976); Nicos Poulantzas, *Fascism and Dictatorship*, (London, 1977); and in the work of Reinhard Kühnl, notably *Texte zur Faschismusdiskussion: Positionen und Kontroversen*, (Reinbek bei Hamburg, 1974).

23. Hans-Peter Schwarz, *Vom Reich zur Bundesrepublik. Deutschland im Widerstreit der aussenpolitischen Konzeptionen in den Jahren der Besatzungscherrschaft*, new ed. 1981, p. 11.

24. Sigmund Neumann, 'Einführung' in Max-Gustav Lange (ed.), Parteien in der Bundesrepublik, (Stuttgart and Düsseldorf, 1955), p. xxiii.

25. Badstubner, *op. cit.*, p. 89.

26. For the churches' role vis-a-vis the Third Reich, see Friedrich Baumgartel, *Wider der Kirchenkampflegenden*, (Neuendettlersau, 1959); Hans Müller, *Katholische Kirche und Nationalsozialismus*, (Munich, 1963); Gunter Lewy, *The Catholic Church and Nazi Germany*, (London, 1964).

27. Mimeographed copy available from CDU party headquarters, Bonn. The Bavarian CSU, from the outset the CDU's coalition partner, never really espoused the notion of Christian Socialism; early documents in sekretariat der CSU in Bayern (ed.), *10 Jahre CSU in Bayern*, (Munich, 1955).

28. Gerhard Schutz, 'Die CDU—Merkmale ihres Aufbaues', in M.G. Lange (ed.), *op. cit.*, p. 123.

29. Ralph Miliband, *The State in Capitalist Society*, (London, 1969), p. 187.

30. A term borrowed from the title of the excellent collection of essays, G. Schäffer and C. Nedelmann, *Der CDU-Staat. Studien zur Verfassungswirklichkeit der Bundesrepublik*, (Munich, 1967).

31. The presence of former Nazis at all levels of West German society has been amply documented, and the fact has long been accepted by all social sectors.

32. Reinhard Kühnl, 'Die Auseinandersetzung mit dem Faschismus in BRD und DDR', in Gerhard Hess (ed.), *BRD-DDR: Vergleich der Gesellschaftssysteme*, (Cologne, 1971), p. 269.

33. *Ibid.*, pp. 262-263.

34. Ekkehard Krippendorff, 'Introduction' in E. Krippendorff and V. Rittberger (eds.), *The Foreign Policy of West Germany: Formation and Contents*, (London and Beverly Hills, 1980), p. 2; or as Konrad Adenauer would put it, in a 1954 aside to French High Commissioner Francois-Poncet: 'Don't forget that I am the only German Chancellor who has preferred the unity of Europe over the unity of his own country'.

35. Gordon Smith, among others, evidently accepts this line of reasoning. He writes that although these three elements—anti-communism, christianity, free market economy—'help to characterize the party', '. . . they fail to inject into its policies a strong ideological content which, say, nationalism would supply'. (*Democracy in West Germany: Parties and Politics in the Federal Republic*, (London etc.,

1979), p. 91.
36. Hans Beyer rightly emphasises the militant-aggressive quality of West German anti-communism which he documents extensively; see 'Der Hauptinhalt unserer Epoche und seine Auswirkungen auf die antikommunistische Strategie und Ideologie des Imperialismus', in *Deutsche Zeitschrift für Philosophie*, Vol. 31, no. 4 (1983), esp. pp. 406–407.
37. Major Mauer, *Deutsche Monatshefte*, no. 3, 1960, p. 12.
38. Quoted by Alan Wolfe, *The Rise and Fall of the 'Soviet Threat': Domestic Sources of the Cold War Consensus*, (Washington, D.C., 1979), p. 13; for discussion and analysis of these developments, see pp. 10–20 and *passim*.
39. Quoted in Rudolf Augstein, *Konrad Adenauer*, (W. Wallich, trans., London, 1964), p. 39.
40. Quoted in Beyer, *op. cit.*, p. 407.
41. This is the fruitful line of critique of totalitarianism theories developed by Reinhard Kühnl in, e.g., the two volumes of *Formen bürgerlicher Herrschaft*, *op. cit.*
42. An interpretation later fully developed and set out by C. Friedrich and Z. Brzezinski in the several editions of their *Totalitarian Dictatorship and Autocracy*; further see Hannah Arendt, *The Origins of Totalitarianism*, (New York, 1956).
43. Parenti, *op. cit.*, p. 4.
44. Authors' Collective under the direction of Ludwig Elm, *Konservatismus in der BRD: Wesen, Erscheinungsform, Traditionen*, (E. Berlin, 1982), p. 5.
45. K.O. Hondrich, *Die Ideologien von Interessenverbänden*, (W. Berlin, 1963), p. 168.
46. As summarised and discussed, e.g., in Heinrich Hannover, *Politische Diffamierung der Opposition im freiheitlich-demokratischen Rechtsstaat*, (Dortmund-Barop, 1962), pp. 2–3.
47. Reimut Reiche and Peter Gäng, 'Vom antikapitalistischen Protest zur sozialistischen Politik', in *Neue Kritik*, no. 41, April 1967, p. 18.
48. Werner Hofmann, *Stalinismus und Anti-Kommunismus. Zur Soziologie des Ost-West Konflikts*, (Frankfurt, 1967), pp. 152–153.
49. On all this, see *ibid.*, pp. 153–154.
50. Parenti, *op. cit.*, p. 92.
51. A discussion which basically follows Graf, *op. cit.*, ch. IV(3).
52. Kurt Schumacher, *Turmwächter der Demokratie*, (Berlin-Grünewald, 1953), Vol. II, p. 167.
53. B.L., 'Der Antisowjetismus und wir', in *Freie Tribüne*, 9 September, 1950.
54. Crusius and Wilke, *op. cit.*, p. 76.
55. Wolfgang Abendroth, *Antagonistische Gesellschaft und politische Demokratie. Aufsätze zur politischen Soziologie*, (W. Berlin, 1967), pp. 76–77.
56. Wehner's speech reprinted in *Vorwärts*, 8 July 1960, 5 et seq.
57. As will be elaborated presently.
58. Stuby, *op. cit.*, p. 103.
59. 'Abbruch der Beziehungen zwischen SPD und SDS', Party Executive Committee Resolution of 19 July 1960, in *Jahrbuch der SPD 1960/61*, (Bonn, 1961), p. 452.
60. Here see Kurt Kusch, 'Förderung des SDS', in *Sozialistische Politik*, 10 October 1961, p. 5; further see 'Gegen "Sozialistische Förderergemeinschaften" ', Party Executive Resolution of 6 November 1961, in *Jahrbuch der SPD, op. cit.*, p. 477; and the Party Council's confirmation of this decision reprinted in the same volume, p. 477.
61. See, among others, SPD (ed.), *Uber das Wesen und die Absichten der 'Deutschen*

Friedens-Union'. Informationsmaterial, (Bonn n.d., 1961); *Die Freunde Ulbrichts,* SPD Documentation series, (Bonn, 1961).

62. 'Abgrenzung zur "Deutschen Friedens-Union" ', Party Executive Committee Resolution of 9–10 January 1961, in *Jahrbuch der SPD 1960/61,* p. 463.

63. John Saville, 'The Ideology of Labourism', in R. Benwick, R.N. Berki and B. Parekh (eds.), *Knowledge and Belief in Politics: The Problem of Ideology,* (London, 1973), p. 215.

64. Fritz Vilmar, 'Gesamteuropäische Koexistenz und innersozialistische Kritik', in Dutschke and Wilke (eds.), *op. cit.,* p. 34.

65. See Michael Kreile, *Osthandel und Ostpolitik,* (Baden-Baden, 1978), ch. 3.

66. This argument parallels that of Claudia von Braunmühl, *Kalter Krieg und friedliche Koexistenz: Die Aussenpolitik der SPD in der Grossen Koalition,* (Frankfurt, 1973), esp. pp. 146–156.

67. For a summary of opinion polls, see K. Baker, R.J. Dalton, K. Hildebrandt, *Germany Transformed: Political Culture and the New Politics,* (Cambridge, Mass. and London, 1981), p. 119.

68. The 26 May 1965 version is published, in mimeographed form, as: Entwurf eines Gesetzes zur Änderung des Grundgesetzes (Notstandsgesetz), special publication of the Presse- und Funknachrichten, n.p. 1965.

69. H.J. Blank, and J. Hirsch, 'Parlament und Verwaltung im Gesetzgebungsprozess', in Schäffer and Nedelmann (eds.), *op. cit.,* p. 96.

70. See 'Das Hamburger Strategiepapier', in Freimut Duve (ed.), *Der Thesenstreit um 'Stamokap': Die Dokumente zur Grundsatzdiskussion der Jungsozialisten,* (Reinbek bei Hamburg, 1973), ch. A(2).

71. Kreile, *op. cit.,* p. 33.

72. The concept of *Modell Deutschland* has become a central one during the past decade or so, and the relevant literature is enormous. Two good accounts in English are W.E. Patterson and G. Smith, *The West German Model. Perspectives on a Stable State,* (London, 1983); and Frieder Schlupp, *'Modell Deutschland* and the International Division of Labour', in Krippendorff and Rittberger (eds.), *op. cit.,* ch. 2.

73. Kreile, *op. cit.,* p. 32.

74. Michael Kreile, 'Ostpolitik Reconsidered', in Krippendorff and Rittberger (eds.), *op. cit.,* p. 138.

75. *Ibid.,* p. 134.

76. *Ibid.,* p. 134.

77. Reproduced in Claudia von Braunmühl, 'The Enemy Within: The Case of Berufsverbot in West Germany', in *The Socialist Register 1978,* p. 58.

78. R. Steinke, W. Süss, and U. Wolter, 'His Refrain is Heard Around the World: An Initial Assessment of the Bahro Congress', in Ulf Wolter (ed.), *Bahro: Critical Responses,* (White Plains, New York, 1980), p. 218.

79. Von Braunmühl, 'Berufsverbot. . .', p. 67.

80. Still the best comprehensive study of the workings of the extermination programme, Raul Hilberg, *The Destruction of the European Jews,* (New York etc. 1961).

81 Hannah Arendt, *Eichmann in Jerusalem: A Report on the Banality of Evil,* (New York, 1963).

82. Franz Hegmann, 'Toeing the Line in West Germany', in *CAUT Bulletin,* February 1982, p. 12.

83. *Ibid.,* pp. 13–14.

84. Dieter Deiseroth, 'Kontinuitätsprobleme der deutschen Staatsrechtslehre(r)? Das Beispiel Theodor Maunz', in D. Deiseroth, F. Hase, and K.-H. Laduer (eds.), *Ordungsmacht? Uber das Verhältnis von Legalität, Konsens und Herr-*

schaft, (Frankfurt, 1981), p. 103.

85. See the huge catalogue of 'reasons for doubt' given in von Braunmühl, 'Berufs-verbot. . .', pp. 64–65.

86. Wolfgang Abendroth, 'Das Bundesverfassungsgericht und die Berufsverbote im öffentlichen Dienst', in *IMSF Informationsbericht Nr. 22: Berufsverbote in der BRD, eine juristisch-politische Dokumentation,* (Frankfurt, 1976), p. 31.

87. *Ibid.*

88. Theo Schiller, 'Stellungnahme zum Entwurf eines Gesetzes zur Änderung dienstrechtlicher Vorschriften', in *ibid.,* p. 38.

89. 'Die Stellung der CDU/CSU', in *ibid.,* p. 80.

90. Friedhelm Hase, ' "Bonn und Weimar": Bemerkungen zu der Entwicklung vom "okkasionellen" zum "ideologischen" Staatsschutz', in Dieseroth *et. al.,* (eds.), *op. cit.,* p. 70.

91. Quoted in Detlef Lehnert, *Sozialdemokratie zwischen Protestbewegung und Regierungspartei 1848–1983,* (Frankfurt, 1983), p. 205.

92. Hans Kremendahl, 'Die Freiheit-Sozialismus-Diskussion im Bundestagswahl-kampf 1976 und das Verhältnis von Konsens und Konflikt im Parteiensystem der Bundesrepublik Deutschland', in Gerhard Göhler (ed.), *Politische Theorie. Begründungszusammenhänge in der Politikwissenschaft,* (Stuttgart, 1978), p. 119.

93. Union of Democratic Jurists in the Federal Republic, 'Zusatzbericht der VDJ über die Berufsverbote an die UNO und die nationalen Sektionen des IVDJ vom Januar 1975', in *IMSF Informationsbericht no. 22, op. cit.,* p. 26.

94. These and other cases abundantly documented in *ibid.,* 50 *et seq.*

95. Press release of SPD Party Executive Committee, 11 June 1975, reproduced in *ibid.,* p. 88.

96. Quoted in Kremendahl, *op. cit.,* p. 120.

97. Kreile, *Osthandel und Ostpolitik,* p. 165.

98. Eleonara Cebotarev and Jorge Nef, 'Economic Development and Terrorism: Some Empirical and Theoretical Generalisations', paper presented to 16th annual meeting of Canadian Peace Research and Educational Association, Halifax 1981, mimeo., p. 4.

99. A distinction made by Jorge Nef and David Moore, 'The Terrorist Weapon: An Appraisal', in *Laurentian University Review,* special issue on 'Politics and Violence', Vol. XIV, no. 1, (November 1981), pp. 27–37.

100. Cebotarev and Nef, *op. cit.*

101. In a letter to then Federal President Walter Scheel, Amnesty International wrote that West Germans were singularly hesitant to sign petitions, even those opposing genocide and torture: 'The reason given to us is that the person approached worked in the public service, or intended to apply for a position in the public service and was afraid that signing a petition would work to their disadvantage.' (Sebastian Cobler, *Law, Order and Politics in West Germany,* (trans. Francis McDonagh, Harmondsworth, 1978), p. 66.

102. John Dornberg, 'West Germany's Embattled Democracy: the Anti-Terrorist Threat from the Right', in *Saturday Review,* 10 June 1978, p. 20.

103. Ovid Demaris, *Brothers in Blood: The International Terrorist Network,* (New York, 1977), pp. 233 and 255.

104. Again without pushing the parallel too far, precisely the same could be said of the Third Reich which also practically eliminated anti-state terrorism.

105. Cobler, *op. cit.,* pp. 10–11.

106. *Ibid.,* ch. 4(4). The arguments contained in this, and the subsequent paragraph closely follow Cobler's well-documented case.

107. *Ibid.,* p. 97.

108. *Ibid.*, p. 104.
109. *Ibid.*, p. 110.
110. *Ibid.*, p. 111.
111. *Ibid.*, p. 146.
112. Several of these studies are summarised in Baker, Dalton and Hildebrandt, *op. cit.*, p. 27.
113. See Hermann Scheer, 'Der Mythos des Privaten: Kurt Biedenkopfs Funktion für die "neue" CDU', in Martin Grieffenhagen (ed.), *Der neue Konservatismus der siebziger Jahre*, (Reinbek bei Hamburg, 1974), p. 183.
114. Slogans which prompted one's colleague and friend to affix a bumper sticker to his car which read *Sozialismus ist Freiheit*—thus earning him hostility from supporters of all three parties!
115. Quoted in Kremendahl, *op. cit.*, pp. 111–112.
116. Rudolf Bahro, 'The SPD and the Peace Movement', in *New Left Review*, no. 131 (1982), p. 21.
117. Hondrich, *op. cit.*, p. 172.

THE IRONY OF ANTI-COMMUNISM:
IDEOLOGY AND INTEREST IN POST-WAR AMERICAN FOREIGN POLICY

Alan Wolfe

Since 1945, US leaders have pointed, with depressing regularity, to Soviet actions as proof that communism is an evil force destined to spread around the globe unless stopped by a firm hand. Of all Soviet actions, the one that perhaps had the greatest effect in solidifying the Cold War was the coup that brought a pro-Soviet leadership to power in Czechoslovakia in 1948. Yet the very same case can also be used to illustrate another fascinating feature of the Cold War: the degree to which aggressive actions by the Soviet Union were literally welcomed by the United States in order to build a domestic consensus around anti-communism. Consider the history.

In early 1945, Soviet troops, sweeping westwards, occupied Moravia and Slovakia. On May 5th, Prague residents took to the streets and began to fight the last remaining Nazis. General Patton and the US Third Army were fifty-six miles away. Although American military commanders and OSS activists urged General Eisenhower to move into Prague, the Allied Commander, after consultations with Soviet Chief of Staff, Alexei Antonov, turned them down. By political agreement, the US had already conceded Czechoslovakia to the Russians.

The only problem with the agreement lay with the Czechs themselves. Although the Czech Communist Party was genuinely popular, the last hope for the divided and defeated country was a coalition government including both the communist leader Klement Gottwald and Czech patriots Jan Masaryk and Edward Benes. In May 1946, elections were held and the Left—split between Communists and left-wing socialists—won a tiny majority. For the next two years, Gottwald and his allies intensified the pressure to move Czechoslovakia closer to the Soviet Union. American policy seemed almost intentionally designed to help them. Washington rejected a request from Masaryk for wheat, undermining his domestic support. President Truman and Secretary of State George Marshall deliberately refused to see the Czech hero on his trip to Washington. On October 6th 1947, Marshall informed the US Cabinet that Moscow 'will probably have to clamp down completely on Czechoslovakia, for a relatively free Czechoslovakia could become a threatening salient in Moscow's political position'. Soviet efforts to control the country, Marshall concluded privately, were 'purely defensive'. [1] Masaryk, disappointed and uninformed of Washington's write-off, returned to Prague to face a

214

communist-inspired coup. Without any support in the US, his position was helpless, and Gottwald, backed by the NKVD and 18,000 nearby Soviet troops in Austria, soon took power. Czechoslovakia had become a Soviet 'satellite'.

Responding to the February 1948 crisis, the Truman administration invoked the metaphor of appeasement. 'We are faced with the same situation with which Britain and France were faced in 1938–39 with Hitler', Truman wrote to his daughter. In March, after the news of Masaryk's mysterious death reached the West, a mood of near hysteria swept over Washington. On March 17th, Truman addressed a joint session of Congress and denounced Soviet aggression: '. . . the Soviet Union and its agents have destroyed the independence and democratic character of a whole series of nations in Eastern and Central Europe. It is this ruthless course of action, and the clear design to extend it to the remaining free nations of Europe, that has brought about the critical situation in Europe today. The tragic death of the Republic of Czechoslovakia has sent a shock-wave through the civilized world.'

The domestic consequences of Truman's speech were immediate and dramatic. Henry Wallace, a potential threat to Truman's re-election from the Left, was isolated and eventually marginalised. In April 1948 Congress approved the Marshall Plan and the appropriations followed in June. A three billion dollar supplement to the defence budget, intended to expand the Air Force, won approval in April and it was soon increased. By the time the Czech crisis subsided, the budget of the Air Force had doubled. No other twelve month period witnessed as many changes in the structure and operations of the US military establishment as those that followed February 1948. An uncertain, quasi-isolationist economic giant had become a military superpower as well.

From the standpoint of international relations, the US reaction to the Czech crisis is difficult to understand. As George Kennan would write, there was 'nothing unexpected, nothing out of the ordinary, in any of the communist behavior—the Czech coup, and the Berlin blockade—that caused so much alarm in Western capitals. . . Washington's reactions were deeply subjective, influenced more by domestic political moods and institutional interests than by any theoretical considerations of our international position'.[2] Indeed, from the standpoint of domestic politics, the Czech crisis initiated a process that would be repeated time and again throughout the history of the Cold War. The significant elements of that process include the following:

1. Unquestionably, the Soviet Union acted like a major military power. It attempted to take advantage of every situation in order to establish control over any area of the world deemed essential to the national interest.

2. Far from contesting such Soviet control, the United States tacitly urged

it, comfortable with such Soviet moves and almost relieved to see them take place.

3. In public, however, the United States stated the exact opposite of what it came to expect in private.

4. In short, Cold War rhetoric and anti-Soviet hostility were never directed against the Russians but were for the benefit of the American public and congressional leaders, and the European Allies. Such rhetoric became essential to the process of stalemate-breaking, producing action where before resistance had existed.

While American policymakers saw an analogy with Munich, there was one essential difference between Prague's fate in 1939 and in 1948. Neither Chamberlain nor Daladier denounced Nazism while granting it legitimacy, but Truman and his advisors publicly excoriated the very society whose control over Czechoslovakia they tacitly accepted. In this sense, the Cold War began with a clearly recognised gap between ideology and interest. Anti-communism, as an ideology, demanded military action and a state of permanent readiness against the enemy. Yet in reality, Americans were not prepared to go back to war. Capitalists were beginning to profit from peace, and stability, not counter-revolution, became the West's ultimate objective. For US policymakers, one problem above all others would come to monopolise their attention: how to 'manage' anti-communism, to keep the flame high enough to serve domestic political objectives without turning it so high that it would lead to a conflagration.

I will argue three propositions in this essay. The first is that the US foreign policy establishment, a generation after the Cold War began, has failed to manage the gap between ideology and interest. The ideas advanced purely for public consumption in 1948 have become the private belief system of the policymakers themselves in 1984. Put another way, Washington has become more and more enamoured with one particular reading of contemporary history as the rest of the world is beginning to accept it less. The advent of the Reagan administration has resulted in a process by which the objects of a propaganda campaign become its subjects.

My second proposition is that the confusion between ideology and interest has transformed the nature of the superpower rivalry. In the late 1940s, both the United States and the Soviet Union sought strategic advantage while cloaking their ambitions in humanitarian rhetoric. In America, however, this was denied. The Russians, it was said, as perpetrators of a totalitarian ideology were forced by circumstances to act as their chiliastic vision demanded. The notion that a 'totalitarian' state would always follow the dictates of ideology turned out, in retrospect, to be a false displacement of the Nazi experience onto the Soviet Union. In actual fact, Soviet leaders, conservative to the core, demonstrated a remarkable ability to finesse the rules of realpolitik. A fact as disappointing to the Left as it was welcome to capital. It was the United States, a society convinced of its pragmatism and realism, that began to base its foreign policy on theories of how the world worked rather than the real world itself.

Third, and most troublesome, I contend that the belated triumph of anti-communist ideology, its ability to become the very reality it was invented to distort, occurs at the precise moment when a theory of nuclear strategy compels nation states to make policies based on perceptions rather than capabilities. Deterrence, as it has evolved between the super-powers, accords a much greater importance to the subjective perception of intentions than it does to the intentions themselves. The Soviet leader-ship, presiding over an authoritarian state with little if any internal free-dom, has much less need to concern itself with the ideological distortion of its antagonist's nature than does the American leadership. Ironically, then, the Soviet Union's very undemocratic structure makes it less susceptible than the United States to the displacement of interest into ideology; contrariwise, in America, leaders are constantly forced by the dynamics of electoral campaigns to simplify the world and reach down for the lowest common understanding of their antagonist's motives. Thus a democratic society is more likely to become captivated by ideology than an authoritarian one, and as a result, its foreign policy in the nuclear age is far more likely to be unpredictable and unstable. And, since in deter-rence theory, the perception of intentions has become elevated to strategic importance, it is also far more dangerous.

American policymakers were retrospectively candid about their deliberate exaggeration of the Soviet threat in the late 1940s. The Truman administration, as we have seen, shared a private understanding of Soviet conduct that differed markedly from its public statements. Two years after the Czech crisis, Paul Nitze, Leon Keyserling, and others in the administra-tion completed work on NSC-68, their top-secret review of Soviet intent-ions. Dean Acheson later spoke of the importance of being 'clearer than truth' in writing the document, so as to better 'bludgeon the mass mind of "top government". . .', while Nitze told a later interviewer that bureau-cratic infighting demanded a certain sharpening of the language of 'the Soviet threat'.[3] In other words, once a decision was taken to deceive the public about what officials knew to be true regarding Soviet intentions, it was a short step toward self-deception and the need for even highly placed officials to agree among themselves over the image of Soviet expan-sion. An image that would become official. As John Lewis Gaddis writes of NSC-68, 'Imprecision, its drafters believed, was necessary to gain action. . .'[4] Thus, America's overall foreign policy in the Cold War was to be quite rationally based on an imprecise and bureaucratically distorted view of its antagonist.

There was nothing remarkable or unique about the decision of the

Truman administration to deceive the public. Political elites throughout history have said one thing while doing another with unbending consistency. What is worthy of comment is the process by which America's leaders came to forget that they were lying. The explanation for this forgetfulness is rooted in the peculiarities of American political culture.

Economically, the United States became a global power as early as World War I, if not sooner. Were economics the sole explanation for the behaviour of nation states, the growth and expansion of the American economy would have led uneventfully and predictably to the assumption of global political ambitions as well. But that process was anything but smooth, for even though America had become an economic giant, its political system and assumptions about the world remained embedded in the eighteenth century. Isolationism, decentralisation, localism, balanced budgets, low taxes, the separation of powers and other American homilies were thin material for the creation of an imperial state. America's uniqueness as a world power stems from the massive discrepancy between a cosmopolitan capitalism and a parochial democracy. A pre-modern political culture has been combined with a post-modern economic system, and as a result, American policy is characterised by frequent swings from one pole to another, as if each change in a cycle requires the complete repudiation of what came before.

Although American capitalists revolutionised the means of production in the late nineteenth and early twentieth century, they were, when compared to Europe, reluctant to modernise the state, preferring to articulate a *laissez-faire* ideology that became more obsolete with time. This repudiation of a political project by the economic elite placed a real burden on elected officials. Their choice was to capitulate to conventional wisdom and be forgotten or to strive for 'leadership', which meant state-building and modernisation. What came to be called Progressivism (or reform, or today, liberalism) was this latter course: the building of government capable of responding to the national and international needs of capital as a whole despite the strenuous objections of capital itself.

One method of overcoming entrenched short-sightedness was to rally public opinion behind a popular modernising crusade. By carrying an appealing message to 'the people' in some plebiscitary fashion, public opinion could be mobilised to undermine the entrenched opposition to state expansion that existed in local government, the US Senate, and the courts. The trouble lay in discovering an appropriate appeal. Populistic candidates often found themselves in touch with a mass base, but their agenda (controlling banks and railroads and attacking the profit motive) asked for trouble in respectable places. In the search for a programme of mass appeal that would expand the scope of government, yet at the same time would not court dangerous passions, public officials soon discovered the realm of foreign policy. In the period between the administrations of Theodore Roosevelt and Woodrow Wilson, the modern American state was invented.

Although Roosevelt and Wilson were both expansionists, there was one significant difference between them. The former was an unabashed imperialist whose explicitly stated goal was the triumph of American power and prestige. The latter, whose global ambitions were fully as strong, consistently subsumed his objectives under more appealing rhetoric, including even anti-imperialist notions. Of these two models, the Wilsonian one soon established its superiority. Americans seemed not to object to the creation of an empire, but they never wanted it acknowledged that this was what they were doing. Theodore Roosevelt's explicitness was his undoing. Wilson implicitly understood that American political culture was parochial and pacificist, therefore requiring that humanitarian symbols be used to explain actions in the national interest.

Of these two approaches, there is little question that Franklin Roosevelt, the next American president to take the country into war, borrowed Wilson's and not his cousin's method. The great political genius of F.D.R. was the elaborate ritual he developed to involve the American people in the European war gradually without seeming to do so.[5] More than any other president in this century, F.D.R. established the tradition of stating one thing ideologically and doing the opposite in his international actions. As John Milton Cooper comments:

> The main lessons that Roosevelt's successors have drawn from his foreign policies have been that the public usually has to be either hoodwinked or inflated into pursuing the right course and that attempting to educate the people only invites trouble. The much-discussed and frequently condemned 'imperial presidency' of the middle of the twentieth century has been Franklin Roosevelt's chief legacy to his presidential successors.[6]

Franklin Roosevelt's shadow was enormous, and it included, as William E. Leuchtenberg has noted, the birth of the military-industrial complex as well as the welfare state.[7] The capacity of the Truman administration to maintain both a private and a public view of Soviet intentions—a capacity shared by its successors—had its origins in the way F.D.R. managed domestic public opinion during World War II.

The liberal presidents who cultivated an atmosphere of international crisis in order to build up support for their version of expanded state power (Truman, Kennedy, and Johnson in recent times) were taking a calculated gamble. They hoped, or at least assumed, that over time Americans would grow into their role as imperial protector, shedding their isolationism and quaint political customs in favour of the economic and material benefits they would gain from leadership in the world economy. When that point was reached, when the American political system was revised to bring it into line with what the American economy had achieved, then presumably, the kind of anti-communist hysteria distastefully cultivated for domestic political reasons could be dropped. What democratic liberals never seemed to understand, and what Ronald Reagan and the Republican Right understood brilliantly, was the remarkable staying power of political culture, its ability to live on as an anachronism even as the economy seemed to dictate otherwise.

Neither American political culture nor the US state ever modernised the way that liberal reformers hoped. In the 1980s, America retains its global ambitions, but its domestic politics still linger in the past. The public is narcissistic, concerned with its own condition, barely cognisant of the rest of the world. When, for example, President Reagan's national security advisor, the most powerful position in government, did not know the names of the countries and leaders he would be dealing with, his ignorance was no obstacle to his appointment.

A rampant desire to keep taxes low affects both parties, even though all imperial ambitions are expensive and must ultimately be paid for from tax revenue. Ethnic considerations at home shape foreign policy decisions abroad, a process no self-respecting empire can tolerate for long. Partisanship is bitter, government divided, consensus fractured and the elite in disarray. In short, rather than America's global participation shaping its political system, the unique American political system has shaped America's imperial behaviour.

The result of the persistence of pre-modern politics into post-modern economics is a hybrid system that can only be described as isolationist imperialism. Americans want to be militarily strong, but they refuse to see their sons die in wars. They have Spartan longings for discipline combined with an Athenian taste for instant gratification and pleasure. They swing rapidly back and forth from belligerence to an overwhelming reluctance to use force. A nation that admires courage is constantly consumed by fear. When fear of war dominates, Americans search for controls on arms. But when fear of the Russians dominates, they urge their politicians to build the very arms they previously wanted controlled. It is as if there are two Americas, each one corresponding to different visions of the Soviet Union. Anti-communism brings out the worst of those two Americas, encouraging parochialism, self-righteousness, religious millenarianism, ideological rigidity, and excessive moralism. A society that combines isolationism with imperialism is a society that imposes itself on the world twice, once to control it economically, and then to preach to it morally.

The anti-communism fashioned at the end of World War II to smooth the transition from isolationism to imperialism has taken on a life of its own. To such a degree, in fact, that it has become counterproductive to capitalist needs themselves. The phantasmagorical increases in military spending contemplated by the Reagan administration, for example, while of striking benefit to specific constituencies, threaten to undermine sustained economic growth for generations to come by creating permanent deficits. The challenge to American capital from Japanese and German firms is exacerbated by the reliance on cumbersome technology and top-down innovation inherent in a militarised economy. Any hopes for a kind of trilateral economic management of the world economy—the latest word in capitalist planning just a few years ago—have been doomed by the overt nationalism of the Reagan administration.

In the 1980s, in other words, anti-communism threatens to undermine the Western alliance. It leads to eventual economic stagnation, reduces America's capacity for innovation, pegs interest rates at exorbitant levels, creates future inflation, and convinces the rest of the world that America is an unstable partner. Yet anti-communism is so firmly entrenched in the incumbent administration that it would be barely relaxed should a new administration come to power. Men like George Kennan in the late 1940s saw anti-communism as a temporary device that would increasingly become less necessary. Rarely has a gamble proved more wrong, and with such serious consequences.

The persistence of anti-communism long past the time when its inventors hoped it would disappear must be regarded as testimony to the strength of democracy. There have been many empires in world history. There have also been many societies with universal suffrage. America is the first to combine them both for any length of time and with extraordinary results.

In the late 1940s, men like Reinhard Niebuhr and Hans Morganthau worried about whether Americans could be convinced to live up to their imperial responsibilities. Fully aware of the latent isolationism in American political culture, these so-called 'realists' questioned whether democracy was compatible with globalism. Let the people decide through some kind of mass politics, they reasoned, and Americans being as they were, people would opt for privatism and parochialism over sophisticated participation in world affairs.[8] The concern of these men was well founded, but it had a twist they never understood. American democracy did permit a mass society, composed of an essentially unsophisticated public, to elect their political leaders. But instead of retreating from the notion of empire, such mass participation kept alive the anti-communism that was its rationale, even as the realists themselves, such as Morganthau and Kennan, came to question the very imperial premises they once advocated.

Democracy at home and imperial management abroad create an extremely unstable combination. Surely this is why the Soviet Union, with little need to worry about domestic dissent, contested elections, journalistic leaks, and public debate, can sign treaties with the United

States and expect to see them ratified; a simple matter that no American leadership can ever count upon. Surely this is also why America's most ambitious globalists (from the gentlemen free-traders of the late 1940s to the conservatives around Reagan today) are men uncomfortable with democracy, engaged in a perpetual quest to curb the press, place limits on public access to government, and rely on the most covert possible agencies of the state. Those Americans most hostile to the Soviet Union are also those who most emulate the anti-democratic character of the Soviet system.

There are limits to how far any American administration can go in placing restrictions on democracy for the sake of imperial ambitions. There is, and for most of this century has always been, a far more attractive alternative. Instead of narrowing the scope of democracy to dull its effects, one can achieve the same objective by expanding it. Since the days of Napoleon III, it has been no secret that a mass public can be mobilised to register support for elite objectives, so long as the elite takes sufficient care to flatter popular prejudice, play to public ignorance, and reinforce traditional symbols. The coexistence of empire and democracy has not abolished the latter but transformed it. Americans have little conception of democratic citizenship except a passive obligation to vote, and not even all Americans do that. The kind of democracy that has developed as a by-product of the Cold War is one that elites need not fear. Incumbents, so long as they are willing to pander to the public have unlimited opportunities to distort the national 'debate' and to win support for their programmes. Such leeway is not completely unrestricted; there was nothing Ronald Reagan could do to keep US troops in Lebanon, for example. But the passive, plebiscitary form that democracy has taken in the United States, especially since the late 1940s, is one that, with just a little bit of work, can become another aspect of proper imperial management. The American people can be treated in roughly the same way that one finds a new government for Chad.

The persistence of anti-communism and the transformation of democracy into plebiscite is, in reality, the same process. In the late eighteenth and early nineteenth centuries, the American political elite created a system intentionally designed to prevent the concentration of political power. Government was to be shared between state capitals and Washington, with, if anything, a preference towards the former. At every level of government, power was to be divided between executive, legislative, and judicial functions. Private factions—later to be called interest groups—were recognised to play a public role. Although a distrust of political parties was present, given the other assumptions of the system, it was inevitable that they too would divide and fracture power. Few of the early theorists of American democracy understood that such eighteenth century notions of the polity would prove incompatible with national aspirations, though Alexander Hamilton was one conspicuous exception and John Marshall another. Many understand it now, however, and as a result, there are roughly three schools of thought seeking a solution to the problem.

1. There are those who would essentially 'reform' or abolish fractured political power and replace it with a national, modernised state. This is an especially popular view among Kennedy-type liberals like Theodore Sorensen.[9] It is akin to rationalisation in the economic sphere, which appropriates the language of efficiency for the sake of more deliberately pursued objectives.

2. There are those who would keep fractured political power and be prepared to forego imperial adventures incompatible with it. At one time this position was lodged in the extreme Right. Now it has, with the exception of a kind of libertarianism, shifted to the Left. But in any case it is a minority tendency that has little weight in the national discussion on these matters.

3. Finally, one can keep the forms of decentralised political power—and even praise them constantly—while stripping them of power in favour of less accountable but more streamlined covert agencies or private concentrations. Thus, the Reagan approach, represents an updated version of Walter Bagehot's distinction between the 'dignified' and 'efficient' parts of government. For it to succeed, it must rely on crusades like anti-communism both to give unity and to deflect public scrutiny.

Expressed in this way, it becomes possible to offer an explanation of why it came to pass that the gap between anti-communism as ideology and as interest has been lost. It will be recalled that the theme of this analysis is not that policymakers in the late 1940s deliberately distorted the Soviet threat; it is in the nature of holders of political power to distort their objectives. The far more challenging phenomenon to explain is *why the foreign policy establishment ultimately came to believe in private what it once offered only to the public.* It seems clear that the reason for this failure is connected to what Allen Matusow has called 'the unravelling of America'. That is, the process by which the hegemony of the American liberals in the post-war period was undermined, which was mainly due to their misreading of the mood of the times.[10]

The Cold War liberals of the Truman administration, epitomised by men like Dean Acheson and Averill Harriman, were essentially nineteenth century elitists operating in a twentieth century, democratic political culture. Their vision of the state was one in which a small, well-bred, and informal elite would, through the appropriate channels, make decisions in conjunction with similar elites in other countries. In this, Great Britain was their model. Unable to contain their contempt for the public and its ways, and distrustful of the fractured and decentralised government that made coordinated decision-making outside the public

view close to impossible, they invited opposition from the more conservative interests which had their roots in local institutions. The
McCarthy period, for example, had far more to do with the conservative
distrust of men like Acheson that it did with any serious hunt for Communists or subversives. And it was because the liberal foreign policy
establishment was so elitist by temperament, that the conservative opposition could monopolise democratic symbolism. From McCarthy to
Reagan, the conservative attack on foreign policy liberalism has traditionally been cast in a populistic and democratic language. When liberals
essentially lied about their true objectives—writing off Czechoslovakia, or,
of far more importance to the Right, conceding Korea and China to
socialism—they were being realistic in international terms but naive in
domestic politics. They enabled the Right to accuse them of arrogance,
and prepared the way for a counter-elite, that really believed in its rhetoric,
to take power.

The triumph of anti-communism as ideology is the revenge of the
American Right. Since the New Deal, there has been a die-hard conservative movement in the United States waiting for an opportunity to end its
isolation from American life and to roll back the gains achieved by working people and minorities.[11] Ironically, it was foreign, not domestic
policy, that gave them their chance. To this day, public opinion polls
show that the specific programmes of the New Deal are still popular. No
conservative government ever could have come to power in the United
States by arguing for limits on social security and other New Deal programmes. Had liberals stuck to their domestic objectives, they might still
be in power. But they did not. They possessed unquenchable imperial
ambitions. And following their mentors Woodrow Wilson and Franklin
Roosevelt, they were never willing to state those ambitions openly. So
long as they did not, so long as they told the public one thing while
doing another, they ran the risk of losing not only their foreign policy
agenda but their domestic one as well. Anti-communism could not be
turned on and off at a moment's notice. Liberals' distrust of democracy
gave rise to an anti-democratic Right that could achieve its anti-populistic
objectives in the language of populistic democracy. Hubris has its place
in Greek tragedy, but in a democratic political culture, it is political
suicide.

If there is a tragedy in this story, it comes not from the fall of liberalism,
but from the fact that anti-communism as an ideology reached its culmination at a time when an important shift in strategic theory was taking
place. The rivalry between the Soviet Union and the United States, after
all, is unlike any previous national rivalry in world history. When land-
based, labour intensive, gruelling wars were fought between many different

states, capabilities ultimately determined victory or defeat. In the Cold War, where the existence of nuclear weapons between major powers makes such wars impossible, capabilities lose their meaning at a certain point. As this began to dawn on policymakers, intentions rather than capabilities became the key element in the theory of deterrence.

Once each side in the Cold War developed even a relatively small number of nuclear weapons capable of destroying the major cities of the other, national security considerations focused on second-strike retaliation. Once, that is, it was sufficiently clear that there was no effective defence against a nuclear first-strike. Deterrence logic held that the only secure method of preventing the other side from launching first was to convince it that enough retaliatory potential would remain to wreak total havoc. The premise of deterrence theory was that no leader of a superpower could be so irrational as to risk the inevitable destruction of his own society by launching first. There was substance to this argument. For a generation, deterrence seemed to prevent a nuclear war, or, to be more precise, no nuclear war took place while deterrence was practised. Moreover, there seemed to exist, especially from about the mid 1960s to the mid 1970s, a roughly stable pattern of mutual expectations between the superpowers.

Over time, however, something seemed to go wrong with the theory of mutually assured destruction. For one thing, new technologies offered fantastic new potentialities: MIRVing increased the number of targets, fire power was increased, and computerisation led to promise of pin-point accuracy. In addition, strategic theorists began to argue that each side should begin to target each other's weapons (counterforce) in addition to their cities. A suggestion which seemed to run against the grain of second-strike planning. Third, both sides, but especially the US, began a fascination with weapons that contained the potential for a pre-emptive first-strike. The MX missile was the most notorious instance, with the Soviet SS-20s being somewhat more ambiguous but certainly destabilising. Finally, the US took the lead once again and planners began to think about reviving anti-ballistic missile systems. President Reagan's fascination with Star Wars technology is an aspect of this. These systems, however, because they seek to prevent an incoming first-strike, undermine the basic premise of mutually assured destruction.

There is a technological explanation for the gradual undermining of mutually assured destruction. It is that once certain first-strike or ABM systems can be developed, they will be developed. Ironically, one can take heart from such a technological determinism, for it implies that human beings themselves did not choose to bring the world a step closer to nuclear destruction but were forced to do so by means over which they had no control. Unfortunately for such optimism, the technological explanation is not sufficient, both because ABM and first-strike technology is still imperfect and because it was also imperfect fifteen years ago. The breakdown of MAD, in short, must be located somewhere else, and I wish to suggest that a major cause, at least on the American side, lies in the dynamics of its domestic political system.

In retrospect, the flaw in MAD was political, not technological. It lay, not with the enemy's leaders, who could easily understand that there was no defence against a nuclear war, but with one's own population, which found it difficult to understand the proposition at all. For deterrence to work, a political leader would have to patiently explain to his own people that they must accept the reality of being left undefended against a first-strike in order to ensure that the other side did not launch one. Put another way, those state officials responsible for national security would have to confess, if MAD were to survive, that in the nuclear age there is no such thing as national security. No democratic leader, and certainly no American one, could make such a confession and survive politically.

Deterrence led directly to a situation in which the leaders of the two superpowers shared an understanding of the nature of nuclear war that they were incapable of sharing with their own people. There was only one solution to this problem, and that was not to share it at all. In the Soviet Union, the elitism implied by deterrence was not even conceptualised as an issue, since democratic expectations did not exist. But in the United States, national security considerations that precluded the discussion of their nature became an essential component of liberal arrogance. Men like Robert McNamara and his 'whiz kids' went along blissfully making the US more vulnerable to a Soviet first-strike in order to insure deterrence. They did not, however, offer any credible explanation of why they were doing this, even though it made perfect sense globally. In other words, the very factors that made deterrence work between states, made it unworkable within states, or at least within democratic ones. It was precisely because deterrence meant the creation of two political realms that it was incompatible with democracy. That is, the creation of one realm between the superpowers that was based on a logic totally different from the other, that between the leaders of a single superpower and its own people. Thus, in an age of nuclear war planning, a closed society can be more 'responsible' globally than an open society. At some point, a democratic society will have to choose whether democracy is important, in which case it can no longer practise deterrence, or whether nuclear superpower status is important, in which case it can no longer practise democracy.

America chose to forego deterrence, at least that version of it premised upon mutually assured destruction. As the anti-communist ideology that was launched for instrumental reasons in the late 1940s penetrated through both its society and leadership, it raised an obvious question that liberals committed to MAD could not possibly answer: if the Soviet Union is as bad as you have been telling us since 1948, then why are we sitting here waiting for them to attack us first? For a surprisingly long time, that question was not asked, only because almost no questions about nuclear strategy were asked in the public realm. But as the conservative Right gathered strength and prepared to take power, it could not avoid such vulnerability for long. From the perspective of the Reagan administration (a perspective shared by conservative Democrats as well) the conversion of anti-communist ideology into policy meant living with the end of mutually assured destruction.

From this point forward, deterrence, if it exists at all, exists with a new set of premises. In order to prevent the other side from launching a first-strike against us, the new logic suggests, we must convince them that we are contemplating a first-strike against them. Thus, the clear strategic importance of the MX missile, leads directly to launch-on-warning concepts and to pre-emptive first-strike thinking. This shift in deterrence theory is perhaps the single most important event in international relations that has taken place in the last decade. It represents a major heightening of the danger of nuclear war. And a major reason for it lies with the fact that ideology interfered with interest in the articulation of strategic doctrine. If both superpowers had been authoritarian societies with no need to explain their global actions at home, we might still be living without first-strike planning. But to its credit, one of the superpowers was not authoritarian and, as a result, it found itself unable to live with what appears to be in retrospect a marginally safer logic than the one it is beginning to practise.

Unlike wars fought before the advent of nuclear weapons, mutually assured destruction shifted the focus of interest from capabilities to intentions. Now the shift from MAD to first-strike planning shifts the focus again from intentions to perceptions of intentions. A subtle, but vitally important, distinction. It is not enough, under the Reagan doctrine, to build first-strike weapons, one must also increase the hostile rhetoric associated with them in order to convince the Russians that we might just use them. This process is similar to the so-called 'mad man' theory of Henry Kissinger and Richard Nixon, which was premised upon a willingness to convince the enemy that they were capable of even the most irrational acts. Thus, MAD was premised, however tangentially, on a theory of human rationality, assuming that no rational leader would launch first if that meant the destruction of his own society. On the other hand, the newly emerging strategic doctrine builds an expectation of irrationality into the mind of the antagonist. It is important, in the new logic, that the antagonist's perceptions of what we are capable of doing remain uncertain, so as to guarantee they will take no offensive action. In short, the shift from MAD to its successor is a shift from giving the antagonist the greatest possible assurance that he will know what we are going to do to one of maximising his uncertainty about what our intentions are.

As perceptions of intentions replace intentions, in the logic of strategic theory, the final and most unsettling point in the narrative is reached. At the start of the Cold War, when the United States possessed a monopoly on nuclear weapons, its leaders created an ideology which differed substantially from what they knew to be the reality. Then, as parity between the superpowers and mutually assured destruction took hold, the United States began to believe its own ideology about Soviet intentions, becoming the victim of its own propaganda campaign. In this second phase of the Cold War, the Soviet Union as a closed society, was not susceptible to the process of substituting ideology for interest, its foreign policy could therefore stabilise around a pure balance of power model.

In the third stage of these developments, when the perceptions of intentions become more important than the intentions themselves, the ideological construct developed by one superpower becomes the model for the other. Faced with a relentlessly ideological campaign directed against them—one that even questions their right to exist as a society— the Soviet leaders respond in kind, reviving their own long-dormant ideological visions of the United States. This, of course, acts as a self fulfilling prophecy for American leaders, who can now point with pride to Soviet ideological behaviour as positive proof that American ideological perceptions were correct all along. In summary, if the Cold War began with one power acting on ideology and the other on interest, and then reached a period when the two roles were reversed, it has culminated in a process where both act on ideology and neither on interest. That, surely is the point where there is no longer any innocence and vicitimisation marks the relations between the superpowers. Each has become part of the other's worldview, each necessary for the other to justify itself.

The process begun when anti-communism became the public rationale for America's global ambitions has, in the 1980s, come full cycle. American leaders not only believe what they once hoped just the public would believe, but they have also managed to convince the Soviet Union to believe it, thereby reconfirming their own beliefs. Ideology needs such cyclical movement to keep it alive, especially, as in the case under discussion, when the ideology has less and less to do with the way the world actually works. It is a dangerous enough business, this process by which ideologies bring into being the behaviour upon which they are predicated. It is doubly dangerous when the parties concerned possess the kinds of weapons they do. Evidently, the cycle will only be broken when a political movement with an interest in survival and not with an ideology of apocalypse can assume enough power to force a shift in the dynamic between the two nuclear superpowers.

NOTES

1. Interesting accounts of the Czech events are contained in Richard Mayne, *Postwar,* (New York: Schocken Books, 1983), p. 118–139 and Daniel Yergin, *Shattered Peace,* (Boston: Houghton Mifflin, 1978), p. 343–357.
2. Quoted in Robert Dallek, *The American Style of Foreign Policy,* (New York: Knopf, 1983), p. 176.
3. Dean Acheson, *Present at the Creation,* (New York: Norton, 1969), p. 375–76; Paul Y. Hammond, 'NSC-68: Prelude to Rearmament'', in Warner Schilling, ed., *Strategy, Politics, and Defense Budgets,* (New York: Columbia University Press, 1962), p. 309.
4. John Lewis Gaddis, *Strategies of Containment,* (New York: Oxford University Press, 1982), p. 99.
5. See Robert A. Dallek, *Franklin Delano Roosevelt and Foreign Policy,* (New York: Oxford University Press, 1979).
6. John Milton Cooper, Jr., *The Warrior and the Priest,* (Cambridge, Mass: Belknap Press of Harvard University Press, 1983), p. 361.
7. William E. Leuchtenbert, *In the Shadow of FDR,* (Ithaca, NY: Cornell University Press, 1983), p. 245.
8. See Ernest W. Lefever, *Ethics and U.S. Foreign Policy,* (New York: Meridian Books, 1957) for a discussion.
9. Theodore Sorensen, *A Different Kind of Presidency,* (New York: Harper, 1984).
10. Allen Matusow, *The Unravelling of America,* (New York: Harper and Row, 1983).
11. On this point, see Michael Miles, *The Odyssey of the American Right,* (New York: Oxford, 1980).

WAGING IDEOLOGICAL WAR: ANTI-COMMUNISM AND US FOREIGN POLICY IN CENTRAL AMERICA

Philip Brenner*

The Bolshevik leaders have had very definite ideas with respect to the role which Mexico and Latin America are to play in their general program of world revolution. They have set up as one of their fundamental tasks the destruction of what they term American imperialism as a necessary prerequisite to the successful development of the international revolutionary movement in the New World. . . Thus Latin America and Mexico are conceived as a base for activity against the United States.
> —*Secretary of State Frank Kellogg, 'Bolshevik Aims and Policies in Mexico and Latin America', 1927*[1]

In Guatemala, international communism had an initial success. It began ten years ago, when a revolution occurred in Guatemala. The revolution was not without justification, but the Communists seized on it, not as an opportunity for real reforms, but as a chance to gain political power. . . If world communism captures any American State, however small, a new and perilous front is established which will increase the danger to the entire free world and require even greater sacrifices from the American people.
> —*Secretary of State John Foster Dulles, 1954*[2]

As Nicaragua is already doing, additional Marxist–Leninist regimes in Central America could be expected to expand their armed forces, bring in large numbers of Cuban and other Soviet bloc advisors, develop sophisticated agencies of repression and external subversion, and sharpen polarizations, both within individual countries and regionally. . . The crisis is on our doorstep.
> —*National Bipartisan Commission on Central America, 1984*[3]

A haunting echo emerges from the solemn warnings today about the potential communist domination of Central America. For more than half a century US officials have harped on a similar theme and have followed it with intervention in the region. During much of this time journalists and scholars focused on the interventions, and treated the alleged threat of communism as little more than a pretext for US domination. The *New York World*, for example, exclaimed in response to the 1927 State Department memorandum:

> One can only characterize this as a degrading form of propaganda aimed either to save Mr. Kellogg's face. . . or as part of a concerted effort on the part of the State Department to mislead and inflame American opinion as the prelude to a diplomatic rupture and an armed intervention.[4]

---

* I very much appreciate the advice of Peter Kornbluh and William LeoGrande.

230

The claims of protecting the hemisphere from a communist threat by Secretary of State John Foster Dulles, when the US assisted in the overthrow of the Guatemalan government, have been similarly dismissed by most scholars as little more than a weak justification for other American purposes in Central America.[5] Indeed, the anti-communist theme has been repeated so often to cover up the true intentions of the United States in Central America that many analysts have viewed it only as a pretext— and nothing more—for US intervention in the region.

The current fervour against communism is not the same as the pretexts of years past. It has taken on a new dimension. Ridding the hemisphere of communism has become an end in itself for the United States; it has become a religious crusade, an ideological war. For this reason the contemporary anti-communist campaign should not be dismissed as sheer hypocrisy. As it has gathered momentum, the campaign has become a crusade against which the mere exposure of its associated fallacies or the recitation of rational argument provides little resistance. To be sure, anti-communist posturing retains many elements of rationalization, whereby it serves other interests. But this alone does not describe its character or suggest its importance as an animating force of US policy in Central America.

This article will examine the nature of the United States' ideological war against communism in Central America today. The first section will describe the way anti-communism has become associated with a multiplicity of goals that are involed to justify US intervention. The description suggests the crusade-like quality of the anti-communist campaign. The parallels to a crusade will be drawn up explicitly in the second section, which focuses on the distortions that are propagated in order to bind the faithful together. The third section explores why anti-communism has taken such a firm hold on Washington. In the concluding section the way in which the crusade has been manifested in policy will be examined, because this suggests the significance of the crusade, which will be considered.

I—Intervention and anti-communism

During the twentieth century the United States has intervened in the Caribbean and Central America for a variety of reasons in pursuit of at least as many interests. Although scholars differ in their emphases on particular reasons, most include three prominent ones: to keep out foreign powers, to ensure access to sea lanes, the Panama Canal, raw materials and markets, and to maintain stability. A consensus on these is evident across the political spectrum from scholars on the left to those on the right.[6] To be sure, explanations differ as to why the three have been sufficiently important to the United States to warrant intervention. Walter Lafeber, for example, points to the US interest in its own security and the desire to develop and maintain a system of neo-dependency. Cole Blasier suggests the US has had an interest in control, or dominant political influence, for its own sake.[7] In each case, particular interests also may have been factors. They range from the particular interests of the people involved in the bureaucracy, to the electoral insecurity of presidents.[8]

The three prominent reasons are clear in many of the cases of US intervention. Concern about a foreign power appears to have prompted the US to occupy Haiti in 1914, because it feared German control of the Windward Passage, and to invade Mexico in 1916, because of Mexican relations with Germany.[9] In both cases the concern turned around security matters. Attention directed at the Panama Canal and Caribbean sea lanes has at times been less a matter of security than commerce, though it would be difficult to disentangle the two. The United States has equated open commerce with its security in this century for several reasons. First, commerce provides the raw materials necessary for domestic industry and development. Thus in 1950, when Ambassador George Kennan underlined the importance of Latin America to the United States, he pointed to the protection of 'our raw materials', but he suggested a security context: were Europe to turn against the United States, he said, 'Latin America would be all we would have to fall back on.'[10] Indeed, Latin American raw materials were used extensively in the arms build-up during the Korean War.

Second, commerce provides markets for US industries, which have been important for the US economy. Finally, open commerce has meant invest-ment by US capitalists who would maintain Latin American countries in a position of dependency vis-à-vis the United States. Dependency reduced the ability of these countries to turn away from the United States and to welcome a non-hemispheric power into a relationship that might threaten the US.

Certainly the dynamics of neo-dependency were not clear to many US policymakers. Neo-dependency may have been understood, if at all, only at an intuitive level. It appears that policymakers often opted to intervene merely at the behest of private interests.[11] They may have done so on the crude basis of their own personal and pecuniary relations with threatened companies, or on the basis of a shared outlook about the sanctity of private property, and about the responsibility of the United States govern-ment to protect American property. Regardless of the source—whether it was a sophisticated calculus about dependency or a simpler notion about American owned property—the concern for private investors seemed for the most part compatible with US security interests.

Likewise, stability has been prized because it seemed to ensure US security and commercial interests. Repressive governments that suppressed dissent—which often took the form of strikes—and that were aligned with the United States, thus became more desirable than democratic governments. The latter had more tolerance for disruption, and were more difficult to control because they were less autocratic.[12]

The common thread that runs through most of the explanations of US intervention is the sense that the United States has viewed the Caribbean and Central America from the perspective of a great power, and has seen the region as within the US sphere of influence. All great powers, the conventional wisdom holds, act from a logic that dictates a power must maintain hegemony over an area it sees as in its sphere. Great powers define their security partially in terms of such maintenance, and resort to techniques such as neo-dependency to promote and perpetuate hegemony.

The assertion that the United States treats Latin America as a protectorate, as a region under its sphere of influence, does not resonate well with the American vision of itself as a non-imperial—and even an anti-imperial—power. Americans hold a profound belief in their exceptionalism, a belief that in the New World they built a society that rested on neither the class divisions nor the imperialism of the Old World, and that was guided by a moral vision. Indeed this faith has tinged public pronouncements about US intervention in Latin America. As the eminent conservative historian Dexter Perkins observes:

> Again and again, in the controversies that arose, the emphasis is on ideology, rather than on security. American statesmen have believed, and acted on the belief, that the best way to rally American opinion behind their purposes is to assert a moral principle.[13]

In part this accounts for the repeated use of an alleged atheistic communist threat to justify intervention. A fight against communists required no other moral justification. It became the equivalent of earlier rationalizations for US intervention, which characterized the United States as a noble missionary out to civilize or Christianize backward populations.

The point at which this missionary overlay—the crusade to rid the hemisphere of communism—took on a life of its own is difficult to specify precisely. As noted, anti-communism was invoked before World War II. In the decade after the war anti-communist appeals with respect to Latin America gained greater frequency as they coincided with the Red Scare of the period. There is evidence, for example, that a crusade-like mentality animated US intervention against Guatemala in 1954 even more than the desire to restore United Fruit's property. Blasier observes that 'Dulles' policies toward Guatemala were in part a religious crusade against atheistic communism, in part an ideological struggle on behalf of free enterprise, and in part a battle with Soviet expansionism'.[14] What is clear is that today the crusade is wholly coincident with professed US concerns for security, the maintenance of neo-dependent relations, and hegemonic domination. Where these interests might have been distinguishable at one time from an anti-communist posture, they are now one and the same. This equation has enabled anti-communism to take on a life of its own as the guide for US policy.

It is revealing to examine the official reasons for US military activities and expanded presence in Central America and the Caribbean today.[15] In each instance, the foreign threat—that is, the threat from outside the hemisphere—is the Soviet Union, which has allegedly injected itself into the hemisphere directly by assisting and controlling its agents, and indirectly through its ideology, communism.[16] Marxism–Leninism and communism are seen as one and the same, as a consistent ideology with a clear associated political programme, and most importantly, as foreign.[17] Starting from these premises, the logic of the US concern becomes apparent with respect to the traditional reasons for US intervention.

1. *Foreign power:* Little distinction is made between US security and keeping the Soviet Union out of the hemisphere. Of necessity, because Cuba and Nicaragua are in the hemisphere, a ready equation is made between these two countries and the Soviet Union. Cuba and Nicaragua are linked to the Soviet Union as 'surrogates', 'mercenaries', 'part of the Soviet intelligence network', 'partners', and 'collaborators'.[18] At times, an activity is referred to as 'Cuban–Soviet', or the three countries are contextually linked as in: 'Cuba, Nicaragua and the Soviet Union aided. . .'[19] This sleight of hand enables Cuba and Nicaragua to be the focus of arguments about protecting Central America from a non-hemispheric power. These 'foreigners' threaten the United States for several reasons. Their presence allegedly undermines US credibility in the eyes of allies, who presumably could not trust the United States to come to their defence if the US is unwilling to attack enemies so close to home.[20] In a time of war with the Soviet Union, the US would be hampered in sending supplies and reinforcements to the battlefield (which presumably would be outside the hemisphere), because the Soviet navy could attack US deployments from bases in Central America and the Caribbean, and could block up the Panama Canal.[21] Short of war, such bases would improve the Soviet capability to gather intelligence about the United States, and to pursue their expansionary aims through the hemisphere.[22] Their goal, it is said, is to control all of Central America and then Mexico, which would place a hostile power directly on the US border. The United States has been able to develop as a democracy and as the strongest country in the world because it has been in the fortuitous position of never having to defend its borders. The necessity of a border defence would change the American way of life.[23] Such an aim is facilitated by the nature of these foreigners. They are ruthless and untrustworthy. They do not respect coalition government, and they take advantage of 'liberal' open systems the way in which the Bolsheviks were able to undermine Eastern European governments.[24] Their weapon is terror, and to permit their terror in this hemi-

sphere is to encourage the international terror network that the Soviet Union sponsors.[25]

2. *Access to markets, etc.:* The Soviets understand how vital the Caribbean sea lanes are to the United States. Half of US 'shipping tonnage and imported oil passes through Caribbean shipping lanes', President Reagan exclaimed in 1984, 'and nearly half of [U.S.] foreign trade passes through the Panama Canal and Caribbean waters.'[26] The emphasis on oil is a version of the old concern about protecting US sources of raw material, even though much of the oil is not produced in the region. An increasing amount is refined in the Caribbean basin. While the old concern was largely economic, the new emphasis is both commercial and strategic. Similarly, open sea lanes and an accessible Panama Canal have had simultaneous security and commercial casts placed on them. This is the case even with respect to private investment. The denunciation of Marxist–Leninist regimes for their lack of pluralism is based on a complex link between security and commercial interests.[27] The regimes in question are Cuba, Nicaragua, and the potential governments that would be ruled by guerrillas fighting in El Salvador and Guatemala. Such regimes are said to deny the unfettered penetration of US capital, which makes their countries inhospitable climates for investment. Investment is one of the bonds that tie a country to the United States, and make it less susceptible to Soviet penetration. US investment is also seen as the only route to economic development in the region, and without development the countries provide 'ripe conditions' for exploitation by Marxist–Leninist subversives.[28]

3. *Stability:* These subversives appreciate that ripe conditions are unstable ones, which is why 'an explicit purpose of guerrilla violence is to make matters worse'.[29] The consequences of instability in the region are not only the likely takeover by the Soviet surrogates, but the massive migration of Central Americans to the United States.[30] Such a flow of immigrants threatens even the stability of the United States and so poses a security problem. While official statements avoid explicit racial references about the nature of the refugees, they muster up images that have been used for more than a century to describe undesirable aliens who do not fit into the mainstream population of the United States.

4. *Moral goals:* Implicit in this litany of threats to the United States and the hemisphere is the moral purpose that attaches to a struggle against communism. But what can be made explicit should not be left to the imagination, so the moral case has been spelled out. To fight totalitarian communism in the hemisphere is 'a moral duty and a solemn responsibility', President Reagan told the US Congress. To be idle would mean that the United States would 'stand by passively while the people of Central America are delivered to totalitarianism'.[31] Indeed, the Kissinger Commission declares the primary US interest in the region is the preservation of 'the moral authority of the United States'. This includes the require-

ment that the United States 'be perceived by others as a nation that does what is right *because* it is right. . .'[32] What is right is to help 'our friends' who are fighting communism. 'The people of El Salvador,' the President admonished, 'are earning their freedom and they deserve our moral and material support to protect it.'[33] Moreover, the other democratic countries in Latin America are looking to the United States to protect their freedom from the dangers of totalitarianism in their midst.[34]

In sum, by official reckoning, a war against communism in Central America comports with the historic interests and values of the United States. Anti-communism throughout the century equates perfectly with the reasons for US intervention in the region. With such a unitary correlation, anti-communism can be readily substituted at all times as the rationale for US action. In the process of such substitution, anti-communism has slowly become the end itself.

II—The anti-communist crusade

Political crusades are no new phenomena in the United States. Many movements in the last two hundred years have taken on an evangelical fervour.[35] They have been accompanied by an ideological world view that explains events in terms of conspiracy; that reduces complex issues to a struggle between good and evil, and that exaggerates the evil to the point of paranoia; that prompts a self-righteousness on the part of the faithful; and that ultimately rests on a blind faith. The current anti-communist crusade directed at Central America fits this mould quite securely.

A conspiratorial view of events in Central America runs rampant through the official declamations reviewed in the last section. The Soviets, Cubans and now Nicaraguans have a plan to take over Central America, officials allege, and so all turmoil in the region can be traced directly to this source. 'The Soviet–Cuban thrust to make Central America part of their geostrategic challenge,' the Kissinger Commission asserts, 'is what has turned the struggle in Central America into a security and political problem. . .'[36] Concomitant with the conspiratorial view is a portrait of the enemy that takes on fantastic proportions. As William LeoGrande observes: 'In this envisioned conspiracy, the communists are omniscient and omnipotent, the noncommunists ignorant and impotent.'[37]

Having enlarged the enemy to frightening dimensions, crusaders then register enormous fears about the monster. The communists in Central America hate the United States, officials charge, see control of the region as a first attack on the United States, and finally seek to destroy America and 'its way of life'.[38] Such fears lead to a rigidity that cannot tolerate any deviation, because to accept any accommodation is to expose Good to Evil. 'President Jimmy Carter's Ibero–American policies', the Committee of Santa Fe sermonized, are the culmination of this accommodation process whereby. . . Latin American regimes are abandoned to extracontinental attacks by the international Communist movement.[39]

To wage war against this enemy thus becomes a moral obligation as much as it is self-serving. The Kissinger Commission proudly proclaims that 'in Central America today, our strategic and moral interests coincide'.[40] The United States can self-righteously arrogate to itself, therefore, the prerogative to determine which regimes in the region are legitimate and which are not. Cuba and Nicaragua fail the tests.

The tests have a mystical quality to them. They do not rely on ready proofs, but emerge from a fabric of distortions and blind assertions. To believe these requires a leap of faith, which is what all crusades demand of their followers as a condition to join the fold. Richard Hofstadter explains that

> The typical procedure of the higher paranoid scholarship is to start with such defensible assumptions and with a careful accumulation of facts, or at least what appear to be facts, and to marshal these facts toward an overwhelming 'proof' of the particular conspiracy to be established.[41]

Six articles of faith constitute the 'proofs' of the anti-communist crusade over Central America. Repeated regularly, they are: (1) the United States is supporting democracy in Central America; (2) US credibility is at stake in Central America; (3) there is a Soviet/Cuban/Nicaraguan nexus that makes Nicaragua and Cuba surrogates of the Soviet Union; (4) Nicaragua is a threat to its neighbours and the United States; (5) the countries of the region are potential 'dominoes'; (6) the anti-Nicaraguan guerrillas are fighting for democracy.

The six shibboleths do emerge from some undeniable facts, as Hofstadter suggests is often the case. The facts are invoked to affirm the veracity of the web that is spun out of them, and to obscure the leaps of faith that constitute the web itself. There is no question, for example, that Cuba is a Marxist–Leninist state, and that it views the Soviet Union as a 'natural ally'. Nearly three-fourths of Cuba's trade is with Comecon (Soviet and Eastern European trade bloc) countries. The Soviet Union provides significant amounts of economic and military aid to Cuba along with large subsidies, on the oil and machinery it exports to Cuba and on the sugar it imports. Cuba has supplied arms to Nicaragua, and has given extensive assistance in the form of teachers and medical professionals. In the ruling Sandinista directorate there are some people who consider themselves to be Marxist–Leninists, and this is true as well of some leaders among the insurgents in El Salvador and Guatemala. What is questionable are the conclusions that are developed on the basis of these facts. Consider each of the six.

1. Democracy in Central America may be the most often stated goal of the Reagan Administration, but incantation does not substitute for action. In El Salvador, which is the main focus of the policy, it has promoted three elections since 1982. But in each instance, the choices were limited by the exclusion of candidates associated with the FDR (Democratic Revolutionary Front). This meant that many Christian Democrats and Social Democrats who had run for office even in earlier disrupted and discredited Salvadoran elections were kept off the ballot. The last election, in May 1984, was further distorted by the intrusion of the US through its massive support for Jose Napoleon Duarte. Still, the United States has maintained the fiction that the elections were democratic, because at least the 'centre' and right participated fully. This fiction rests on the claim that the El Salvador government is a centre regime which had instituted reforms beginning after the October, 1979 coup, and that it has been continuing those reforms. In fact, the government that came to power in October, 1979 lasted for three months, and most of the reforms it tried to develop were undermined by the military and right wing, which regained power by March, 1980.[42] Most of the people involved with the first junta are now in exile, and many of them are working actively with the FDR. The lack of real progress in democratizing El Salvador prompted President Reagan to veto the military aid bill he had requested at the end of 1983, because it would have required the President to certify continuing progress towards democracy.[43]

What the Administration would have to overlook in such certifications is the close link between the 'death squads' and the government. The death squads are not the rogue groups of right-wing extremists Administration officials describe. They have been organized and directed by high military officials and form a part of the apparatus the government uses to control the populace.[44] There is some evidence that they may be even linked to the Central Intelligence Agency.[45]

Democracy in the other Central American countries also appears to be of little real concern for the Administration. It points to the 1981 Honduran election as a movement away from authoritarian rule, and then ignores the way in which real control of the government has remained in the hands of the military.[46] Worse, it obscures the way in which increasing US military assistance to Honduras has strengthened the military's control, and how US plans for a permanent base there are likely to nullify the civilian rule it upholds rhetorically.[47]

The obfuscation with respect to Guatemala is the most callous. President Reagan already has resumed the sale of military equipment there despite congressional bans, and has proposed a military aid package for the junta of $10 million. He claims that the rate of killing by the military has diminished and elections are in the offing. But the sales were begun during the rule of General Efrain Rios Montt, who increased the murder rate for rural Indians, and the 'hope' for democratic reform is pegged on the regime of General Oscar Meija Victores, who was involved with the so-called rural pacification during the Rios Montt era. He is a member of the officer corps that had prevented free elections and produced the blood-baths in the 1970s.[48]

2. If the pursuit of democracy and the associated prevention of dictatorship express the moral component of US policy, the most important self-interested component is insuring US credibility. Central America is a 'vital' US interest, numerous officials have declared. If the US were to give up a vital interest to its enemy, then its credibility with allies who depend upon the US would wither. However, it is far from clear to which allies the officials are referring. Major European allies repeatedly have told the Administration that neither do they see the stirrings in Central America as vital to US interests, nor do they believe the US should pursue a military solution to secure what it alone perceives is in its interest. One French diplomat said in 1983:

> Just because the United States believes that every problem that arises in the Southern hemisphere has the Russian hand behind it, that doesn't mean it is so.[49]

Western leaders are far more concerned that the United States might actually become enmeshed in a Central American war and thereby reduce its military commitment to Europe. In that sense the Administration is correct about its credibility, but for the wrong reasons. US credibility as a rational and responsible international actor is at stake in Central America and the Caribbean.[50] Even Conservative Prime Minister Margaret Thatcher publicly rebuked the United States for its 1983 invasion of Grenada, and for the mining of Nicaragua's harbours in 1984.

Europeans have been advising the Reagan Administration to rely on the Contadora countries (Mexico, Panama, Colombia and Venezuela) to mediate the conflicts in the region. These four US allies grouped together precisely to encourage the United States to reduce its involvement in the Central American wars. Along with other Latin American countries, they have told the United States both that its credibility would not be affected if the guerrillas won in El Salvador or the Sandinistas remained in power, and that its credibility would be harmed if it did intervene militarily.[51] The United States has turned a deaf ear to its allies' entreaties. It has not responded positively to Contadora proposals, and it continues to base its actions on what it perceives are worst case scenarios, which the Latin Americans find are highly problematic. The worst case is that Nicaragua and other so-called Marxist–Leninist regimes would open bases for the Soviets, which might endanger free US access to the Canal and Caribbean sea lanes. However, Nicaragua has asserted time and again that it will not permit any foreign base on its soil, and the Soviet Union has shown no inclination to seek such a base. It appears unwilling, or unable, to pay the cost that such a base would entail, which would be the case in El Salvador and Guatemala as well.[52]

3. The 'worst case' scenarios turn on the important and unsupported assumption that Nicaragua and Cuba are surrogates of the Soviet Union, as would be any Marxist-Leninist state. It is an assumption, born in the simplistic pre-Sino/Soviet split era, of a monolithic communist world. It is also an assumption on which the Administration relies only with respect to Central America. Elsewhere, as in China and Yugoslavia, it recognizes that not all Marxist–Leninist regimes are alike, or are pawns of the Soviet Union. China and Yugoslavia, for example, carry on a greater proportion of their trade with the Soviet Union than does Nicaragua. Nicaragua has received aid and weapons from the Soviet Union; it also has received these from several Western countries. Unlike Comecon countries, it has not organized its economy along a Soviet model, and it has maintained a large private sector, a relatively uncensored press, and religious freedoms.[53] But its internal organization is less critical for the assumption than its external relations, because supposedly it is Nicaragua's foreign policy that worries the United States. In this regard, there is no evidence that the Soviet Union has been able or even has tried to direct Nicaraguan foreign policy. Charges that Nicaraguan support of the Soviet Union in the United Nations demonstrate its slavishness are credible only if one accepts the premise that a country could never vote with the Soviets without being a Soviet pawn. In fact, Nicaragua has taken a non-aligned stance in the UN. Cuba has also respected Nicaragua's sovereignty. The best evidence suggests that when Cuba has advised Nicaragua how to handle its foreign affairs, it has told the Sandinistas to avoid Cuba's mistakes and not to alienate itself from the United States.[54]

Assertions about Cuban puppetry did not originate in the Reagan Administration. They have been prevalent for twenty years, and most prominently since the 1970s, when Cuban support for the MPLA in Angola and the Ethiopian government in its war against Sudan began to involve troops. The evidence points to a mixed record: that Cuba took the lead in enlisting Soviet support for the MPLA and agreed to the Soviet request for assistance to the Ethiopians.[55] Other cases also paint a picture of two independent countries who have similar goals at times and who might work in concert when their goals coincide.[56] Most importantly, however, there is no evidence that either country has any plan to control Central America or desire to do so. Indeed, the Soviet Union has tended to be far more respectful about US domination over its sphere of influence than the US has been of the Soviet Union's.[57]

4. Similarly, there is no evidence of a Nicaraguan plot to overthrow

other countries. The United States has maintained the most sophisticated reconnaissance of the El Salvador border, yet has produced no solid proof to support its claims that Nicaragua is shipping arms and ammunition to El Salvador. The weakness of the Administration's case was articulated succinctly by an especially well-informed Central American analyst in mid-1984, shortly after he left the Central Intelligence Agency. He said,

> The whole picture that the Administration has presented of Salvadoran insurgent operations being planned, directed and supplied from Nicaragua is simply not true.[58]

The Salvadoran insurgents appear to receive most of their arms and ammunition from the Salvadoran army.[59]

In part the Administration's case revolves around the large build-up of Nicaraguan military forces. What the case omits is the obvious need for such a large force to protect Nicaragua from daily incursions by CIA-supplied contra forces. Moreover, the Nicaraguans reasonably anticipate even heavier fighting in the future, directly against the United States or Honduras.[60] The weapons they have received are defensive, though clearly they were insufficient even to prevent the mining of key ports by the CIA in 1983 and 1984.

5. The Nicaraguan threat to its neighbours is an element in the complex scenario of how Central America is likely to fall under Soviet domination. In effect it is a modern version of the 'domino' thesis. Three versions of the domino effect have been propounded by the Administration. In the first, the countries of the region are said to be ripe for direct Soviet/Cuban/Nicaraguan aggression, which occurs through agents sent in for this purpose. In a second version, the countries might fall by 'contagion' or by a 'ripple effect', again because they are ripe or lack sufficient stamina. The third version is a variation of the first: the insurgents may be locals but they are controlled by foreign forces and in effect are not indigenous.

All of the versions rest on the vivid metaphor of dominoes, and little else. Dominoes are each carved alike, and fall from the same pressure. In reality, countries have different histories, different forces at work in their midst, different reasons for turmoil and stability. Each country must be understood in its own terms to appreciate whether revolution is likely at a particular time. Costa Rica, for example, with a long democratic tradition and little repression was less affected by the Sandinista victory than was El Salvador.[61] Mexico, which is seen as the ultimate domino, is a stable country with enduring political institutions. This is one reason why it has given so little credence to Administration worries about falling dominoes.[62]

Undoubtedly, guerrillas in El Salvador and Guatemala were heartened by the Sandinista victory. But in such cases the focus should be placed on the reasons for revolution—the oppression and poverty—and not on the example that heartens them. They might well draw sustenance as well from successful revolutions in other parts of the world. As in other revolutions, including the American Revolution, they also rely on a range of ideas to energize their followers. Some form of Marxism–Leninism has been embraced by nearly all successful twentieth century revolutions, and Central American revolutionaries should be expected to embrace these ideas, too. But as in other countries they have adopted those ideas that suited their particular conditions and meshed them with other relevant concepts. Liberation theology, with its emphasis on democracy, the grievances of the poor, and bearing witness, has also engendered the struggle against tyrannies in El Salvador and Guatemala.

The argument that the Central American insurgencies are not indigenous because only a foreign-supported revolution could be sustained starts from an unsubstantiated assumption.[63] It also bears little relation to the reality of these cases. The roots of the Guatemalan struggle emanate from the repression that followed the US-sponsored overthrow of the Arbenz government in 1954. It gained momentum in the 1970s, precisely during the period when Cuba had turned its attention to Africa and was harmonizing relations with Latin American countries.[64] Similarly, the guerrilla movement in El Salvador developed strength during the 1970s, following the military's nullification of the 1972 election.[65]

6. The web is fully enmeshed with the final claim of the anti-communist crusaders, which draws attention back to the opening proposition. The United States is said to be fighting for democracy in Central America against foreign totalitarian forces that aim to take over the countries and weaken the US. Therefore, whatever means the United States uses is ultimately democratic in character because its aim is democracy. In this way the contras who are attempting to overthrow the Nicaraguan government with US support are 'freedom fighters', and their goal must be the creation of democracy in Nicaragua, because they oppose the present regime.

There is little doubt any more that the aim of the contras is the overthrow of the government. Even the Administration has shifted its rationale for support of them from the flimsy claim that they intended merely to interdict arms.[66] The official intention now is to pressure the Sandinistas to fulfill their 'promises' of creating a democracy. But would the contras provide democracy if they succeeded? Nicaragua has not had any experience with democracy in half a century, so that none of the contra groupings can claim to spring from democratic roots. Of the three major groupings, moreover, the two based in Honduras—and which are the most powerful—have direct ties to the repression of the Somoza dictatorship.[67] This is especially true of the FDN (Nicaraguan Democratic Force), whose military command structure is entirely drawn from the Somoza National Guard. Their alleged fidelity to democratic freedoms is hardly credible.

Indeed, their sabotage is aimed partly at the Nicaraguan effort to hold democratic elections in November, 1984. The defence against the contras has forced Nicaragua to impose some curbs that could distort a process of free elections. Preparation for the elections has included a successful literacy programme and long consultation with several US universities about procedure. Thus the US professes its support for democracy by blindly sanctioning the efforts in El Salvador, Honduras and Guatemala, and by discounting the efforts in Nicaragua while aiding the guerrillas who are trying to undermine these efforts.

The durability of the six propositions, especially in the face of serious criticism from scholars, journalists and commentators, indicates that they have become articles of faith. It is possible that the Reagan Administration is ignorant of the reality it pretends to describe in Central America. Administrations do tend to arrive in Washington with a type of 'amnesia', a lack of historical memory about what has happened before it arrived. As Eldon Kenworthy explains, 'Washington confuses its discovery of the guerrillas, *its* awakening, with what has actually been going on in these countries.'[68] Indeed, several of the key policymakers on Central America in the early days of the Administration were ignorant about the region. But this perspective does not explain why the Administration chose to be ignorant. Nor does it explain why the Kissinger Commission, which consulted with more than seven hundred people by its own reckoning, persisted in propagating the myths.

An alternative explanation is that the distortions are the result of a deliberate campaign of misinformation. Evidence for this comes from numerous examples, such as the first 'white paper' that the Administration issued to support its Central America policy.[69] A *Wall Street Journal* inquiry into the document determined, in the words of the White Paper's principal author, that parts are deliberately 'misleading' and 'over-embellished'.[70] Similarly, one official explained to me in a 'background' interview how the fictitious claim materialized that there were 250,000 Nicaraguans under arms. He said, 'Someone happened to use that figure one day in a briefing for reporters, and no one questioned it. So we stuck with it.'

While it is widely accepted that all administrations attempt to manipulate the media to some extent, and distort information especially with regard to military operations,[71] it would take a grand conspiracy to maintain so consistently the six assumptions of US policy. They cannot be merely the result of ignorance and deliberate distortion. They have become the ready catch phrases of officials throughout the foreign policy bureaucracy and in Congress. Without evidence of a conspiracy at work, it strains credibility that such predominance for the myths is the result of a conspiracy. A far more plausible explanation is that a religious mindset has enveloped official Washington, an anti-communist framework that has the earmarks of a paranoid crusade, and that the six propositions have become its intellectual glue.

III—The politics of anti-communism

So first of all, let me state clearly that on some very important things, all Americans stand in agreement. We will oppose the establishment of Marxist states in Central America. We will not accept the creation of Soviet military bases in Central America. And we will not tolerate the placement of Soviet offensive missiles in Central America—or anywhere in this hemisphere.
                        —Sen. Christopher J. Dodd (Democrat, Connecticutt), 1983[72]

Anti-communism pervades and sets the limits on all debate about Central America in Washington today. Senator Dodd had been the leading opponent of the Reagan Administration's military approach in Central America when he delivered the above address. Even with this opening, he was criticized severely by House Majority Leader Jim Wright (Democrat, Texas), because the address minimized the communist threat and challenged the President's programme. Now, when critics of the Administration policy comment on Central America, they feel compelled to begin their remarks by reciting canons about the horrors of communism.

What accounts for this ideological straitjacket is unquestionably the anti-communist fervour of Reagan Administration officials. But their success is only partly explained by their ardour. Anti-communism has taken hold throughout the policymaking apparatus because it serves a variety of interests at this particular time. To appreciate how anti-communism has become a crusade in Washington, it is necessary to examine ideological, domestic political, and particularistic factors that are at work.

A. *Ideological Factors:* Like previous anti-communist crusades, the current one could count on a vast popular prejudice against communism. By the 1980s popular culture no longer was dominated by the anti-communist themes of the 1950s, but residual fears and fantasies from earlier propaganda barrages remained. Thus facile equations between Marxists, Marxist–Leninists, and communists are accepted readily. For example, Chilean President, Salvador Allende, was a self-described Marxist. The description bore a closer relation to his intellectual critique of Chilean capitalism than it did to a Marxist–Leninist political programme, as the MIR (Left Revolutionary Movement) in Chile frequently reminded him. In Central American countries, Marxist–Leninist insurgents have been at odds frequently with the Communist Party of each country, because the communists have tended to eschew armed struggle. Such distinctions are easily blurred when the three terms are used interchangeably by US officials.

What gave anti-communism its greatest popular force at the end of the

1970s was its inherent xenophobia. Communism was linked to a foreign power—the Soviet Union—and was seen as a foreign ideology. At a point when national pride had deteriorated, and the United States seemed to be reeling from blows in Southeast Asia, in Iran, and at the Panama Canal, a foreign devil explanation provided easy comprehension for the state of affairs. The foreign devil theory replaced a national debate that might have occurred and never materialized about the United States' role in the world. It obscured the nature of US hegemony in Central America for the previous eighty years, and the dynamic of de-colonization that was occurring there. The American people had never acknowledged that the US treated Central America as a protectorate, and so could not understand why movements for sovereignty would involve hostility towards the United States. They had been misled about the structural sources of oppression in Central America, and so could not understand how these structures would generate indigenous rebellions.[73]

Anti-communism facilitated a peculiarly American explanation of social unrest to emerge once again: the germ theory of turmoil. The theory rests on the metaphor of a healthy human body, which is equated to the supposedly well functioning systems of Central America. A healthy body, in this view, is not upset by its normal operation from the inside. Sickness comes only when a foreign agent, a germ, enters. Notably, one version of this theory dominated US social science during the anti-communist crusade of the 1950s, and it lasted into the 1960s. 'Consensus' historians, for example, contended that significant social movements, such as abolitionism, were the product of people who felt they were outside the system— in effect, people who were abnormal.[74] The system itself, they suggested, could not produce such turmoil, because it rested on a consensus about fundamentals.

A corollary to the theory is that germs can spread and make sickness contagious. Interestingly, the notion that communism is contagious in Central America emerged during the Cold War of the late 1940s and 1950s. It has re-emerged as a dominant metaphor today.[75] The germ theory and its corollary justify hostility towards communists, especially as they engender the American spirit of messianism, a spirit of cleansing the temple. Anti-communism thus appeared as a way for Americans to recall their best instincts, the instincts to help others and to prevent the imposition of tyranny. Americans had risen to the challenge in World War II against totalitarian Nazism, and could do the same against totalitarian communism.

For some Americans, totalitarianism was evil less because of its alleged effects on the societies in question than because of their reduced ability to penetrate these societies. For similar reasons that the Soviet Union opposes pluralism in Eastern Europe—because its domination occurs through the Party—so American business and political leaders have championed pluralism in Central America. US control occurs through the economy, which it wants separated from politics. Herein lies Jeanne Kirkpatrick's distinction between authoritarian and totalitarian regimes that President Reagan found so compelling.[76] Authoritarian governments have permitted US businesses to operate with relatively little restraint. This suggests that anti-communism serves some domestic US interests especially well.

B. *Domestic Factors:* At the moment when ideological factors were coalescing towards a crusade against communism in Central America, the capacity of the US Congress to resist such a campaign was deteriorating. Campaign spending had skyrocketed in the 1970s, with several House races costing in excess of $500,000 and many Senate races running over $1 million. No incumbent felt immune from the potential threat of a well financed opponent, and all sought ways to reduce their vulnerability. Thus one senior House member, who was involved in Central American policy formation, explained his pessimism about congressional efforts to curtail the US commitment. When asked in a personal interview why Representatives continue to vote for military aid to El Salvador even though their constituents opposed it, he said, 'They may be against it today, but who knows what they'll think tomorrow. Constituents are easily swayed on these matters, and no one here wants to risk being caught on the wrong side of this war.'

A major factor in increased campaign costs has been the rise of political action committees (PACs).[77] While PACs encompass the conventional political spectrum, the best coordinated and richest are those which support right-wing candidates. Some, such as the Committee for the Survival of a Free Congress, ostensibly focus on 'social' issues. But their effect has been to defeat legislators who have opposed military intervention in the Third World, and to elect virulent anti-communists. Increasingly campaigns have emphasised foreign policy issues, with right-wing candidates charging that incumbents who are not vigorously anti-communist are tacitly supporting the enemy. With Republicans in control of the Senate since 1981, and prominent anti-communists such as Jesse Helms (Republican, North Carolina) chairing Senate subcommittees related to foreign policy, the legitimacy of the anti-communist rhetoric has been enhanced. Meanwhile, potential resisters to the tide feel increasingly powerless.

The career civil service has been similarly weakened as a potential source of opposition to the anti-communist crusade. The bureaucracy had tended to place a brake on major departures by new Presidents in the past.[78] To some extent it has prevented President Reagan from implementing fully all that he has said he would like to do in Central America. But when Assistant Secretary of State for Inter-American Affairs Thomas Enders was dismissed in 1983, because he had advocated a 'two-track' approach that included dialogue with the El Salvador insurgents, it sent a chill through the bureaucracy. The removal of US Ambassador to Nicaragua Anthony Quainton in early 1984 firmly signalled to career bureaucrats what they had suspected already. Quainton, a career foreign service officer, met with displeasure because he refused in his reporting to bow to the official line that Nicaragua was in the grip of intractable communists. For those who wanted to retain any influence or advance their careers, it was clear that a vigilant anti-communism with respect to Central America had to be manifest. The bureaucracy was disposed towards anti-communism already.[79] What it might have opposed were adventurist actions that were inconsistent with US interests in the region. But it had few resources on which to rely, especially with Congress so weakened and public debate so oriented to a new Cold War.[80] The Reagan Administration's cold war orientation placed even greater pressure on career service officers in the Latin American bureau to conform to the anti-communist posturing that was emerging throughout the State Department.

President Reagan did not invent the posture of the Cold War. It had begun to gain strength in the 1970s as 'Cold War liberals' grouped together to oppose detente with the Soviet Union and the slower rate of growth in military spending.[81] They also shared an outspoken and long-standing commitment to fight communism, and they preached a 'militant containment' of the Soviet Union. Though the Committee on the Present Danger—their major forum, organised in 1976—received no money from defence contractors, Committee members had extensive links with the defence industry and military establishment. Their prestige also lent credibility to appeals from the New Right, which in turn reinforced the Committee's efforts through conservative PACs. Notably, the Cold War liberals and the New Right had kept their distance from each other prior to the 1970s. Each had viewed the other with suspicion and hostility, because of differences over domestic issues. An anti-communist crusade enabled them to make common cause and grow together symbiotically. It was also their route to power, as several members of the Committee on the Present Danger joined the Reagan Administration along with New Right disciples.

C. *Particularistic Factors:* President Reagan's appointees who had been members of the Committee on the Present Danger were located throughout the foreign policy machinery.[82] The President himself had been a member. This is not to suggest that a conspiracy was at work, because the Committee itself had no control over these people. Their common membership does suggest a like-mindedness with respect to communism.

Though the media described some of the new Latin American policy-makers as 'pragmatists'—Thomas Enders, for example, was opposed by Sen. Jesse Helms because of his prior association with the detente-tainted Nixon and Ford Administrations—all of those associated with Latin

American policy accepted the Cold War prism that the President and Secretary of State Alexander Haig immediately imposed on the US perspective of Central America. Still, some were more ideologically inclined than others, and the ideologues were well situated at key locations. They were people who had developed their careers as anti-communists, and they were single-minded in their devotion to the cause. For example, Roger Fontaine, a co-author of the vitriolic Santa Fe report, was Latin American specialist on the National Security Council. Constantine Menges, who had propounded the Central American domino thesis in the 1970s (and who was severely criticized by several senators in 1981 for ideologically biased and deceptive reports), was responsible for the CIA's National Intelligence Estimates on Latin America. Whether the anti-communist crusade could have been mounted with different people is of course difficult to evaluate, even with the ideological and domestic political factors coinciding to give anti-communism its force. It is clear that the particular people who made up the Reagan Administration were such vigorous anti-communists that credit for the crusade must be given to them in the first instance.

Their task was made easier by the pleas for help to ward off the communist menace, which came from conservatives in Central America. This coincided with Reagan's ascension, because the guerrilla movement in Guatemala and El Salvador had gained strength in the 1970s. Local oligarchs may not have believed that the guerrillas were communist and directed by Moscow, or they may have believed their own propaganda. In any case they had learned from experience in the 1950s and 1960s that the alarm of a communist threat could be sufficient to generate US assistance. In these countries the military and local police were generally inclined to see communist threats, because of a well developed anti-communism within their ranks.[83] Businessmen in El Salvador and Guatemala were closely allied to the military, and also tended to embrace a rigid anti-communism, as a defence against any reforms that they believed would reduce their power.[84]

A final factor at the end of the 1970s uniquely fuelled the broad ideological and domestic political movements that were being shaped into a crusade. President Jimmy Carter prepared the way for the anti-communist crusade by introducing and propounding many of the very same assumptions that the Reagan Administration had used so forcefully. In this respect, the development of the anti-communist crusade of the 1980s followed the pattern of the crusade in the 1950s. President Harry Truman had paved the way for McCarthyism by focusing the terms of the foreign policy debate on anti-communism and through his attempts to ferret out communists in the government. When conservatives attacked him for being an insufficiently diligent anti-communist, he had little to offer in defence. He himself had identified the 'menace', and he shared the critics' assumptions.[85]

The Carter legacy is evident with respect to three key countries: Cuba, Nicaragua and El Salvador. Consider in each case how Carter paved the way for Reagan's policies.

+Cuba: The Carter Administration moved quickly to reduce hostility towards Cuba in 1977,[86] UN Ambassador Andrew Young characterized the Cuban presence in Angola as a 'stabilizing' influence. US and Cuban diplomats began to staff the 'interests sections' that had been operated previously by the Swiss and Czech embassies. Tourist and cultural exchanges flourished. But by the end of 1978 coolness prevailed again. Cuba and the US had been on opposite sides of the Sudan–Ethiopian war, and Presidents Carter and Fidel Castro had had a personal blow-up over the invasion of Zaire by Shaba rebels. Strains grew in September, 1979 as Carter exaggerated the importance of a Soviet brigade in Cuba and denounced Cuba for threatening the United States. To underscore the now official view that Cuba was a major enemy, the President issued a policy statement, PD-52, that ordered national security agencies 'to devise strategies for curbing Cuba's activities [in the Third World] and isolating it politically'. The new attitude shaped the agenda of demands that Carter developed as the basis for a normalization of relations. These focused on bilateral issues such as migration, unsettled claims, and the Soviet military presence in Cuba, and international issues such as Cuba's involvement in Angola, Ethiopia, and Caribbean Basin countries. Reagan adopted both the agenda and the view that Cuba is a major enemy of the United States. The Reagan Administration has taken more active measures against Cuba than were undertaken in the Carter years. But the measures follow from an orientation towards Cuba that Reagan inherited from Carter.

+Nicaragua: The revolution in Nicaragua offered the Carter Administration an opportunity to act in accord with its professed human rights goals, and its claim that it sought new ways of relating to anti-colonial forces in the Third World.[88] Charges by conservatives that Carter's policy drove Somoza from office and handed over Nicaragua to the Marxist-Leninist Sandinistas suggest that, at the least, his orientation differed from Reagan's. In reality, the Carter Administration acted on premises that are not far from those of the conservatives. Until the eve of the Sandinista victory, the Carter Administration attempted to prevent the FSLN (Sandinista National Liberation Front) from gaining control. In June 1979, the US called for an emergency meeting of the Organization of American States, to install a multilateral force in Nicaragua that would 'preserve order'. The Latin Americans refused to support the ruse. A White House spokesman called for the retention of the National Guard, that is, somocismo without Somoza. The National Security Council emphasized Cuba's role in the struggle, and introduced the idea that the Sandinistas were puppets of the Cubans. The Administration never repudiated these premises. But with the coming to power of the FSLN in July, Carter attempted to find a way of working with the revolution. He quickly sent emergency assistance of $20 million to Nicaragua, and he proposed a $75 million aid package to Congress. However, by September the Administration again was criticizing Nicaragua for its anti-US statements at the summit of non-aligned nations, and in December, the Administration reacted angrily when Nicaragua refused to condemn the Soviet Union over the invasion of Afghanistan. It seemed to them that Nicaragua was falling into the Soviet camp, and they said so. This hardly helped the $75 million aid package sail through Congress. Indeed, Administration lobbyists devoted little effort to securing congressional approval of the bill, which passed finally in October, 1980. Ultimately, the Reagan Administration chose not to expend the full amount of the package, on anti-communist grounds that echoed the Carter sentiments.

+El Salvador: While the Reagan Administration may not conceive of El Salvador as the jewel in the crown, it has focused on this war-torn country as the place to halt the forward advance of international communism—the site where the US had drawn the line. Such was the conception of the Carter Administration too. Following the Sandinista victory in July, 1979, Carter policymakers feared that revolution might spread to El Salvador because of the brutality of the Romero dictatorship there. There is evidence that the Administration encouraged junior military officers in their plans to stage the October, 1979 coup. The October junta unsuccessfully tried to implement a series of major reforms, and the Carter Administration applauded the efforts with economic aid and with military assistance designed to mount a campaign of 'clean counter-insurgency'. But the old line military quickly moved to consolidate its power, and the aid only buttressed their strength. The Carter Administration refused to acknowledge the changes that returned control to the most repressive forces in El Salvador, and introduced the fiction after March 1980 that the regime was a continuation of the October, 1979 junta. As violence increased in 1980—dramatized by the assassination of Archbishop Oscar Romero— the Carter Administration developed the position that the government stood at the centre, and that the violence was a product of extremism on the left and right. Links between the government and the right were obscured, and Carter continued military aid with the justification that military stability provided a 'shield' for social reforms. When four American churchwomen were assassinated brutally on December 2, 1980, the aid was suspended. But in mid-January, just days before he left office, Carter resumed the assistance. The State Department declared, in its explanation for the resumption, that

We must support the Salvadoran government in its struggle against left-wing terrorism supported covertly with arms, ammunition, training, and political military advice by Cuba and other Communist nations.[89]

Carter thus provided Reagan with virtually every premise that has undergirded the anti-communist crusade. In each of the three cases, he rationalized his actions by reference to a communist threat, and he focused on communism as the source of the problem he confronted. His reasons for taking this approach may have involved his own anti-communist inclinations, his fear of electoral defeat in a growing anti-communist climate that had developed from the broad ideological and political factors discussed above, and his reliance on National Security Council director Zbigniew Brzezinski, who had long advocated an East–West orientation for US–Third World relations. Whatever the source of his approach, though, it served to reinforce the anti-communist climate, and to pave the way for the crusade that Reagan has led.

IV—Ridding the hemisphere of communism

The war against communism in Central America is rooted in neither security nor commercial interests. Fear about threats to these interests often prompted US intervention in the past. Now officials focus the fears wholly on communism, which they have substituted in a meaningless way for the traditional threats. Hegemony may still be an underlying interest that animates the Reagan Administration's crusade. But Administration officials have tended to discount cavalierly those critics—including prominent members of the foreign policy establishment[90]—who focus on the seeming irrationality of the Administration's approach to preserving US hegemony in the region. It can do so because the critics are not speaking to the Administration's principal objective, which is to wage ideological war against communism and rid it from the hemisphere.

An ideological war can be waged on several fronts: in a battle of ideals, in economic competition, and in military confrontation against those who might embrace 'unacceptable' ideals and economic arrangements. The United States is now engaged on all three fronts against communism in Central America.

The war has been pursued on the first front by Reagan Administration demands for elections and pluralism in Central America. These have become the ideals on which the US is relying to counter the idealistic appeal that it believes communism holds out for the poor. In this way the US hopes to develop a glue that will bind countries ultimately to the United States without coercion. Though actions by the US belie its democratic intentions, this aspect of the anti-communist war embraces a positive thrust. It expresses an idealism that would be beneficial to the mass of people in the region if the necessary concomitants to real democracy—adequate health care, education, housing, food, and jobs— were also pursued. But such concomitants would require fundamental structural changes that the US has opposed, and so the aim of removing communism from the hemisphere has rested minimally on the hope that this front will be victorious.

On the economic front, the Administration has proposed programmes that would provide some development to counter the Cuban model, which has had a high regard in Latin America. But the main effect of its two major proposals—the Caribbean Basin Initiative and the aid package based on the Kissinger Commission recommendations—would be to reproduce the dependency status of the region's countries while recreating conditions for profitable investment by US multinationals.[91] Neither consequence would have much impact on reducing poverty in Central America. Even with the $8 billion assistance programme that Kissinger advocated, internal reforms would be piecemeal, and would not alter the structures of economic power that generated and maintain the poverty.

Given the weaknesses of the first two fronts, militarization has thus become the linchpin of the war against communism in Central America. Here the Administration has adopted the very practices that it alleges the communists have used.[92] The military war against communism includes: the training, supply and direction of guerrillas who are attempting to overthrow a government (Nicaragua); the development of a government's (Honduras) capability to support the invasion of another country (Nicaragua); the regionalization of the war; and the introduction of foreign troops into direct combat. The aims of these practices became clear by 1984.[93]

The first aim has been to establish a new military base in the region from which the United States could readily intervene or direct military operations. Existing bases in Panama, Cuba and Puerto Rico were considered too insecure or distant for this purpose. This has been accomplished in Honduras, where the US has built and improved airstrips to handle large transport planes, constructed barracks, dredged harbours, and installed sophisticated communications facilities. As Michael Klare reasons, 'By the conclusion of Big Pine II, the United States had a fully developed combat infrastructure in Honduras capable of supporting any level of military operations through Central America.'[94]

Such a base may not be used by US forces in large numbers, but it would be difficult for the United States to achieve its second aim without direct intervention. That aim is the total destruction of all guerrilla forces in El Salvador, Guatemala and Honduras. It has discouraged all efforts to establish a dialogue with armed opposition, and has declared a 'victory' over the guerrillas as 'vital' to US interests. A large obstacle in the way of achieving this objective has been the weakness of the El Salvador army. The army has been unable to defeat the guerrillas militarily or to gain effective control over the four provinces that guerrilla forces dominate. Morale in the El Salvador military has been low, and retention of the best trained troops has been difficult. The US worked especially hard to secure the election of Duarte in May, 1984, so that the eventual call for US troops would come from a government that appeared both legitimate and centrist. The United States recognizes that total victory will require the involvement of US military forces.

However, victory over the guerillas would be only temporary, US officials reason, if Nicaragua continues to be governed by the Sandinistas. They see Nicaragua as a sanctuary for rebels who might rise again after a short respite.[95] The lesson they apply from their Vietnam war experience is that total victory depends on 'no sanctuaries and no Ho Chi Minh trails'. They see the war as a regional conflict, and victory must entail the overthrow of the Nicaraguan government. This became their third aim.

Overthrow of the Nicaraguan government has required a complex strategy, because the military there is well trained and armed, the government still enjoys broad support, the contras are associated with the still hated Somoza national guard, and past US intervention resulted only in repression and deprivation. The strategy draws on lessons learned in the 1983 invasion of Grenada. Administration policymakers saw that its victory there was secure when the press reported that the Grenadian populace welcomed the invaders. Indeed, Grenadians had suffered from the economic sabotage of US perpetrated against the island. The invasion was triggered by dissension within the ruling party that led to the assassination of Prime Minister Maurice Bishop. The anti-Nicaragua strategy, then, is to reproduce in Nicaragua the conditions that worked to the US advantage in Grenada.

The US plan, it appears, is to weaken the Nicaraguan economy so that the populace would welcome conquering US troops who were accompanied by promises of massive relief. It also hopes to divide the military so that it could not effectively combat the invaders.

In order to effect this plan, the United States has first engaged in economic warfare against Nicaragua.[96] Western allies have been encouraged to reduce trade and deny credits. The US set an example when it cut back 85 per cent of Nicaragua's sugar quota in 1983, and opposed loans in international banks. In part, the activities of the US-supported contras have been aimed at the Nicaraguan economy. The destruction of oil depots prior to harvest and the threat to international shipping has reduced its hard currency earnings significantly.

Second, it has directed the contra military actions towards demoralizing the Nicaraguan army and instilling fear in the populace.[97] The hope is that repeated contra success will engender recriminations and feuds in the military. US bravado in defying international law over the port mining was an effort to intimidate a peasantry that is beginning to grow war-weary. Continued actions, it is thought, will ultimately turn the peasants against a Sandinista government that cannot protect them.

The ideological war against communism in Central America thus involves a far greater commitment than any previous war of this sort. It is a war on three fronts, and its aims are total victory. Prosecution of the war has included the relentless bludgeoning of domestic opposition into an anti-communist mindset. Significantly, the war also has led to the re-assertion of unbounded presidential power, which had been associated with the era of 'imperial' presidents. Congressional limitations on CIA support for the contras, on the use of US troops in combat, and on the construction of permanent facilities in Honduras have been ignored.[98] The Administration has shown a wanton disregard for international law as well, in the mining of the Nicaraguan ports. The mining highlighted the fact that President Reagan had approved a general resumption of the type of discredited CIA covert activities which had been curtailed in the 1970s.[99] In effect, he had declared that no obstacle would stand in the way of victory in the struggle to rid the hemisphere of communism.

What makes this war especially dangerous is its ideological character. The enemy, that is, the object of the struggle, is amorphous, because the communist label has been applied so indiscriminantly. The enemy may be Cuba, countries which ally themselves with Cuba, or even those which merely trade with and recognize Cuba and the Soviet Union. But the bounds of the crusade have not been clearly established, because paranoid fears are unrelated to real threats. It has been the dangers of such craziness that have led elites to urge the Reagan Administration to stop its crusade.[100] In a sense, the objective of the crusade is the traditional US goal of hegemony. Yet by translating this aim into an anti-communist crusade, the US now wildly searches for communists to destroy. This has the effect of generating resistance among potentially hospitable countries, of creating enemies where none existed, and so of undermining US hegemony in the region.

United States engagement in the war is still unfolding, and the Administration's determination may not be sufficient to bring the United States fully into the Central American conflict and to pursue the war as it would wish. It has not yet convinced the public, important sectors of the business community, and significantly, its Latin American and European allies of the need to wage this ideological war. These centres of power hold out the possibility that the Reagan Administration could be forced to end its crusade.

NOTES

1. *US Congressional Record—Senate,* January 14, 1927, p. 1649.
2. John Foster Dulles, 'The Kremlin Out to Destroy the Inter-American System', in *Guatemala in Rebellion: Unfinished History,* eds. Jonathan Fried, *et al.,* (New York, Grove, 1983), p. 78.
3. (Washington, D.C.; January, 1984), p. 93. [Hereafter cited as Kissinger Com-

mission.]

4. 'If You Want Peace. . .', *New York World, January 13, 1927,* reprinted in *US Congressional Record—Senate,* January 14, 1927, p. 1651.

5. On Guatemala see: Walter LaFeber, *Inevitable Revolutions: The United States in Central America,* (New York, Nortin, 1983), pp. 122-123; Richard Immerman, *The CIA in Guatemala,* (Austin, University of Texas Press, 1982); Stephen Schlesinger and Stephen Kinzer, *Bitter Fruit,* (Garden City, N.Y., Doubleday, 1982).

6. For representative examples of each orientation, see: LaFeber, *Inevitable Revolutions,* pp. 79-80, 106-111; Cole Blasier, *Hovering Giant: US Responses to Revolutionary Change in Latin America,* (Pittsburgh, University of Pittsburgh Press, 1976), pp. 211, 229-231; Howard J. Wiarda, *In Search of Policy: The United States and Latin America,* (Washington, D.C., American Enterprise Institute, 1984), p. 24.

7. Abraham Lowenthal suggests that the orientation towards domination, which he aptly labels 'the hegemonic presumption', was less a conscious definition of US interest than a consequence of the overwhelming US influence in Latin America that developed from a coincidence of changes favourable to the US. See 'The United States and Latin America: Ending the Hegemonic Presumption', *Foreign Affairs,* October, 1976.

8. Abraham F. Lowenthal, ' "Liberal", "Radical", and "Bureaucratic" Perspectives on US Latin American Policy: The Alliance for Progress in Retrospect', in *Latin America and the United States: The Changing Political Realities,* (eds.) Julio Cotler and Richard Fagen, (Stanford, Stanford University Press, 1974), pp. 227-233; Richard J. Barnet, *Intervention and Revolution,* (New York, World, 1968), chapter 2; Blasier, *Hovering Giant,* p. 232.

9. Jenny Pearce, *Under the Eagle: US Intervention in Central America and the Caribbean,* (London, Latin America Bureau, 1982), p. 19; Blasier, *Hovering Giant,* pp. 108-110.

10. Quoted in LaFeber, *Inevitable Revolutions,* p. 107.

11. Blasier, *Hovering Giant,* p. 220; LaFeber, *Inevitable Revolutions,* pp. 60–63. This pattern was described most vividly in the famous statement by General Smedley D. Butler: 'I spent thirty three years in active service as a member of. . . the Marine corps. . . And during that period I spent most of my time being a high-class muscle man for Big Business, for Wall Street and, for the bankers. . . . Thus I helped make Mexico and especially Tampico safe for American oil interests in 1914. I helped make Haiti and Cuba a decent place for National City Bank to collect revenues in. . . I brought light to the Dominican Republic for American sugar interests in 1916. I helped make Honduras "right" for American fruit companies in 1903.' Quoted in Pearce, *Under the Eagle,* p. 20.

12. LaFeber, *Inevitable Revolutions,* p. 107. In a clear recent articulation of this view, former State Department Policy Planning Staff member, Susan Kaufman Purcell, observed—without condoning the tendency—that the US 'is hostile to revolutions even before we see how they turn out. . . We know that authoritarian regimes will not be hostile to us, while democratic governments will be less subservient, and perhaps more hostile.' Forum, 'Can the US Live with Latin Revolutions?' *Harper's,* June 1984, p. 43.

13. Dexter Perkins, *The United States and Latin America,* (Baton Rouge, Louisiana State University Press, 1961), p. 19.

14. Blasier, *Hovering Giant,* p. 229.

15. The following were used as a representative sample: (1) President Reagan's televised address, May 9, 1984; text in Congressional Quarterly *Weekly Report,* May 12, 1984 [hereafter cited as Reagan address, May 1984] ; (2) President

Reagan's address to the US Congress, April 27, 1983; text in Congressional Quarterly *Weekly Report,* April 30, 1983 [hereafter cited as Reagan address, April, 1983] ; (3) Kissinger Commission; (4) Testimony of Under Secretary of Defense for Policy Fred Ikle, March 11, 1982, in US Congress, Senate, 'The Role of Cuba in International Terrorism and Subversion', Hearings Before the Subcommittee on Security and Terrorism, 97th Cong., 2nd Sess., Serial No. J-97-97 (Washington: 1982) [hereafter cited as Ikle testimony] ; (5) Testimony of Assistant Secretary of State for Inter-American Affairs Thomas Enders, March 12, 1982, in *ibid.* [hereafter cited as Enders testimony] ; (6) Nestor D. Sanchez (Deputy Assistant Secretary of Defence for Inter-American Affairs), 'United States Security Interests and Concerns in Latin America', Remarks before a workshop sponsored by the American Bar Association (San Diego, December 11, 1981), mimeo. [hereafter cited as Sanchez speech] ; (7) 'Background Paper: Central America', Paper released by the US State Department and Defense Department (Washington, May 27, 1983) [hereafter cited as Background Paper] .

16. Reagan address, May, 1984, p. 1131; Reagan address, April, 1983, pp. 853, 855; Kissinger Commission, pp. 4, 12, 14, 15, 38, 84; Ikle testimony, pp. 85, 96, 105; Enders testimony, pp. 143-47; Sanchez speech, pp. 3, 5-9; Background Paper, pp. 3-5, 15-17.

17. Reagan address, May, 1984, p. 1131; Reagan address, April, 1983, pp. 853, 855; Kissinger Commission, pp. 12, 14; Enders testimony, p. 146; Sanchez speech, p. 3.

18. Reagan address, May, 1984. p. 1131; Reagan address, April, 1983, p. 855; Kissinger Commission, pp. 14, 30, 88-91, 107, 113; Ikle testimony, pp. 89-93.

19. Reagan address, May, 1984, p. 1133; Background Paper, p. 6.

20. Reagan address, April, 1983, p. 855; Kissinger Commission, pp. 37, 93, 107; Ikle testimony, p. 97; Enders testimony, p. 159; Sanchez speech, p. 2.

21. Reagan address, April, 1983, p. 853; Kissinger Commission, pp. 91-93; Ikle testimony, pp. 88-89, 137; Sanchez speech, pp. 11-13.

22. Kissinger Commission, pp. 12, 38, 92; Ikle testimony, pp. 85, 137; Background Paper, p. 15.

23. Reagan address, May, 1984, p. 1131; Kissinger Commission, pp. 91-92; Ikle testimony, p. 89; Enders testimony, p. 159. Also see 'Kirkpatrick on the "Contagion" ', *Newsweek,* March 14, 1983, p. 22; William J. Casey, 'The Real Soviet Threat in El Salvador—And Beyond', *US News & World Report,* March 8, 1982, p. 123.

24. Reagan address, May, 1984, p. 1132; Kissinger Commission, pp. 30, 85-88; Ikle testimony, pp. 95-96; Background Paper, p. 4.

25. Reagan address, May, 1984, p. 1131; Kissinger Commission, pp. 14, 37, 85; Ikle testimony, pp. 93, 97; Enders testimony, pp. 145-146.

26. Reagan address, May, 1984, p. 1131. Also see: Kissinger Commission, p. 92; Ikle testimony, pp. 88-89; Sanchez speech, p. 11.

27. Kissinger Commission, p. 41; Ikle testimony, p. 93; Background Paper, p. 3.

28. Kissinger Commission, pp. 4, 86-87; Enders testimony, p. 143.

29. Kissinger Commission, p. 87.

30. Reagan address, May, 1984, p. 1131; Reagan address, April 1983, p. 855; Kissinger Commission, p. 93; Ikle testimony, p. 115. Also see, Alfonso Chardy, 'Salvadoran refugee flood threatens US, Shultz says', *Miami Herald,* March 7, 1984.

31. Reagan address, April, 1983, pp. 856, 855, respectively.

32. Kissinger Commission, p. 37 [emphasis is theirs] . The second interest is, 'To improve the living conditions of the people of Central America', and the third

is, 'To advance the cause of democracy, broadly defined, within the hemisphere'. *Ibid.*

33. Reagan address, April, 1983, p. 854.

34. Kissinger Commission, p. 113; Enders testimony, p. 155.

35. Richard Hofstadter, *The Paranoid Style in American Politics and Other Essays,* (New York: Knopf, 1965), Introduction.

36. Kissinger Commission, p. 12. The report later concludes (pp. 86–87) that 'Cuba and Nicaragua did not invent the grievances' on which turmoil feeds, but that insurgencies could not exist without foreign sustenance, which ultimately generates 'a totalitarian regime in the image of their sponsors' ideology.'

37. William M. LeoGrande, 'Through the Looking Glass: The Kissinger Report on Central America', *World Policy Journal,* Winter, 1984, p. 261. Such imagined omnipotence is precisely the pattern Hofstadter describes as typical of political paranoia: *The Paranoid Style in American Politics,* p. 36.

38. Reagan address, May, 1984, p. 1131; Kissinger Commission, p. 38.

39. The Committee of Santa Fe, 'A New Inter-American Policy for the Eighties', (Washington: Council for Inter-American Security, 1980). Three of the five authors of the report took on significant Central American policy roles shortly after publishing this report. For a probing critique of the Reagan Administration's ideological rigidity, see Richard E. Feinberg, *The Intemperate Zone,* (New York: Norton, 1983), pp. 191–194.

40. Kissinger Commission, p. 37.

41. Hofstadter, *Paranoid Style in American Politics,* p. 36.

42. Kenneth E. Sharpe and Martin Diskin, 'Facing Facts in El Salvador: Reconciliation or War', *World Policy Journal,* Spring, 1984, pp. 520–527; Cynthia Arnson, *El Salvador: A Revolution Confronts the United States,* (Washington: Institute for Policy Studies, 1982), pp. 40–56; 'Locked in Battle', NACLA, *Report on the Americas,* March/April, 1984, pp. 14–17.

43. Joanne Omang, 'President Vetoes Bill Tying Aid to Salvadoran Rights', *Washington Post,* December 1, 1983. Reagan previously had issued certifications of progress, but these had been criticized severely in Congress.

44. Craig Pyes, 'A Dirty War in the Name of Freedom' and 'Right Built Itself in Mirror Image of Left for Civil War', *Albuquerque Journal,* December 18, 1983; LeoGrande, 'Through the Looking Glass', p. 271.

45. Philip Taubman, 'Salvadoran Said to be Informant for CIA', *New York Times,* March 23, 1984.

46. LeoGrande, 'Through the Looking Glass', p. 262; PACCA (Policy Alternatives for the Caribbean and Central America), *Changing Course,* (Washington: Institute for Policy Studies, 1984), p. 31.

47. George Black, 'Fortress Honduras: Delivering a Country to the Military', *The Nation,* January 28, 1984, pp. 90–92; Fred Hiatt and Joanne Omang, 'US Honduran Base at Last, Study Says', *International Herald Tribune,* February 3, 1984; 'Democratic Honduras: The Crisis of Legitimacy', *Update,* July/August, 1982 (Washington: Washington Office on Latin America, 1982), pp. 1, 9.

48. LeoGrande, 'Through the Looking Glass', p. 261; Victor Perera, 'Guatemala Under Siege: Chaos in the Scorched Earth', *The Nation,* January 28, 1984, pp. 92–94; 'Guatemala: The Roots of Revolution', *Special Update,* February, 1983 (Washington: Washington Office on Latin America, 1983).

49. Tom Arms, 'US Latin manoeuvres prompt deep concern among overseas allies', *Miami Herald,* July 29, 1983. Also see: Alfonso Chardy, 'US Warns Paris not to aid Sandinistas', *Miami Herald,* April 7, 1984; Arthur Schlesinger, Jr., 'Kissinger Report Lacks a Sense of Reality', *International Herald Tribune,* January 21, 1984; Eldon Kenworthy, 'Central America: Beyond the Credibility Trap',

World Policy Journal, Fall, 1983, p. 197.

50. In March, 1984, over 600 parliamentarians from seven Western European countries sent a letter to House Speaker Thomas P. O'Neill that expressed alarm over US actions against Nicaragua.
51. '9 Latin Nations Report Tentative Accord on Isthmus', *Washington Post,* September 11, 1983.
52. LeoGrande, 'Through the Looking Glass', p. 269.
53. Saul Landau, 'Inside Nicaragua's Class War', *Socialist Review* No. 71 (1983), pp. 14–25; PACCA, *Changing Course,* p. 28; Kenworthy, 'Central America: Beyond the Credibility Gap', pp. 189–190; Stephen Kinzer, 'Soviet Aid to Managua is Seen as Crucial but Cautious', *International Herald Tribune,* March 29, 1984.
54. Kenworthy, 'Central America: Beyond the Credibility Gap', pp. 186–187.
55. Philip Brenner, *The Limits and Possibilities of Congress,* (New York: St. Martin's Press, 1983), p. 80; William LeoGrande, *Cuba's Policy in Africa, 1959-1980,* Institute of International Studies, Policy Papers in International Affairs No. 13 (Berkeley: 1980), pp. 17–22, 39–40; Jorge Dominguez, 'Cuban Foreign Policy', *Foreign Affairs,* Fall, 1978, pp. 83–84, 94–97.
56. Robert A. Pastor, 'Cuba and the Soviet Union: Does Cuba Act Alone?' in *The New Cuban Presence in the Caribbean,* (ed.) Barry Levine, (Boulder, Colo.: Westview, 1983); Alfonso Chardy, 'Analyst: Cuba, Soviets at odds over Grenada', *Miami Herald,* February 9, 1984.
57. The Soviet reticence may be due to their incapacity to direct revolutionary movements and their experience of failure. See, Feinberg, *The Intemperate Zone,* ch. 3.
58. Philip Taubman, 'The CIA: In From the Cold and Hot for Truth', *New York Times,* June 11, 1984.
59. Raymond Bonner, 'Report Says El Salvador is Unable to Prevent Diversion of US Aid', *New York Times,* February 15, 1984; Charles Mohr, 'Salvador Rebels Reported to Get Little Arms Aid', *New York Times,* July 31, 1983; Christopher Dickey, 'Nicaraguan Aid Called Not Vital to Salvadorans', *Washington Post,* February 21, 1983.
60. Sam Dillon, 'Hondurans urge invasion of Nicaragua', *Miami Herald,* November 8, 1983; Alfonso Chardy, 'Report calls US bases in Honduras "grave risk" ', *Miami Herald,* February 17, 1984; Bob Woodward and Fred Hiatt, 'Wider CIA Effort in Nicaragua Seen Planned if Reagan Wins', *International Herald Tribune,* April 11, 1984.
61. Feinberg, *The Intemperate Zone,* p. 189.
62. William Long, 'Mexico doesn't buy the domino theory', *Miami Herald,* August 21, 1983; LeoGrande, 'Through the Looking Glass', pp. 267–268.
63. Kissinger Commission, pp. 86–87.
64. John Dinges, 'Why We Are in Guatemala', *Inquiry,* November, 1982, pp. 21–22; George Black, 'Guatemala—The War Is Not Over', NACLA *Report on the Americas,* March/April, 1983, pp. 2–10; Fried, *et al., Guatemala in Rebellion,* Part III.
65. Tommie Sue Montgomery, *Revolution in El Salvador: Origins and Evolution,* (Boulder, Colo.: Westview, 1982), ch. 5; Arnson, *El Salvador,* pp. 27–31, 54–62.
66. 'A Furor Over the Secret War', *Newsweek,* International Edition, April 23, 1984.
67. Christopher Dickey, 'Rebel Odyssey: Foes of Sandinistas Seek to Purge Somoza Stigma', *Washington Post,* April 4, 1983; Landau, 'Inside Nicaragua's Class War', pp. 11–14; LeoGrande, 'Through the Looking Glass', p. 262.
68. Eldon Kenworthy, 'Reagan Rediscovers Monroe', *Democracy,* July, 1982, p. 82. [Emphasis in original.]

69. US Department of State, Bureau of Public Affairs, 'Communist Interference in El Salvador', Special Report No. 80, February 23, 1981.
70. Jonathan Kwitny, 'Tarnished Report? Apparent Errors Cloud US "White Paper" on Reds in El Salvador', *Wall Street Journal*, June 8, 1981.
71. Dan Hallin, 'The Media Goes to War—From Vietnam to Central America', NACLA, *Report on the Americas*, July/August, 1983, pp. 2–21. Also see: Philip Knightley, *The First Casualty*, (New York: Harcourt Brace Jovanovich, 1975); David Halberstam, *The Powers That Be*, (New York: Knopf, 1979).
72. Congressional Quarterly *Weekly Report*, April 30, 1983, p. 856.
73. LaFeber, *Inevitable Revolutions*, ch. 3.
74. For examples see: David Donald, *Lincoln Reconsidered*, second edition (New York: Knopf, 1965), ch. 2; Daniel Bell, *The End of Ideology*, revised edition (New York: Collier, 1962), ch. 6.
75. Blasier, *Hovering Giant*, p. 9; Watson, 'Kirkpatrick on the "Contagion" '.
76. Jeanne Kirkpatrick, 'Dictatorships and Double Standards', *Commentary*, November, 1979; LaFeber, *Inevitable Revolutions*, p. 104.
77. For a thorough description of their operation see Elizabeth Drew, *Politics & Money: The New Road to Corruption*, (New York: Macmillan, 1983). Also see: Gordon Adams, *The Iron Triangle: The Politics of Defense Contracting*, (New York: Council on Economic Priorities, 1981), ch. 8.
78. Abraham F. Lowenthal, 'Ronald Reagan and Latin America: Coping With Hegemony in Decline', in *Eagle Defiant*, (eds.) Kenneth Oye, *et al.* (Boston: Little Brown, 1983), pp. 322–325.
79. Barnet, *Intervention and Revolution*, pp. 26–27; Blasier, *Hovering Giant*, p. 249.
80. LaFeber, *Inevitable Revolutions*, pp. 274–278; Fred Halliday, *The Origins of the Second Cold War*, (London: New Left Books, 1983).
81. Jerry Sanders, *Peddlers of Crisis: The Committee on the Present Danger and the Politics of Containment*, (Boston: South End Press, 1983), ch. 6; Alan Wolfe, *The Rise and Fall of the 'Soviet Threat': Domestic Sources of the Cold War Consensus*, (Washington: Institute for Policy Studies, 1979); Peter Shaw, 'The New Right, Neo-Conservatives and US Policy in Central America', Senior Thesis, Bucknell University, 1984, pp. 7–14.
82. Sanders, *Peddlers of Crisis*, pp. 282–289.
83. LaFeber, *Inevitable Revolutions*, p. 298; Juan Jose Arevalo, *Anti-Kommunism in Latin America*, trans. Carleton Beals (New York: Lyle Stuart, 1963), pp. 34–35.
84. Arnson, *El Salvador*, p. 76; 'Guatemala: The Roots of Revolution', pp. 3–4.
85. David Caute, *The Great Fear: The Anti-Communist Purge Under Truman and Eisenhower*, (New York: Simon & Shuster/Touchstone, 1979), pp. 25–30, 268–279; Athan Theoharis, *Seeds of Repression: Harry S. Truman and the Origins of McCarthyism*, (New York: Quadrangle, 1977).
86. For an elaboration of this review see: Philip Brenner, 'The Unchanging Agenda in US–Cuban Relations', Paper delivered at the 11th International Congress of the Latin American Studies Association, Mexico City, September 30, 1983. Also see: Brenner, *Limits and Possibilities of Congress*, pp. 49–52, 84–88; Max Azicri, 'Cuba and the United States: What Happened to Rapprochement?' in Levine, *The New Cuban Presence in the Caribbean*, pp. 176–184; Wayne Smith, 'Dateline Havana: Myopic Diplomacy', *Foreign Policy*, Fall, 1982.
87. For an elaboration of this review see: LaFeber, *Inevitable Revolutions*, pp. 229–242; Richard R. Fagen, 'Dateline Nicaragua: The End of the Affair', *Foreign Policy*, Fall, 1979; Jan Knippers Black, 'Government and Politics', in *Nicaragua: A Country Study*, (ed.) James Rudolph, US Army Area Handbook Series

(Washington: Department of the Army, 1982), pp. 177–178.
88. For an elaboration of this review see: Arnson, *El Salvador*, pp. 50–54, 64–70; LaFeber, *Inevitable Revolutions*, pp. 247–255; Montgomery, *Revolution in El Salvador*, pp. 19–20; William LeoGrande, 'A Splendid Little War: Drawing the Line in El Salvador', *International Security*, Summer, 1981, pp. 29–32, 37–43.
89. Quoted in Montgomery, *Revolution in El Salvador*, p. 179.
90. George W. Bell, 'Brezhneved By the US', *New York Times*, June 14, 1983; Arthur Schlesinger, Jr., 'The Central American Dilemma', *Wall Street Journal*, July 20, 1983; Kenworthy, 'Central America: Beyond the Credibility Gap', p. 183.
91. Sidney Weintraub, 'A Flawed Model', and Richard E. Feinberg and Richard S. Newfarmer, 'A Bilateralist Gamble', in *Foreign Policy*, Summer, 1982; LeoGrande, 'Through the Looking Glass', pp. 264–266; Philip Brenner, 'Comments prepared for the National Bipartisan Commission on Central America', delivered to the Commission, September 15, 1983.
92. Hofstadter describes this sort of pattern vividly: 'The enemy seems to be on many counts a projection of the self. . . A fundamental paradox of the paranoid style is the imitation of the enemy.' *Paranoid Style in American Politics*, p. 32.
93. Much of it was evident already in 1983 with the disclosure of National Security Decision Directive 17. See Raymond Bonner, 'President Approved Policy of Preventing "Cuba-Model States" ', *New York Times*, April 7, 1983. Also see: Don Oberdorfer, 'Applying Pressure in Central America', *Washington Post*, November 23, 1983.
94. Michael T. Klare, 'Central America War Games: Manoeuvres in Search of an Invasion', *The Nation*, June 9, 1984.
95. 'Background Paper: Nicaragua's Military Build-Up and Support for Central American Subversion', Released by the Departments of State and Defense, July, 1984.
96. John Cavanagh and Joy Hackel, 'Squeezing Nicaragua's Economy', *Washington Post*, March 25, 1984, p. C5.
97. Richard J. Barnet and Peter Kornbluh, 'America's Covert Operations Are Really State Terrorism', *Los Angeles Times*, April 8, 1984; Martha Honey, 'The CIA digs in with the contras', *The Sunday Times*, (London), April 22, 1984.
98. Martin Tolchin, 'CIA Said to Overspend Its Budget on Nicaragua', *New York Times*, June 6, 1984; Philip Taubman and Jeff Gerth, 'Reagan Administration Moves to Bypass Curbs on Latin Aid', *International Herald Tribune*, May 19, 1984; US General Accounting Office, 'Funding of Joint Combined Military Exercises in Honduras', Appendix to Comptroller General Decision B-213137, June 22, 1984, p. 16.
99. William Ellsworth-Jones, *et al.*, 'CIA: Back to Dirty Tricks', *The Sunday Times*, (London), April 15, 1984; Peter R. Kornbluh, 'The born-again CIA', *San Jose Mercury News*, April 15, 1984, p. 1C.
100. See for example, Inter-American Dialogue, *The Americas in 1984: A Year for Decisions*, (Washington: Woodrow Wilson Center for International Scholars, May, 1984).

ANTI-COMMUNISM IN GUATEMALA: WASHINGTON'S ALLIANCE WITH GENERALS AND DEATH SQUADS

James F. Petras & Morris H. Morley

Introduction: Liberal and Conservative anti-communism

In the contemporary US social formation, both liberal and conservative political, economic and social forces have made the issue of anti-communism central to the domestic and foreign policy debate. Conflicts between political and economic nationalist regimes in the Third World and the US imperial state, over the conditions for capital accumulation and the nature of Third World class relations, have been conceptualized by post-World War II American policymakers in terms of anti-communist ideology in order to justify an interventionist foreign policy. The utility of the notion is precisely that it allows the US to disguise the basis of its ties to client regimes and ruling classes: economic interests are obscured and national-class struggles are redefined as East–West conflicts. Foreign policy is not discussed in terms of a secure environment for multinationals to extract the economic surplus or political-strategic concerns, but largely with reference to Third World allies' opposition to 'communist subversion'.

While the resort to anti-communist ideology has functioned to divert attention from the systemic concerns of the US imperial state, it has also served to rationalize the impact of large-scale violence perpetrated by allied regimes against their own populations. In countries such as post-1954 Guatemala, the most heinous acts of pro-US military rulers are subsumed within the anti-communist struggle. The requirement that liberal forces in US society develop politics from the terrain of anti-communism in a context where the most reactionary groups have been, and remain, dominant has had profound consequences for liberal efforts to promote a reformist anti-communist option in the Third World. Ultimately, the liberal and conservative variants have generated similar outcomes: political terrorist regimes; social and economic regression; massive state-centred corruption; fraudulent elections; foreign economic domination; and rulers who collaborate with US regional and global objectives.

During the Kennedy and Carter presidencies, the White House launched major efforts to combine reformist policies with anti-communist ideology in Guatemala. Each, however, proved incapable of bringing about reforms or modifying the pattern of state-authored mass repression. Essentially the liberal version of reformist anti-communism differs from its conserva-

261

tive variant in terms of programmes, political allies and the scope of regime violence. Liberals propose to carry out changes that improve the standard of living of the masses at the cost of local elites, without adversely affecting the US multinationals, their local economic partners, or the institutional position of the military and police. The conservative anticommunists seek to unify all sectors of the local ruling class and downplay reforms in favour of an exclusive military approach. Hence, while American liberals try to forge an alliance between the middle class and the military, American conservatives promote a power bloc in which the traditional oligarchical-military Right is dominant. The third difference between liberal and conservative anti-communists has to do with the scope of repression. The former support violent regime measures against radical class-based organisations but hope to exclude Christian Democratic and other centre-based groups from the wave of terror. The latter do not usually draw these fine distinctions. Instead, they support each and every effort by military or military-controlled governments to stamp out independent organized forces in society.

While these distinctions between liberals and conservatives have surfaced in US public debate, one major factor has unified them, feeding similar policy consequences: an ultimate reliance on the military establishment and police forces to establish dominance in the target country. In the case of Guatemala, the policies of all administrations from Eisenhower to Reagan, whatever their initial intentions, have consolidated the repressive forces in society and, in so doing, strengthened precisely the most significant obstacles to any serious and sustained programme of socio-economic change. The reformist anti-communism promoted by imperial state liberals has been repeatedly undermined by the Guatemalan military who have destroyed the very social movements capable of instituting such changes. The unwillingness of either the Kennedy or Carter White House to break with these armed forces, despite criticism of the latter's 'excesses', indicates that in their order of priorities, defeating radical social movements was paramount over and against social and economic reforms. In the process of supporting the destruction of these movements, however, the liberals have strengthened the groups opposed to all changes—thereby also undermining the 'centrist' option. Thus the logic of US liberal anti-communism converged with the results of their conservative counterparts generating a continuous pattern of unrelieved repression sustained and supported by one set of imperial state policymakers after another. The Guatemalan experience offers a striking illustration of this convergence and its outcome: the persistence of one of the most brutal regimes in modern history.

Anti-communism as a destabilizing mechanism
Anti-communism has served as a mechanism to destabilize democratic and

nationalist regimes which attempt to carry out reforms that adversely affect US propertied interests. In this context, anti-communist ideology transforms a conflict between poor peasants and workers, and multi-nationals into a confrontation between Communist Terror and the Free World. This transformation of reality is central to gaining domestic support in the US because as an imperialist democracy it must secure the consent or acquiescence of its citizens. (Anti-communist demonology is thus a necessary accompaniment of a manipulated democracy.) The use of anti-communism as a destabilizing mechanism probably offers no clearer instance than that of Guatemala during its brief decade of democratic rule beginning in the mid-1940s.

The overthrow of the brutal Ubico dictatorship in 1944 by a coalition of urban workers, dissident military officers and sectors of the bourgeoisie created the basis for the freest elections in Guatemalan history. The liberal democratic government of Juan Jose Arevalo (1945–1950) presided over a period of discrete but significant social and economic advances for the country's workers and peasants—as well as the revival of a competing political party system. The wage levels of the urban working class were increased and a labour code was enacted giving workers the right to strike, establish trade unions and engage in collective bargaining. Arevalo also introduced a social security system, passed a law forcing the oligarchy to lease unused land to the peasants, and at least established the conditions for social organization to take place in the countryside. But the resistance of the oligarchy and the United Fruit Company prevented the implementation of any changes in the highly concentrated pattern of landownership (2 per cent of the population owned over 70 per cent of the farm land) in a society where the mass of the population—mestizos and Indians—were landless and forced to sell their labour power to maintain a precarious existence and were, therefore, at the mercy of the large landowners who had ties with the coercive power of the state.

Amidst the rise of the Cold War and the ideology of anti-communism as a driving force in American foreign policy during the Truman administration, the basis of Washington's policy toward Guatemala remained essentially economic, reflecting, above all, the enormous weight exercised by United Fruit throughout the local economy where its investments were valued at $60 million. Schlesinger and Kinzer provide a concise description of the Company's reach: 'It functioned as a state within a state, owning Guatemala's telephone and telegraph facilities, administering its only important Atlantic harbor and monopolizing its banana exports. The company's subsidiary, the International Railways of Central America (IRCA), owned 887 miles of railroad track in Guatemala, nearly every mile in the country.'[1]

The election of Colonel Jacobo Arbenz as president in 1950 accelerated the process of social and economic change in Guatemala initiated by his predecessor. The centrepiece of the Arbenz programme was an agrarian reform law which resulted in the expropriation of 1.5 million acres of uncultivated land belonging to approximately 100 plantations, including over 400,000 acres of United Fruit property—with compensation to be determined on the basis of 1952 tax declarations and paid in 25 year government bonds. By 1954, 100,000 families or approximately 500,000 individuals had received land as well as access to bank credits and state technical assistance.[2] Arbenz further sought to end the dominance of United Fruit and other American companies in the public utilities and transportation sectors (docks, railways, highways, electric power) of the economy. The government also fostered the development of industrial and agricultural labour organizations, increased the minimum wage, and began to elaborate an independent foreign policy within regional and global political forums. Despite these efforts to reshape the Guatemalan society and economy, Arbenz did not seek to challenge decisively the capitalist mode of production. The goal of the agrarian reform, for instance, was not structural changes in the existing landholding pattern but increased efficiency and higher production levels on the plantations. Nonetheless, this comparatively modest challenge to American capital accumulation in Guatemala and concern over the possibility of a 'revolution in the revolution' anchored in the newly mobilized workers and peasants led the Eisenhower administration to define the popular nationalism of Arbenz as a threat to imperial regional hegemony and world stability.

US policymakers (including Secretary of State John Foster Dulles and CIA Director Allen Dulles whose business and personal ties to United Fruit were longstanding) devised a multitrack strategy to disintegrate the Arbenz government and restore an environment for optimal capital accumulation and expansion. Washington placed an embargo on military assistance to Guatemala; economic and technical aid programmes were withdrawn; an extensive media-propaganda campaign jointly financed by the US government and United Fruit accused Arbenz of having permitted 'international communism to gain a political base in the hemisphere'; and great pressure was exerted by the White House to mobilize regional support for the imperial objective. High-ranking American officials characterized the expropriation of United Fruit lands as 'discriminatory', denounced the compensation formula as unsatisfactory, and promised United Fruit executives that the restoration of the Company's pre-Arbenz empire would be given the greatest priority under a new regime:

> At some point during the preparations for the invasion, a United Fruit official. . . met privately with Allen Dulles to discuss the status of United Fruit properties following Arbenz's downfall. Dulles promised that whoever was selected by the CIA as the next Guatemalan leader would not be allowed to nationalize or in any way disrupt the company's operations.[3]

Although the takeover of United Fruit lands and the proliferating labour and agricultural laws were instrumental factors in the August 1953 White House decision to overthrow Arbenz by military force, the destabilization policy was consistently rationalized in terms of the ideology of anti-communism and the need to respond to an 'external threat' that might lead to Guatemala's withdrawal from the capitalist politico-economic orbit. Internal Truman administration memoranda expressing concern over the 'ascending curve of Communist influence'[4] during the early months of the Arbenz presidency laid the basis for an evolving policy of diplomatic, political and economic hostility toward the nationalist regime. By the time of the Eisenhower White House, Arbenz's 'drift toward Communism' had become an established 'fact' among Washington policymakers. The notion that indigenous Communist Parties were agents of, or the transmission belts for, expansionist international communism was given explicit voice in relation to Guatemala in a draft paper prepared by the State Department in August 1953 for consideration by the National Security Council: 'In Guatemala Communism has achieved its strongest position in Latin America, and is now well advanced on a program which threatens important American commercial enterprises in that country and may affect the stability of neighboring governments. Continuation of the present trend in Guatemala would ultimately endanger the unity of the Western Hemisphere against Soviet aggression, and the security of our strategic position in the Caribbean, including the Panama Canal.'[5]

In October, Assistant Secretary of State for Inter-American Affairs John Moors Cabot castigated Arbenz for 'openly playing the communist game' and declared that there could be no 'positive cooperation between the two countries'.[6] Another high-level inderdepartmental report on Guatemala (May 1953) concluded that Communist political influence was 'far out of proportion to their small numerical strength' despite the fact that they lacked any influence within the key coercive fractions (army and police) of the state and had no ministerial representation.[7] Their influence centred largely around the leadership of some urban based unions, the participation of individual party members in the administration of the agrarian reform, and the Party's capacity to organize and mobilize popular support for the government's programmes.

Following the tenth Inter-American Conference of Foreign Ministers in Caracas, Venezuela in March 1954 where the US delegation led by Secretary of State Dulles steamrollered through a declaration which 'established anti-Communism as the principal criterion for legitimizing and delegitimizing governments and judging their hemispheric policies'[8] the CIA received its 'marching orders' from the White House and NSC, together with an estimated $20 million in funds, to plan and train an invasion force of Guatemalan exiles to overthrow the Arbenz regime. United Fruit and other American corporations with major economic investments in Guatemala were briefed on the project by senior administration officials on an ongoing basis until the ouster of Arbenz.

Washington's assessment of the Guatemalan situation was simply confirmed by the nationalist government's decision to purchase a shipment of arms from Czechoslovakia in May 1954. This 'discovery' provided a convenient pretext for unleashing Colonel Castillo Armas and his exiles training under CIA direction on a United Fruit plantation in Honduras. In early June, a senior State Department Middle America official wrote to the US Ambassador to Guatemala, John Peurifoy: 'There is 100 per cent determination here, from the top down, to get rid of this stinker [Arbenz] and not stop until that is done.'[9] Some days later, Secretary of State Dulles announced that Guatemala was in the grip of a 'Communist-type reign of terror'.[10] Before the end of June, Arbenz was overthrown, the social and economic experiment terminated, and a pro-US right-wing anti-communist regime installed in power.

Through the skillful use of anti-communist ideology, Truman and Eisenhower policymakers were able to mobilize domestic support for a policy of antagonism toward Arbenz. In the process they were able to obliterate the fundamental conflict over property ownership and obscure an array of social and economic issues which created conflicts between the regime and foreign capital and provided the substantive basis for US imperial state actions leading to the downfall of the nationalist government. As Walter LaFeber cogently points out, Washington's preoccupation with anti-communism in Guatemala, especially during 1953 and 1954, 'overlook[ed] the previous seven years of growing confrontation that had centred on issues of private property and personnel for the Guatemalan agencies that exercised power over property'.[11]

Anti-Communism as a legitimizing mechanism

Anti-communism as a legitimizing mechanism has the virtue of obscuring the nature of Washington's principal allies, their methods of rule and their policy objectives. Under the vague rubric of anti-communist can be found the members of the death squads, military dictators, secret police tortures, and the like. The pursuit of anti-communist policies provides a cover for all the repressive activities as well as the massive corruption and pillage that has characterised arbitrary military rule. Washington's focus on the Communist–Anti-communist dichotomy has been central to the effort to redirect attention away from basic class and national dichotomies, thereby preventing any attempts by popularly-based Third World governments to mobilize international support and solidarity. The imperial state emphasis on anti-communism also serves an important domestic function: It weakens the anti-interventionist impulse among the liberal US public, thus neutralising internal opposition to foreign policy initiatives and alliances with totalitarian client regimes. The period in Guatemala after 1954 provides us with an excellent example of the way in which Washington used anti-communist ideology to mobilize US public opinion to support its ties with successive dictatorial rulers by redefining issues in terms ('anti-communist', 'anti-subversion' instead of economic/strategic interests) favourable to the creation of a bipartisan foreign policy. Moreover, the common use of anti-communism as a legitimizing mechanism by both liberals (e.g., Kennedy and Carter) and conservatives (e.g., Eisenhower and Nixon) indicates that the issue of protecting the status quo in Guatemala through the aegis of the armed forces (the country's major anti-communist force) is the overriding priority for US policymakers.

Having utilized the ideology of anti-communism to justify the over-throw of Arbenz, American officials now wielded it to legitimate the rightist military regime of Colonal Carlos Castillo Armas (1954–1958) which terminated all efforts at social and economic reform, destroyed the newly organized workers and peasant unions, abolished the political party process, and initiated a period of repressive capitalist development 'from above and outside' based on large-scale infusions of US public and private capital. Castillo Armas cancelled the legal registration of 533 unions and revised the labour code to make future union organizing virtually im-possible. Hundreds of labour leaders were murdered and within a year union membership declined from 100,000 to 27,000.[12] In the political arena, Castillo Armas summarily disenfranchised the approximately 70 per cent of the population who were illiterate. Meanwhile, the new regime moved quickly to recreate the conditions for optimal capital accumulation: almost all the labour legislation of the 1944–1954 period was abrogated; a new petroleum law eased restrictions on exploration by foreign com-panies and some of the largest US oil multinationals received concession rights to begin operations; a pact negotiated directly with the military rulers restored to United Fruit all of the property expropriated by Arbenz; taxes on interests and dividends were abolished; efforts at agricultural and industrial diversification were terminated, and the traditional authority of the agro-commercial (principally coffee) oligarchy and United Fruit was restored. Under Castillo Armas, however, the period of economic growth came to an end and Guatemala experienced a reversion from balance of payments surpluses to substantial trade deficits. Nonetheless, the decisive factor shaping the Eisenhower administration response to the new regime was the reconstruction of the state and economy to serve the interests of private capital accumulation. US economic assistance to Guatemala during the Castillo Armas presidency totalled $80 million which contrasts sharply with the miniscule $600,000 authorized for the whole Arevalo–Arbenz period.[13]

The presidency of General Miguel Ydigoras Fuentes (1958–1963) witnessed no decisive break with the pro-US policies of the previous military government. Domestically, however, Ydigoras Fuentes presided

over a period of deepening class-economic inequalities and rural im-
poverishment in a context where there no longer existed political channels
for social reform through elected leaders. Political closure and economic
marginalization created the objective basis for the emergence of revolutionary politics in 1960 in the form of guerrilla movements led by US-trained
military officers hostile to the revival of traditional landlord dominance
and the expanded American economic and politico-military presence.
These movements established a base of support precisely among those
peasants and Indians most directly affected by the 'rollback' of the social
and agrarian reforms of the 1944–1954 period.

The rise of the guerrillas definitively resolved the tension inherent
within the Alliance for Progress between the reformist anti-communist
goals of the Kennedy administration and the right-wing conservative
(military-oligarch) anti-communists embraced by Washington in the post-
Arbenz era. The White House shifted all of its political and military
support to the most reactionary elements in Guatemalan society in order
to defeat the guerrilla challenge for state power. By this time, however,
US policymakers were growing increasingly disenchanted with Ydigoras
Fuentes' seeming incapacity to contain the guerrillas despite the fact that
his regime continued to accommodate US political and economic interests,
and even allowed Guatemala to serve as a strategic base for American
interventionary actions in the region (e.g. Cuba 1961). His decision to
allow Arevalo to return from exile and participate in the proposed
December 1963 presidential elections was the last straw as far as both
the country's military high command and the Kennedy White House were
concerned. In March 1963, the army, supported and, indeed, encouraged
by Washington ousted Ydigoras Fuentes from office, cancelled the elections and installed former Defence Minister Colonel Enrique Peralta Azurdia
as the new Head of State. Peralta Azurdia immediately dissolved Congress,
banned all political activities, and rigorously enforced the existing 'state
of siege' under which the country was already being governed.

Although the new military president was determined to vigorously
prosecute the war against the guerrillas, his 'nationalist' orientation soon
created frictions with Washington over the scope of direct Pentagon
involvement in struggle. While he sought and accepted increased levels of
US military assistance, Peralta Azurdia opposed on-the-ground participation by American counterinsurgency experts in the war against the rural
antagonists of the military state—contending that the Guatemalan armed
forces were quite capable of defeating the guerrillas without foreign
combat support. Meanwhile, this period featured a consolidation of the
power of the Guatemalan military throughout society, including the
economic sphere where it deepened its linkages with the oligarchy through
large-scale property purchases. During the latter part of his rule, Peralta
Azurdia moved to create the conditions for a revival of a limited form of

electoral politics. A new constitution, enacted in 1965, provided for restricted political party competition and laid the groundwork for the election of a 'progressive' civilian Julio Cesar Mendez Montenegro as president in 1966. Paradoxically, however, the Mendez Montenegro government (1966–1970) was responsible for the disintegration of the progressive liberal political option in Guatemala, clearing the path for a period of violent military rule. A forced alliance between the ultra right-wing forces and the liberal elements represented by the new president, promoted by the US with the cooperation of Mendez Montenegro, had devastating consequences for the mass of the Guatemalan populace.

Although the rightist military and oligarchy were wary of Mendez Montenegro's 'liberalism' and doubted his capacity to eliminate the guerrilla threat, Washington believed he would be more likely than his predecessor to allow Pentagon counterinsurgency specialists to play battlefield roles in the anti-guerrilla struggle. American officials participated in discussions between the president-elect and the army high command that established the conditions under which Mendez Montenegro was allowed to take office.[14] The military would be allowed to prosecute the war without restrictions, the existing structure of command would be left intact, and the political Left would be excluded from participation in the government. Mendez Montenegro's decision to foresake his liberal anti-communism under military-US pressure, from the outset of his tenure in office, led directly to a period of wholesale massacres which had the practical effect of eliminating any differences between liberal and right-wing anti-communist forces in Guatemala.

During the Mendez Montenegro presidency (1966–1970), the US military commitment to Guatemala expanded dramatically, not only in the form of direct assistance (equipment and supplies) and manpower (counterinsurgency experts), but also through a US Office of Public Safety (OPS) programme to instruct and arm the National Police—which increased in numbers from 3,000 to 11,000.[15] The OPS funding to Guatemala during this period constituted the second largest (after Brazil) programme in Latin America. When the Guatemalan army launched its brutal 'pacification' strategy in 1967 under the command of Colonel Carlos Arana Osorio in the Department of Zacapa, it was advised by US military attache Colonel John Webber and approximately 1,000 US Green Beret Special Forces.[16] An estimated 15,000 individuals (mostly peasants) were killed in the Department of Zacapa alone over the next three years.[17] Complementing this officially sanctioned violence were even more brutal forms of repression perpetrated by extreme rightist organisations with the complicity of the regime. 'With President Mendez's consent, and despite constitutional prohibitions,' writes one authority, 'private right-wing groups formed their own units to murder students, Indians, and labor leaders [even as the number of labour unions and rural cooperatives actually increased under Mendez Montenegro] suspected of sympathizing with the rebels.'[18] More than twenty anti-communist 'death squads' composed of off-duty police and retired military officers proceeded to eliminate not only leftists and liberals but all those who in any way supported programmes of social change. A leading Christian Democratic official estimated that 6,000 political murders occurred during the 'liberal' president's tenure.[19] The enormous amount of physical force applied by the state and its imperial benefactors partially destroyed a divided guerrilla movement while the vigilante terrorism of the oligarchy-supported death squads, created a more profound polarization in Guatemalan society.

In 1970, Colonel Carlos Arana Osario won the presidency, due to a split among the Left-liberal parties which received a majority of the votes, and immediately launched a ferocious campaign of terror in an effort to permanently eliminate all segments of the urban and rural opposition to military rule. Martial law was imposed and the right-wing death squads and the security forces were given carte blanche to literally cut a swathe through the heterogeneous political antagonists of the Arana presidency. As many as 1,000 people were murdered in the first three months of the regime but this did not dissuade the Nixon administration from looking favourably on Arana Osario's government as an important regional ally and showering it with military and economic aid. 'During the height of one particularly bloody repression in 1971,' according to an account of the period, 'twenty-five officers and seven former US policemen worked with that military'.[20] In 1972, Washington dispatched $32.2 million in economic assistance, the second largest annual total ever provided to a Central American country. Meanwhile, the authoritative *Amnesty International* reported that between 1970 and 1973 over 15,000 people were killed or 'disappeared' by the regime.[21] The majority of the victims were peasants, but they also included large numbers of trade unionists, students, journalists, social democratic politicians and representatives of various professional groups. The complicity of the Nixon–Ford administrations, in this period of uncontrolled terror waged by the military state against its own population during the late sixties and early seventies, is strikingly illustrated by the fact that between 1967 and 1976 almost all of Guatemala's foreign military assistance—$35 million worth—came from the United States.[22]

In 1974, General Kjell Laugerud, the preferred candidate of the military leadership, became president in one of the more fraudulent elections in contemporary Guatemalan history. Under Laugerud, the level of state-authored violence experienced a *relative* decline during the first two years of his tenure and was accompanied by the reinstitution of political activity, a growth in union membership from 28,000 in 1974 to approximately 80,000 in 1976 (still below the Arbenz period),[23] and the formation of rural cooperatives. In the urban centres, this controlled political 'opening' led to a recomposition of the opposition forces and the emergence of a growing mass-based popular movement representing disparate political, social and ideological forces. In the countryside, following the violent repression of the Arana Osorio period, guerrilla movements reemerged and began to concentrate on the development of labour and peasant unions. Land conflicts (the growth of a landless or near landless peasantry had reached enormous proportions) and government terrorism of the preceding years had fostered an increased militancy among the Indians and peasants and the development of linkages with the guerrillas, especially in the northern province of Quiche. The radicalization of these highland Indian communities, the growth of a broad based urban opposition, and the renewed effectiveness of the guerrillas forced Laugerud to resort to a policy of selection assassinations, beginning in 1977, to eliminate the leadership of this burgeoning opposition to military rule and repression.

The response of the Carter administration was an attempt to influence changes in the method of Laugerud's rulership that did not threaten any serious rupture in bilateral relations. While careful not to risk actions that might endanger the large US economic stake in Guatemala, the Carter White House applied some pressures, primarily in the form of a cutback in military credits, to force the regime to modify the scope of its repressive policies: to be more selective in their application and to combine state control with limited social reforms. The refusal of the clientist ruling class to modify the more extreme features of its policy of terror created friction between Washington and Guatemala City and the suspension of military assistance, (although previously authorized weaponry and funds continued to flow until 1980)—but the flow of economic assistance was not disrupted.

Carter's effort to elaborate an anti-communist foreign policy 'with a human face', like Kennedy's earlier attempt to combine counterinsurgency warfare with reformist anti-communist regimes, ultimately foundered on the existence of a hegemonic anti-communist ruling class in Guatemala opposed to any kind of social and economic change and, therefore, to the type of heterogeneous political coalition that Washington viewed as the basis for instituting reforms. In both instances, the White House sought to separate and disassociate liberal anti-communism from right-wing anti-communism in Guatemala, but the imperial state's capacity to pursue this type of flexible anti-communist policy (Christian Democratic-reformist military-centrist Social Democrats, etc. coalition) was obstructed by the totalitarianism of the military-oligarchy forces which controlled the state and Washington's (liberal and conservative) first priority: sustaining the capitalist state in the context of a rising guerrilla challenge.

The fraudulent election of General Romeo Lucas Garcia in 1978 signalled the total collapse of the reformist anti-communist option pursued by the Carter foreign policymakers. Lucas Garcia instituted a reign of terror that can be compared with the worst excesses of the early 1970s. Between 1979 and mid-1980, over 3,000 unarmed combatants were slaughtered by the army and the death squads, including peasants, labour organizers, religious workers and priests, lawyers, teachers and journalists.[24] During the subsequent ten months, 76 leaders of the Christian Democratic Party and 10 officials of the Social Democratic United Revolutionary Front were murdered.[25] Meanwhile, army massacres of entire Indian villages was a not uncommon occurrence. By early 1981, 'killings of people in opinion-making positions [had] decimated university faculties, student groups, moderate and left-of-centre political organizations, rural cooperatives, newspaper and radio staffs, peasant leagues, unions and churches'.[26] At this time, *Amnesty International* released a detailed report on Guatemala which documented in great detail the military government's role as the *only* author and practitioner of the 'official' and 'unofficial' terror: '. . . the selection of targets for detention and murder, and *the deployment of official forces for extra-legal operations,* can be pinpointed to secret offices in an annex of Guatemala's National Palace, under the direct control of the President of the Republic.'[27]

With the advent of the Reagan presidency, the tension evident in the US imperial state at certain historical moments between promoting the interests of liberal anti-communism as opposed to alignment with right-wing anti-communist regimes was unambiguously resolved as the new group of Washington policymakers sought immediately to provide legitimacy for the murderous Lucia Garcia regime. 'It is very important to our interests in the region to re-establish relations with the Government of Guatemala,' remarked a senior State Department official at the beginning of Reagan's tenure, 'and we are actively pursuing ways in which to do so.'[28] In May 1981, Secretary of State Haig's special emissary, General Vernon Walters, visited Guatemala where he dismissed human rights criticisms as without foundation and expressed US support for the military's efforts to defend 'the constitutional institutions of this country against the ideologies that want to finish off those institutions'.[29]

Emboldened by this public display of Washington's support, the repression continued apace, reaching its zenith in 1982 when the army, security forces, national police, intelligence services and death squads, working in concert or individually perpetrated several hundred documented massacres.[30] This terror 'offensive' was conducted largely under the auspices of General Efrian Rioss Montt who succeeded Lucas Garcia as president following an internal military coup in March 1982. In early April, he approved a secret army plan for a major escalation of the counter-insurgency war in the countryside which 'focused upon eliminating the insurgent's popular base by massacring whole communities of suspected sympathizers. . .'[31] Indiscriminate and generalized murder became the order of the day in the months that followed. Military and paramilitary forces engaged in random executions, selective assassinations of community leaders and massacres of whole indigenous villages suspected of guerrilla sympathies.[32] Between March and September, almost 8,000 non-combatants were killed, disappeared or were victims of collective holocausts.[33] Rioss Montt's scorched earth policy against peasant and Indian villages was largely responsible for the more than 100,000 Guatemalan refugees that have entered Mexico since January 1981 and another one million displaced persons who remain in the country as internal refugees or in forced 'relocation centres' (concentration camps).[34]

Within the Reagan anti-communist Cold War schema, Rioss Montt was a valued regional client. The Guatemalan military's war of annihilation, especially in the countryside, was of limited concern to Washington when contrasted with the regime's pro-capitalist orientation, its acceptance of the Reaganites bipolar view of the world, and the nature of the local political antagonists—a guerrilla movement with a growing popular constituency. The Reagan White House exploited loopholes in Congressional restrictions on military aid to Guatemala, directly and indirectly, to bolster the firepower of the armed forces.[35] To facilitate US corporate sales, it reclassified such items as jeeps and trucks as non-military forms of assistance in order to circumvent the letter of the Foreign Assistance Act. Between December 1980 and December 1982, Bell Helicopter Company, acting under a licence authorized by the White House and issued by the Commerce Department, sold Guatemala $25 million worth of civilian helicopters that were subsequently used for military purposes.[36] In January 1983, the Reagan administration formally approved export licences for the sale of $6.3 million worth of helicopter parts. The imperial state exhibited similar determination to continue economic assistance to the Guatemalan rulers. In October 1982, the White House declared that the US would no longer vote against multilateral development bank loans to Guatemala on human rights grounds because, according to State Department officials, human rights in the Central American country had actually improved under Rioss Montt![37] Reagan concluded a trip to Guatemala in December with a ringing declaration of support for Rioss Montt whom he described as 'totally dedicated to democracy in Guatemala' and the object of 'a bum rap' in regard to accusations of widespread human rights violations committed during his presidency.[38]

Defence Minister General Oscar Humerto Mejia Victores who replaced Rioss Montt in August 1983 following another army coup has continued, although with not the same high level of intensity, the brutal policies of his predecessor. During the first four months of his rule, killings and disappearances of regime opponents were also accompanied by a massive programme of arbitrary arrests which affected more than 7,000 persons in Guatemala City alone. The change in military leadership had no effect on Washington's policy and Reagan's efforts to increase the still relatively limited flow of economic and military assistance to Guatemala, even though Congress continues with some success to obstruct administration objectives. US representatives in the international banks, for instance, have vigorously supported Guatemalan loan requests since the October 1982 policy shift. In September 1983, they voted in favour of loans to their right-wing anti-communist allies totalling $70.5 million.[39] The Reagan desire to normalize military and security ties was writ large in the administration fiscal year 1984 security assistance proposals which included a request for $10 million in Foreign Military sales credits and loan repayment guarantees for Guatemala. In February 1984, the White House lifted a two month freeze on the sale of $2 million worth of helicopter parts, ostensibly imposed to pressure the Mejia Victores regime to improve its human rights performance, even though more than 800 persons were reported assassinated or 'disappeared' during the first three months of the year.[40]

Conclusion

US policymakers bear direct responsibility for the ascent to political power of the Guatemalan military in 1954; and the policies of successive Republican and Democratic administrations have been instrumental in the armed forces' calculated escalation of military control and state-authored repression over three decades. On the one hand, presidents from Truman to Reagan have opposed progressive democratic governments and movements in Guatemala. On the other, they have lavishly financed and supported right-wing military and military controlled regimes receptive to US corporate interests at the expense of the country's vast majority of workers and peasants and who were prepared to align themselves with Washington's regional and global objectives. US direct private investment in Guatemala rose from $131 million in 1960 to $186 million in 1970 to $260 million in 1980—the largest US multinational commitment in Central America.[41] The ideology of anti-communism has been utilized by Washington policymakers, time and again, to justify opposition to agrarian reform, organized worker-peasant movements and nationalist development projects, and to legitimate the repressive policies pursued by rightist military rulers. The results have ranged from the reversal of democratic and social reform based on parliamentary politics to the blockage of all avenues of political expression and opposition based on force and violence; from growth through national development benefiting the mass of the population to growth through national exploitation based on state terror financed and supported by Washington which enriched the military-oligarchy ruling class and impoverished the country's Indians and peasants.

The social consequences of US-financed and supported military rule in Guatemala since 1954 has been profound: a concentration of land owner-

ship and wealth in the hands of the army, oligarchy and US corporations;
a decline in virtually every area of social welfare—education, public health,
drinkable water, access to electricity; widespread malnutrition and low
life expectancy levels in rural areas; a persistent and serious infant
mortality problem (35 per cent of children nationwide and up to 60 per
cent in rural Guatemala die before the age of 5); massive illiteracy; extensive unemployment and underemployment; the growth of urban slums;
and a decline in the minimum wage to below the level of the Arbenz
period (the purchasing power of the urban workers fell by one third
between 1970 and 1980 alone).[42] Between 1950 and 1978, the share of
national income obtained by the poorest 50 per cent of the population
declined from 9 per cent to 7 per cent while the top 5 per cent of the
population increased its share from 48 per cent to 59 per cent.[43]

Since the US orchestrated destabilization and overthrow of the reformist
Arbenz government in 1954, every Guatemalan regime has engaged in
large-scale extrajudicial execution of noncombatant civilians. In December
1983, *Amnesty International* which has closely monitored the human
rights situation in Guatemala since the early 1970s, issued a report which
concluded on the following note:

> Under successive administrations, the regular security and military forces in
> Guatemala—as well as paramilitary groups acting under government order or
> with official complicity—have been responsible for massive instances of human
> rights violations, including 'disappearances' and extrajudicial execution, directed
> at people from all sectors of Guatemalan society [Indians, peasants, teachers,
> students, trade union leaders, health services personnel, journalists, other pro-
> fessional groups, etc.] . . . although there have been fluctuations in the volume of
> killings and 'disappearances', the policies and structures responsible for these
> violations have remained virtually the same.[44]

In the three decades since democratic popular rule in Guatemala, the
institutionalized terror of the rightist anti-communist regimes supported
by conservative and liberal Washington administrations has claimed over
100,000 victims.

Anti-communist ideology in both its liberal and conservative guises
has been the key mechanism destabilizing the emergence of independent
political forces and legitimizing a succession of repressive military rulers in
Guatemala for more than three decades. The notion has functioned to
undermine the class analysis of class conflict and substitute fictitious
world-system ideological conflicts. Every imperial administration from
Eisenhower to Reagan has employed it to mobilize domestic support for
these totalitarian regimes that have shown themselves willing to accommodate US economic, political and strategic objectives throughout the
Central American–Caribbean region. Moreover, anti-communist ideology
has served to empty the language of Western democracy of all of its

cognitive meanings: anti-communist terror and massacres have been continually associated with the defence of free institutions. Clearly, no return to a democratic foreign policy in the United States and elsewhere in the capitalist world is possible without a complete rejection of the ideology of anti-communism and the policies associated with it.

NOTES

1. Stephen Schlesinger and Stephen Kinzer, *Bitter Fruit: The Untold Story of the American Coup in Guatemala,* (New York: Doubleday & Company, 1982), p. 12.
2. See Richard M. Immerman, *The CIA in Guatemala: The Foreign Policy of Intervention,* (Austin: University of Texas Press, 1982), p. 66; Walter LaFeber, *Inevitable Revolutions: The United States in Central America,* (New York: W.W. Norton & Company, 1983), p. 116.
3. Stephen Schlesinger and Stephen Kinzer, *op. cit.,* p. 120.
4. Quoted in Walter LaFeber, *op. cit.,* p. 114.
5. Draft Policy Paper Prepared in the Bureau of Inter-American Affairs, Top Secret, 'NSC Guatemala', August 19, 1953, in US Department of State, *Foreign Relations of the United States, 1952-1954, Volume IV, The American Republics,* (Washington: US Government Printing Office, 1983), p. 1074.
6. Quoted in Stephen Schlesinger and Stephen Kinzer, *op. cit.,* p. 135.
7. National Intelligence Estimate, Secret, 'Probable Developments in Guatemala', May 19, 1953, in *Foreign Relations of the United States, 1952-1954, Volume IV, The American Republics, op. cit.,* p. 1061. On the limited influence of the Communists within the state and governing regime, see Stephen Schlesinger and Stephen Kinzer, *op. cit.,* pp. 58-61; Cole Blasier, *The Hovering Giant: US Responses to Revolutionary Changes in Latin America,* (Pittsburgh: University of Pittsburgh Press, 1976), p. 227.
8. James Petras, *et al.,* 'The Monroe Doctrine and US Hegemony in Latin America', in James Petras (ed.), *Latin America: From Dependence to Revolution,* (New York: John Wiley & Sons, 1973), p. 257.
9. Quoted in Richard M. Immerman, *op. cit.,* pp. 157-158.
10. Quoted in Stephen Schlesinger and Stephen Kinzer, *op. cit.,* p. 11.
11. Walter LaFeber, *op. cit.,* p. 119.
12. See Stephen Schlesinger and Stephen Kinzer, *op. cit.,* p. 219.
13. See *Ibid.,* pp. 232-233.
14. See Suzanne Jonas and David Tobis, (eds.), *Guatemala,* (Berkeley: North American Congress on Latin America, August, 1974), p. 105.
15. See Stephen Schlesinger and Stephen Kinzer, *op. cit.,* p. 247.
16. See Walter LaFeber, *op. cit.,* p. 169.
17. See Thomas P. Anderson, *Politics in Central America,* (New York: Praeger Publishers, 1983), p. 26.
18. Walter LaFeber, *op. cit.,* p. 170.
19. See Thomas and Marjorie Melville, *Guatemala: The Politics of Land Ownership,* (New York: Free Press, 1971), pp. 247-248.
20. Walter LaFeber, *op. cit.,* p. 257.
21. See Jenny Pearce, *Under the Eagle: US Intervention in Central America and the Caribbean,* (Boston: South End Press, 1982), p. 71.
22. See Walter LaFeber, *op. cit.,* p. 257.
23. See Thomas Anderson, *op. cit.,* p. 29.

24. See Walter LaFeber, *op. cit.*, p. 260; Lars Schoultz, *Human Rights and United States Policy Toward Latin America*, (Princeton: Princeton University Press, 1981), pp. 352–354.

25. See Warren Hodge, 'Repression Increases in Guatemala As US Is Seeking To Improve Ties', *New York Times*, May 3, 1981, p. 3.

26. *Ibid.*, p. 3.

27. 'Guatemala: A Government Program of Political Murder—The Amnesty Report (Extracts)', *The New York Review of Books*, March 19, 1981, p. 38.

28. Quoted in Warren Hodge, *op. cit.*, p. 3.

29. Quoted in Christopher Dickey, 'Haig's Emissary, in Guatemala, Discounts Charges of Rights Abuse', *Washington Post*, May 14, 1981, p. A1.

30. See Richard Alan White, *The Morass: United States Intervention in Central America*, (New York: Harper & Row Publishers, 1984), p. 104.

31. *Ibid.*, p. 97.

32. See *Ibid.*, p. 100–101.

33. See Comite Pro Justicia Y Paz de Guatemala, *Human Rights in Guatemala*, February 1983, p. 21.

34. See David B. Lawrenz, 'Rearming the Guatemalan Military: "Reagan Refugees" for Mexico and the US', *COHA Memorandum*, (Washington, D.C.: Council on Hemispheric Affairs, February 13, 1984). 6 pp; 'Refugees are everywhere', *Central America Report* (Guatemala City), Vol. XI, no. 6, February 10, 1984, pp. 42–43; United Nations, General Assembly Report of the Economic and Social Council, *Situation of Human Rights in Guatemala*, 38th Session, Agenda Item 12, A/38/485, November 4, 1983, pp. 32–34.

35. See Richard J. Meislin, 'US Military Aid for Guatemala Continuing Despite Official Curbs', *New York Times*, December 19, 1982, pp. 1, 18; Bruce P. Cameron and Christopher D. Ringwald, *Aid to Guatemala: Violating Human Rights*, (Washington, D.C.: Center for International Policy, May 1983), 6 pp.

36. See Christopher Dickey, 'Guatemala Uses US "Civilian" Copters in Warfare', *Washington Post*, January 23, 1982, pp. A1, A11.

37. See Raymond Bonner, 'US Now Backing Guatemala Loans', *New York Times*, October 10, 1982, p. 17. Also see Jim Morrell and William Jesse Biddle, *Central America: The Financial War*, (Washington, D.C.: Center for International Policy, March 1983), pp. 6–7.

38. Quoted in Steven R. Weisman, 'Reagan Denounces Threats to Peace in Latin America', *New York Times*, December 5, 1982, p. 1.

39. See *MesoAmerica*, (San Jose, Costa Rica: Institute for Central America Studies), Vol. 3, no. 5, May 1984, p. 2.

40. See, for example, 'Government sanguine about violence problem', *Central America Report* (Guatemala City), Vol. XI, no. 7, February 17, 1984, pp. 51–52.

41. See 'Garrison Guatemala', Special issue of *NACLA Report on the Americas*, Vol. XVII, no. 1, January-February 1983, p. 12.

42. See Washington Office on Latin America, 'Guatemala: The Roots of Revolution', *Special Update*, (Washington, D.C., February 1983), pp. 2–6; Walter LaFeber, *op. cit.*, pp. 167–168, 259; Stephen Schlesinger and Stephen Kinzer, *op. cit.*, pp. 253–254.

43. See Washington Office on Latin America, *op. cit.*, p. 2.

44. Amnesty International, *Guatemala Update: Amnesty International Human Rights Concerns in Guatemala Since the August 1983 Coup Which Brought General Oscar Humberto Mejia Victores to Power*, (London, December 23, 1983), p. 1.

SOVIET EXPANSIONISM AND EXPANSIVE ANTI-SOVIETISM

Xavier Zeebroek

'Western capitalist societies and socialist societies simply represent different stages of development; there are differences between them, but they are not fundamental differences.' Nowadays, no one would dare to come out with such a statement in a political meeting of any kind. Anyone who did so would be laughed out of court and would look like a schoolboy trying to cause a sensation rather than a responsible adult. Yet it is in fact a fairly accurate summary of the views held by a number of distinguished economists, sociologists and political observers in the sixties and early seventies. Walt Rostow,[1] Jan Tinbergen,[2] and Sorokin[3] all predicted that in economic and social terms the capitalist and socialist systems would converge and that the technological revolution would transcend them both and produce a synthesis of capitalism and socialism: the affluent society. Other famous figures like Galbraith[4] and Marcuse[5] also took a sympathetic view of this thesis, even though the latter did draw pessimistic conclusions from it, and developed it in various ways. Even Sakharov predicted a scientific and technological revolution in both systems which would, by the year 2000, lead to a world government and to the elimination of contradictions between nations.[6] It might seem easy to sneer at the euphoria of such theories. They flourished almost exclusively in capitalist countries and were the product of an extremely favourable historical environment. The golden sixties meant not only full employment and a standard of living that would have been inconceivable only a few years earlier, but also the conquest of space. At least in its early stages, the conquest of space meant that, in scientific and economic terms, the USSR was catching up with the West. At the same time, the long, slow process of detente had produced a whole series of agreements and treaties in a wide range of areas. It was very tempting to interpret what was in fact only an ephemeral trend as an irreversible movement. It would, however, be a mistake to think that the theoreticians of convergence felt any sympathy towards the Soviet Union. In that sense, the early ideologues of the death of ideology were quite clearly products of their own system.

We now live in an age of disillusionment. The 'technostructure' simply maximizes austerity. The only growth area is in unemployment, which is quietly ushering in an era of enforced leisure. For many people, there is no longer any possibility of improving their standard of living. Even the crisis itself is in crisis; detente is collapsing under the sudden impact of divergent conceptions of 'security'. It is one of history's ironies that the scientific revolution which gave rise to so many hopes should have been subordinated to the needs of the arms race. Technology is used primarily for the manufacture of armaments. With all due respect to the alchemists of the sixties, the eighties are likely to be an age of lead rather than an age of gold.

New prejudices for old

Times change, and discourses change with them. The dream of world government is gone for ever, shattered by the prismatic reflections of new conceptions. New clichés are turning old commonplaces inside out. Curiously enough, however, the prevailing pessimism applies to only one vector of the old convergence. As a result, the megalithic struggle between the bourgeois state and the dictatorship of the proletariat has undergone a metamorphosis. Like certain archaic clauses in the penal code, the term 'capitalism' has fallen into disuse. It belongs to the nineteenth century and is 'no longer applicable'. To replace it, the most archaic allegories of the bourgeois revolution have been pressed into service: pluralism, democracy and freedom. These are now the three spectres that haunt our whole social system.

Socialism never existed, except in the naive writings of idealists. For seventy-five years, a barbaric system deceived us by usurping the name of the socialist utopia. It can no longer hide the fact that it is an obscene society, that it is the living embodiment of the very worst form of dictatorship. It can no longer conceal the horrors of the Gulag or the fact that it is a vampire which feeds on democracy, a new form of imperialism. George Orwell, who prophesied this gigantic struggle between good and evil, is enjoying a posthumous triumph with books that are scarcely older than NATO itself, books which read like Nostradamus rewritten by La Fontaine.

Given these conditions, there can be no question of waiting peacefully for the unification of the world. Not only do we have to take sides; we have to dig in as soon as possible. The most constant part of the anti-Soviet discourse is the military theme or, to use the stock phrase, 'the evaluation of the threat'. NATO has been making the same point for the last thirty-five years. 'The military might of the Warsaw Pact is so great that it cannot reasonably be justified in terms of defence needs. . . It still gives great importance to the element of surprise and to rapid offensive operations. Warsaw Pact forces are organized, trained and equipped to take the offensive from the very outset of any conflict'.[7] NATO, of course, is a purely defensive organization 'designed to prevent war; its ultimate political objective is to achieve a lasting peace based upon appropriate guarantees of security. In order to achieve that objective, it must have sufficient power to discourage attacks on any of its members'.[8]

Involuntary peace

There is nothing new about this polemic. If we invert the terms of the equation, we find a mirror image of the same picture, but this time it is the Soviet Union that is in the right. It may well be a truism to say that no weapon has ever been used for purely defensive purposes, but it is also more pertinent than ever. The invention of the atom bomb and of the formidable combination of a missile and one or more thermonuclear warheads was the result of a technological breakthrough that gave offensive thinking an indefinite lead over defensive thinking. It also meant that any offensive would be unimagineably violent, devastating and uncontrollable. The military, and much less the politicians, have never liked anything they cannot control. Both pacts claim to have kept the peace in Europe for the last thirty-five years, but both have created and maintained tensions which have at times come close to causing a general conflagration. It is difficult to avoid the conclusion that both sides are simply taking the credit for the achievements of their weapons and that they are in fact dismayed by the incredible speed, range and destructive power of their strike forces. Peace can only last until such time as one of the protagonists sees through the charade. The one thing that transcends confrontation and restricts their bellicose ambitions is the likelihood of their being annihilated in any intercontinental exchange. In that sense, deterrence is nothing more than a codified form of blackmail masquerading as a point of law. It is not a doctrine which ensures perpetual peace, but a de facto situation which temporarily prevents war.

Comparisons are odious

There is of course nothing new about the idea that only the Warsaw Pact is an aggressive military alliance. A more recent assumption has, however, darkened the picture even further. It is generally assumed that since the 1970s, the Soviet Union has developed the means to carry out its policy of worldwide expansion. Not a single meeting of the Military Committee, the Nuclear Planning and Defence Groups or the North Atlantic Council goes by without this principle being reiterated or without a review of the new weapons systems introduced by the Soviet Union. In 1982, a 'comparison of opposing forces' was for the first time published for the benefit of both the media and the general public. It has recently been updated and republished by NATO's information service. The stated aim of this publication is to underline the rapid build-up of Soviet power in every domain. The build-up is very real. But this publication is also designed to prove that it poses a threat to world nuclear parity and to demonstrate that the USSR has a crushing superiority in the European theatre. Thus, it is claimed that 'The quantitative and qualitative improvement in the USSR's strategic forces means that it now has the potential to upset the strategic balance.'[9] The only way NATO can reach this conclusion is to stress numbers of vectors (missiles and aircraft) and their power as opposed to number of warheads and their accuracy. Describing the balance of strategic power in these terms is rather like judging a nation's economic power in terms of the surface area of its factories rather than in terms of *real production* and *quality of production.* In terms of numbers of warheads, the USA's vast superiority (in 1975, the ratio was three to one in its favour) has not been reversed, even when calculated in purely numerical terms (9,665 warheads as opposed to 8,800).[10] Given the surplus nuclear capability of both sides, this has no military significance. The USA also has the advantage in terms of accuracy and the speed with which its missiles can be launched.[11] The Soviet Union is also at a disadvantage in other areas; US warheads, for instance, are more evenly distributed between the three services (Army, Navy and Air Force). 71 per cent of all Soviet missiles are land-based Intercontinental Ballistic Missiles which are highly vulnerable because they are easily detected by satellites. The equivalent figure for the USA is 22 per cent. The Soviet ICBMs can only be used for a first strike or for launch on alert.

The Soviet Union's weak second strike capability completes the picture; it consists mainly of weapons which would be likely to survive a first strike, in other words submarines and strategic bombers. The Soviet Union has virtually no strategic airborne forces, which account for only 3 per cent of all nuclear tests carried out (they represent 27 per cent of all US forces and 49 per cent of all megatonnage). This is quite understandable, given that a Soviet bomber has very little chance of reaching any target in the USA. Submarines carry 32 per cent of the Soviet Union's warheads; the equivalent figure for the USA is 51 per cent. The Stockholm International Peace Research Institute (SIPRI) also notes that: 'Only 15 to 20 per cent of the Soviet Union's submarine forces are deployed on a permanent basis, largely because the Soviet Union is unable to keep more of them in service. Almost 50 per cent of the USA's strategic submarines are permanently on patrol. Whereas the twenty American submarines which are always at sea are thought to be invulnerable to Soviet anti-submarine warfare, the nine or ten Submarine Launched Ballistic Missiles which are based in Soviet ports are under constant US surveillance. . . Soviet submarines are much noisier than their American equivalents and are therefore more vulnerable to anti-submarine warfare. Given this, the geographical advantages it enjoys and its technological superiority, the USA can be considered the dominant side in terms of anti-submarine warfare.'[12]

The methods used to evaluate the balance of power constantly give rise to misunderstandings and tend to give credence to over-simplifications.

Three truly discriminatory methods are used. The criteria chosen for comparisons systematically reinforce NATO views. No weight is given to the fact that in qualitative terms, the West has a definite advantage. Finally, neither French nor Spanish forces are taken into account on the grounds that neither country is a member of NATO's integrated military structure. As a result of these omissions, only Soviet missiles and land-based US missiles are taken into account in calculating the balance of power in Europe. Whereas organisations like SIPRI and the London-based International Institute for Strategic Studies always use world figures, the strategy used by NATO gives credence to the argument that it has nothing in Europe to counter the Soviet Union's SS44s, SS5s and SS20s. But as is the case with ICBMs, most theatre missiles are carried by French, British or US submarines, the latter being based in Great Britain.

In terms of conventional weapons, NATO always omits to mention that the USSR has a lot of old weapons as well as more sophisticated weaponry. Thus, a great deal is made of the threat posed by the Soviet Union's 50,000 tanks. But whereas T72s and T80s may be comparable with the West's best tanks, the Soviet Union also has 35,000 T54/55s and T62s (80 per cent of the total), whose design dates back to the early sixties. Their operational weakness was confirmed when large numbers of these tanks were destroyed in the clashes between Israel and Syria in the Lebanon in 1982.[13]

An asymmetrical balance
For the last thirty years the Soviet Union has been catching up with the West, but by the 1990s we are likely to see the completion of a whole series of American research programmes and a large-scale use of advanced technologies which will allow the US to regain the ground it has lost. The reliability of automatic guidance systems and the fearful accuracy of targetting systems will make all the difference and, together with the ability of electronic counter-measures to outwit decoys and evade increasingly sophisticated warning systems will determine a projectile's ability to reach its target. Battlefield weapons will simply be so many parts of an overall technological structure and generic terms for them will have no operational meaning in terms of comparative evaluations.

No serious historian would even contemplate assessing the threat posed by a state in terms of how many battalions it has. If battalions were that important, the Roman Empire would never have fallen to the Goths, Napoleon would have lost all his battles, Nazi Germany would have had considerably more difficulty in conquering France[14] and the war in Vietnam would have been no more than a training exercise for the USA. On the other hand, history is full of examples of states which have—for all sorts of political, economic and ideological reasons—deliberately started conflicts, even though they were in purely military terms weaker than their enemies. They have been victorious because they were able to exploit the advantage of surprise or their tactical superiority.

NATO calculations inevitably take into account the heartlands of the USSR, as 60 to 80 per cent of its military capability is concentrated there. American territory is never taken into account. This reflects a real geographical imbalance, but it has nothing to do with the world balance of power. It has become fashionable to discuss conventional forces solely in terms of Europe. This implies that part of NATO and less than one third of all American forces should be equivalent to the Warsaw Pact and two thirds of all Soviet forces. If that balance were ever achieved, it would be intolerable to the Soviet Union.

NATO plays upon our strong Eurocentric sympathies and exploits this concentration on Europe in order to conceal the fact that the military choices made by the two great powers are radically different. The USA has had unchallenged military control over the American continent for decades. The only direct threat has to come from the sea or the air. The only country in the world which stretches over the greater part of two continents faces hostile powers on two fronts. The Soviet Union is not protected by any natural barriers.

Since 1945, the USA has dominated the world in terms of expeditionary and air-sea power. The USSR has achieved land and air superiority along its frontiers and in two potential theatres of operation: China and Europe. The dominance of land-based forces has for a long time been a constant feature of Soviet history and goes back to Russia's imperial traditions. This can also be explained in terms of the vast area of territory that has to be defended (22,402,200 square kilometres; 2.5 times the surface area of the USA) and in terms of the length of the border and lines of communication which are not broken by any oceans. To describe the largest country in the world as a 'regional' super power may seem provocative. But two thirds of the surface of the earth is covered by water; those who remain on land will never be the strongest.

Given that, in territorial terms, the existing status quo with both NATO and China is unlikely to change, the USSR's capacity for expansionism is usually evaluated in terms of its military presence in the Third World rather than in terms of the possibility of a war between the super powers degenerating into a worldwide nuclear conflagration. The main issue we have to look at, then, is the USSR's ability to intervene rapidly and in force far away from its own frontiers. We also have to look at the results it has obtained in that area. In these terms, the classic Western argument, which concentrates upon conventional forces (conventional and nuclear), is rather less than convincing. Any power which wants to rule the world—and this, it is claimed, is the Soviet Union's aim—has to deploy its forces throughout the world. That means that it must rely upon air and sea power and must have military bases throughout the world. We will therefore concentrate upon this aspect of the strategic confrontation.

NATO countries are increasingly disturbed by the Soviet Union's ability to 'project' its military power to every continent in the world. 'The Soviet Union's ability to react to crises or favourable opportunities, and its ability to make its power and influence felt in zones that are far away from its own frontiers have caught the attention of the whole world. . . Recent analyses of the Soviets' tendency to increase their capabilities have brought out the current and projected development of the Soviet navy, its improved air and amphibious capabilities, the organizational flexibility of its forces, and improvements in command, control and communications (C^3I) and logistic support.'[15] 'In the first stage of their attempt to acquire facilities, the Soviet Union had major successes in Ethiopia, South Yemen, Angola and Vietnam and lesser successes in Syria, Tunisia and Guinea.'[16] The conclusions reached by the highly competent Military Committee are very pertinent, but they can lead to assumptions which are diametrically oppposed to the motives that are normally ascribed to the Kremlin leaders. NATO makes no secret of the fact that it sees the Soviet Union as having 'A fundamental philosophy according to which all resources, military and otherwise, have to be used together to establish a flexible network of influence and to open up a window on the world.'[17] According to former NATO Secretary Joseph Luns, 'The Soviet Union has never restricted its ambitions to equality and the maintenance of the status quo'[18] and has 'used the theoretical pretext of peaceful coexistence to begin psychological warfare and subversion.'[19]

The real world is both more complex and less Machiavellian than this. The constraints which have governed the spectacular development of the Soviet navy, which in 1945 was simply a coastal defence force and which is now a deep water fleet, are, for instance, very different to those governing the growth of the American fleet. The US Navy's powerful task forces are deployed in every ocean in the world and are headed by gigantic aircraft carriers with a displacement of 70 to 90,000 tonnes, each of them capable of housing some one hundred aircraft. The four Soviet fleets do not have anything like the same capabilities. In the event of a major war breaking out, they would immediately be cut off from one another and would have to make for their home ports. And as a result, the USSR would be cut off from the rest of the world. The tasks assigned to the Navy in wartime are therefore astonishingly modest. Their initial and most important task is to protect the coast and to prevent any landings from taking place. They then have to ensure that the strategic nuclear submarines have unchallenged supremacy in the inland seas controlled by the USSR (the Arctic Sea, controlled by the Northern Fleet, and the Sea of Okhotsk, controlled by the Pacific Fleet). Finally, they would do their best to overcome natural obstacles (occupying straits and keeping open channels through the ice fields) and the blockades set up by the West to keep Soviet ships penned up inside territorial waters. Then, and only then, would they begin to disrupt enemy sea communications and to attack the task forces.

Although the Soviet Union has developed its navy to such an extent that it can interdict coastal areas to any Western invader and can carry out certain attrition missions against enemy communications, it has only 12,000 marines (6 per cent of the American total) and has little amphibious capability. It is, then, its increased *peacetime* capabilities which worry the capitalist countries. It is not the Soviet Union's ability to protect sea communications with friendly Third World countries that worries them so much as the fact that its ships now cruise the oceans of the world and have both a certain deterrent capability and a far from negligible ability to spy on the Western navies and gather intelligence on their tactics and operational capability.

In the event of crisis or even tension, this means that the West can no longer make even a limited intervention with the certainty that it would not lead to a major confrontation with Soviet warships. But although this may make the American admirals reluctant to threaten Soviet interests too openly, what NATO describes as 'an offensive force capable of making its effects felt throughout the world'[21] was not enough to stop them bombarding Beirut, invading Grenada, blockading Nicaragua and mining its ports, all within the space of a year.

TABLE I

Military Forces and Bases Abroad

Locations of Foreign Forces	US and Allies*		Countries of Origin USSR and Allies*		Other**	
North America						
1 Bermuda	US	1,550	—			—
2 Canada	US	710	—			—
	UK	##	—			—
Latin America						
3 Antigua	US	120	—			—
4 Ascension Is.	UK	##	—			—
5 Belize	UK	1,800	—			—
6 Cuba	US	2,270	USSR	2,800		—
7 Falkland Is.	UK	7,000	—			—
8 Honduras	US	300	—			—
9 Nicaragua		—	—		C	2,000
10 Panama	US	9,130	—	—		—
11 Puerto Rico	US	2,980	—			—

TABLE I *(contd)*

Military Forces and Bases Abroad

Locations of Foreign Forces	US and Allies*		Countries of Origin USSR and Allies*		Other**	
NATO Europe						
12 Belgium	US	2,390	—		—	
13 Germany, West	US	257,980	—		—	
	UK,F,B.N.	150,100	—		—	
14 Greece	US	3,470	—		—	
15 Iceland	US	3,110	—		—	
16 Italy	US	13,920	—		—	
17 Netherlands	US	2,120	—		—	
18 Norway	US	210	—		—	
	UK	n.k.	—		—	
19 Portugal	US	1,670	—		—	
20 Turkey	US	5,310	—		—	
21 United Kingdom	US	28,540	—		—	
Warsaw Pact						
22 Czechoslovakia		—	USSR	78,000	—	
23 Germany, East		—	USSR	406,000	—	
24 Hungary		—	USSR	50,000	—	
25 Poland		—	USSR	50,000	—	
Other Europe						
26 Spain	US	8,410	—		—	
27 Greenland	US	320	—		—	
28 Gibraltar	UK	2,100	—		—	
Middle East						
29 Bahrain	US†	—	—		—	
30 Cyprus	UK	4,900	—		—	
	G	1,300	—		—	
	Tu	24,000	—		—	
31 Egypt	US	150	—		—	
32 Iraq		—	USSR	1,200	J	3,000
			EG	160		
33 Israel	US	110				
34 Lebanon		—		—	S	50,000
35 Oman	US†	—	—	—	—	
	UK	660				
36 Saudi Arabia	US	480	—		—	
37 Syria		—	USSR	2,500	Y	500
		—	EG	210		
38 Yemen, AR		—	USSR	500	—	—
39 Yemen, PDR		—	USSR	1,500	C	800
			EG	320		
South Asia						
40 Afghanistan	—	—	USSR	95,000	—	
41 Diego Garcia	US	1,800	—		—	

TABLE I *(contd)*

Military Forces and Bases Abroad

Locations of Foreign Forces	US and Allies*		Countries of Origin USSR and Allies*		Other**	
South Africa (contd)						
42 Mayotte	F	n.k.		—		—
43 Reunion	F	n.k.		—		—
Far East						
44 Brunei	UK	1,000		—		—
45 Cambodia		—	USSR	300	V	170,000
46 Canton Is.	US	#		—		—
47 F. Polynesia	F	n.k.		—		—
48 Gilbert Is.	US	#		—		—
49 Guam	US	8,760		—		—
50 Hong Kong	UK	7,650		—		—
51 Japan	US	50,740		—		—
52 Johnston Atoll	US	120		—		—
53 Korea, S.	US	38,630		—		—
54 Laos		—	USSR	500	V	45,000
55 Midway Is.	US	#		—		—
56 Philippines	US	14,950		—		—
57 Thailand	US	100		—		—
58 Trust Territory	US	#		—		—
59 Vietnam		—	USSR	5,000		—
60 Wake Is.	US	#		—		—
Oceania						
61 Australia	US	700		—		—
Africa						
62 Algeria		—	USSR	1,000		—
			EG	250		—
63 Angola		—	USSR	200	C	18,000
			EG	450		
64 Benin		—	USSR	1,200		—
65 Cen.Afr.Rep.	F	1,500		—		—
66 Chad	F	n.k.		—	L	3,000
67 Congo		—	USSR	350		—
			EG	750		
68 Djibouti	F	3,700		—		—
69 Eq. Guinea		—		—	M	400
70 Ethiopia		—	USSR	1,350	C	13,000
			EG	250		
71 Gabon	F	450		—		—
72 Ghana	UK	150		—		—
73 Guinea		—	USSR	380		—
			EG	120		
74 Guinea-Bissau		—	USSR	600		—
75 Ivory Coast	F	450		—		—
76 Kenya	US†	—		—		—

TABLE I *(contd)*

Military Forces and Bases Abroad

Locations of Foreign	US and Allies*		Countries of Origin USSR and Allies*		Other**	
Africa (contd)						
77 Libya		—	USSR	1,800		—
			EG	400		
78 Madagascar		—	EG	300	NK	400
79 Malawi		—		—	SA	100
80 Mali		—	USSR	200		—
81 Mauritania		—	USSR	200		—
82 Morocco	US†	—		—		—
	F	150				
83 Mozambique			USSR	300	C	750
			EG	100		
84 Namibia		—		—	SA	67,500
85 Sahara, W.		—		—	M	90,000
86 Senegal	F	1,170		—		—
87 Seychelles		—		—	T	250
88 Somalia	US†	—		—		—
89 South Africa		—		—	I	200
90 Sudan		—		—	E	700
91 Zaire	F	130		—		—
	B	350		—		—
92 Zimbabwe	UK	100		—	Ch	120
					NK	200

```
*       NATO and Warsaw Pact
#       Less than 100 personnel      ##   Several hundred personnel
†       Facilities under construction
**      Key to country names, see table opposite
n.k.    not known
```

TABLE II

Countries with Forces Abroad

Key to table above

B	Belgium	25,350
C	Cuba	34,550
Ch	China	120
E	Egypt	700
EG	E. Germany	3,310
F	France	58,750
G	Greece	1,300
I	Israel	15,200
J	Jordan	3,000
L	Libya	3,000
M	Morocco	90,400
N	Netherlands	5,500
NK	North Korea	600
S	Syria	50,000
SA	South Africa	67,600
T	Tanzania	250
Tu	Turkey	24,000
UK	United Kingdom	93,860
US	United States	461,130*
USSR	Soviet Union	700,880
V	Vietnam	215,000
Y	Yemen, PDR	500
	Total	1,855,000

*   Does not include 284,000 US service personnel afloat.

Over 1,800,000 of the world's armed forces are currently on foreign territory. About one-third are abroad to fight wars or serve as occupying forces. The majority are based on foreign territory to project national power and serve as the eyes and ears of the forces at home.

Naval presence and naval supremacy

The fact that the balance of power at sea is still in favour of the US and other NATO naval powers like Britain and France has less to do with numbers of ships and tonnage than with bases in foreign countries. Even a modern squadron of nuclear propelled ships and ocean-going auxiliaries cannot undertake an engagement thousands of miles away from its home port. It needs at least one permanent forward base capable of supplying it with fuel, munitions and large quantities of food at short notice. And according to *Flottes de Combat,* (the French equivalent to *Jane's Fighting Ships*), 'Despite continuous diplomatic efforts, the Soviet Navy has not yet succeeded in finding a foreign base worthy of the name, and the few staging posts and other facilities it has acquired here and there cannot compensate for what would in wartime be a very serious handicap.' Moreover, 'Nothing new has been introduced into the auxiliary and support fleet, which, despite all the efforts of recent years, is still the surface fleet's weak point.'[22] The fifteen or so ports which are usually described as fall-back bases are in fact little more than anchorages with a few supplementary facilities. Only the old American base at Cam Ranh in Vietnam appears to have been refitted to take a score of warships, about six hunter-killer submarines and long-range reconnaissance aircraft on any permanent basis.[23] On a much smaller scale, Ethiopia has also been able to provide some purely military facilities. Third World countries which receive aid from the Soviet Union are usually reluctant to grant it such facilities, precisely because of the radical nationalism and desire for independence that led them to break with their pasts. In the West, Angola, for instance, is usually described as a puppet of the Soviets and the Cubans, yet its constitution bans the construction of any foreign bases in the country. The Soviet Union pays a high military price for its anti-imperialist policies. The Americans, on the other hand, have spun a real spider's web of 360 major bases and 1,600 installations in 36 countries. In the event of war breaking out, the Mediterranean, the Pacific and the Atlantic would immediately become Western lakes. Guantanamo, which is actually on Cuban soil, houses almost as many American troops (2,270) as there are Soviet troops on the rest of the island (2,800).[24] Only the Indian Ocean is not under exclusive US control, not because American, French and British forces are numerically inferior, but because the Soviets appear to be able to ensure a permanent presence there thanks to Ethiopia and South Yemen.

In addition to the American forces based in Europe, it requires 142,000 men to man and maintain the euphemistically named forward based system. This dense and complex network is the result of forty years of tireless application of the 'containment doctrine' developed by Truman and Dulles. In both peacetime and wartime it plays an indispensable support role for the 284,000 naval personnel who are permanently based at sea, the 194,000 marines and the 400,000 men of the Rapid Deployment Force. Whilst medium-size naval powers like Britain and France cannot be compared with the USA, they have retained a string of island colonies scattered across the oceans of the world. These provide staging points for their fleets, which could usefully complement one another in time of war. Britain has 26,000 troops based outside the NATO zone; France has 10,000 (see Table I).

The Socialist community's military presence outside the frontiers of the Warsaw Pact is much more varied. That presence includes the massive troop concentrations that are the classic symptoms of armies of occupation (leaving aside the issue of political justification). The Soviets have 75,000 troops in Mongolia and a further 100,000 in Afghanistan; there are 170,000 Vietnamese troops in Cambodia and 45,000 in Laos. Here, we are talking about land-based forces in countries bordering on the powers concerned. From a purely military point of view, these territories represent only a marginal extension of Soviet expeditionary capabilities. These interventions were not in fact motivated by expansionist ambitions. There are also 21,800 Soviet troops and 3,310 East Germans in a score or so of Third World countries, but their mission is very different. They are advisers, technicians and instructors and their primary task is to train local armies in the use of Soviet equipment.

The Cuban interventions in Angola and Ethiopia were on a very different scale. In both cases, one Third World country gave aid to another in order to protect a Socialist revolution which was threatened by foreign intervention. But what struck observers most was the rapidity and efficiency of the airlifts organised by the USSR and the excellent Soviet–Cuban coordination which ensured rapid and decisive victories. In the case of Angola, Cuba's decision to respond to the MPLA's call for aid on 5 November 1975 came twelve days after the South African intervention. It led to a decisive victory in late November and to the complete defeat of the FNLA and UNITA in mid-January 1976. At the end of January, the South African forces decided to pull out. In Ethiopia, the Ogaden was reconquered only a month after the start of the counter-offensive. In both cases, the Cuban forces were relatively small and totalled only 20,000 men, or barely a division.[25] The resources used by the Soviet Union were, however, impressive. The Red Army's airborne capacity was not exactly unknown; in 1968, a whole division was moved into Prague overnight and every strategic bridge in the country was occupied within six hours. During the 1973 Arab–Israeli war huge quantities of supplies were flown in in record time. All these operations took place on the periphery of Soviet territory and there was no need for refuelling. In the case of both Angola and Ethiopia the distances involved meant that refuelling halts were inevitable and authorization to fly over a number of countries had to be obtained. This was the first long-range intervention made by the Socialist camp.

The astonishing development of Soviet air transport can largely be explained in terms of the virtual disappearance of other modes of transport (rail, road and ship). Aircraft are often the only means of ensuring communications in all weathers, especially in Siberia.[26] The operational importance of this axiom has not escaped the Kremlin; the airborne force soon became an auxiliary command and then a strategic command.

Although Soviet naval capabilities have definitely increased since 1960, it is difficult to accept NATO's claims that it has moved from coastal defence to control of the seas. Naval supremacy is still mainly an American monopoly and the Soviets have yet to show any desire to challenge that monopoly. Their fleet is still primarily an anti-ship force designed to prevent the USA controlling the seas rather than to challenge it directly.

In this context, access to port facilities has not been a determining factor in Soviet Third World policy. On three separate occasions, the Red Army has lost important bases which would otherwise have allowed the fleet to be refuelled in the Mediterranean. After the break with Yugoslavia in 1948 it lost access to Cattaro, and the break with Albania in 1966 cost it other facilities. Finally, Egypt's defection in 1971 denied it access to Alexandria. A similar reversal occurred in the Indian Ocean in 1977, when the Soviet Union lost access to the Berbera base in Somalia. The ease with which Third World countries have expelled their Soviet advisers and changed sides without a shot being fired indicates the fragility of the 'extension of Socialism'. These events ought to make those who still claim that once the Soviets set foot in a country they are there for ever think again. History teaches us that poor countries find it much easier to break off their links with the Kremlin than to repay loans from the West. In that sense, the IMF is a much more efficient and discrete policeman.

Unlike the USSR, the Americans have made their forward base system a major priority and have used the pretext of ensuring the survival of the rest of the world to set up bases on the Warsaw Pact's doorstep. They have in fact assumed the right to open fire at point blank range. This, combined with the doctrine of containment, means that, for the Soviets, strategic operations begin at the border. For Moscow, any increase in the Soviet Union's ability to make long-range interventions means increased room for manoeuvre. For Washington, it is an intolerable challenge. All the symptoms of this neurosis can be seen in a single phrase chosen at random from the prolific literature of Atlanticism: 'NATO does not have a great enough numerical *advantage* to ensure a satisfactory *balance* of naval power.'[27]

Domination or influence?

Luns is simply expressing the convictions of his Western colleagues when, in the midst of all this desolation, he finds at least a crumb of consolation in the fact that 'The Communist regimes have lost both their monolithic structure and their ideological and political appeal because they have failed on every count, except in terms of military prowess.'[28] According to the former Secretary General, the USSR's so-called failure condemns it to being a one dimensional power. In terms of international relations, this leaves little room for the motivations of Third World countries which turn to the Soviet Union for aid; no political ideal is involved and all they can import is destabilization. This simplistic vision of the rules governing East–West relations simply confuses the issue. The model is discredited and only the threat remains.

The arms trade with the countries of the South is of course much more important to the USSR than it is to the West, but its absolute value is less important than its relative effect on the balance of trade. Between 1979 and 1983, the Third World absorbed 70 per cent of all the Soviet Union's exports of heavy armaments, 50 per cent of US exports and up to 80 or 90 per cent of French and Italian exports. NATO countries have always sold more weapons to more countries than Warsaw Pact countries, but this sector represents only 3 per cent of their total foreign trade; arms account for 10 per cent of Soviet exports.[29] This structural difference is becoming more marked, and half of all Soviet exports to the Third World now consist of arms. The change has been decisive, but it would be inaccurate to claim that it represents a complete militarization of trade with the Third World.

The change has more to do with admiration for Soviet weaponry than with admiration for the USSR itself. Soviet weapons are easy to use and maintain and stand up well to the harsh combat conditions found in most poor countries. They are also cheap and can therefore be bought in larger quantities than the more sophisticated and more fragile weapons produced in the West. Finally, they tend to be supplied more rapidly. Conflicts in the Middle East have consistently shown that their operational performance is poorer than that of American or European arms, but many governments are less interested in quality than in maintaining large armies at low cost and without excessive technological dependence on outside forces. Their nationalist and anti-imperialist aspirations are more important than their commitment to the Socialist ideal. The Soviet Union and the USA have a similar balance of trade with the Third World, but only twenty-six countries trade with the Soviet Union, whereas seventy-three trade with the USA.

Although the arms trade helps to improve profitability and provides the hard currency which the Soviet Union needs so badly, this highly specific form of aid cannot in itself change the basic nature of the regimes to which it goes. Sukarno's Indonesia, Nasser's Egypt and Indira Gandhi's India all had highly developed public sectors, but they were still basically capitalist countries.

Even Third World countries which have political and military links with the Soviet Union trade more with the West than with the USSR. Ethiopia and Angola are classic examples of this paradox. In 1981, only 9.8 per cent of all Angola's imports came from the USSR; 56.6 per cent came from Western Europe and a further 11.1 per cent came from South Africa.[30] 27 per cent of Ethiopia's imports that year came from the USSR, whereas 54 per cent of its foreign trade was with the US and EEC countries.[31]

It is of course true that the USSR is trying to promote its interests throughout the world and that it therefore comes into conflict with the US and its allies, but it is far from true that it takes control of all the countries with which it establishes favourable relations. This is why many observers argue that the Soviet Union's sphere of effective dominance is restricted to Eastern Europe. The integration of the political and the military indicates that the international division of labour rests upon a very narrow economic base. The USSR's primary objective is the maintenance of the status quo with NATO and it tends therefore to react to any major opposition by breaking off relations or, in extreme cases, by military intervention. On the other hand, it would be difficult for an objective observer to describe those Third World countries in which the Soviet Union has exploited situations it did not create as constituting a sphere of influence. Alliances have been reversed, and the Soviet Union has been unable to influence events to any great extent. The fact that it expanded its sphere of influence in Africa and Asia substantially during the seventies does not in itself alter that fact. On the other hand, the challenges posed by Poland and Rumania may have revealed that its sphere of influence is increasingly fragile, but they have not breached it to any great extent.

Two other processes are also at work. One is gradual and goes by stages, but the other has been surprisingly rapid. Most European Communist Parties have, to varying degrees, distanced themselves from the Soviet Union and have left its 'sphere of domination' but not its 'sphere of influence'. Afghanistan, which was for a long time within the Soviet sphere of influence, has been dragged by force into its sphere of domination.

The Canadian Kremlinologist Jacques Levesque notes that, in economic terms, 'Local revolutions have extended Socialism beyond the borders of the Soviet Union, but they have not helped it to recover from its economic inferiority. On the contrary, the China of the fifties, Vietnam, Cuba, Angola and Ethiopia have all been economic burdens for the Soviet Union. In other areas of the Third World, the Soviet Union paid dearly for the extension of its influence in the fifties and sixties. Since the fall of Khrushchev, Soviet leaders have tried to make trade with the Third World more profitable, and have been criticised by their partners for doing so, but they have not caught up with the West to any significant extent.' He concludes that, 'Until now, the extension of Socialism beyond the frontiers of the Soviet Union has resulted primarily but not exclusively in political and strategic gains. . . In that sense, the spread of communism. . . does help to consolidate and legitimize Soviet power.'[32]

The fantasies of anti-communism

The anti-Soviet discourse of NATO is both logical and understandable coming from an organization of states which, in both ideological and military terms, is hostile to both the USSR and to Communism in general. The fact that NATO's one-sided arguments are being taken up by many intellectuals and by most of the Western media is a sign of the times. Some of their arguments look more like a frenzied crusade against the forces of evil rather than a careful and objective attempt to analyse the complex mechanisms that govern the workings of any society. In France, this tendency is represented by best-selling authors like Glucksmann, Morin, Ellenstein, Castoriadis, Léy, Besançon and, to a lesser extent, Hélène d'Encausse. The amazing thing is that this crude warmongering discourse enjoys such popularity and is accepted by people of such widely differing views. More balanced and detailed analyses by Kremlinologists and observers of East–West relations like Kennan, Bialer, Hough, Lavigne, Julien and Levesque receive much less attention and are blithely ignored by the popular ideologues. There is something alarming about the mass interest whipped up by these apocalyptic prophets and their oversimplified picture of the Soviet threat, especially when more open-minded people are dismayed by the uniform greyness of the terms in which the inextricable complexity of the world is described. Novices are confused or disappointed by any analysis of world diplomacy or technology that does not read like an adventure novel or a political pamphlet. But when analyses are couched in those terms, objectivity flies out of the window.

Anti-Sovietism is rather like the Loch Ness monster. From time to time it reappears in the distance, refreshed after a few years' sleep. But it never dies because it is the USSR itself that makes its heart beat. Anti-Sovietism sounds the death knell for reasoned debate and for any rational debate and marks the beginning of an emotional campaign. Unfortunately, it takes hindsight to realize how much emotional intensity and irrationality is involved. On the other hand, these outbursts of irrepressible emotion allow the authorities to take concrete decisions, and the absurdity of their long-term implications is equalled only by the haste with which they were taken.

The incident involving the South Korean Boeing may well have revealed the paranoia and tactlessness of the Soviet military, but it certainly cannot be interpreted as evidence of any increased operational capability or of expansionist ambitions on the part of the Soviet Union. But it had a considerable impact on the thinking of the US Congress, which had until then been reluctant to vote the exorbitant military credits demanded by the Reagan administration. Yet again, an emotional response confused the real issues.

A detailed examination of the US defence budget reveals that it has less to do with any real increase in the military capabilities of the USSR than with the short-term needs of the US itself. The Soviet budget has been rising steadily since the fifties, whereas the growth of the US budget has been characterized by the series of leaps reflecting the wars in Korea and Vietnam. This has not, of course, prevented the US from using the USSR as a pretext. In 1960, Kennedy used the terrifying prospect of a 'missile gap' to justify his huge nuclear programme. Although most commentators now accept that the 'gap' was purely imaginary, it is still part of NATO's arsenal of arguments. The same argument has successfully been used to prove that Europe is completely defenceless against the Soviet Union's SS20s. Reagan's attempt to use the 'window of vulnerability' argument to make Congress swallow the bitter pill of the Ballistic Missile Defence programme was less successful, but experts at the Laurence Livermore research centre in California are already preparing dossiers on a worrying 'beam gap' that is expected to appear in the 1990s.

Anything that comes from the East is portrayed in negative terms. Vices are turned into virtues and vice versa. The USSR is only a great economic power because it wants to improve its army and export its revolution. If its economy stagnates, it will be tempted to invade the West in order to acquire our technology. Trade with the Soviet Union is dangerous as it is tantamount to feeding an enemy. If the Soviet Union achieves self-sufficiency, it will become even more dangerous and nothing will stop its growth. The development of the Soviet threat means that we have to have arms control, but as soon as an agreement is reached it becomes a status quo which can only work to the advantage of the USSR. Its leaders are old and have established a gerontocracy which reflects the fossilization and stagnation of their system. They are ready to do anything. If—and everything suggests that this is in fact the case—a younger generation emerges and takes over from the old men, it will consist of Young Turks who will do anything to make their presence felt on the international scene, regardless of the consequences for the existing balance of power.

Propaganda techniques in fact have very little to do with the subject under discussion. The subject under discussion simply provides them with something to denounce and pretexts for polemics. Those who attack the Soviet Union most savagely are often those who know least about it.

Balanced counter-arguments have to rely upon a much higher degree of documentation. But the outcome of any debate with those who simultaneously hold state power, have the power that only money can give and control the media is a foregone conclusion. It is like the battle between David and Goliath. But this time, David has no sling.

NOTES

1. W.W. Rostow, *Les Etapes de la croissance économique; un manifeste non-communiste,* (Paris: Seuil, 1963).
2. J. Tinbergen, *Convergence of Economic Systems in East and West,* (Rotterdam, 1965).
3. P.A. Sorokin, *Russia and the United States,* (London: Stevens, 1950).
4. J.K. Galbraith, *The New Industrial State,* (London, 1967).
5. H. Marcuse, *One Dimensional Man,* (London: RKP, 1964).
6. In C. Zorgbibe, 'Espoir et illusion d'un rapprochement des structures économiques et politiques', *Le Monde diplomatique,* August 1975, p. 10.
7. Service de l'information de l'OTAN, *L'OTAN et le Pacte de Varsovie; Comparaison des forces en présence,* (Brussels, 1964), p. 3.
8. *Ibid.,* p. 1.
9. *Ibid.,* p. 34.
10. Stockholm International Peace Research Institute, *World Armaments and Disarmament: SIPRI Yearbook 1984,* (London, 1984), pp. 24, 27. The figures are all taken from the same source.
11. For a more detailed study see Xavier Zeebroek, *La Puissance militaire soviétque,* Groupe de Recherche et d'Information sur la Paix (GRIP), *Dossier Notes et Documents,* No. 71, (Brussels, 1984), Part 1.
12. *Course aux armements, contrôle des armements,* (French translation of *SIPRI 1983 Pocket Yearbook*); GRIP, *Gyroscope,* Summer–Autumn 1983, pp. 80–81.
13. For a more detailed study see Xavier Zeebroek, 'Liban, Qui a peur des armes soviétiques?' *Gyroscope,* Winter 1982-1983.
14. France and England had 3,267 planes between them, as opposed to the Third Reich's 3,959. On paper, the Allies in fact had the advantage in terms of fighters (1,420 against 1,264), but unfortunately only 690 fighters and 1,120 other aircraft were actually in France in June 1940. In terms of numbers of tanks, Hitler was at an even greater disadvantage in June 1940 he had only 2,574 tanks, as opposed to the Allies' 4,100. No German tank weighed more than 20 tons; the Allies had 330 of that weight. For further details see J.Sapir, 'Comment apprécier la menace soviétique?' in *Eviter la Guerre* (collective), (Paris: Maspero, 1983), pp. 52-53.
15. 'Expansion de la puissance militaire soviétique', *Nouvelles Atlantiques,* No. 1372, 10 December 1981, Annexe A, p. 1. (Press release from North Atlantic Military Committee.)
16. *Ibid.,* p. 2.
17. *Ibid.,* p. 1.
18. J.M.A.H. Luns, 'Un Regard d'adieu sur l'OTAN', *Revue de l'OTAN,* (Brussels, April 1984), p. 2.
19. *Ibid.*
20. For a more detailed study see D.M. Gormley, 'The Direction and Pace of Soviet Force Projection Capabilities', *Survival,* (London: IISS, November–December 1982), pp. 266-276.
21. *L'OTAN et le Pacte de Varsovie,* p. 18.

22. J. Labayle-Couhat, *Flottes de combat 1983*, (Paris), pp. xxiv, xxv.
23. 'Bombardiers nucléaires soviétiques déployés au Viet-nam', *La Wallonie*, 2 March, 1984.
24. R. Leger Sivard, *World Military and Social Expenditures 1983*, (Washington D.C.), pp. 8-9. Cf. Tables I and II.
25. As will be seen from Table I, there are now 34,550 Cubans based abroad, most of them in Africa.
26. Cf. S.I. Sikorsky, 'Make it Simple. . . Make it Work', *Air Force Magazine*, (Washington D.C., March 1984), pp. 92–95.
27. *L'OTAN et le Pacte de Varsovie*, p. 5.
28. Luns, 'Un Regard d'adieu', p. 5.
29. *SIPRI Yearbook 1984*, p. 177.
30. F. Gèze, A. Valladaö and Y. Lacoste, (eds.), *L'Etat du monde. Annuaire économique et géopolitique mondial*, (Paris: Maspero 1982), p. 320.
31. *Ibid.*, p. 262.
32. J. Levesque, *L'URSS et sa politique internationale de 1917 à nos jours*, (Paris: Armand Colin, 1980), pp. 328-329.

Translated by David Macey

FROM THE WRETCHED OF THE EARTH TO THE DEFENCE OF THE WEST: AN ESSAY ON LEFT DISENCHANTMENT IN FRANCE

Jean-Pierre Garnier & Roland Lew

'There is no such thing as imperialism. There never has been. . . The only places where I have come across it are the Eastern bloc countries and the totalitarian countries of the Third World.' This ironic description of one of the major features of the 'cultural revolution', brought about by the French intelligentsia in the seventies, comes from the authors of a study of audio-visual media in the age of transnational capitalism: 'A complacently ignorant Third Worldism has given way to a convinced Westernism which is steeped in rhetoric.'[1] And it is indeed a striking contrast.

Just over a decade ago, the French Left was full of enthusiasm about the Third World. Progressive intellectuals believed that the Third World's struggle against imperialism and neo-colonialism was a world-wide struggle and that its liberation would signal the world revolution. The 'proletarian nations' which had for so long been excluded from a history that went against them, had now entered history in spectacular fashion and taken the torch from the 'bourgeoisified' working classes of the industrialized world, from classes which had been seduced by the delights of 'consumer society' and betrayed their mission of emancipation.

According to the self-styled Marxist theoreticians of the Latin Quarter, the epicentre of political revolution had shifted from Europe to the 'storm zone' and it would not be long before a tidal wave would flood the Old World and sweep away a system of exploitation which had had its day. Major feats of arms appeared to justify this prophetic messianism: Dien Bien Phu, the 1968 Tet offensive in Vietnam, the triumphal entry of the *barbudos* of the Sierra Maestra into Havana. . . An incandescently lyrical and militant literature set alight the imagination of French academics and journalists and artists of the French Left. The writings of Frantz Fanon, Che Guevara and Mao Tse Tung were sparks starting prairie fires in the small world of Parisian publishing and journalism; Sartre's preface to *The Wretched of the Earth* is a typical example.

The wind blowing across the decadent capitalist West was from neither the East nor the West; it came in gusts from the South, from the lands of the wretched and starving 'periphery', from the vast rebel camp that was besieging the citadels of the 'centre' and the final ramparts of 'the existing order of things'. The destruction of that order would soon be a reality.

299

But the *Internationale* did not unite the human race. The vast majority of the population of the Third World still lives in misery and is still oppressed. What has changed is the 'world view' of those who once thought that the Third World was a redeemer which could save not only itself but the whole of mankind. The fraternal warmth and exaltation of the past has given way to scorn, hostility and even hatred; at best to indifference. Famines and scarcity rage in Africa, Asia and Latin America, but the only response in the West is a fatalistic sort of pity. The exactions of corrupt and repressive governments trying to maintain order in the various 'backyards' of the 'free world' no longer provoke the individual protests and the mass mobilizations of the sixties; nor does our own government's support for their discredited elites. As for resistance and rebellion on the part of the victims, they are now seen as minor skirmishes in the battle between East and West; as side effects of the sinister manoeuvres of the Soviet 'Empire of Evil'. 'Totalitarianism' is equated with 'communism' and 'North–South' struggles, and struggles between dominators and dominated in specific countries, are accordingly seen simply as a projection of East–West relations. With very few exceptions, the leaders and ideologues of the French Left, far from rejecting both 'liberal' capitalism and state capitalism (which they mistakenly equate with 'actually existing socialism'), have resolutely taken sides. They are, that is, on the side of the West which, for the purposes of the moment, they refer to as 'Democracy'. From now on, 'Democracy' is the model for the Third World. As one of the new crusaders who has forsaken his *gauchisme* and rallied to capitalism puts it: 'There is nothing beyond democracy. If the peoples of the Third World are to become themselves, they must become more Western.'[2]

How are we to interpret the process whereby most of the French Left has moved from 'blind enthusiasm to systematic denigration'?[3] We could of course follow the usual pattern and justify their change of heart in terms of the post-victory vicissitudes of the revolutionary process. How could anyone not be disappointed, sickened or disgusted with the retreats made by the regimes that emerged from the liberation struggles? Then we could listen to the self criticisms of an intelligentsia which allowed itself to be blinded and which lived in a dream rather than in the real world. And we could end by joining in the celebrations as the same intelligentsia congratulates itself on its decision to have done with 'mobilizing myths' and 'mystifying ideologies'. Having got over its illusions and its infantile dependency on ideology, the intelligentsia is now ready to take a 'new look' at the real world and its 'complexity'. Its watchword is now 'lucidity'.

There is, however, another way of analysing why yesterday's Third Worldists decided to set off on a new crusade, this time beneath the banners of the capitalist West. We can, that is, *relate their ideological trajectory to the political and social trajectory of the social group to which they belong.* That group has abandoned the fight for socialism in defence of a neo-conservatism decked out in all the trappings of 'modernity'. Third Worldism was a phenomenon found throughout the Western world, but it was at its most extreme in France, as is the unrestrained Westernism which has succeeded it. France is exemplary in that the features of similar movements in other advanced capitalist countries can be found there in almost caricatural form. But 'French-style' Third Worldism is also exemplary in that it is highly specific. France differs from other advanced countries in that, for a time, progressive opinion put revolution on the agenda once more, both as a political demand and as an immediate practical demand. We therefore have to ask two questions. What was being projected in a desire for 'revolution' that was both aroused and satisfied by Third Worldism? And which social group was projecting itself in that 'desire for revolution'?

We may well live in an age of disenchantment, but what was it that enchanted people in the heyday of radical Third Worldism? Who fell under the spell? Of course hopes have been frustrated. But which hopes? And whose hopes? It is common knowledge that any discourse on society has something to do with the position one occupies in society, even if we often feign ignorance of the fact. The theoretical or practical positions we take are not entirely unrelated to the positions we occupy in the social field. Like any other ideological production, the discourse of Third Worldism has, then, to be related not only to the social reality it constituted as an object, but also to its *social subject*. If, in other words, we want to understand the underlying reasons why the French intelligentsia converted to Third Worldism and then converted back to Westernism, we have to look at what was happening in the centre and especially in France itself, rather than at what was happening on the periphery.

1. Origins of the problematic
An Uncomfortable Encounter

The 'Third World', which has been known by a variety of names at various times, has always been seen through a blurred and shifting image, if not an imagery. Without going back to the Ark, it is obvious that East–West relations have for centuries been hampered by misunderstandings, misconceptions and even non-perceptions. 'The East', a generic term meaning 'non-Western', usually referred to the Islamic world, although the focus sometimes shifted to China or India. For the pre-capitalist West it was an object of fear and a realm of imaginary demons. Sometimes, however, it did become a more edifying model, as when the kings and emperors of the enlightenment began to take lessons from Asian despotism and the wisdom of the sages.[4] Islam took a somewhat disdainful view of the West, but in fact knew very little about it.[5] The relationship between the two was never easy and was often based upon mutual suspicion, if not hatred. Even those who took a more kindly view knew little about the distant countries they tried to describe.

Whatever East-West relations may have meant in the past, for 'the conscious and systematic Eurocentrism of the nineteenth century. . . the only conceivable meaning of universality was the wholesale adoption of the European model'.[6]

The nineteenth-century revolutionary tradition in the West was not, however, entirely unambiguous when it came to the East, a term which now applied to those vast areas of the world which were threatened by a vigorous process of colonization. In its attempts to come to terms with the colonial question, the Second Socialist International (1889) had to reconcile its universalist discourse and its Eurocentric tendencies, not to mention the colonialist tendencies of a considerable number of its members, base and leadership alike.

The long-awaited marriage between the movement for social liberation and the peoples who wanted liberation from the colonial yoke did not take place, either theoretically or practically. In practical terms, there was not sufficient mass action on the part of the colonized, and in conceptual terms, the European socialist movement was simply unable to comprehend the vast size of the non-Western world.

Prior to the establishment of the Third International in 1919, meetings between East and West usually took the form of violent imperialist expansion. The values and specificities of the colonial and semi-colonial world were brutally suppressed and subordinated to the white man's imperatives, which were themselves governed by the demands of an expanding capitalism.

The intrusion of modern colonialism was a new challenge and a powerful stimulus to change in the non-Western world. The balance of power was, however, in the West's favour—to an extent which has probably never been equalled, either before or since—and it is that which explains the colonizers' ability to impose their will and the absence of any rapid response, with the possible exception of Japan.

For a long time, neither colonists nor progressive militants, however well intentioned, had anyone to force them to modify their views of the colonized or their behaviour towards them. Indeed, their views were reinforced by the fact that the notion of the white man's superiority was actually shared by old civilizations like China which had once been convinced of their *own* superiority. The West was not seen simply as a cruel and unwanted master, but also as a fascinating pedagogue.

It was only with the Third International that relations between East and West took on a more positive look. The International inherited an actively anti-colonial minority trend from its predecessor. At its second congress in 1920, it did devote a lot of time to discussing the problems of the East and the colonial countries and readily agreed to give the anti-colonial struggle a major role in its revolutionary strategy. A definite majority, however, led by Lenin—argued that the major issue was the revolution in the West and rejected the Indian Communist Roy's thesis that the heartlands of the world revolution now lay in the colonial sphere.

The Russian Revolution soon had repercussions in the East. The East responded to the anti-colonial call that came from the West, particularly in so far as those intellectuals who wanted to modernize their societies saw the Russian Revolution as a simultaneous acceptance and rejection of the West. The victory of Bolshevism seemed to prove that it was possible to take the best that the West had to offer and turn against it; its 'best' being a fraternal call to prepare for world revolution and break with the egotistical interests which had previously dominated East–West relations.

In the various countries of the Third World, a number of men and women, most of them intellectuals, were carried away by an intoxicating hope. They dreamed of nothing less than a merging of civilizations in which the anti-imperialist West and the insurgent East would be on equal footing, of an era in which the people would gain their social and national liberation, in which their creative potential would at last be unleashed. Initially, their vision found its incarnation in Russia, the natural mediator between East and West. The intellectual and anti-imperialist upsurge of the May 4 Movement in China was a powerful expression of this ethos. The country's modernist intellectuals and the leaders who launched the May 4 Movement—at once a patriotic movement and China's first cultural revolution—moved rapidly from liberalism to Bolshevism. For them, Bolshevism was the final proof that a backward country could rebel against its backwardness ('the weight of the feudal past') without necessarily falling prey to the appetites of the imperialists.

The marriage between East and West was not a success. There were to be many disappointments, but there were also some positive gains. The intellectuals had good reason to be disillusioned: the meanders of Soviet policy, which was rapidly dominated by Stalinism, left little room for dreams about the merging of civilizations. It was more a question of manipulating the struggles of the East. In China, the intellectuals who had been radicalized by the May 4 Movement thought that their country was about to undergo a renaissance and were at the same time looking for a road to communism. But before long they had to begin a painful apprenticeship in realism and become accustomed to manoeuvres between great and small powers, to the ruses of militant struggle and to the tortuous tactics of class warfare.

Despite all these misunderstandings, Bolshevism did, even in its Stalinist form, make a decisive contribution. It helped to introduce a new practice of political struggle into what had yet to become known as the Third World, and that was much more important than grandiose theories about the merging of civilizations and the advent of world socialism. It made it possible to combine the anti-imperialist struggle with avant-garde practices. The terms are so familiar and so hackneyed that it is easy to forget how novel they once were and to forget that they lie at the very heart of radical Third Worldism. To take the example of China, which played such an important role in the emergence of anti-imperialism and then Third Worldism: once the universalist fever of 1919 had died down, the radicalized intellectuals became Party militants and learned to harness the anti-imperialist potential of the masses. There were of course many reversals, culminating in the counter-revolution of 1927, a disaster for which their Soviet mentor was certainly largely responsible, but a *small minority* of activists did learn to mobilize the *broad masses.* That was the vital discovery which was to inform the triumphant Third Worldism of the fifties and sixties. The disinherited masses of the Third World had to be mobilized and could be mobilized, provided that the impetus came from an organized centre, provided that the avant-garde was organized as a party that could stir up the masses. The formulae are now so familiar that it is difficult to remember how novel they once were.

The disinherited masses can and must be mobilized. Nothing could have been less obvious than this conception—the result of a rapid but painful process of maturation on the part of the intellectuals of the crisis-ridden colonial and semi-colonial countries. Nothing could have been more unexpected or more dangerous than this sudden appeal to the broad masses. The threat must indeed have been serious for the intellectuals to contemplate calling for a popular armed uprising—a process which is by definition difficult to control. That they did so was in a sense an admission of defeat rather than a positive decision. The 'normal' forces of modernization were conspicuous by their absence from the scene. The appeal to the people was addressed to the poorest and most populous sectors. It was even addressed to women, to a social category that was 'less than nothing' rather than 'half of heaven' in a country like China. It was not addressed to modernist social forces: the bourgeoisie and the proletariat were either simply not there or too embryonic and too irresolute to transform society and respond to the imperialist threat.

Ever since its origins in 1927, Maoism has always meant the mobilization and utilization of millions of impoverished peasants by a small number of militants, most of them from the towns or at least educated in the towns. Beggars who were simply oppressed rather than in revolt were transformed into active revolutionaries because they were acted upon, and they acted in the name of a cause which, the agrarian question aside, escaped them.

The essential elements of the Third World problematic thus emerged long before the Second World War. On the one hand, Stalinism led to serious errors and to the most serious defeats ever inflicted upon the proletariat. On the other hand, the huge conglomerate of countries which came to be known as the Third World were subjected to immense social strains which prevented them from being stabilized even when there was no solution to the crises affecting them. The ravages of Stalinism were powerless to hold back social upheavals which did in some cases lead to great revolutions, like the Chinese Revolution of 1946–49. Moreover, the weight of backwardness and the premature decay of the local bourgeoisie allowed—or forced—the small urban petty bourgeoisie to lead the national struggle.

The difficulties of the anti-colonial struggle thus created the conditions, which were admittedly highly specific, that allowed the petty bourgeoisie and especially its urban fraction to take historical revenge. It was able to lead the struggle rather than remain subordinate to the bourgeoisie and the proletariat, which were both larger and more important in terms of the industrial process. The weakness of the proletariat and the bourgeoisie, combined with the inertia of the peasantry, which was interrupted only by sporadic revolts, gave the radicalized petty bourgeoisie an unhoped-for historical opportunity. It also provided an effective, if unexpected, solution to what looked like a social impasse.

The radicalized intelligentsia, a group representing a tiny fragment of the nation, underwent a metamorphosis. Traditionally, the intellectuals had been scribes or scholars who were dependent on a traditional centre of power—or in the case of the mandarins of China, part of the ruling class of the past—and they now became modern intellectuals, often faced with a loss of class status and almost always threatened with losing their privileged relationship with power (and wealth). As a group they were both aware of the general social crisis and alert to the fact that they were in the uncertain position of being rejected both by those who traditionally held power and by the colonial authorities. They were in a transitional position, midway between their old and new roles, but they were also conscious of the effects that stagnation was having on their countries. They increasingly realized that there was no obvious solution and that they could not function as an organic group of intellectuals simply because no new and dynamic class was emerging. In a very short space of time they were forced to explore new practices and intellectual conceptions (just think of the last years of the nineteenth century or the first years of the twentieth in China, Vietnam or Latin America) and began to be auto-nomously active in a way that would have been inconceivable in the West. The process culminated in the emergence of a revolutionary avant-garde party, a party of militant intellectuals with a popular social base. By the twenties and thirties, the major components of Third Worldism had already appeared in the Third World itself; on the one hand, the Party militant, who was often an intellectual who feared for the future, on the other, a vague entity known as 'the people' rather than differentiated classes. And between the two, the upheavals of a society in crisis.

Radical Third Worldism in the Third World

The vogue for Third Worldism is of course a post-war phenomenon, as is the term itself. The term's popularity might seem surprising, given its many and vague connotations. It is in fact more current in the West than in other parts of the world, where terms such as 'the movement of non-aligned countries' and 'the tricontinental movement' tend to be used instead. The term 'the Third World' was coined by the economist Alfred Sauvy in an article which appeared in 1952. It referred both to a sort of worldwide third estate which was nothing and wanted to be something[7] and to a Third World which was neither capitalist nor socialist. Some countries within the Third World, however, either already belonged to a markedly Stalinist socialist camp or were about to join it; others were undeniably capitalist. Although the concept of the Third World was vague and encompassed a variety of themes and referred to a number of very different national realities, it did also refer to a key idea and to a force which was so powerful that the volcanic metaphors often used to describe it are not entirely without foundation. The process of national and anti-colonial liberation meant both a world in eruption and its irruption on to the world scene.

It is the very extent of the phenomenon that explains the success of a qualifier which in fact qualified very little indeed. The word does, however, accurately pinpoint an essential aspect of the emerging ideology of Third Worldism, namely the notion of a proletarian nation or even a proletarian continent. The disinherited majority was identified with the nation itself and the nation became synonymous with the unity of the insurgent people. The Third World struggle was seen as the key to all the problems facing the nations and continents which had rebelled against colonialism. At the same time, an inverted missionary spirit meant that it would also be seen as the solution to the problems of mankind as a whole.[8]

The proletarian nation took the place of the proletariat in Marx's theory; it was both its own liberator and the liberator of the entire human race. The messianic universalism of the West was still there, but the direction of the flow had been reversed. As Fanon put it in 1961, 'The Third World today faces Europe like a colossal mass whose aim should be to try to resolve the problems to which Europe has not been able to find the answers.'[9] His book ends with an exhortation: 'For Europe, for ourselves and for humanity, comrades, we must turn over a new leaf, we must work out new concepts, and try to set afoot a new man.'[10]

The way in which the problematic was identified and displaced did much to popularize a term which was in itself vague. The vagueness of the concept had the further advantage of concealing the identity of the small group that promoted this populism. For Third Worldism is also a phenomenon with a very localized base. The term refers to the convergence of a broad and irresistible movement for national liberation and a social force with a very narrow base. The radicalized intelligentsia, that is, used and harnessed the broad movement. The Bolshevik heritage was too remote from the realities of the Third World to be used as it stood and was therefore adapted in a variety of ways to suit a very broad mobilization which often ignored class barriers. By doing so, the intelligentsia could mobilize considerable social forces without being subordinated to them. The Leninist heritage had to be modified because the rapid process of Stalinization had destroyed Bolshevism's last vestiges of internationalism and had subordinated it to the national interests of Russia and its new rulers.

The changes can also be explained in terms of the difficulty of applying the concept of class struggle in developing countries where classes were ill-defined and where neither enemies nor allies could easily be fitted into the 'orthodox' nomenclature. Matters were further complicated by the fact that the driving force was an avant-garde party which preached a populism that did little to clarify the precise basis on which the battle was being fought. The slowness with which new classes matured encouraged the survival of older social relations, especially amongst the peasantry, and the vitality of traditional forms of communal solidarity made it possible, if not essential, to use the concept of 'the people' as an overall structure rather than that of class.

Third Worldist populism—according to which the only groups which are not part of the people are the local *compradores* and the direct agents of colonialism—was not the artificial creation of a group that was so small that it had to work in concealment. On the contrary, Third Worldism was a real solution to real problems (a low level of class differentiation, amongst other things) and used real materials: the nationalist and anti-imperialist radicalization of broad sections of the nation. The radicalization was often uncontrolled and had neither a clear sense of direction nor a clear content; the massive upsurge required a unitary structure capable of replacing ineffective structures (traditional elites, state or dynastic power). In some countries, the intelligentsia was obviously destined to lead the movement, as in China, where the mandarin intellectuals had formed a ruling elite for centuries. But even in countries where that was not the case, the concrete experience of two or three generations pointed to the urgent need for a new solution. It also suggested where that solution might be found. The path that had been cleared with such difficulty had to be one that the intelligentsia could take; it had to be adapted to its needs.

The very scale of Third Worldism and the huge range of experiments that derived from the same matrix prove that the solution was neither artificial nor simply a flash in the pan. But the complexity of Third Worldism and the variety of forms it took in practice also prove that the general concept of the Third World was not adequate to the variety of terrain in which it had to be applied. Nor should it be forgotten that the original meaning of the term—a third world which is neither capitalist nor socialist —is illegitimate.

Even so, both the 'non-aligned movement' and the 'tricontinental movement' of the fifties did express a definite desire to find a third way. It took a variety of forms, ranging from a search for an alternative to both capitalism and communism to an attempt to find a specific revolutionary path equidistant from both Soviet Russia and Maoist China.

In practice, Third Worldism has been identified with every possible variety of socialism and capitalism. It is true that the very nature of the mobilization and the difficulties of the struggle often forced it to take radical, or apparently radical, forms which did lead to social upheavals (China, Vietnam). It also led to more or less militant forms of anti-imperialism (Nasser's Egypt, Algeria). The former identified with 'real socialism' and the latter with a real state capitalism that evolved sooner or later into private capitalism. But there was no question of a third way. The near caricature of Stalinism that China exhibited at the time of the Bandung Conference[11] or after the long 'interlude' of Maoism; Cuba's support for the Soviet Union in 1968 and, conversely, the pro-Western position of certain Third World countries, all point to the impossibility of locating the Third World in any specific place and to the impossibility of any coherent discourse or any practical solidarity between its countries.

It is the most radical and dynamic forms of Third Worldism that reveal its component elements and its internal chemistry most clearly; and which did most to feed the fervour of Third Worldism in the West. If we restrict the argument to those forms, a number of features emerge, both during the years of struggle and after the victory.

The first and the most fascinating feature is the very strength of the movement. Ludicrous as it may seem in terms of our traditions, the mobilization of the broad masses by a small number of militants was effective. A few thousand radicalized intellectuals did mobilize millions of individuals. Radical Third Worldism combined a certain kind of class struggle (anti-feudalism, anti-capitalism) with the millenarian aspirations of the whole people.

The emergence of a leading bloc is equally striking. A group of radical intellectuals which was too small to assume all the functions of leadership on its own incorporated certain sections of the population. The intellectuals themselves underwent a major transformation and became militant cadres who rejected the temptation to become critical or universalist intellectuals. The transformation of radical intellectuals into a ruling group is inseparable from the destruction of the critical function of the intellectual, who is by definition distanced from or opposed to the ruling powers. This confusion between the intellectual—a member of a social group with specific interests—and the intellectual function—which has no specific social site—lies at the origin of many misinterpretations of the real evolution of the intellectuals. It also explains the common failure to understand what happened when they became practical militants and began to perform ignoble tasks that were far removed from the envied status of the 'great intellectual'. As Mao well knew, the intellectuals had to be forged anew, with all the energy and force that a blacksmith puts into forging iron. Both processes are at once creative and destructive and they presumably both mean working at a very high temperature. The transformation which allowed a loosely knit group to become leaders of a social movement and finally a potential ruling class or group, also legitimized a social group which was not 'naturally' (in the sense that new relations of production define the 'natural') a ruling class. In this context, the state was an essential staging post in the long march to power. Initially, the party-state centralized the impulse towards mobilization and homogenized the contradictory tendencies which coexisted amongst the people. It then became responsible for ensuring industrial accumulation; accumulation was either inadequate or even non-existent and capitalism itself was not in a position to generate it. The party-state became a strong state. Anti-imperialist nationalism became a state nationalism that was quick to take offence and a mystical exaltation of the nation. The basic characteristics of many forms of Third Worldism soon became obvious and the great speeches of the past were often jettisoned and replaced by empty rhetoric. Their other features—and there were many other features—derived from the ethos of specific nations and civilizations, from the role played by religious traditions in Third Worldist mobilizations—or demobilizations—and from traditional values which were recovered and adapted to nationalism as and when required.

Sometimes, however, the emphasis is placed on terms with more modern connotations; hence the popularity of the term 'socialist', even though it is devoid of its true content and demands. Some new terms, like 'African socialism' were used to refer to realities that were far from new. Others referred to realities that had been constituted elsewhere: Vietnamese, Korean and Chinese 'socialism' means nothing unless it is related to the Soviet model.

What initially looked like a shapeless movement did, then, produce specific if variable results. One of its most unexpected accomplishments often goes unnoticed, but it has had lasting effects in the Third World and an ephemeral effect in the West itself. A small group of radical intellectuals came to power, even though they probably never expected that their universalistic rhetoric and militant practices would transform them into a ruling class in the strict sense of the term or would forge very statist societies which corresponded to their social being. The historical merit, and therefore the legitimacy, of their accomplishment is all the more remarkable in that the task was far from easy. These states emerged in a world that was dominated by a Stalinism that was both counter-revolutionary and chauvinistically national and by an imperialism which may have been weak in the sense that it was losing its colonies but which was at the same time developing into a powerful imperialism which did not need actual colonies. Internally, the peasantry was in revolt, but it often remained passive and was in no sense revolutionary, whilst the embryonic proletariat took a not unambiguous view of foreign interests and at times tried to take command of the movement itself. They were caught up in the rivalry of the great powers and had to rely on the sometimes dubious friendship of their allies, the former colonial countries. They indulged in a rhetoric of purification and at the same time had to adapt to the realities of the balance of power and the opportunities open to them. In the midst of all these difficulties, a relatively new social group succeeded in forging the destiny of nations and in facing up to some of the challenges of the age in which they lived. In its own way, it performed some of the tasks that should have been incumbent upon others, notably the bourgeoisie. The universalism which was sung so lyrically by Fanon and then echoed so brilliantly by Jean-Paul Sartre and Régis Debray did not, however, survive the successes and failures of actual existing Third Worldism and actual active capitalism. It was at this point that a relationship begun so enthusiastically began to break up. The outcome was the anti-Third Worldism we see today.

2. Third Worldism in the West: The French Example

France was the classic home of Third Worldism. There are a number of good reasons as to why that should have been the case, but some of the most important are rather less than obvious. Decolonization was obviously not specific to France alone. But the chaotic conditions in which it took place and France's reluctance to give up its colonies meant that the country was involved in two of the major events in the Third Worldist odyssey: Dien Bien Phu, which was the final outcome of seven years of war in Vietnam, and then a further seven years of war in Algeria. And when the Americans took over in Vietnam, the French could hardly remain indifferent to what was happening in a former colony which, by the end of the sixties, had become the last great Third World cause.

France came a long way between 1945 and 1975. Third Worldism was of course very widespread in the seventies, but colonial attitudes were equally widespread, if not more so, in 1945 when the nationalist revolt in Constantine was crushed with such brutality.

There were few anti-colonialist protests to be heard when the French army came to blows with Ho Chi Minh's Vietminh in 1945. And during the Algerian war—at least until 1960—public opinion was largely in favour of Algeria remaining French or at least of a continued French presence in Algeria.

The subsequent strength of Third Worldism was initially the result of a bad conscience and a moralistic rejection of a colonial reality that had previously been accepted by the majority of people in France. On the Left, it also derived from a somewhat belated rejection of social democracy's commitment to colonialism and from the recantations of the Parti Communiste Français, whose anti-colonialism had always been luke warm. After all, the PCF did describe the Constantine revolt as fascist and had watched the rebels being bombed into submission, just like the rebels in Madagascar. The PCF was in the government when war broke out in Vietnam. In 1956, it voted special powers to Guy Mollet's socialist government to help it increase the repression in Algeria.

Under these conditions, the rejection of anti-colonialism could only come from the *gauchiste* fringe and from outside the labour movement (the Christians). Anti-colonialism soon became combined with a virulent anti-capitalism when General de Gaulle came to power after a military putsch in 1958 and when a right-wing regime which refused to relinquish power established an increasingly authoritarian reign. In an attempt to reinforce their anti-capitalism, the Third Worldists of the sixties looked to the Third World for models to replace a socialism that had been discredited by its compromises with the bourgeoisie and a Stalinist 'communism' whose horrors had been revealed by the Twentieth Congress of the CPSU. A year after the great victory of Dien Bien Phu, the Bandung Conference proclaimed loudly that there was a 'third way', and that proved very attractive to certain groups among Christians who were becoming radicalized and to militants who were looking for an alternative to a bankrupt Stalinism. For those intellectuals who had already broken with Stalinism, there was a great temptation to abandon the 'orthodox' schema and to look overseas for a 'good' proletariat to replace a proletariat which had, under the leadership of the PCF, betrayed its revolutionary vocation.

The populist component—the notion that an upsurge amongst the wretched of the earth would purify the privileged Western world—fitted in perfectly with the search for a new catholicity and the celebration of the redeeming fraternity that was going to embrace the whole of mankind and set the whole of the world alight.

The lyrical power of Fanon's *The Wretched of the Earth*—and the title itself—is a perfect expression of the pathos of an inverted universalism, of the belief that the East was going to enlighten the West. It also expresses the desire for a new historical subject to replace that of the socialist tradition with its belief that the new liberator would come from a humiliated world that had become a storm zone, and that the liberator was an entire people not just the proletariat. It is scarcely surprising that this discovery should have turned new converts into proselytes. Initially, very few people felt they had a vocation, but they made up for their lack of numbers with their zeal, their courage—especially during the Algerian war—and their enthusiasm. When intellectual stars like Jean-Paul Sartre became committed and put their verve and their talents at the service of the anti-colonial struggle, Third Worldism became a real mass movement amongst the rising generations in schools and universities.

All this may sound very obvious and very familiar, but today's anti-Third Worldism makes it all too easy to forget that there were very good reasons for the rise of Third Worldism in France. It was slow to emerge, but if anything was all the stronger for that. The colonizers came face to face with the colonized and admitted that they too had their own existence and their own dignity, if not a superior essence. The day of arrogant Eurocentrism seemed at last to be over. The white man paled at the sight of colonized peoples who were bursting with life.

At a deeper level, however, the Third Worldist movement in France was more complex and was linked to the specific context of French society itself. The dazzling success of Third Worldism in France and the exceptional impact it had on the political life of the country can also be seen as a result of another encounter—although it was in fact largely mythical—the encounter between the intellectuals of France and their counterparts in the Third World. If we examine the milieu in which Third Worldism developed, we can in fact find certain analogies with the social groups which gave birth to the avant-garde leaders of the anti-imperialist struggles in the Third World. France, too, had its frustrated intellectual elite, the representatives of a modernist petty bourgeoisie whose increasing importance in demographic, economic and cultural terms was in contradiction with its marginalization at the political level. Although the dirigiste policies of the Fifth Republic speeded up the economic reconstruction that had begun after the Second World War, France was still an archaic country, both in terms of its institutions and its dominant values.

One of the specific characteristics of bourgeois hegemony in France, as compared with the forms of domination that existed in other advanced capitalist countries, was the survival of a class alliance with a traditional petty bourgeoisie that was still linked to earlier stages of social evolution: small peasants, artisans, small shopkeepers, the liberal professions and the heads of small firms. The alliance became more and more anachronistic as capital became increasingly concentrated, and it also became more difficult to maintain, given that the tendency towards monopolization implied the liquidation of traditional sectors which had, since the mid-nineteenth century, always been the traditional rampart against the 'dangerous' (working) classes. But rather than abandoning its traditional supporters and turning to the managers, technicians, teachers and social workers who were being secreted by the modernization of capitalism and increased state intervention, the French bourgeoisie made the strategic mistake of trying to govern alone. Gaullism bypassed the representative instances of parliamentary democracy and exercised power in an authoritarian manner, combining the personal charisma of the Head of State with the efficiency of technocratic management. Furious at being ousted from the political responsibilities to which it was entitled as a class fraction destined for the task of conceptualization, control, supervision and legitimation, the intellectual petty bourgeoisie became radicalized. Its opposition to De Gaulle evolved into opposition to the regime established in 1958 and finally into opposition to capitalism itself. Its resistible rise had been blocked and Third Worldism became an ideological outlet for its aspirations.

The new petty bourgeoisie felt out of place in a society which was still living in the colonial past and whose official ideology was permeated with a reactionary ethos that was more appropriate to a disappearing rural world than to the new urban generations produced by industrialization. Its exasperation was all the greater in that there was no alternative; neither social democracy nor the practices of the PCF were acceptable to it, even though the latter had attracted a good number of intellectuals at the end of the war and in the immediate post-war period. The traditional Left was incapable of modernizing France and of bringing the essential process of decolonization to a successful conclusion. The formation of the PSU in 1960 and its subsequent development testify to the centrality of these questions. The PSU was to a large extent responsible for giving conceptual and sometimes practical shape to the aspirations of those affected by the modernist currents.

Neither state nor party structures could allow the French petty bourgeoisie to fulfil its ambitions and it was unable to integrate itself into society. It therefore chose to reject society. In its attempt to escape from a capitalist system in which it had no power—as might have happened in a country where it is the norm for social-democratic and conservative parties to hold power alternately—it looked to the Third World, not only to express its solidarity with the hopes of people who were fighting for their emancipation, but also to express its own hopes. Perhaps the most important aspect of its fascination with the Third World is the one thing that is never mentioned. The French petty bourgeoisie could not make a revolution in France, but by identifying with the revolutionary intelligentsia it could make a revolution by proxy. Being cut off from the French proletariat, it made itself the representative of the disinherited masses of the Third World, thus compensating at the level of fantasy for its feeling of isolation at home.

The lyrical illusion of Third Worldism was not, then, simply a phantasmogoria, a populist passion or the fantasy that divergent interests could converge in an upheaval that would create a new society. More prosaically, it was a process of mimicry: the petty bourgeoisie of France wanted to imitate the intellectual elites of the Third World which, although they were in a minority, had finally taken power in progressive countries like China, Vietnam and Cuba.

From a strategic point of view, the Third World provided an adequate model for the seizure of power and proved that a minority which had no obvious historical destiny could create its own destiny and leave its mark on history. And that was a considerable consolation for a petty bourgeoisie that had been condemned to political impotence by the Gaullist France of the sixties.

Basically, the lyrical illusion was the battle hymn of a group of intellectuals, most of them from the lower intelligentsia, who were convinced that they had found a way to gain an unheard of status as an intermediate class in an advanced capitalist country. They thought that they could oust the bourgeoisie and become the ruling class. It is not difficult to explain the appeal of Third Worldism. It seemed to provide a solution to all the problems. As suffering humanity liberated itself, a minority which was intellectual, dissatisfied and sometimes humiliated would find its own road to success. The Western model as such would no longer apply, but some aspects of it would be revitalized by the actions of the Third World peoples who provided the liberating dimension. A movement which had begun in the insurgent areas of the Third World would sweep away France's anachronisms. People have become excited about much less than that!

It is, however, also true that it took a great deal of verbal conjuring to conceal what was going on; it is not easy for a small group to lead a potential revolt and harness the energy of the masses. It was of course May '68 which detonated all the tensions in French society. It was then that all the constituent elements of Third Worldism came together to form an ideology for the West. May '68 was the moment for mass intellectual radicalization and for a search for radical solutions, simply because it was then that the frustration was at its height. In the heat of the moment and with intoxicating slogans like 'l'imagination au pouvoir', those whose job it was to imagine began to demand intellectual power. Like China, which was then in the throes of a cultural revolution, France was a blank page, and those whose function it was to write and think filled it with their writings and their thoughts. The slogan 'We were nothing but we will be everything' has to be taken quite literally; they wanted to be masters of everything in society. The Third World was a Western ideology and, more specifically, a French problematic.

The Morning After
The dreams of May '68 have vanished without trace. And not even the most imaginative participants could possibly have foreseen how France and the Third World itself were to develop.

For some people, however, the balance sheet is not entirely negative. The demands of the modernist intellectuals have in part been met. 'Modernization'—by far the most fashionable slogan of the moment—has become a reality. The archaisms of rural France are disappearing and giving way to a society which is subject to the imperatives of a vigorous capitalism rather than to its traditional stagnation. France has become more open to the outside world, even if the 'outside' world does simply mean America and perhaps Japan. They are the new models for good capitalist housekeeping. Some of the demands of the new petty bourgeoisie have been met. It has got the recognition it wanted and even a place in the apparatus of power. All the excitement of May '68 has had a prosaic but tangible outcome, namely a new class alliance in which the new middle classes can make their voices heard and even negotiate for a share in power. Their central demand has not, however, been met and they have had to abandon one of the central elements of their Third Worldism: their ambition to become the ruling class. The world is dominated by capitalism writ large and not by the bourgeoisie writ petty. Modernization means that capitalism must finally penetrate every sphere of society. The valorization of bourgeois values (the market, profits, the firm) has become the dominant ideology and its praises are sung—or hammered out—by all the media. While there would be nothing new or unusual about this in a country like the United States, it is somewhat unexpected in France, where the identity of the Left has always been largely based on its rejection of capitalism. Being up to the minute has come to mean being competitive, being the most successful competitor in a world where everyone has to compete with everyone else. This ideological modernism has swept away the generous and altruistic impulses of Third Worldism. Capitalism has once more revealed its domineering temperament and its self-confidence. Like the rising capitalism described by Marx it has destroyed all pretence of 'living differently'. Instead it glorifies egotistical instincts and subordinates everyone and everything to economic laws which are made to look like immutable principles.

With capitalism in command, the modern petty bourgeoisie had to be content with a subordinate but far from negligible position. At best, it can become a subordinate group within the ruling class. But it has been generously rewarded for its loyalty and has been able to become the dominant group within the dominated group.

Because it occupies a position midway between the ruling class and the working classes, whose role is restricted to taking orders, the intellectual petty bourgeoisie is the mediating class *par excellence*. It is responsible for the training and supervision of the working classes, though most of its members sublimate their function into 'education', 'training', 'information', 'social work', 'youth work' and so on. The advent of the media society gives them an ideal opportunity to fulfil their vocation for mediation.

In a society where the traditional mechanisms for reproducing the relations of production have a tendency to jam, 'communication' has to lubricate capitalist social relations, not least because the explosion of cultural industries and the state of the art technologies they produce are one of the main launching pads for a new process of accumulation. In Western societies which are now faced with an unprecedented structural crisis, the manipulation of public opinion has become one of the arts of government, and the intellectual petty bourgeoisie has an important role to play at this level too. It may not be able to take power, but it can do much to help the bourgeoisie retain power by making an imaginary assault on the powers it has been granted in the media. Those powers have encouraged them to give up their dreams of a world revolution and to adopt a new attitude of realism—the realism of those who have at last found their rightful place in the reality of capitalism.

This situation allows the new petty bourgeoisie to insert itself into society; it may well have been forced to accept its subordination to the capitalist social order and its masters (who tend to be more impersonal and anonymous than they used to be) but it also tends to dominate the dominated classes. To a certain extent, it is even trying to dominate society as a whole by taking control of ideology and communications. The importance of ideology and communications, that is, allows a section of the new petty bourgeoisie to climb higher in the power structure than it would otherwise be able to do.

In that sense, someone like Serge July, the editor of *Libération* and an active and prolific apostle of modernization, can be said to have fulfilled the old dream of becoming a member of the ruling class. Such successes are, however, the exception rather than the rule. The new petty bourgeoisie is still haunted by its traditional fear of proletarianization. Unlike the old petty bourgeoisie, it is usually salaried and is therefore threatened with being excluded and demoted by the harsh process of capitalist reconstruction.

It is of course unlikely to have to put on overalls and to be fully proletarianized, if only because the working class itself is shrinking. But there is no guarantee that it will not be impoverished or socially demoted. Such fears operate at the level of everyday life and are far removed from the dream of a new society or even a society tailored to the needs of the new petty bourgeoisie.

Ten years in a rapid evolution of capitalism have been enough to cast the new petty bourgeoisie out of heaven—which it stormed only in its imagination—and bring it down to earth and to the constraints of capitalism. The theme of modernization may well be very dear to this social group, but it has not opened up the gates to paradise. Indeed, some of its members live in a purgatory, but they are still a good deal more comfortable than those who are forced to live lower down. They live in a limbo midway between the hell of possible social demotion and the delights of upward mobility and joys of the capitalist El Dorado. A mirage for the many and a possibility for the few. But for almost everyone, this implies allegiance to their master and loyalty to the divine existing social order, come what may.

The Spell of Disenchantment

Those who have become disillusioned with their Third Worldism have justified their disappointment so often that there is no need to listen to their litanies. An alibi is not an explanation.

According to the 'realist' vulgate which passes for a world view on the 'renovated' French Left, the decline and fall of Third Worldism is the logical outcome of the collapse of certain 'revolutionary myths'. The myths were shattered by the sombre realities of the post-revolutionary era, and the lyrical illusion could not survive the brutal revelation of the 'truth'. Everyone has a tale to tell about the disappointments they encountered on the painful road that brought the 'lost generation' of May '68 to the bosom of a society it once rejected.

Many of them saw the Cuban experiment, for instance, as opening up the promise of a third way which could avoid the dictatorship of profit and that of bureaucracy. But when tens of thousands of people flooded into the gardens of the Peruvian Embassy to wait for their exit visas, they proved, if final proof were needed, that the only difference between Fidel Castro's tropical socialism and its Soviet counterpart was the weather.

Thirty years of struggle did nothing to turn Vietnam into an earthly paradise. On the contrary, the boat people were prepared to risk being eaten by sharks or murdered by pirates rather than to help construct the 'new man'. Their Cambodian neighbours were also being led to a glorious future by infallible leaders, but many of them fell by the wayside. They were not killed by the bullets and bombs of the American army, or even by a puppet army, but by their own liberators.

Our students and their academic mentors also placed great hopes on China, but the 'great proletarian cultural revolution' was found to have swept a lot of corpses along in its wake. It was a repetition (though fortunately only a partial repetition) of the demographic feats of the Great Leap Forward[12] which, only a few years earlier, had had the finest flower of the Parisian intelligentsia dancing for joy. It had not at that time finally recovered from the Twentieth Congress's revelations about Stalin's 'errors', but it later drained its cup to the last drop when it learned from Mao's designated—or self-appointed—successors that the Great Helmsman had indeed clung to the rudder come hell or high water, but in order to retain power rather than to guide his people into any safe harbour of prosperity.

And what can one say about the lesser divinities in the Third Worldist pantheon, the varieties of 'African socialism'? In terms of tyranny and incompetence there is little to choose between them, and the scorn and indifference they display towards their starving peoples almost rivals that of the old colonists.

It would of course be absurd to paint a black picture of all the actual non-existent socialist countries over which, according to the Third World-ists, the red flag once flew. With the exception of Cambodia and a few ephemeral dictatorships in Africa,[13] the record of governments which emerged from the liberation struggle is not as bad as our apostate Third Worldists like to claim; they are simply burning their old gods. In com-parison with the fate of the workers and peasants of countries to the south of the Rio Grande, that of the Cuban proletariat is quite enviable.[14] Those who cheerfully reckon up the number of Cubans who have fled their country for the delights of the consumer society would do well to check the statistics for emigration from Puerto Rico, Mexico and Haiti.

Be that as it may, there is no society which has really freed itself from capitalist domination—state or private—or which can be taken as a model for mankind. In that respect, the Third World is not better qualified than the Old World to give anyone lessons in emancipation.

Besides, how could the Third World speak with one voice when it is internally divided by all kinds of oppositions and splits and when they are made serious by the internationalization of capitalism? The false debate between North and South, which has been promoted by incompetent 'experts' in geopolitics, should not be allowed to conceal something that the Third Worldists ignored for far too long: that the diversity of the Third World is greater than its unity. Although the term 'the Third World' is still used, no one would deny that it in fact refers to a host of very different situations. It includes 'new industrial countries' which are exper-iencing a rapid expansion of capitalism because the extension of market relations permits the super-exploitation of the proletarianized masses; African countries which have been abandoned by the multinationals and left to rot in poverty; 'Marxist–Leninist countries' in which the party-state uses centralized planning to accumulate capital; countries in which 'wild' capitalism suggested that an economic miracle was about to take place and which then went bankrupt. . . Countries with oil wealth and countries which have nothing but their deserts, countries which thought they were great powers and which cannot pay their debts (Brazil), countries which cannot fulfil their very modest ambitions. . . Virtually the only things they have in common are the persistence of dependency, hunger and poverty for the vast majority of the population, and repression of varying degrees of brutality. But neither the horrific realization that the revolutionary leaders led their countries into so many blind alleys when they finally took power, nor the fragmentation of what was once thought to be the unity of the Third World can justify our turning our backs on it. Nor can they justify anyone going back there to play 'explorers', to look for the exotic and the picturesque and to claim that the worsening inequalities and injustices to be found there are simply expressions of the 'right to be different'.[15]

First-hand knowledge of the realities of life in these countries does not necessarily lead to a better understanding of their position. Those who are now trying to proclaim 'the white man's innocence' often argue that it was easy to be mystified about the Third World precisely because it was so far away. And it is in fact true that it took a great deal of wilful blindness and crass ignorance to claim that the position of Chinese women during the Cultural Revolution showed how far their European sisters had to go before we could talk about women's liberation.[16] Increased opportunities for travel and the availability of charter flights may have allowed the Third World itself to test its preconceived ideas against concrete realities, but they have done little to overcome the mania for projection. The first contact with reality was of course something of a shock, but rather than analyze what they found in greater depth or lucidly coming to terms with their mutual ambivalence, the militants became travellers or even tourists, allowed themselves to be seduced by the exotica of poverty and used the poverty of exotica to compensate for their political disappointment.

After their 'purifying journey into the mythology of *gauchisme*' a number of May '68 militants abandoned their progressive baggage and decided to go back to the Third World and look at it anew, without 'the blinkers of dogma'. It was once more a matter of freeing people, but from the 'Marxist categories' which 'prevent us from seeing how people really live', rather than from capitalism. As a result, we now have a rash of demystifing travellers' tales. One of our intrepid globe-trotters, for instance, tells us a fundamental truth that was for a long time concealed by 'all the abstract grandiloquence about under-development' and our 'nice sermons about worldwide poverty'. He tells us that in fact the wretched of the earth live 'differently' but 'with dignity'.[17] Too bad if they don't live—or survive— too long.

Something Stirs on the Western Front

The anti-Third Worldism that is now so widespread would not have taken such a virulent form were it not that it is a component part of an ideological counter-offensive designed to legitimize the economic and political restructuring of capitalism at a time when it is becoming a transnational phenomenon. There is no need to dwell at length on the reactionary climate that has prevailed in France for the last ten years. The prevailing wind which blows through the intellectual milieu no longer comes from the South or the East but from the West, from the United States, which has become a technological and cultural Mecca for a directionless intelligentsia which wants to tune into modernity. It has taken a major effort on the part of the intellectual leaders and the intelligentsia's spokesmen to disguise their enthusiastic conversion to the values of the market, profits and the firm, as a cultural revolution on the part of the Left. It was not enough to get rid of their past illusions. They also had to hold the past itself in contempt and exorcize it.

Third Worldism, with all its unspoken ambitions, was an expression of a desire for radical change. It did represent a vision of a society that would be different, even if it was ruled by an avant-garde which governed for and in the name of the masses. In its own way it was part of the critical traditions of the French intelligentsia. It was heir to a secular tradition of opposition to the established order and the intelligentsia now has to get rid of this embarrassing heritage. It has to do away with the explicit anti-capitalism which was the very basis of the French Left's identity. Hence the determination with which the 'new philosophers' and the spokesmen of the so-called 'New Left' try to deny the need to look for an alternative to capitalism and the very possibility of there being any such alternative. What they loathe most is not the errors, illusions or falsehoods of Third Worldism, but its demand for liberation, even though the latter did appear in a somewhat distorted form. Ultimately, the utopia of liberation and emancipation has to be both rejected and rendered literally unthinkable.

The horizons of the new petty bourgeoisie are now limited to their dream of a modernized capitalism. They are therefore satisfied with being a junior partner to the bourgeoisie, a sub-contractor who carries out the task of domination on its master's behalf. As a result, their secret dream that a revolution would allow them to become the ruling class has turned to scorn or even hatred for those who were more successful in other countries. In May '68, the petty bourgeoisie nourished the unrealistic hope of being able to use 'people's power' or 'workers' control' as a means to oust the bourgeoisie, and it now execrates the radicalized middle classes of the Third World who did, thanks to a specific combination of circumstances, become a state bourgeoisie and gained a privileged position which the intelligentsia could never hope to attain in an advanced capitalist country. In France, the petty bourgeoisie has been trapped into being a subaltern agent in the reproduction of the capitalist system, and when it trots out its grievances about the treachery of the ruling elites of the Third World, it is simply settling accounts with its own past.

Forgetting Third Worldism is not enough. Anti-Third Worldism itself is not enough, as it could easily look like hostility towards the countries and peoples of the Third World. The case against Third Worldism is therefore linked with an attempt to rehabilitate 'values' which are supposed to transcend 'outdated divisions' at the international level, just as they have transcended divisions at the national level. The values in question are 'freedom' and 'human rights' and it is a mere coincidence that they should be the slogans on the banners carried by these new crusaders from the capitalist West.

Yesterday's anti-imperialism has already given way to a more positive view of Western domination, past and present. A triumphant capitalism has rehabilitated the Eurocentric moralism which once played its part in justifying the civilizing mission of colonialism. 'The white man's sobs' are now anathema to Gérard Chaliand, who is proud of having dispelled the illusions of Third Worldism in favour of 'an objective and non-complacent examination' of the balance of power in the modern world. He has lost no time in jumping on the human rights bandwagon and riding off with the knights of the free world as they go into battle against the 'totalitarian empire'. 'I think that the age of guilt is coming to an end', claims our strategic expert. Now that decolonization is over [sic] and that we can see the type of regime that can masquerade as 'socialistic', 'revolutionary' or 'progressive', there can be no more feelings of guilt. In this context, 'human rights' has to be seen as Western ideology's first serious counter-offensive against Marxism for decades. For the first time, the Western world is not under attack, but is actively fighting back and saying 'Listen, we too have values that are important, if only because you are in-capable of living up to them.'[18] It is only a short step from that to justifying such neo-colonial adventures as the expansion of capital might require.

In France, the defrocked priests of Stalinism and Maoism have already taken that step. Bernard-Henri Lévy, for instance, can use the excuse of 'protecting people against their own states' and transcending ideological and partisan quarrels to proclaim that our states have a right to interfere and a legitimate and imperative duty to intervene in Chad, Cambodia and Grenada. But not, of course, in Chile, the Philippines or Gabon.

It might seem surprising that people with a progressive reputation should come out with the hackneyed arguments which have always served as an alibi for an internationalism that has nothing to do with the proletariat. But it would be wrong to put their ideological excesses down to naivety. On the contrary, their lucidity about their past commitments is rivalled only by their lucidity about their present commitments. They simply reflect a cynical acceptance of the fact that the interests of all privileged groups are inter-linked, that the interests of all exploiters are inter-linked, even if the petty bourgeoisie itself can hope for no more than crumbs from the table of the real exploiters.

Pascal Brückner deserves to have the last word. Having expressed his indignation at the fact that the UN does not regard anti-Westernism and anti-white racism as 'crimes against humanity', this worthy successor to Kipling goes on to issue a warning to the wretched of the earth who dare to rise against the West: 'There is nothing beyond democracy. If the peoples of the Third World are to become themselves, they must become more Western.'[19] Replace 'democracy' by 'capitalism' and we have it all. History is being rewritten by people who thought they were making history and then realized that they were being remade by history. For them, capitalism is the ultimate horizon of the modern world. And anti-Third Worldism is always there to liquidate the one thing that the 'new course' of history cannot tolerate in either word or deed: a mode of being Western which is not simply Atlanticist. For if the French Left had remained true to itself, it could have taken up the torch of revolution and shown that 'more Western' can also mean 'less capitalist'.

NOTES

1. A. Matterlat, X. Delcourt and M. Mattelart, *La Culture contre la démocratie?* (Paris: La Découverte, 1983).
2. Pascal Brückner, *Le Sanglot de l'homme blanc,* (Paris: Le Seuil, 1983).
3. Paul-Marie de la Gorce, 'Le Recul des grandes espérances révolutionnaires', *Le Monde diplomatique,* May 1984.
4. M. Rodinson, *La Fascination de l'Islam,* (Paris: Maspero 1981).
5. Bernard Lewis, *The Muslim Discovery of Europe.*
6. M. Rodinson, *La Fascination,* p. 88.
7. Alfred Sauvy ends his article 'Trois mondes, une planète' with the words: 'The Third World has, like the Third Estate, been ignored and despised and it too wants to be something.' Cited, Yves Lacoste, *Unité et diversité du tiers monde,* (Paris: Maspero 1980), Vol. 1, p. 14.
8. 'The radical, virulent challenge of *The Wretched of the Earth* is still couched in the language of the colonizers and uses their code and their stated values.' Gérard Chaliand, *Les Faubourgs de l'histoire: tiermondismes et tiers mondes,* (Paris: Calmann-Levy 1984), p. 34.
9. Frantz Fanon, *The Wretched of the Earth,* trans. Constance Farrington, (Penguin Books, Harmondsworth, 1967), p. 253.
10. *Ibid.,* p. 255.
11. 1955 was the year of China's first five year plan (which should have begun in 1953); it was a carbon copy of the Soviet five year plans.
12. Calculations based upon a 1964 census show that between 1958 and 1961, more than sixty million Chinese failed to answer the roll call. Thirty million of them had died of hunger and a further thirty million were not born.
13. The record for longevity amongst the African regimes which emerged in the former French colonies was until very recently held by the grotesquely brutal Sekhou Touré. For a time his regime too was popular with the anti-colonialists of the metropolis.
14. On the Cuban economy, see Joseph Cassas, 'De la médiocrité au décollage', *Le Monde diplomatique,* June 18, 1984, pp. 20–21.
15. Jean-Pierre Garnier, 'Les nouveaux explorateurs', *Le Monde diplomatique,* August 1980.
16. Claudie Broyelle first came to fame with her *Women's Liberation in China,* trans. Michèle Cohen and Gary Herman, (Harvester Press, Hassocks 1977), a hymn of praise to Maoist style women's liberation. Since then both she and her husband Jacques have begun a second career in moral rearmament. Their *China: A Second Look,* trans. Sarah Matthews, (Hassocks: Harvester Press, 1980) shows

that they now believe that the only thing about the East that is red is the blood.
17. Jean-Claude Guillebaud, *Un Voyage vers l'Asie,* (Paris: Le Seuil, 1979).
18. Gérard Chaliand, interview in *Libération,* 29-30 November, 1980.
19. *Le Sanglot de l'homme blanc.*

Translated by David Macey

THE STALINISTS OF ANTI-COMMUNISM

Pascal Delwit & Jean-Michel Dewaele

'Paris today is the capital of European intellectual reaction', writes Perry Anderson in his recent *In The Tracks of Historical Materialism*.[1] His formulation is terse, provocative and quite justified. An intelligentsia which was, almost by definition, considered to be on the left has packed up its bags and gone over to the other side. It now addresses its criticisms, not to French society, but to those who dare to think of transforming it. It no longer turns its anger against the injustice of a system which dominates, exploits and alienates the people of France, but against the injustice which prevails 'elsewhere', and in the present context 'elsewhere' means the other side, the Communist camp. Anti-communism has helped to reconcile many Parisian intellectuals—Anderson rightly notes that provincial intellectuals have not been affected to the same extent—to 'western pluralist democracy'. It is probably difficult for an outsider to imagine the degree of anti-communism that now prevails in France. Except for the Communists themselves, almost everyone has been affected by it.

Until recently the newspaper *Libération* was an eloquent mouthpiece for anarchistic protests; not long ago it described the Communist ministers in the Mauroy government as 'the KGB's agents in France'. In his *La Nature de l'URSS*, Edgar Morin, a brilliant sociologist who was for a long time regarded as a man of the left, describes Soviet power as 'a spider which controls everyone and everything' and the Soviet Union itself as 'a historical monster', as 'a monstrous reality which is out of all proportion and which defies all norms', which 'defies all reason'. M.F. Garaud is of course a right-wing politician, but she is on excellent terms with Charles Hernu, the Socialist Minister for Defence (for and with whom she has organized a number of seminars on foreign policy); in a televised debate she can claim that 'The Soviets are Martians, real Martians. Their system could never have been devised by human beings.'

One could give many other examples. Such extreme statements are not merely examples of individual hyperbole. They are typical of the prevailing climate in France and even of the concrete policies of the government. Compared with Mitterand's Atlanticism, Gaullism looks positively anti-American and De Gaulle himself looks like a trouble maker. Not content with adopting a pro-American diplomatic line, Mitterand also attacks European peace movements and socialist parties which dare to distance

324

themselves from Washington.

The presence of Communist ministers in the French government from 1981 to 1984 has done nothing to change this state of affairs. Their loyalty to the state, their 'managerial seriousness' and their 'sense of responsibility' have done nothing to placate an anti-communism which still sees them as 'foreign agents'. Anti-communism has done so much to stir up the right's hatred for the left that a former *gauchiste* pamphleteer like J.E. Hallier can even claim that Mitterand is 'a Russian lackey and deserves to be put up against a wall and shot'.

It is true that the Parti Communiste Français (PCF) takes a soft line on the Soviet Union, especially compared with the line taken by the PCI. But it has completely rejected the notion that Moscow can provide a 'model' for the international labour movement. It is also true that the extreme sectarianism displayed by the PCF between 1977 and 1981— particularly towards the Socialists—did a lot to tarnish its image. It cannot be denied that its tone and its rigidly authoritarian practices help to fuel anti-communism. But anti-communism relies upon false comparisons, invective, groundless accusations and slander. It has no scruples about applying double standards and never qualifies its statements. As in the darkest days of the Cold War, anti-communism is more virulent in France than in any other country in Europe. Its best spokesman is a singer, the most popular singer in France. His success is the most striking demonstration of the strength of anti-communism. Yves Montand was once known for his close connections with the PCF, but the radically anti-communist and anti-Soviet positions he has recently adopted have brought him such fame that it was actually rumoured that he would be standing in the presidential elections. His inspiration comes from none other than Jorge Semprun who was, until about fifteen years ago, a prominent member of the Spanish Communist Party in exile.

In other words, former Communists are playing an important role in the anti-communist and anti-Soviet campaign that is sweeping across France. They have been joined by a younger generation of Marxists who, in the heyday of Maoism, looked to the People's Republic of China rather than to the Soviet Union for their inspiration. Their adulation of revolutionary China had an almost religious intensity. These renegades from 'Marxism–Leninism' have not simply abandoned their old convictions and their ardent faith. They have rallied with equal passion to the anti-communist and anti-Soviet camp. Their passion is as great as ever; only its object has changed. Whatever they may say and despite appearances to the contrary, the continuity in their attitude is more real than their change of heart.

It would take a long time to list all the former Stalinists and former Maoists who have become self-proclaimed enemies of Marxism, Maoism and the revolution (and of the left and of even a reformist notion of change). In France, the list includes the names of the most prestigious members of the intelligentsia. The media flatter them with their best attentions and promote them to stardom. Morin, Leroi-Ladurie, Ellein-stein, Robrieux, Sollers, Glucksmann and many others have all become energetic, even aggressive defenders of a free world which is, they claim, faced with a 'totalitarian threat'.

In the article that follows, Pascal Delwit and Jean-Michel Dewaele examine the case histories of two former Communists who have become virulent anti-Communists: Annie Kriegel, the historian and sociologist, and Pierre Daix, the writer and journalist. Their individual cases are not especially outstanding. But in terms of their general tendencies, their intellectual weaknesses and their ideological impact, they are typical of the murky phenomenon of French anti-communism. It is also an important phenomenon, so much so that it might be seen as one of the major planks in today's bourgeois hegemony.

M.L.

I

Annie Kriegel (née Annie Becker) was very active in the Résistance and joined the PCF during the war. At that time she used the name Annie Besse. Despite her youth (she was not yet twenty), she already had major responsibilities and worked with immigrant workers in Grenoble. It was in these circumstances that she discovered the PCF. Her courage, her youth and her conviction soon brought her to the notice of the Party's leaders. After the war she was promoted rapidly. She was initially a student organizer, but soon became the cadre responsible for intellectuals in the vitally important Fédération de la Seine, the largest and most prestigious concentration of intellectuals in the PCF. Our young star was also on the editorial board of the PCF's theoretical journal, *La Nouvelle Critique, revue du marxisme militant*. '*La Nouvelle critique* had been founded alongside *La Pensée*, considered too soft and academic in order to supply a more juvenile, ardent and more militant tone.'[2] *Les Cahiers du communisme*, the PCF's other journal, described its appearance in the following terms: 'A new journal is about to appear in response to the new needs of the ideological battle. It appears at a time when the forces of reaction are making a major effort to spread their lies, slanders and unhealthy ideas. . . in order to denounce the lies and falsifications of the ideologues of reaction, answer them and promote our arguments and explanations.'[3] *La Nouvelle critique* was to be—and became—the spearhead of the ideological counter-offensive. It attacked politicians and writers in identical terms: Jules Moch, David Rousset, Bidault, Sartre, Blum, Truman, Mauriac, Malraux. . . The style of its denunciations is *La Nouvelle critique*'s immediate hallmark: 'They are not the unwitting instruments of the great fear of capitalism or the wretched playthings of objective contradictions whose hidden mechanisms and deeper roots remain invisible to them. Far from it! The orders they are following are clear and they know whose purposes they are serving. *They are lying and they know that they are lying.* They lie because they know that their lies are useful to their masters. They stink of lies. They use their falsifications to create splits, but they are at peace with their bad consciences. They will stoop to anything and rummage through any dustbin.'[4] The famous style is the journal's hallmark: groundless accusations, permanent invective, bizarre comparisons and real paranoia. It has to be said that the style was, amongst other things, seen as a response to equally crude anti-communist propaganda which was equally unconcerned about ideological niceties. This was after all the height of the Cold War. The western bourgeoisie was determined to divide the left and isolate the Communist Parties. The Communist Parties therefore adopted the familiar tactic of defending the besieged citadel. The more isolated the PCF became, the more it turned in upon itself. In any study of this period it has to be remembered that it was not only the Communists who were manichaean, dogmatic and sectarian. Nor were they the only ones to take orders from abroad. That does not, however, excuse the PCF's policies or the speed with which its members retreated back into a citadel they had been able to leave during the Resistance. This, then, was the prevailing climate when Annie Kriegel joined *La Nouvelle critique.* She worked mainly alongside men like Casanova, Daix and Leduc, and all four 'were required to act as intellectual policemen'.[5] There was also talk of the 'thought police'.

Annie Kriegel wrote many articles on a wide variety of subjects for *La Nouvelle critique.* Her style was lively, alert, fiery, aggressive and unsubtle. In short it was perfectly in keeping with the journal's general tone. In 1952, for example, Kriegel was given the task of attacking a new book by Jules Moch, an SFIO minister of evil memory: in 1947 he had given the order to open fire on striking miners. Her article is so virulent that the attack finally becomes blunted. 'The care with which Monsieur Moch records all the dirty tricks of the bourgeoisie is significant. He is brilliantly continuing the dirty work of *Gringoire.*'[6] Moch and *Gringoire* are attacked in the same terms. Kriegel is implying that there is no basic difference between social-democracy and the extreme right: *Gringoire* was the best known newspaper of the pro-fascist fringe in the thirties. And, like any good socialist, Moch is a liar. 'His account of the facts is a lie, pure and simple. "In 1935, a young Communist assassinated Kirov." Wrong, Monsieur Moch; it was in 1934, not in 1935. Why should Moch lie? In order to introduce another lie: "After the great trials of 1935, tens of thousands of people were executed and millions were deported." '[7] Jules Moch obviously knew that Kirov was assassinated in 1934. And so he lies in order to serve his masters! And Annie Kriegel catches him out!

But Jules Moch is not the only traitor amongst the Socialists. The hatred expressed in Annie Kriegel's attack on Léon Blum is at once ludicrous and odious. 'Hitler refrained from attacking the Jews of the big bourgeoisie. Who will ever forget that Léon Blum, his wife at his side, contemplated from the windows of his villa the smoke from the ovens of the crematoria.'[8] This is particularly odious: Léon Blum was deported to a concentration camp and those members of the Jewish bourgeoisie who did not choose exile ended up in Auschwitz. Kriegel must have known that. In 1953, she again refers to Blum: 'This was Léon Blum's clever formula. He was always wrong, but he was "so intelligent". He always recommended policies that were opposed to the interests of the working class and the people, but his arguments were so "subtle".'[9] Blum's political record may be debatable and patchy, but this is a somewhat oversimplified description of the man who led the Popular Front.

The Socialists were not the only targets for these Stalinist-tipped arrows. Marxists who are not members of the Party, like Mascolo, also come under attack. First of all, how can anyone be a Marxist without being a member of the Party? Mascolo must be a splitter. She rains insults down on him. In just a few pages he is accused of being a mere caricature of a dialectician, of being a sophist and of acting irresponsibly. His book is obscure and pretentious. Mascolo is naive, shameless and eclectic. And when he dares to raise the question of the role of intellectuals in the PCF, the reply is stinging, insulting and brooks no reply. 'It is simply comical for the most dubious representatives of the French intelligentsia, café adventurers who are part writer, part philosopher and part artist and who always have an eye for the main chance, to set themselves up as judges who are qualified to pronounce on matters of science and culture.'[10] In the eyes of prosecutor Kriegel, Mascolo's only good point is that he too condemns and attacks Gide and Malraux. Kriegel concludes her article with the words: 'This is a perfect example of petty bourgeois spite. He would rather slander the party of the working class by accusing it of harbouring suspicions about the intellectuals than objectively analyse the relationship between the Communist Party and the intellectuals.'[11] Fortunately, the PCF, Annie Kriegel and La Nouvelle critique are there to 'Preserve the unity of our Communist doctrine and denounce splits.'[12]

Annie Kriegel is not content with attacking men. When the occasion arises, she can also denounce ideas. Thus, the idea of constructing a European community is pilloried and described as nothing less than a process of fascisization. 'The construction of a European community will encourage the process of fascisization and will paralyse science and culture.'[13] Naturally enough, no evidence is produced to support her argument. When Kriegel talks about fascism, she should know what she is talking about; after all she did fight it in the resistance. But words seem to have lost all meaning. In some of her flights of oratory, Kriegel contrives to combine hate-filled diatribes with sycophancy and the most banal eulogies of Stalin. Her attacks on the authors of the history books used in French schools is a typical example. 'The people who write these text-books will stoop to anything. Stalin is a good and generous man to whom millions of men and women have turned. He is Lenin's disciple and heir, the builder of socialism, the leader of the anti-fascist struggle and the champion of peace. Stalin's name is honoured and his face is loved by the workers of the whole world; in every country the working class and the people take him as their model and their guide. They wish him a long life and have sworn their loyalty to him. The wretched lackeys of the bour-geoisie paint him in the colours of the only men they know and mix with: cunning, cruel exploiters whose hands are stained with the blood of the workers and evil dictators like Hitler and Pétain, whom they helped to power in capitalist states.'[14] It is difficult to imagine a more manichean vision of the world. Annie Kriegel was not, of course, the only person in the PCF to indulge in such excesses. But it is also true that not all French Communists displayed the same shortcomings. Kriegel was in the forefront of the battle and therefore in the forefront of Stalinism and sectarianism.

Throughout this period, Kriegel's defence of the 'purity of Marxism' is not limited to the printed word. She also carried the good word to Party branches in person, explaining the line, convincing those who had doubts, attacking the recalcitrant and even closing down branches which had become too derelict or which had succumbed to the gangrene of criticism or doubt. Despite her youth, her authority, her rigidity and her power meant that she made enemies as well as friends in the PCF. While she was head of the Communist student organization for instance, she played a controversial role in the expulsion of Marcel Prenant, a member of the Central Committee. Although Prenant was an inter-nationally known biologist, he was criticized for his lukewarm support for Lysenko and his 'proletarian science'. It was in fact Kriegel who attacked him and blocked his re-election to the Central Committee. When she now refers to the incident, she claims to have been the victim of a plot and says that she intervened at the request of Thorez himself. 'Do you really think that a young Communist of twenty-two would have dared to take the floor in front of the Party's main leaders without being told to?'[15] When Marcel Prenant later mentioned the incident, he summed it up laconically: 'As soon as she saw where her interests lay. . .'[16]

Like all the Party officials of the day, she took part in the campaign against Marty, a famous Party leader who had fallen into disgrace. 'Annie Besse, one of the leading figures in the Fédération de la Seine went in person to address a meeting of Communist students in the Latin Quarter and to justify the accusations against Marty. She spoke from the plat-form in the little room in the rue Lhomond, arms raised, fists clenched, eyes blazing. She was a convincing little hothead.'[17]

Annie Kriegel quietly left the PCF in 1956 or 1957. What was the reason for her sudden departure? Perhaps she was disturbed by the Soviet intervention in Hungary. Perhaps, as she now claims, it was the doctors' plot, though it was in fact Kriegel who organized the petition got up by Jewish Communists to denounce the bourgeois press's 'new slander'. She told her friend Dominique Desanti that 'on the night of 26 May 1955 neither she nor her husband could sleep for worry and kept asking themselves the same question; if Tito was a true socialist, what about those who had been executed?'[18]

Whatever the reasons for her departure from the PCF, Kriegel avoided all political activity for a time. She retired from politics to work on her thesis on the origins of the PCF. Its publication in 1964 marked her entry into the scientific world. The militant had become an academic who was respected throughout the French intellectual world. Her thesis, which has been republished in a cheap edition, is still regarded as the authoritative work on the subject. It is even considered a classic. Not only Kriegel's status had changed; arguments replace the old insults and she relies upon abundant documentation rather than unfounded assertions. Summary and peremptory judgments give way to qualified statements, details and precision. Her thesis is also one of the first works to study the PCF from the inside. It is the first example of a genre which was to produce an astonishing number of similar studies, many of which helped to fuel anti-Communism in France. At the time, however, Kriegel was very much an innovator. What she was trying to prove or establish was that the birth of the PCF was the result of a historical accident, that the Party is an alien phenomenon which has been grafted on to France.

From this point onwards, Kriegel came to be regarded as the leading specialist on the French labour movement. Her reputation was consolidated by the publication of several other books on the CGT, the First World War and the French labour movement and related topics. Quite apart from the undoubted scientific qualities of her work, many people thought that Kriegel had an extra advantage: 'She knows what she is talking about. Like Racine's Acomat in *Bajazet,* she grew up in the harem and she knows her way around it.'[19] Kriegel's *Les Communistes français* is, then a classic example of the 'Inside the PCF' genre. Such books explain the workings of the 'apparatus', with each author contributing his piece on democracy, political education, the cadres, the bureaucrats, and above all on money, the party's secrets and its relations with Moscow. Written in 1968 and revised in 1970, *Les Communistes français* is considered a classic. It has to be said from the outset that the book is very accessible, extremely well-documented and simply written. All these factors contributed to its success. But alongside some very interesting passages we find others that are, to say the least surprising coming from a specialist of this stature: '[in the PCF] anything that smacks of swagger, stands out as exceptional or unusual or catches the attention is suspect. This is of course a source of hypocrisy, but it is a very specific kind of hypocrisy. Everyone tries to hide their vices and their past slips. But within the PCF, everyone tries to model their behaviour on a type whose dominant feature is known to all: normality'.[20] She later adds: 'The eccentrics who are so common in anarchist organizations—bastards, hunchbacks, homosexuals, butterfly collectors, drug users, fetishists—all feel ill at ease in Communist organizations, as does anyone obsessed by personal problems, as do philosophical, sexual and cultural minorities and as does anyone who is too enthusiastic about music, the cinema or the countryside.'[21] Quite aside from the absurdity of stating that, for some unknown reason, hunchbacks and butterfly collectors feel ill at ease in Communist organizations, it is noteworthy that Kriegel once more fails to provide even a shadow of proof. Such passages simply serve to reinforce the notion that the PCF is made up of robots or zombies who are devoid of any feelings. Nor does Kriegel attempt to provide any explanation for her claims. The fact that the PCF is a predominantly working class organization may to some extent explain why it finds it difficult to accept certain minorities or marginal situations. Kriegel's assertions are unproven; the documentation and detail that characterize the work as a whole are noticeably absent from this chapter. Finally, even if we did have proof that there are no 'eccentrics' in the PCF, we would still need to be able to compare it with other major parties in France. Then, and only then, we might be able to draw some scientific conclusions.

The Party moulds its members and its leaders are simply mediocrities: 'A Communist leader does not merely try to look like the man in the street. Most of them are mediocre through and through. And their mediocrity causes problems.'[22] Coming from a famous specialist, this is a truly astonishing statement. Communist leaders are said to be mediocre, but the criterion for mediocrity is never defined. Proof, explanations and examples are nowhere to be found.

The major thesis of both this study and Kriegel's other books is that the PCF is a 'counter society'. 'A Communist Party based in a country where it does not hold power functions as a party-society. The counter society it forms within the wider society prefigures the socialist society it intends to substitute for existing society when it has seized power.'[23] The notion that the PCF is a counter society is definitively associated with the name of Annie Kriegel. It is an attractive idea and has found many supporters. But first of all we have to decide and agree upon what is meant by 'society'. And to state baldly and without qualification that the PCF is a prefiguration of the socialist society it wants to see is something of an oversimplification. It is, of course, not unreasonable to argue that if the

PCF gained power (and precisely what that means remains to be seen), some of the Party's characteristic features would have a major influence on both power and society. Kriegel, however, concentrates on those features to the exclusion of others. It is perfectly obvious that the very process of the seizure of power and the conditions under which it occurred would inevitably have major effects on the party concerned. The same could be said of the exercise of power itself. None of these obvious points are made. It is as though the PCF were a timeless body on which social reality has no effects.

The danger of this kind of 'argument' is that it leads to some very dubious comparisons. Thus, Kriegel concludes her discussion of the party-society as follows: 'We can thus explain how it is that so many characteristic features of Soviet Society reappear in the French Party.'[24] How can a sociologist of Kriegel's standing compare a political party with a society? Just what features do they have in common? What is the nature of those features? Neither of these questions is ever answered. Yet Kriegel's reputation in the intellectual world remains untarnished.

Such arguments have the obvious advantage of reinforcing a pre-conceived image of the PCF. The reader finds precisely what he expects to find in the form of what appear to be scientific arguments.

In the seventies, *Le Figaro* offered Kriegel a job and she accepted the offer. She thus became a specialist on the French labour movement working for a conservative newspaper. From now on the political shift becomes very obvious; Annie Kriegel has definitely moved to the right. The columns of *Le Figaro* provide her with a platform and a mass audience for her increasingly militant anti-communism and for her ultra-Zionism. Her passion for Israel and Judaism have also led her to write for *L'Arche*, a very conservative newspaper which is virtually the official organ of the Jewish community of France. In 1979, Kriegel published a collection of the major articles she wrote for *Le Figaro* between 1976 and 1979. They are worth looking at, if only because the author's decision to republish them suggests that she sees them as more than reports on current events. She also feels it necessary to explain why she agreed to write for *Le Figaro*, which she describes in her introduction as 'a thinking and courteous newspaper which is both courageous and liberal'.[25]

Kriegel's image of the PCF leaves one speechless. 'The 93,879 members who were recruited in 1975 joined, then, a classic Leninist party.'[26] How can anyone writing in 1975 claim that the PCF is a classic Leninist party? Besides, what is a classic Leninist party? Since its foundation, the PCF has undergone such major changes and modifications that it is impossible to speak of it simply as a classic Leninist party. To describe it as such means blotting out the entire history of the Party and the labour movement. But Kriegel is perhaps more concerned with satisfying the expectations of *Le Figaro*'s readers, who all too often explain the PCF's line in terms of what is happening in Moscow.

As for the record of the Soviet Union, it is, as one might have expected, completely negative. 'The record of the Soviet regime does not include any positive changes in economics, politics or culture. There is no point in stressing the issue; the stagnation and inertia are self-evident. No one doubts, for instance, that industrial life is severely handicapped by the delays and the incoherence of a centralized and bureaucratic system of planning, by the absence of a qualified and conscientious work force, by overmanning and bad management and by the corruption of middle-rank officials. Agriculture is in an even worse state. Soviet society still displays the same negative features. The small party apparatus dominates an increasingly undifferentiated and stagnating society which has never been fully urbanized or properly educated. The population is incapable of imagining any collective project. Alcoholism is alarmingly widespread, particularly amongst the younger generation. Its cultural bankruptcy is irredeemable and the contrast between the shapeless entity known as Soviet culture and the vitality of both Samizdat publications and the intelligentsia makes it even more obvious.'[27]

In just a few lines we have all the classic clichés about the Soviet Union. No one would deny that it has serious problems with agriculture. It is quite obvious that alcoholism is a scourge and that the system of planning is at times incoherent goes without saying. But it is neither serious nor scientific to describe a country solely in terms of alcoholism, incoherence, inadequacy and failure. No regime can maintain itself in power by repression alone. If everything is chaos and stagnation, how are we to explain the fact that the Soviet people give the regime at least passive support? It is of course true that *Le Figaro*'s readers are not interested in the detailed figures and impartial accounts provided by specialists like Maric Lavigne or Alec Nove.

Soviet foreign policy is of course determined by all the classic objectives. 'The Soviet Union cannot give up the one thing that justifies it and its power. Not content with ruling Russia and its satellites, it wants to be at the heart of a whole system. The ultimate aim is still the establishment of a world wide socialist republic which would, by definition, be peaceful.'[28]

To conclude this discussion of foreign policy, it should be noted that Kriegel agrees with Raymond Aron that the USA has definitely abdicated its responsibilities. She has also drawn an astonishing comparison between the Russian revolution and Khomenei's revolution in Iran: 'A revolution which is definitely a remake of a glorious model; the revolutions of February and October 1917.'[29]

In terms of French domestic politics, Kriegel attacks not only the Communists but also the Socialist Party, and especially its Marxist wing (CERES): 'There is no difference—or no coherent difference—between social-democracy and Communism.'[30] CERES's leader Jean-Pierre Chevènement is a 'democratic socialist, as his party label indicates, but he thinks solely in terms of Leninism'.[31] Chevènement's Leninism is 'a poor man's Leninism, even more impoverished than Communist Leninism'.[32] She supplies no arguments, but she is happy to indulge in ad hominem attacks: 'Althusser is too innocently speculative for what he has to do. Elleinstein is too obviously a schemer for what he has to say.'[33]

Kriegel's 'scientific' period is over. We are back to the mordant tone, the attacks, accusations and clichés of the pamphleteer rather than the language of the author of scientific works.

We have already discussed Annie Kriegel's anti-Soviet views, her anti-communism and her anti-socialism. We now have to look at her ultra-Zionism. It the seventies and eighties Judaism becomes a fundamental assumption for Kriegel. It does not, however, appear to have been very important to her during her Stalinist period. In 1953 she even went so far as to argue for the complete assimilation of the Jewish community: 'Jewish solidarity is a subjective illusion and a product of the diaspora. The Jews have always been an exploited minority. . . Jewish solidarity allows the French bourgeoisie to keep the Jewish masses and Jewish workers under its thumb. It is also an obstacle to total assimilation, which would be a real disaster for the bourgeoisie. . . Like any other nationalist ideology, Zionism is therefore basically racist. It distracts Jews from the class struggle.'[34]

Nowadays, she cannot condemn anti-Zionists strongly enough and claims that they are nothing but anti-semites. In 1982, Kriegel's Zionism reaches a paroxysm with *Israël est-il coupable?* which appeared in Raymond Aron's 'Libertés 2000' collection. The book claims to be an analysis of the effects of the war in the Lebanon on western public opinion, but its tone can only be described as hysterical. We might be reading something written thirty years earlier. Words have again lost all meaning. Kriegel's targets may have changed, but her methods are the same. 'Anti-Zionism is to Communism what racist anti-semitism was to Nazism. It reveals its true essence and is at the heart of its strategy of conquest and expansion.'[35] Kriegel launches an attack on a whole host of organizations which are, she claims, controlled or manipulated by the Communists; they range from anti-racist organizations to the World Council of Churches. The Communists and their allies are at work everywhere. Moscow and the socialist bloc used the Israeli invasion of Lebanon to see how Europe would react to a major brainwashing campaign. 'It became a full-scale experiment. The socialist camp is perfectly capable of turning freedom of information, which is the ultimate criterion of democracy, against the democracies themselves.'[36] She goes on: 'But that is not the main point. The main point is that a world-wide brainwashing campaign, a systematic campaign of disinformation on a world scale has developed unimpeded. The western news system has been destroyed and used against the West.'[37] The media lent themselves to this campaign: 'Because of their leftist sympathies, European journalists all too often reported events quite uncritically and dug up anything that could be used against Israel.'[38]

For the benefit of the Mitterand government, she then adds: 'French foreign policy has been shown to be broadly in line with the desires of Moscow and those of the French communists.'[39] Since the left came to power, Franco–Soviet relations have in fact been cooler than ever before. In terms of foreign policy, Socialists and Communists disagree over many issues: Chad, Lebanon, disarmament, Israel, Afghanistan, Poland. . . Kriegel never mentions their disagreements. She then goes on to explain the 'real aims' of 'anti-Jewish terrorism': 'The fact is. . . that those who are killing Jews are not killing "substitute" Jews, in other words Israelis. They are killing Jews because they want to kill Jews, and if they could do so they would kill all Israeli Jews and all the Jews of the diaspora. . . The terrorist campaign against Jews in European synagogues means only one thing: anti-Zionism is the concrete expression of anti-semitism and the aim of anti-semitism is the extermination of the Jews.[40]

Judaism has in fact become an essential reference point and a source of identity for Kriegel. In her book, she tells us that she has wept for political reasons three times in her life: when the Soviets invaded Hungary in 1956, when De Gaulle spoke of the Jewish people as an elite people and described them as domineering and self-confident, and when John Paul II granted an audience to Yasser Arafat. The latter reaction would appear to have more to do with hatred for the PLO leader than with disappointment because the trust she placed in the head of the Catholic Church had been betrayed. The fact that she can react to the 1956 events in Hungary and to a diplomatic gesture on the part of the Vatican reveals the extent to which she has entered the realm of the irrational.

How, in the last analysis, can one explain a career which begins with ultra-Stalinism, followed by an academic interlude and then by a definite move to the right? How can we explain how someone can move through all these phases? It seems obvious that Kriegel's individual psychological makeup must have a lot to do with the way she has changed. Psychology might provide at least a partial explanation of certain of her reactions. In an account of a conversation with one of her students, she remarks, 'I wonder to what extent I have forgotten certain things, because one of my pupils spitefully told me last week that in 1947 I had written an article on "Zionism and Anti-Semitism". You could have knocked me over with a feather, I did not remember any more.'[41] It is difficult not to see this as an example of amnesia in the psychological sense. But such explanations are clearly not enough. Kriegel's extreme Stalinism and her subsequent departure from the PCF can perhaps be explained in terms of the generation to which she belongs. Annie Kriegel joined the Party, it will be remembered, during the war. And as she herself writes: 'No one who looks at statistics on how long people have been in the Party can fail to be struck by one curious percentage: of the present membership, only 3.1% joined the Party during the war.'[42] According to other figures supplied by Kriegel, only one in ten of those who joined at that time are still members. She belongs to a generation that has been ravaged: 'A generation which has been decimated. It is also a warped generation. The conditions under which they joined have left their mark on them and they are still fascinated by the two techniques they had to learn: clandestinity and partisan warfare.'[43]

The motivations of those who joined the PCF during the war also have to be taken into account. Did they join because of the PCF's major role in the Resistance or because they wanted to transform society? Not, of course, that there is any necessary contradiction between the two.

A study of the theoretical training these new members received—or did not receive—would be of great interest. During the war they can have received little training and any training they were given after the war must have been very Stalinist. In those conditions, our young militant can have had only a very vague notion of Marxism and would have been unlikely to have been able to resist the simplistic arguments of the day.

Kriegel's decision to join the Party must also have had a lot to do with the climate of the war. When the war and its immediate aftermath (the Cold War and the defence of the besieged citadel) gave way to a less heady period, the basis of her commitment rapidly disappeared, particularly as a considerable degree of naivety was also involved. But other factors must also have been at work. Kriegel's career was compromised once the PCF was forced, however reluctantly, to question the more aggressive aspects of the Stalinism with which she identified. It was not for nothing that the Party completely changed *La Nouvelle critique*'s editorial board.

Finally, the denunciation of Stalin's crimes at the Twentieth Congress of the CPSU, the rehabilitation of the 'traitors', the self criticisms and the questioning must also have increasingly given rise to doubts which eventually led to a complete change of heart.

Personal factors aside, Annie Kriegel belongs to a group of former Stalinists who, as Maxime Rodinson puts it, 'Combat their former faith with the zeal of the neophyte, and who, moreover, employ just the same sort of reasoning, the same virulent tone and lack of subtlety, that they had formerly placed in the service of the cause they now combat.'[44]

Kriegel has moved from one extreme to another, from Communism to anti-Communism. Her fervour remains constant. As with many other Stalinists who have gone over to absolute anti-Sovietism, her career could in many ways be described in religious terms. This conclusion is a comment rather than a condemnation. It is, however, to be regretted that Annie Kriegel has never seen any need to explain her past actions. It is of course true that no one has ever put her in the position of having to do so. Anti-Communism is now so fashionable in France that it does not have to be justified. It is so much part of the political climate that its ideologues can do and say anything. Even though it is the work of intellectuals, it borders, however, on the irrational. It is in that sense that the case of Annie Kriegel is so exemplary.

II

'The Marxist doctrine is omnipotent because it is true. It is comprehensive and harmonious and provides men with an integral world outlook.' (Lenin, 1913).[45]

'The PCF clings to this ideal more tenaciously than ever. And yet, seventy-five years after the event, what remains of these flamboyant assertions? the invasion of Czechoslovakia, the Gulag Archipelago, the crimes of Lin Piao and the Gang of Four, Ethiopia's new head of state consecrated as a revolutionary by Brezhnev when he arrives in Moscow, his hands still dripping with the blood of the students, the cultural genocide directed against the peripheral peoples of the USSR, a crude denial of human rights in Belgrade. The only constant features of Marxism in power are despotism and cultural underdevelopment. What is the point of going on with the list? Every adjective used by Lenin has been turned into its caricatural opposite. Poor old PCF!' (Pierre Daix, 1978).[46]

'The greatest crime of all is man's exploitation of man. The Nazi camps took that exploitation to a paroxysm, to its logical conclusion. But the Soviet Union's reeducation camps are the logical conclusion of something very different; the complete suppression of man's exploitation of man. . . They are one of the Soviet Union's most glorious achievements.' (Pierre Daix, 1949).[47]

'Marxism, the science of politics, is based upon the liberation movement led by the proletariat, the most exploited of all social classes. The Communist Party is based upon the same science. It is both the vanguard of the proletariat, a form of consciousness and a scientific tool. *It brings together the best elements within the proletariat.* It has educated the whole class and is therefore capable of forging the militants it requires if it is to shoulder its responsibilities.' (Pierre Daix, 1949).[48]

'Let me tell you straight away that if the Soviet Union had been a hundred times worse, and if Stalin had committed a hundred times more crimes than he did commit, the struggle I am speaking of would not have been any different. . . The Communist Parties are human tools created in the image of the Party forged by Lenin.' (Pierre Daix, 1949).[49]

'Marcel Liebman listed Lenin's illusions in his *Le Léninisme sous Lénine* and I added a few more to the list in my *Le Socialisme du silence.*

You do not have to look far to find further proof of the naivety, ignorance, simplism and weakness of Leninism.' (Pierre Daix, 1978).[50]

Make no mistake about it. We are not trying to justify the events of the forties and fifties, and we will come back to them later. Nor are we trying to ridicule the author. On the contrary, we are trying to reveal the mechanism behind the evolution of Pierre Daix who, after thirty-four years in the PCF, now takes what Philippe Robrieux describes as 'a position based upon a fundamentalist anti-Communism.'[51]

Pierre Daix was born in Ivry-sur-Seine in 1922. As a *lycée* student he was successively influenced by his history teacher André Meynier, who was a Socialist, by his mathematics teacher P. Labérenne, who was a member of the PCF and, in his final year at school, by René Maublanc, who was one of the PCF's philosophers.

He joined the PCF on 26 September 1939, the day that it was proclaimed illegal by the Daladier government. He played an important role in the clandestine work of the Communist student organization. He was arrested in November 1940 and again in January 1942. He then spent two years in French prisons before being deported to Mauthausen in March 1944. In the camp, he played an active role in organizing international Communist resistance. According to his own account, it was then that he became a Stalinist: 'When I finally began to ask myself how I could ever have become a Stalinist, I realized that it must have happened in Mauthausen.'[52] It was also in Mauthausen that he first learned of the existence of the Soviet reeducation camps. 'In 1937 he [Pavel Loukov, a Russian he had met in the camp] had been in a camp, a Soviet labour camp. He told me that it had made a man of him.'[53]

This somewhat curious account was to be a vital part of the arguments used by Pierre Daix in the campaign against David Rousset.[54]

After the war, Daix was given a post in the *cabinet* of Charles Tillon, the Communist Minister for Aviation. He held that position until May 1947. He then worked for a while on *L'Avant Garde,* the Communist student newspaper and for Editions Sociales, the PCF's publishing house. He did not, however, remain there for long. At the time the PCF was trying to gain ideological control over a number of publications. In January 1948 Daix therefore took over from Loys Massons as editor in chief of *Les Lettres françaises.* That this was a planned operation has been confirmed by many witnesses and analysts of the PCF. According to Jeanine Verdès Leroux, for instance, 'During this period the PCF, which published a number of titles itself and which had also launched some new titles, gained control over certain papers. In other cases, open-minded editors were replaced by men who were *unconditionally loyal.* They were rewarded for guaranteeing the *strictest orthodoxy* without having to be told what to do. This is what happened when Pierre Daix replaced Loys Massons as editor in chief of *Les Lettres Françaises.*'[55] According to the paper's editor Claude Morgan, 'Casanova wanted to get his own man in. Pierre Daix dragged Marxism into everything and *Les Lettres Françaises'* sales began to fall.'[56] Renaud de Jouvenel: 'Pierre Daix may well have been lulled into a sense of security because he had a sleeping partner he could rely on. He was certainly not interested in the commercial fate of the newspaper. Advertising was the least of this bright team's concerns. The only thing that mattered was putting it to bed early enough to get it out on the streets, but I would be prepared to bet that no one ever worried about sales or wondered why the number of unsold copies was rising so alarmingly.'[57]

When Pierre Daix joined the editorial board of *La Nouvelle critique* it did nothing to alter the widespread view that he was a 'Party policeman'. Jeanine Verdès Leroux describes the journal as follows: 'Official positions on everything were expressed in the crudest of terms. This was the only place that the "two sciences" theory was fully developed and that the pro-Lysenko campaign became most extreme. It was *La Nouvelle critique* that theorized socialist realist painting and praised it to the skies. *The journal perfected the deliberate use of polemic; its virulence and inventiveness are difficult to imagine and almost impossible to describe. Polemic was the norm and it took outrageous forms.* This was not the result of excesses on the part of a few individuals; it was a tactic, as one of our interlocutors saw only too well; "It really was a way of putting the boot in. It was a military tactic designed to stop the majority of intellectuals coming under the influence of our interlocutors".'[58]

Pierre Daix was very active in all this. There is no need to go into everything that he wrote. One event, which is as important as it is dramatic, is enough to tell us a great deal about the climate described above: the Rajk affair.

In 1948, Rajk, the Hungarian Minister for the Interior, was accused of Titoism and of plotting to overthrow socialism. He was tried, found guilty and executed. There was no proof and the only evidence against him came from unconvincing 'confessions'. Pierre Daix wrote an account of the trial and analysed the whole question for *La Nouvelle critique*. Leaving aside his stupidly sectarian comments on the Yugoslav regime,[59] one passage in particular gives us a very clear picture of the author's state of mind: 'The evidence is there for all to see. The Hungarian government has just published a blue book containing a full transcript of the Rajk trial. A French translation appeared recently. (*Les Lettres Françaises* had already published Rajk's statement.) If we look at the accused's statement, we learn that Rajk was arrested by the Hungarian police in 1931 and became a paid informer. He initially worked for the Hungarian police, then in Czechoslovakia and was finally sent to Spain. According to Hungarian police records, he was recruited by the French *deuxième bureau* [intelligence service] while he was in the Vernet camp. He was also contacted by an American agent, but he had already been recruited by the Gestapo, who repartriated him. When the country was liberated, he went over to the American intelligence services and was infiltrated into their Yugoslav network in 1947. He himself said that "Rankovich [the Yugoslav Minister of the Interior] told me that the Yugoslav network consisted of himself and Tito". Rajk was a self-confessed intermediary for the Americans and acted on orders from the Yugoslav network. He was plotting to assassinate the leaders of the Hungarian Communist Party and to destroy the People's Democratic regime in Hungary.'[60] Any comments would be superfluous.

This Cold War dogmatism was to give way to a more qualified attitude and Pierre Daix finally began to ask himself a few little questions. His attitude began to change at the beginning of the fifties, when disturbing reports about certain members of Stalin's entourage began to emerge. Stalin himself of course remained above reproach. In his autobiography *J'ai Cru au matin,* Daix describes the atmosphere when the dictator died: 'Like everyone else, I was completely overcome, perhaps more so than others as I had already begun to ask questions. *But that simply meant that I extolled the mythical father who had left us orphaned.* I entitled my article in *Les Lettres Françaises* "He Taught Us To Grow Up".'[61] Relatively soon after Stalin's death news of the turmoil in the Soviet Union began to emerge.[62] Pierre Daix was surprised, even astonished: 'In the autumn of 1954 *L'Humanité* [the PCF daily] published a report which made the ground shake beneath me: the American Noël Field had been rehabilitated in Hungary. Everyone who had been found guilty in the Rajk and Slansky trials had been charged with conspiring with him. This proved that the trials had been put up jobs. I thought I was going mad.'[63] 'So Rousset had been telling the truth.'[64]

The Twentieth Congress of the CPSU confirmed all the rumours that had been circulating. Once more, Pierre Daix felt the ground shake beneath him. Unlike many Communist intellectuals, he did not, however, leave the Party after the Soviet invasion of Hungary, which he describes as follows: 'I accepted the Soviet army's intervention in Budapest as a tragic but inevitable decision.' He then adds: 'When a demonstration in which both Guy Mollet and Antoine Pinay took part ended with an attack on the PCF's headquarters and on *L'Humanité*'s offices, I was with my Party body and soul.'[65]

In the late fifties, Daix continued to work for *Les Lettres Françaises,* but he now took a more openly critical view of the USSR.

In 1963, he took the important step of writing a preface for Solzhenitsyn's *One Day in the Life of Ivan Denisovich,* the book which provided sceptics with the final proof that camps did indeed exist in the Soviet Union. The preface marked the beginning of a gradual estrangement from the Party, a process which became more marked during the

Prague Spring of 1968. Pierre Daix was actually in Prague that spring and what he saw there filled him with enthusiasm. He wrote a moving account of his experiences there in his *Journal de Prague* and updated it in his later *Prague au coeur* (1974). He was deeply shocked by the PCF's acceptance of the Soviet intervention of August 1968 and of the normalization that put an end to the attempt to build a Czech socialism.

His book *Ce que je sais de Soljenytsine,* which appeared in 1973, marked his final break with the Party. He decided not to renew his membership at the beginning of 1974. He had been a member of the PCF for thirty-four years, but now the divorce was complete.

1974 was a turning point in Daix's life. He has subsequently altered both his beliefs and his field of activity. In recent years he has completely revised his position, his beliefs and his ideals. The main theme of his work is now a systematic anti-Communism.

It is of course quite legitimate to question one's former political loyalties. It is, however, unfortunate that many intellectuals have done so only as a result of changing literary and ideological loyalties.

The case of Pierre Daix is particularly unfortunate. He not only paints a very distorted picture of history and doctrine but also makes what can only be described as an unjustified claim to knowledge of matters doctrinal and historical. The tactics he used during his Stalinist period have not disappeared. On the contrary, they are more pronounced and more obvious than ever. It is therefore useful to look at them here.

1. *Insults, invectives and gratuitous slanders.* 'The Party's central school still teaches Engels in the same old way. No one takes any notice of Michel le Bris's protests. The real question is this: How is it that this raving lunatic, this bloodthirsty moron who plays with the massacre of whole races as though he were playing marbles has lasted this long?'[66] There is of course no argument or proof in support of this claim. There is a definitely hysterical quality to these insults.

2. *Lying by Omission.* In his book on the crisis in the PCF, Pierre Daix writes: 'Marcel Liebman listed Lenin's illusions in his *Le Léninisme sous Lénine* and I added a few more to the list in my *Le Socialisme du silence.* You do not have to look far to find further support of the naivety, ignorance, simplism and weakness of Leninism.'[67] This is a very strange view of Liebman's book. Daix suggests that there is very little to it, though it is in fact cogently argued and contains many passages that contradict the 'summary' he gives of it here. *Le Léninisme sous Lénine* does contain many attacks on the deification of the infallible Lenin, but its main target is the way anti-Soviet ideologues have polemically distorted his image: 'The almost desperate will power and paralysed energy he showed in the last weeks and months of his struggle reveal *the authenticity of his democratic aspirations.*'[68] Pierre Daix claims to be using Liebman's arguments, but he turns them into a denunciation of Leninism which is simply not

there in the text.

In a rather different register, we find the following comments on the presence of Cuban troops in Angola: 'How is it that not one member of the PCF, intellectuals included, ever asks about the uninterrupted series of defeats Marxism has suffered wherever it has taken power?. . . Not to mention its role in supplying mercenaries, denying the people of Africa the right to self-determination and handing Africa over to the Cubans.'[69] Once again Pierre Daix is obviously distorting the truth to make it fit in with his a priori assumptions. What about all the interventions that have been made in an attempt to deny the people of Angola their right to self-determination? Does he have to be reminded that the Cubans intervened after the murderous invasion made by South African and Zairean troops and that they intervened at the request of the legitimate representatives of the country? They helped Angola to achieve true political, social and cultural independence. This was in fact the interpretation adopted by the UN Security Council in its resolution 387 of 31 March 1976. Pierre Daix has not a word to say about all this.

3. *Intellectual Dishonesty.* In his *La Crise du PCF*, Daix looks at the problematic of the PCF during the occupation and at the role played by its leaders and others who took part in the events of that period. Here we find a very clear allusion to the death of Fried Clément, Comintern's representative in France. 'Fried's silence was assured when he was murdered by "persons unknown" in Brussels in 1943.' Daix adopts Bruhat's hypothesis that Clément was killed by Communist agents. 'But just to make sure, he was, at the suggestion of Soviet advisers, also posthumously condemned during the 1958 Slansky affair.'[70] Bruhat's hypothesis has yet to be proven, but Daix's next statement is truly astonishing: 'Julien Lahaut was also murdered in 1958.' First of all, he gets the date wrong; Lahaut was in fact murdered in 1950. He was at that time the Chairman of the Belgian Communist Party, and to claim that both men were killed by Communist assassins suggests an amazing ignorance of the historical facts. Lahaut was in fact shot down by two right-wing killers who claimed that he had shouted 'Long live the Republic!' in parliament as Bauduin was being crowned. The murder is one of the most famous and most tragic events to have occurred during the 'monarchy debate' in Belgium. It is famous enough for Daix to have known both of the murder and who was responsible for it. But facts are irrelevant when an insinuation—even a gratuitous and groundless one—can be used to support an indictment that has more to do with ideology than with history.

Like many other intellectuals who used to belong to the PCF, Pierre Daix has a tendency to set himself up as a historian of the Communist movement and as a Marxist theoretician. As we have already stressed, he has every right to do so. But it is difficult not to look for a connection between the new career he has embarked upon and both the current fashion for anti-Communism and the profitability of anti-Communist literature.

The method is always the same. Pierre Daix analyses everything that affects the Communist movement and Marxist theory in terms of three or four set formulae.

Thus, when he looks at the history of the PCF, it is always in terms of Moscow and Leninist theory (or his own version of that theory): 'The real history of the PCF begins in June 1920. It begins, not in France, but in the Kremlin in Moscow, if not in Lenin's mind.'[71]

'Far from signifying a reconciliation between the PCF and the French nation, the turning point of 1934 simply indicates that the USSR thought it to its advantage to back France against Hitler's might or at least to block the possibility of a Franco–German alliance.'[72]

'In 1975–76, the PCF leadership put it about that the Party had changed because it had at last come to terms with the facts about Stalin's repression, but the change was really a means of preserving the continuity of Leninism, both in organizational terms and in terms of political strategy.'[73] It is quite obvious that the PCF has at times acted in accordance with Moscow's wishes. But anyone who attempts to explain sixty-four years in the history of the PCF solely in terms of orders from the Kremlin and never looks at either socio-political conditions in France or at the problems they pose for the PCF is an obsessional rather than a historian.

When it comes to matters of theory, the flimsiness of our author's assertions is little short of astonishing. In 1949 he was loudly proclaiming theses that bore all the hallmarks of extreme certainty and dogmatism. To take only one of many examples: 'Marxism, the science of politics, is based upon the liberation of movement led by the proletariat, the most exploited of all social classes. The Communist Party is based upon the same science. It is both the vanguard of the proletariat, a form of consciousness and a scientific tool. It brings together the best elements within the proletariat. It has educated the whole class and is therefore capable of forging the militants it requires if it is to shoulder its responsibilities.'[74] In 1980 the same Daix can make such categorical and unfounded statements as: 'Because so many of his prophecies appear to have come true we tend to forget that, insofar as he was a scientist, Marx was a scientist of his own time. It was because he applied Darwinism to the study of human societies that he came to the conclusion that the forces of production would produce the material basis for socialism. Marx takes the concept of universal evolution from Darwin because he can use it to support the Hegelian dialectic and put it on a materialist basis. By doing so Marx unwittingly reduces social and economic phenomena, which are, he claims, autonomous, to a biological model. He thus sees the same reductionist approach as those who take natural selection, which is the

motor behind Darwinian evolution, and conclude that capitalism is bio-
logically justified because it practises the survival of the fittest... I would
not take such malicious pleasure in pointing out how crude Marx's anthropology is if it did not have such serious consequences. Because of their
continued belief that the development of the forces of production will
sooner or later make the social superstructure socialist those Communists
who have gained power have no compunction whatsoever about indulging
in a horrific number of acts of cultural genocide. Capitalism has nothing
to learn from them in these matters. On the contrary, they have gone
much further than capitalism has ever done, and their doctrinal generaliza-
tions take us back to the days when the missionaries colonized the
"infidel" and the "pagans".'[75]

The reductionism and the oversimplifications are quite amazing. It
cannot be denied that, in terms of anthropology, Marx and Engels now
look very dated and that their basically evolutionist views have been
proved to be erroneous. But Daix gives us a very summary presentation
of Marx's work and makes it look as though his theory never changed.
He never supports his arguments with specific references to specific texts
and his reasoning is very unsubtle. The similarity between this vision of
Marx and that put forward by Daix forty years ago is inescapable; it is
simply an inverted mirror image of the apologias and eulogies of the past.

The present climate obviously encourages and authorises such views;
indeed it makes them almost compulsory. But Marx's life and work
continue to inspire research. In this domain, there are no certainties and
no dogmas. On the contrary, few authors have inspired such a wide variety
of research.

As everyone knows, Marx once told a French Socialist that he was not
a Marxist. If he saw the caricatures that now pass for Marxism, he would
probably say that he was an anti-Marxist. And Pierre Daix is certainly one
of the more important caricaturists. His eulogies were caricatures and so
are his denunciations. He always was a caricaturist.

III

It is impossible not to be struck by the contrast between the incredible
intellectual irresponsibility of these authors and the audience they have
found, especially (or mainly) in the French intelligentsia. Their writings
display all the classic features of the polemics in which right wing journalists and literati used to excel. They deliberately avoided a rationalist
approach and their sympathies were with the forces of reaction and the far
right. The reactionary pamphleteers won their last and most resounding
victories in the thirties, when the representatives of the school led by
Maurras launched their final attacks on democracy, the Republic, the reds
and the Jews. And then came the divine surprise of Vichy.[76]

The intellectuals of the left are now writing similar pamphlets. And these people are on the left; neither Pierre Daix nor Annie Kriegel have ever shed their liberal veneer, even though Kriegel does write for a major conservative newspaper. They claim, even more so than ever, to be defending the interests of progress and democracy. It does not take much to make them claim to be the representatives of true socialism, the socialism of Jaurès, for instance. They also claim to be serious scientists and honest intellectuals. Their claims are somewhat extravagant, but the critics accept them and accord them a status that bears no relation to their true merits. Anyone who is sceptical enough to doubt them meets with a twofold objection. These people know what they are talking about. And of course they do provide certain publishers with best sellers.

'These people know what they are talking about.' 'They have seen communism from the inside.' 'Their knowledge has all the wealth of first hand experience.' All these arguments could easily be turned against them. If we analyse their writings, we find all the classic reactions of people who have been disappointed in love. But no one dreams of criticising them for their past, even though it has marked them for ever. They may well have been converted, but they have not changed. They are praised because they appear to have undergone a metamorphosis; no one notices the constants, even though they are glaringly obvious. Their best sellers prove, thanks to the support of the most indulgent and slothful critics anyone could hope for, that the public can be fooled. No one denounces or even notices the arrogance of both yesterday's eulogies and today's diatribes; no one cares that there is never any proof and that invective is used in the place of analysis. Their inverted hyper-Stalinism—which takes the usual form of total manichaeanism—is white-washed simply because it is directed against Communism. The hysteria has not really changed, but it gets a better welcome in its present guise. Raymond Aron, who was, or so we are told, the personification of intelligence and reason, gave these renegades both hospitality and support, even though they had yet to recover from their illness.

Kriegel and Daix should be the object of a clinical study, and no doubt psychology will play some part in their future biographies. The indulgent reception they have had is, however, a political phenomenon and any analysis of anti-Communism has to look at it carefully. It shows the extent to which the bourgeoisie is prepared to use anti-Communism as a weapon. It also shows that the petty bourgeoisie, to which most of the Parisian intelligentsia belongs, is moving to the right and is unreservedly joining in the anti-Communist campaign.

This is not the place to look into the many sources of anti-Communism or at the wave of anti-Communism that has flooded across France in recent years. But the examples of Annie Kriegel and Pierre Daix clearly reveal the power of anti-Communism. Their success cannot be explained in terms of the scientific or literary quality of their work. On the contrary, the present climate of self-satisfaction and complacency shows that all that is required of anti-Communism is a mixture of extreme convictions and extreme harshness which can easily coexist with 'common sense' and irrationalism. The anti-Communist ideologue is simply called upon to be a merciless prosecutor who can condemn without any hesitation or any understanding. The eternal enemy is the still-born child of a world revolution, something which has been dying for years and which is still the target for an anger that has lost none of its old force.

NOTES

1. Perry Anderson, *In The Tracks of Historical Materialism*, (London: Verso, 1983), p. 32.
2. Maxime Rodinson, 'Self Criticism', in *Cult, Ghetto, State: The Persistence of the Jewish Question*, trans. Jon Rothschild, (London: Al Saqi Books, 1983), p. 44.
3. Jeanine Verdès Leroux, *Au Service du parti*, (Paris: Fayard, 1983), p. 179.
4. *Ibid.*
5. *Ibid.*, p. 81.
6. Annie Besse, *La Nouvelle critique*, No. 39, September–October, 1952, p. 58.
7. *Ibid.*
8. Annie Besse, cited, Rodinson, 'Self Criticism', p. 43.
9. Annie Besse, *La Nouvelle critique*, no. 46, p. 40.
10. Annie Besse, *La Nouvelle critique*, no. 52, p. 66.
11. *Ibid.*, p. 68.
12. *Ibid.*
13. Annie Besse, *La Nouvelle critique*, no. 42, p. 51.
14. Annie Besse, *La Nouvelle critique*, no. 24, p. 61.
15. Joël Kotek, *L'Intellectuel, Le PC et l'affaire Lysenko ou les avatars d'une science prolétarienne en occident*, Unpublished *Mémoire de licence*, Université Libre de Bruxelles, 1979–80, p. 115.
16. *Ibid.*, p. 116.
17. Philippe Robrieux, *Histoire Intérieure du Parti communiste*, (Paris: Fayard, 1981), p. 331.
18. Dominique Desanti, *Les Staliniens*, (Paris: Seuil, 1970), p. 290.
19. *L'Arche*, 26 March, 1972.
20. Annie Kriegel, *Les Communistes français*, (Paris: Seuil, 1970), p. 135.
21. *Ibid.*
22. *Ibid.*, p. 136.
23. Annie Kriegel, *Communismes au miroir français*, (Paris: Gallimard, 1974), p. 179.
24. Annie Kriegel, *Les Communistes français*, p. 81.
25. Annie Kriegel, *Le Communisme au jour le jour*, (Paris: Hachette, 1979), p. 16.
26. *Ibid.*, p. 23.
27. *Ibid.*, p. 136.
28. *Ibid.*
29. *Ibid.*, p. 325.
30. *Ibid.*, p. 111.
31. *Ibid.*, p. 56.
32. *Ibid.*, p. 205.

33. *Ibid.*, p. 225.
34. Annie Kriegel, cited, Bernard Legendre, *Le Stalinisme français. Qui a dit quoi?*, (Paris: Seuil, 1980), p. 201.
35. Annie Kriegel, *Israël est-il coupable?*, (Paris: Laffont, 1982), p. 16.
36. *Ibid.*, p. 50.
37. *Ibid.*, p. 51.
38. *Ibid.*
39. *Ibid.*, p. 53.
40. *Ibid.*, p. 119.
41. Annie Kriegel, cited, Rodinson, 'Self-Criticism', p. 46.
42. Annie Kriegel, *Les Communistes français*, p. 67.
43. *Ibid.*, p. 70.
44. Rodinson, 'Self Criticism', p. 31.
45. Lenin, 'The Three Sources and Three Component Parts of Marxism', *Selected Works*, (Moscow, 1970), Vol. 1, p. 66.
46. Pierre Daix, *La Crise du PCF*, (Paris: Seuil, 1978), p. 21.
47. Legendre, *Le Stalinisme français*, p. 105.
48. Pierre Daix, 'Le Procès Rajk, les partis communistes et la paix', *La Nouvelle critique*, no. 10, November 1949, p. 29.
49. Legendre, *Le Stalinisme français*, pp. 108–109.
50. Pierre Daix, *La Crise du PCF*, p. 93.
51. Robrieux, *Histoire intérieure*, tome 4, 1984, p. 155.
52. Pierre Daix, *J'ai cru au matin*, (Paris: Laffont, 1976), p. 106. Daix's account of his two years in Mauthausen and of the clandestine organization can be found in his *La Dernière forteresse*, 1950.
53. Pierre Daix, *La Crise du PCF*, p. 116.
54. In 1950, David Rousset began a polemic with *Les Lettres françaises* over the existence of concentration camps in the USSR, which he had denounced in his *L'Univers concentrationnaire*. He was vilified by the entire Communist movement. Pierre Daix, who had already slandered Rousset, defended the interests of the Party but finally lost the argument. This is a contemporary Communist account: 'In Communist circles, intellectual and otherwise, the name of David Rousset was surrounded by a sort of aura of treachery and felony. He was a Tortskyist and a traitor. I had never read his books, but hatred for him was so great that I never even thought of looking at them. The hatred and slander were so great that I believed he had been paid by the Americans to write books like *Les Jours de notre mort* and *L'Univers concentrationnaire* and to invent slanderous stories about so-called concentration camps in the USSR', cited, Leroux, *Au Service du parti*, p. 51.
55. *Ibid.*, p. 105, emphasis added.
56. *Ibid.*, p. 205.
57. *Ibid.*, p. 180.
58. *Ibid.*, emphasis added.
59. 'Tito's national-communist regime uses the same mystifications as national-socialism. It is the new weapon imperialism needs in its fight against the peoples who have just freed themselves from its yoke.' 'Le Procès Rajk', p. 37.
60. *Ibid.*, p. 29.
61. Pierre Daix, *J'ai cru au matin*, p. 317, emphasis added.
62. Most of these reports dealt with the power struggle between Malenkov and Khrushchev, the physical elimination of Beria, the first rehabilitations and Khrushchev's trip to Belgrade in 1955.
63. Pierre Daix, *J'ai cru au matin*, p. 351.
64. *Ibid.*, p. 337.

65. *Ibid.*, pp. 365–367.
66. Pierre Daix, *La Crise du PCF*, p. 106.
67. *Ibid.*, p. 93.
68. Marcel Liebman, *Le Léninisme sous Lénine*, (Paris: Seuil, 1973), Vol. 2, p. 322, emphasis added.
69. Pierre Daix, *La Crise du PCF*, p. 12.
70. *Ibid.*, p. 139.
71. Pierre Daix, *Les Hérétiques du PCF*, (Paris: Laffont), p. 19.
72. *Ibid.*, p. 164.
73. Pierre Daix, *La Crise du PCF*, p. 50.
74. 'Le Procès Rajk', p. 29.
75. Pierre Daix, *Les Hérétiques*, pp. 304–305.
76. This was how Maurras, the apostle of integral nationalism greeted the defeat of his country in 1940. For Maurras and many others like him the defeat of the Republic was an extraordinary source of comfort in those difficult days.

Translated by David Macey

RELIGION AND ANTI-COMMUNISM: THE CASE OF THE CATHOLIC CHURCH

François Houtart

In view of the phenomenon of a bipolar division between a 'free world' and a 'socialist world', it seems appropriate to examine the role played by religion in general and by Christianity in particular. This is of course a vast question and cannot be dealt with exhaustively here, circumstances vary considerably and the positions of those involved are often contradictory. All we can do here is to make some general theoretical comments and then look at a number of concrete examples, all of which concern the Roman Catholic Church.

Theoretical Considerations

A Marxist analysis of the phenomenon of religion brings out the ambivalence of its social functions. It is at once an expression of the protests of the lower classes and a sublimation of an order which sanctions social inequality. It offers an illusory solution to certain emancipation movements and is, at the same time, a source of commitment to liberation. As an institution, it is connected with oppressive powers, but it can also give rise to a vigorous and prophetic denunciation of injustice. It is at times difficult to say precisely what we are dealing with when we talk about religion, and we therefore need to make an historical and dialectical analysis.

In the current situation, the Church has no one line, even though certain tendencies seem to be dominant. In so far as it comprises a number of different representations of the world, religion itself is 'an ideal part of the real'.[1] It is, in other words, one of the elements which enter into the construction of social relations, classes and, therefore, the class struggle. This applies at the level of belief, that of symbolic expressions and ethics, and at the organizational level: at the level of the churches themselves.

The context, of course, varies considerably. In some countries on the periphery of Western capitalism, social relations are still read in terms of religious codes, though this is becoming increasingly rare. On the other hand, almost all predominantly agrarian societies live their relationship with nature in terms of the religious representations and practices which provide them with their main form of protection. Religious beliefs can also be found in industrialized capitalist countries, but here they are no longer bound up with representations of man's relationship with nature or

349

of social relations. They are in fact convictions as to the origins and destiny of man and the universe, and have a wide range of different connotations, both for sections of the bourgeoisie, for the intellectuals, for the working class and for the so-called middle classes.

All this suggests that the religious factor may play a more important role in the dynamics of society than some people are prepared to admit. In itself, the religious factor is ambivalent. We readily associate religion with right-wing regimes: the Catholicism of Marcos or Pinochet and Reagan's Christianity immediately come to mind. Certain religious values can be used to sanction repressive or imperialist policies. On the other hand, many revolutionaries in Central America, the Philippines and Southern Africa find their Christianity a source of commitment to the liberation struggle.

In terms of anti-Communism, it is not, then, surprising to find that religion has more than one function. This is certainly true of Catholicism. In order to gain a better understanding of what is at stake, we will first look at differences on the theoretical level, concentrating upon the religious and the materialist conceptions of history. We will then examine the question of social ethics and, finally, the problem of the religious institution and its autonomous space. The second section of this study will look at a number of concrete practices.

1. Oppositions at the theoretical level

Historically speaking, socialism developed within the framework of a philosophy and is therefore incompatible with religion at the theoretical level. That incompatibility is a constant source of hostility.

A. Religion and Historical Materialism

The assertion that any practice is rooted in a philosophical position, which is in itself an idealist position, means that the divide between historical materialism and religious belief is total. Within the framework of historical materialism it is obviously easy to argue for the rejection of any given praxis or analysis. The argument goes as follows: a class analysis means a Marxist analysis and as such is obviously bound up with Marxist philosophy, which is based upon atheism. It is on this basis that Latin American liberation theology, which is based—explicitly or implicitly— upon a Marxist analysis of Latin American society has been challenged and even condemned. This also explains why it is that Christians who join Marxist-influenced social, political and revolutionary organizations find themselves marginalized. Whilst such analyses and such commitments are not unproblematic, the attitude described above does imply starting out from an idea or a philosophy rather than from social relations. The question of what is understood by social reality and of whether a reading of social reality in terms of conflict is, in fact, the most adequate means to represent it, simply does not arise. The result is a polarization which goes far beyond the philosophical level and which has effects at the level of practice.

This tendency becomes even more marked when a political party or regime adopts historical materialism as a reference or platform. In such cases, the opposition between religion and historical materialism becomes a balance of power which finds expression in institutional policies and in the mobilization of the social base in support of those policies.

Marxist-influenced political formations and social movements often take this attitude. In theory, the religious problem is a conclusion and not a starting point for a praxis or an analysis, but when the terms of the equation are inverted, the struggle against religion and the marginalization of believers becomes a political object which produces the same reactions and the same divisions as before.

B. Social Ethics

All religions, and particularly Christianity, have elaborated a system of social ethics based upon religious convictions. The evangelical basis of Christianity can, for example, lead to a demand for justice for the poor and hence to a condemnation of oppression. Any ethical construct is, however, mediated through a representation of the social. In certain precapitalist societies, social relations were explained and legitimized in religious terms, and their concept of ethics derived from the notion of a divinely ordained social order. With the development of market-based societies and the capitalist mode of production, this kind of representation became obsolete, and more elaborate social doctrines were developed, notably by the Catholic Church.

The Church's social doctrine is determined by a reading of the most immediate aspects of social reality, namely inter-human social relations. Society is seen as a sum of interpersonal relations. Marxist thought, however, marks a qualitative leap in social analysis. This new reading takes in social structures as well as interpersonal relations and insists that structures are more than the sum total of relations. It concentrates upon the significant links between the elements that make up social relations. In a class structure, those elements are necessarily antagonistic.

In terms of the first reading of social reality, which has traditionally provided the basis for the Church's social doctrine, the immediate responsibility of the individual is quite obvious. This leads almost automatically to a call to change reality. Reality is perceived as being unjust and oppressive, and an appeal is therefore addressed to the individual consciences of social actors. The rich and powerful are urged to be generous, and the poor and the oppressed are urged to be more patient in their attempts to change society.

All this is very logical, as the starting point is a refusal to read social reality in terms of class antagonisms and class struggle. Given that this reading itself is based upon interpersonal relations, all struggles and antagonisms are immediately transposed to that register and therefore become unacceptable to those who preach fraternity and love of one's fellow man in the name of religious values. The same starting point can also lead to a confusion between means and ends. The end is the construction of a just, fraternal society, and class collaboration becomes the means to obtain that end, which is defined as the common good. The vast majority of religious groups take this view. It is found in a highly developed form in the social doctrine of the Catholic Church, but it also forms the basis of, say, Greek Orthodox thought. In addition, it forms the ethical basis of the major religions' views on peace.[2]

The result is, then, a theoretical basis for opposition to any form of social ethics which is elaborated in terms of a structural analysis of classes.

One of the most typical of these ethical constructs is John Paul II's encyclical *Laborem Exercens* (on labour). Social reality is read in terms of a stratification and not a structure, and the encyclical therefore remains at the level of description rather than analysis. The notion of a fair wage is, for instance, invoked without any reference to surplus value, surplus labour or socially necessary labour. Capitalism and socialism are described primarily as reflections of economic ideas and as reducing man either to a commodity or to a mere object of economic relations. As a result, both systems are criticised in terms of the ideas and ideologies on which they are based. In terms of an ethics based upon interpersonal relations, socialism is unacceptable because it is based upon the idea of class struggle, whereas capitalism is amenable to improvements.[3]

C. The Place of the Religious Institution

The importance of organization varies from religion to religion. As befits a Church which developed under the Roman Empire and which was strengthened by feudal society, Catholicism is, from a juridical point of view, the most highly developed form of religion. The Second Vatican Council modified its organization to some extent, but it is still a very hierarchical system. Its mode of institutionalization requires considerable material resources for the training of personnel and for the upkeep of places of worship, religious education and regional and international communications.

Since the fragmentation of Christendom and the development of the capitalist system, Catholicism has done more than any other branch of the Christian Church to develop a network of institutions in the fields of education, culture and health. Despite the power struggles of the nineteenth and twentieth centuries, these institutions did develop within the framework of liberal capitalist society. Catholicism was only a threat to the emergent bourgeoisie in so far as it was bound up with the ideological position of the landed aristocracy. With the birth of a new class enemy and the emergence of a new structure of social relations, religious institutions were able to become the allies of the bourgeoisie, even if they were at times critical allies.

The fact that it is the capitalist system that gives religious institutions most space can be explained in terms of theory: religious beliefs and their expressions are no longer essential to the reproduction of social relations. They are still useful, but the new relations of production are explained and legitimized in terms of a socially-based ideology rather than by recourse to the supernatural (a divinely ordained order), as they were in feudal society.

During the transition to socialism, however, the institutional space allotted to the churches is reduced for a variety of reasons. On the one hand, the state takes over the organization of health, educational and cultural networks in order to extend them to the whole population. On the other, the transition is a difficult period in which ideological mobilization may take the form of constraint. Finally, the social space required for the autonomy of religious institutions is defined both by the specific religious model in question and by the degree of social rigidity deemed necessary for the transition to socialism.

The religious sources of anti-Communism have, then, deep theoretical roots and are not simply a matter of tactics. But it would be a mistake to conclude that the attitudes of the churches and institutionalized religions are absolutely monolithic. On the contrary, large numbers of Christians and even certain members of the clergy accept the social analysis developed by Marxism and use it as a means to formulate an ethic. This is true both of the liberation theology which has emerged in certain Third World countries and of those intellectuals or believers who are involved in social, labour or revolutionary struggles. Even within the institutional church itself, there are those who argue for a less hierarchical view of evangelization and for a new definition of social space. The 'Basic Communities' of Latin America, the Philippines and Southern Africa are one such example.

2. The Influence of Church Practices

What, in the present conjuncture, can the practices of the Christian churches and of the Catholic Church in particular do to further the confrontation between the Western world and the socialist world or, on the other hand, to help to demystify the tendency to present it as a conflict between good and evil? In order to answer this question, we will look at a number of ecclesiastical practices within the Roman Catholic Church.

If we wish to reach any conclusions about the practices of the Church, we have first to make a distinction between a number of different sectors. We will look first at the production of values, which in both the Catholic Church and every other religious institution, are defined in terms of a reference to the supernatural. We will, then, consider the institutional practices which reproduce either the institution itself or its relations with other institutions in society, notably the state and social movements. Finally, we will look at the constitution of the church. Its constituents are socially diverse and, to some extent, have their own base in religiously-based social movements and religious movements. We will use these criteria to identify a number of different practices.

A. The Production of Values

This is obviously a vast topic and has to be approached selectively. We will look first at how church documents represent Marxism and then at a very specific issue in social ethics: nuclear weapons. Finally, we will examine the Church authorities' attitude towards liberation theology, which is itself productive of certain values.

(i) The Image of Marxism

The majority of Church documents begin their discussion of Marxism by describing its philosophy and its critique of religion, but the description itself is often simplistic or even caricatural. Official documents rarely give a succinct account of the various positions Marx and Engels adopted with regard to religion and they do not situate those positions in terms of the historicity of their production. It is of course true that the same failing is apparent in a lot of Marxist readings. Church documents, however, tend to caricature Marxist positions in order to criticise them more easily. The French bishops, for instance, outlined their views of relations between Christians and Marxists in a document published on June 30th 1977. They note the fact that many Christians share with Marxists a critical view of society and of social commitment. But they then argue that Marxism wants to have a monopoly on social change and therefore leads to totalitarianism and to the rejection of pluralism. They also claim that it excludes all classes other than the proletariat. This, according to the bishops, means that man is reduced to being a reflection of relations of economic production. Man is, that is, subordinated to a new ruling group and the road to totalitarianism lies open.

The French bishops accuse Marxism of defining individual consciousness simply as 'the ephemeral appearance of a moment in a collective consciousness'. As for the Marxist view of religion, they recall that in Marxist terms, religion is destined to disappear and that any believer who works with Marxists is therefore working for his own destruction. Finally, historical materialism's claim to scientificity is severely criticised and rejected as unacceptable.

The bishops' presentation of Marxism's conception of man, its explanation of society and its attitude to religion is extremely reductive and confuses theoretical positions with the political positions of Marxist-based movements.

In contrast, the document extols the values of Christianity without ever making any allusion to the actual practices of the Church in specific historical circumstances or to those of Christians who hold power. Even though the moderate tone of the document marks a departure from earlier condemnations of Marxism it still relies upon facile comparisons which inevitably sing the praises of Christianity and condemn Marxism as intrinsically evil.

In most of the documents published by the Episcopal Council of Latin America (CELAM), Marxism is usually discussed in terms of 'ideology'. In his inaugural address to CELAM's eighteenth Ordinary General Meeting in 1981, Mgr. Lopez Trujillo denounced 'the ideological use of the tools of Marxist analysis, which goes against the authority of the Church' and then added, 'How can CELAM remain silent?. . . the structure of the Church is being threatened by the indiscriminate—I would even go so far as to say unscientific—use of an analysis which is now one hundred and fifty years old, even though it is presented as something new.' In his report to the CELAM meeting held in Port-au-Prince, the Council's new president, Mgr. Quarracino, described the use of Marxism as an 'ideological manipulation'.

The documents issued by the Congregation of the Doctrine of Faith (formerly known as the Holy Office) are no more explicit. We have already referred to certain papal statements. If we now look at some of the speeches made by John Paul II during his travels, we find allusions not only to Marxism's atheist philosophy, but also to its reduction of man to labour power, to a theory of class struggle which is incompatible with the Christian concept of loving one's fellow man and which is simply an expression of collective egotism. (Speech to the peasants of Panama, 1983.) We are, then, dealing with an ideological struggle in which each side takes a reductive view of its opponent's views. The object is to assert the superiority of a religious view of the meaning of life, man and the universe that is denied by Marxism.

Such positions are not, however, universally accepted by all religious groups or, indeed, within the Catholic Church itself. Although most senior churchmen speak to their congregations in very simplistic terms, some do make certain distinctions. Thus, Cardinal Aloisio Lorscheider, Archbishop of Forteleza (Brazil) and President of the Brazilian Conference of Bishops, has no hesitations about taking a somewhat different view. In an interview published in his diocesan newsletter he remakrs: 'When I hear people claiming that the Church is being infiltrated by Marxism, I ask them what they understand by Marxism. Usually, I get no answer. . . Many people who talk about Marxism do not mean Marxist philosophy, but Marxist analysis [which is] an attempt to understand the society in which we live.' The distinction between philosophy and analysis, which some Marxists would reject, means that Christians do not have to reject Marxism's social analysis and its political project along with its atheism.

It has to be remembered that in his encyclical *Pacem in terris*, John XXIII takes a very novel position. Although he insists that no Christian can accept an atheist philosophy, he also makes a distinction between theories on the one hand and the groups and movements which convey those theories on the other. He thus establishes a basis for a dialogue by opening up new possibilities. Although a number of doors have been closed since the pontificate of John XXIII, similar views can still be found among those who work seriously at systematizing religious values. This is particularly true of Latin American Catholics and African Protestants who are involved in liberation theology. Liberation theology begins by analysing oppression and the liberating message of the gospel. Because it makes a scientific analysis of society and of the practices of the struggles of the oppressed, it sees Marxism as part of an attempt to emancipate mankind. The Christians concerned are involved in the struggles of the oppressed and base their theological reflections upon them.

(ii) The Ethics of Nuclear Weapons

The American bishops' views on nuclear war are expressed in their collective letter of 1983. Given the nature of the East–West confrontation, it is of considerable interest to look at the views of the bishops of one of the superpowers. Their position is very clear. They unequivocally condemn both nuclear war and any deliberate decision to make a first strike, even on a limited scale. They are, however, rather less clear when it comes to the question of deterrence, but they do state that deterrence must not be used as a means to gain superiority. The bishops' position is, then, in conflict with US nuclear policy, particularly as they do not portray the enemy as 'absolutely evil'. President Reagan's views on the matter are well known.

Some of the bishops take their criticisms of Reagan's arms policy even further. Two bishops in the state of Montana have stated their opposition to the MX programme. The bishop of Amarillo, Texas has condemned Pantex, the firm building the neutron bomb, and has asked Catholics to look elsewhere for work. Mgr. Flanagan, the bishop of Worcester (Mass.), is in favour of unilateral disarmament, and Mgr. Hunthauser, the bishop of Seattle, has stated that he will withhold part of his taxes as a protest against the increase in nuclear weapons.

The American bishops have thus taken a qualified view of the nuclear weapons issue, but their counterparts in France do not appear to be taking the same line. In their statement of 8th November 1983, they condemn the use of nuclear weapons, but they also ask: 'Does the fact that their use is immoral imply that the nuclear threat itself is immoral? The answer is not self-evident.' The document implies that the Soviet bloc is obviously aggressive and that the existence of the nuclear threat is therefore justified. The bishops claim that their attitude is logical because 'A dialogue is blocked and sterile. . . superficial and false. . . when certain of the parties involved are nurtured upon ideologies which deny the dignity of human beings.' They even go so far as to claim that an increased level of deterrence is justified by 'the domineering and aggressive nature of Marxist-Leninist ideology'. They add, finally, that 'theoretical materialism is using people's desire for peace. . . to conquer the world.'

It is, then, quite clear that the French bishops are helping to promote anti-Communist and anti-Soviet views and that, in the present conjuncture, they are objectively making a contribution to Western policy. The point has not gone unnoticed in NATO circles. In an article published in the *NATO Review*, Portugal's representative to NATO states that there is no contradiction between NATO policies and the Church's position on nuclear deterrence: 'It is impossible to condemn nuclear deterrence in the same moral terms that one would use to condemn the possible use of nuclear weapons.' In a reference to the position of certain churches he adds, 'Morally, the emphasis is strongly on deterrence.'[4]

(iii) Disapproval of progressive views within the Church

In recent months, progressive views within the Church have come under fairly systematic attack. The main targets have been liberation theology and what has been termed the Popular Church in Latin America. As we have already noted, liberation theology is an attempt to re-think theology and to go beyond social ethics. It begins with the position of the oppressed and re-reads the Gospel from the point of view of the poor. Their situation is not simply described in terms of its effects, but analysed in terms of its causes. Liberation theology therefore touches upon our conception of the role of Christ in human history, the salvation of mankind, our conception of the Church and its role, and evangelization itself. It has much in common with many liberation movements and with the views of the many Christians who are personally involved in social struggles.

In Latin America, the Philippines and certain parts of Africa the Church has developed into a new community of believers. In Brazil, over one hundred thousand people now belong to 'basic communities', and similar communities have played an important role in establishing the social bases for revolutionary movements in Nicaragua, El Salvador and Guatemala. New religious roles have been developed (community leaders, spokesmen), and laymen and laywomen, peasants and workers have become directly involved in evangelical and pastoral work. Some sections of the Catholic hierarchy—certainly John Paul II himself—regard this development, which means much more than decentralization, as a threat to the unity of the Church.

Warnings have been issued and administrative measures have been taken against the basic communities, and some of their positions have been condemned.

Liberation theology has been accused of using Marxist methods of analysis. In his inaugural address to the CELAM Conference in Puebla, John Paul II stated that a distinction has to be made between 'Christian liberation' and 'forms of liberation based upon ideologies which destroy the evangelical vision of man, the world and history'. In his letter of 29th June 1982 to the bishops of Nicaragua and in his sermon of 4th March 1983, he strongly condemns all forms of Church organization which are not subject to the authority of the bishops.

Although these declarations and measures do not refer directly to the confrontation between the socio-economic systems represented by the two superpowers, powers, their implications can only increase the distance between them and thereby escalate the confrontation.

Institutional Practices

In terms of institutional practices, a distinction has to be made between institutional reproduction and relations with other institutions in society.

(a) Institutional Reproduction

The Italian bishops' statement of 15th December 1975 provides a clear illustration of what is at stake in institutional reproduction. They firmly reject the possibility of any alliance with the Communist Party, not only because the Party is atheist, but because any such alliance would threaten the Vatican's concordat with the Italian government as well as Christian institutions in the fields of health, education and culture. They are, in other words, concerned to defend the Church's institutions and are afraid that the social space allotted to those institutions might be restricted.

The document even goes so far as to condemn those Christians who ally themselves with Marxists on the grounds that they are damaging 'the hierarchical and organic community of the Church'. It then refers to the internal reforms taking place within the Christian Democratic Party and argues against any political collaboration with the Communist Party. This was of course the period when the PCI was proposing its 'historic compromise'.

What is at stake is the problem of institutional reproduction. In order to safeguard that reproduction, the bishops ally themselves with a political system which is intrinsically bound up with the capitalist organization of society, with its integration into the economy of the West and with policies which are quite clearly dominated by the United States.

The very explicit position taken by the Italian bishops is not, of course, shared by all their colleagues. The vast majority of the world's bishops do, however, hold broadly similar views. In that sense, the Belgian bishops' positions on the economic crisis, immigrant workers and nuclear weapons are typical. In all three cases, they stress the seriousness of the problem, the unacceptability of certain inequalities and the injustice that does exist in society, but they end up by taking inter-class reformist positions that pose little threat to the structure of the capitalist system.

(b) Relations with Socialist States and Revolutionary Movements

The question of relations with the socialist states and with revolutionary movements is extremely complex. We will therefore restrict our discussion to the main issues, to John Paul II's views and to a brief examination of what might be termed the Vatican's *Ostpolitik*.

(i) The Position of John Paul II

Certain commentators stress the fact that John Paul II appears to have taken very different positions when speaking in Latin America and when speaking in Poland. There is in fact a very logical connection between the two. Although the style is somewhat restrained, it transpires quite clearly from his writings that in terms of both their philosophical positions and their political practice, Marxism and the Communist regimes are the main enemies of the Catholic Church. Where, however, Marxist regimes are in power, as in Poland, he recommends that they be given de facto recognition, despite their differences with the Church. John Paul II's aim appears to be to arrive at a modus vivendi which will give the Church the greatest possible institutional power in any given society. In institutional terms his logic is eminently coherent.

This is why the Church in Poland may well be opposed to the regime in power but is still willing to tone down its opposition and refuses to support Solidarity's more advanced positions. It also explains why the Pope urged Vietnamese Catholics to take part in the reconstruction of their country in the message he sent them when he visited the Far East in April 1984.

But where ongoing social and political struggles might bring a Marxist regime to power, the entire institutional strength of the Church is mobilized to prevent that eventuality becoming a reality. This is the real meaning of the difference between the message John Paul II took to Nicaragua and that contained in the speeches he made during his visits to various Third World countries. He cannot be criticised for not denouncing injustice—he clearly does so at every possible opportunity—but his denunciations are always tempered by a very severe warning as to the dangers of Marxist alternatives.

The Church has to display great institutional, doctrinal, ethical and organizational unity in its dealings with both Socialist states and revolutionary movements. That is why the Pope stresses these different points and translates them into Church policy. He does so firmly but with sufficient subtlety not to have caused any spectacular rifts in Catholic ranks. It should be remembered that it is because of his intervention at the Second Vatican Council that *Gaudium et Spes,* which deals with the Church in the world, contains no direct condemnation of Communism.

In the present circumstances, such an attitude could of course easily be translated into the terms of an East–West confrontation. This is obvious from Reagan's eagerness to establish diplomatic relations with the Vatican and to meet John Paul II in Alaska; from the contacts established between the Vice-President and other senior US officials and Rome in the period leading up to the Pope's visit to Latin America; and from Foreign Minister Léo Tinderman's exploitation of incidents that occurred during the papal visit to Managua to justify Belgium's refusal to cooperate with Nicaragua. There are many other similar examples. It cannot be denied that a number of churchmen and even senior figures in the Vatican sometimes have a direct hand in this subtle diplomacy. But it also has to be accepted that they have for the most part refused to become involved in a theological argument and, unlike Reagan, have not described the Soviet enemy as 'satanic'.

(ii) The Vatican's Ostpolitik

An excellent summary of the Vatican's Ostpolitik will be found in Dennis J. Dunn's recent article.[5] Dunn describes the history of the Vatican's relations with the socialist countries since the 1917 Revolution. He points out that the Vatican organized relief for the population of the Soviet Union during the great famine and that, whilst Pius XII's encyclical does condemn Communism and its international expansion in strong terms, the Pope also condemned fascism shortly before it was written.

It was, however, only after the Second World War that a coherent policy towards the socialist countries developed. The history of the last forty years reveals both a definite continuity in terms of underlying attitudes and a number of changes at the practical level.

The emergence of more socialist countries in Europe was perceived as a direct threat to the institution of the Church. The Church adopted a hostile attitude and the socialist countries took measures against the Church and sometimes against religion itself. Outside Europe, the Vatican saw the process of decolonization and the increase in Marxist-inspired revolutionary movements—not to mention the fact that whole countries like China were going over to Communism—as a basic threat to the Church and its mission work. It was in this context that new Western alliances culminated in the formation of NATO, that a series of religious conflicts broke out in the East, and that Pius XII adopted a hard line towards Communism and the socialist countries. The dialectic of confrontation was present at every level, both theoretical and practical.

The pontificate of John XXIII marked a very definite change at the level of practice. The Pope wanted to build a bridge, both in order to arrive at a modus vivendi between Church and State in the East and to try to open up a dialogue at the personal level by, for instance, receiving Khrushchev's son-in-law. He thus made a certain contribution to the development of detente. It will be recalled that he offered to act as a mediator in the Cuban crisis. He also tried to contribute to the institutional reconstruction of the Church in the social countries.

Paul VI followed a similar policy and, although he took a harder line at the theoretical level, he did accept that a modus vivendi was the best way to promote peace and stability in Europe.

The problem of episcopal appointments in the various Eastern bloc countries was resolved; bishops were appointed in Hungary in 1964, in Yugoslavia in 1966 and in Czechoslovakia in 1972. Monsignor Casaroli was the architect behind these successes. Diplomatic relations between Cuba and the Vatican were never broken off and for many years the Cuban ambassador was the doyen of the Vatican diplomatic corps. Relations with Yugoslavia were re-established at the beginning of the seventies.

The Soviet Union has displayed a certain moderation in its attitude towards the Vatican, not least because it is well aware of the influence that the Catholic Church can bring to bear over the question of peace. It has accepted the need for a modus vivendi with Catholics living in Soviet territory, especially in Lithuania. The Vatican's Ostpolitik has often been harshly attacked by conservative religious groups and by right-wing political parties alike. They claim that the Vatican has made too many concessions in exchange for minimal institutional advantages and for the appointment of bishops who take an ambivalent view of Communist regimes.

The election of John Paul II did nothing to change the overall line of the Vatican's policies, even though he himself came from a socialist country. He has insisted on negotiating from a position of strength, but he has kept the dialogue going. And, as Dunn, points out, it is not a naive dialogue.

(iii) Social Movements Based upon Religion and Anti-Communist Religious Movements

There are, within both the Catholic and the Protestant churches, a number of groups and organizations which see anti-Communism as an important part of their doctrine or even as their doctrinal basis. It would be pointless to list them all, and to do so would probably exaggerate their importance. Some of the movements which provide support for the Church in socialist countries come into this category. There have been reviews and other publications, but most of these movements have lost what strength they once had. It is more important to note that organizations like Opus Dei, which combine religious fundamentalism with right-wing, or even extreme right-wing political views, still receive encouragement and institutional

support from the Vatican. Such organizations naturally promote confrontational ideas and practices and may even be showing the way for
the policies of the future.

There are of course also movements like Pax Christi, whose position
on the arms race and East–West relations reflect those of the modern peace
movement; and the Catholic development and cooperative organizations
which, despite the policies of their respective governments, continue to
finance projects in countries such as Vietnam, Mozambique, Angola,
Cambodia and Nicaragua.

All this only goes to show that the Catholic Church is not a monolith
and that the line taken by its leaders is not always followed by
its members.

Conclusions

As an institution, the Catholic Church is, then, opposed to Marxism. That
is only to be expected in that it is a religious institution which is founded
upon faith in God. When, however, its anti-Marxism is used as a political
argument, the Church itself takes on a political complexion. As in many
other areas, the only way forward is for believers and unbelievers alike to
adopt the same social analysis and to leave the philosophical question
open. The inflexibility of official positions in the field of social analysis
and political projects is an expression of the amalgam we have been
discussing. The positions adopted by many religious authorities are in-
flexible and, to put it mildly, unscientific, and they can lead directly to
the use or even the manipulation of religion to worsen the conflict
between East and West.

In terms of its concrete practices, however, the Church has not become
involved in the logic of confrontation to any great extent. That it has
not done so is a reflection of its institutional interests; after all, the Church
is also present in socialist countries. From that point of view, it can to a
certain extent become a source of moderation.

In terms of the emancipation of exploited classes and of the peoples
of the Third World, it is far from certain that the Catholic Church's
attitude, which is closely bound up with both an idealist definition of
theological orthodoxy and the defence of its own institutional interests,
does correspond to the dynamics of the Gospel, which calls for the
defence and liberation of the poor. Any real fidelity to those objectives
would obviously imply a fundamental revision of both the Church's
thinking and its practice. Indeed, it implies such a fundamental revision
that certain parties are not prepared to take the risks involved.

NOTES

1. The expression is used by Maurice Godelier in his *L'Idéel et le matériel*, (Fayard: Paris, 1984).
2. This also applies to the World Conference for Religions and Peace. Cf. F. Houtart and G. Lemercinier, *Religions and Peace-Analysis of the Statements and of the Members' Opinions of the World Conference for Religions and Peace*, CRSR, Université Catholique de Louvain, Louvain-La-Neuvre, 1984.
3. F. Houtart, '*Laborem Exercens:* Refléxions sur ses logiques théoriques et concrètes', paper read to the Marx Colloquim, Vrije Universiteit van Brussel, 1983.
4. Jose Manuel P. de Villas-Boas, 'Les Perceptions publiques et la moralité nucléaire', *Revue de l'OTAN*, Vol. 32, no. 2, April 1984, p. 18.
5. Dennis J. Dunn, 'The Vatican Ostpolitik', *Journal of International Affairs*, Vol. 36, no. 2, Fall–Winter 1982/83.

Translated by David Macey